"Yong-Shik Lee is moving the study of law and development to a new paradigm which more fully takes on board the insights of institutional economics along with a growing awareness of the issue of state capacity. He understandably has much to say about the East Asian model but his focus is not confined to this important case. He takes a close look at South Africa after the end of Apartheid and, strikingly, examines the contemporary US through a developmental lens. The reader will find much to enjoy and to learn from in this book."

Dr. Simon Deakin, Professor of Law, University of Cambridge

"This book is a very well-written, ambitious and thought-provoking account and treatment of a very complex topic. The theory captures central elements of what makes up the connection between law and development."

Dr. Philipp Dann, Professor of Law,
Humboldt University

"With this new book Yong-Shik Lee has succeeded in providing scholars and students with a robust and insightful analytical framework to re-launch Law and Development as an exciting field of academic research and study. Prof. Lee adopts a universal approach that enables his framework to be used as an analytical framework to discuss the issues related to social and economic inequality and development in developing and developed countries. This is an essential book for both scholars of law and development studies and policy makers."

Dr. Faizel Ismail, Former Ambassador of South Africa
to the World Trade Organization

"If you are looking for a comprehensive and insightful introduction to the very complex subject of the many roles of formal legal institutions in economic growth and social and political development, Y.S. Lee's *Law and Development: Theory and Practice* more than fits the bill. It manages to present both the conventional wisdom and its critics' attacks fairly and with no resort to caricature, an essential but seldom achieved goal of every introduction to complicated legal fields."

Professor Frank Upham, Professor of Law,
New York University

"This rewarding and important book is comprehensive, knowledgeable and deep. It arrives at insightful and new propositions on the role of formal and informal law and the role of government for economic development. Also, the author's intimate knowledge about East Asia leads the reader to a much better understanding of government's potential role for development. This includes not only governmental investor protection if formal law is weak but also a public oversight and steering of private investment. Both generated high and lasting economic growth for low income countries."

Dr. Hans-Bernd Schäfer, Professor of Law,
Bucerius Law School

"The first and second editions of this excellent book have re-opened the theory behind Law and Development, providing renewed impetus for a new generation of interdisciplinary scholars to work systematically in addressing and having an impact upon global poverty, and not just in the so-called Global South. Comprehensive in scope, analytical in approach and clear in exposition, Prof. Lee gives food for thought for students, scholars, activists and policy makers. Drawing upon comparative historical data from the East and the West, this expanded second edition clarifies the importance of prioritising political stability in achieving successful development outcomes. An important work, likely to be a reference for some time to come."

Dr. Salim Farrar, Centre for Asian and Pacific Law,
Sydney Law School

Law and Development

This book examines the theory and practice of law and development. It introduces the General Theory of Law and Development, an innovative approach which explains the mechanisms by which law impacts development. This book analyzes the process of economic development in South Korea, South Africa, and the United States from legal and institutional perspectives. This book also explains why the concept of "development" is not only relevant to developing countries but to developed economies as well.

The new edition includes five new chapters addressing the relationships between law and economic development in several key areas, including property rights, political governance, business transactions, state industrial promotion, and international trade and development.

Yong-Shik Lee is a scholar in law and development. He is currently Director of the Law and Development Institute and Visiting Professor of Law at Georgia State University College of Law. Lee has taught at leading universities throughout the United States, Asia, and Australia. He graduated in economics with academic distinction from the University of California at Berkeley and received law degrees from the University of Cambridge (B.A., M.A., Ph.D.). Author of *Reclaiming Development in the World Trading System* (Cambridge University Press, 2006, 2009, 2016), *Microtrade: A New System of Trade Toward Poverty Elimination* (Routledge, 2013), *Law and Development Perspective on International Trade Law* (Cambridge University Press, 2011), and *Safeguard Measures in World Trade: The Legal Analysis* (Edward Elgar, 2003, 2005, 2014), Lee has published over 100 scholarly articles, book volumes, chapters, and shorter notes in the areas of law and development, international economic law, and economics, with leading publishers in North America, Europe, and Asia. He has also frequently spoken on issues relating to law and development, international economic law, and the WTO.

Routledge Studies in Development Economics

For more information about this series, please visit: www.routledge.com/series/
SE0266

Law and Development

Theory and Practice

Second Edition

Yong-Shik Lee

Routledge
Taylor & Francis Group

LONDON AND NEW YORK

Second edition published 2022
by Routledge
2 Park Square, Milton Park, Abingdon, Oxon, OX14 4RN

and by Routledge
605 Third Avenue, New York, NY 10158

Routledge is an imprint of the Taylor & Francis Group, an informa business

© 2022 Yong-Shik Lee

First edition published by Routledge 2020

British Library Cataloguing-in-Publication Data
A catalogue record for this book is available from the British Library

Library of Congress Cataloging-in-Publication Data
A catalog record has been requested for this book

ISBN: 978-0-367-54685-4 (hbk)
ISBN: 978-0-367-54686-1 (pbk)
ISBN: 978-1-00-309017-5 (ebk)

DOI: 10.4324/9781003090175

Typeset in Galliard
by Newgen Publishing UK

MIX
Paper from
responsible sources
FSC
www.fsc.org FSC™ C013985

Printed in the United Kingdom
by Henry Ling Limited

In memory of Dr. Sang Kook Lee (1929–2019)
My loving father, devoted pathologist, and revered professor

Contents

Figures

Tables

Foreword

The development of "law and development"

The study of law and development has gone through a series of mutations since the middle decades of the twentieth century. At that point, it was confidently believed that economic growth in the developing world would create the conditions not just for the emergence of sustainable liberal democracies and the rule of law, but for the reduction over time of social inequalities. The optimism of the Kuznets curve gave way to the more pessimistic predictions of those economists who argued that the relationship between countries already industrialized and those still industrializing were one of structural dependence and the embedding of inequality within and between nations. In the 1970s, legal scholars, attentive to these debates, gave up on the claim that the path to development outside Europe and North America lay through the adoption of Western institutions and practices. In the 1990s, the debate shifted again as the "Washington consensus" gained ground: now one particular model of growth, associated with deregulation and privatization, achieved ascendancy. After the financial crisis of 2008, it became harder to maintain belief in the self-correcting properties of markets, but no single new paradigm emerged. Rather, facts on the ground began to reshape perceptions: China's rise, in particular, focused attention on the previously neglected role of state capacity. China's experience, however, cannot be considered in isolation from the development of other East Asian economies, in particular Japan, Korea, and Taiwan, since the 1960s.

The story of Korea's recovery, in the second half of the twentieth century, from the effects of war and colonization in the first half, is well known, but perhaps its causes have been misunderstood. Korea's revival is often attributed to the role assumed by an activist state in directing resources to strategic industries. This view is not wrong, but as Yong-Shik Lee shows, it is only part of the story. The use of the legal system to promote development has been a central aspect of the Korean growth model; but the role of the law goes far beyond the functions attributed to it by the Washington consensus, namely supporting property rights and ensuring market access. Applying his new General Theory of Law and Development, Lee shows how the legal system was proactively used in Korea to constitute and reshape markets.

To understand the factors which generate sustainable development entails close examination of the role of law in diverse areas such as intellectual property, labor regulation, and corporate governance. Also central to Lee's theory of law and development is the idea that law is a mode of governance in its own right, rather than an instrument of policy to be deployed at will. Up to this point, development scholarship in general, while frequently acknowledging the limits of law, has paid insufficient attention to its institutional potential. Too often, policy makers in the past three decades have assumed that for markets to expand, law, and the state more generally, must recede. This perspective fails to see that markets, to work well, need to be institutionally bounded. This is a role that the legal system is in principle able to perform, but it cannot do so if it is not well resourced.

The legal system is also well placed to do something that the market alone cannot, which is to strike a balance between economic growth and social cohesion. As many countries are now seeing, growth that produces ever-increasing inequality is not sustainable: the negative feedback effects, which in extreme cases include the rise of authoritarian politics and rejection of the rule of law, will undermine the market itself if allowed to persist. As Lee's case studies show, inequality is a fetter on development not just for middle-income countries such as South Africa, but for supposedly developed ones such as the United States, which is in danger of regressing to a pre-twentieth century state of social division and fragmentation.

With the onset of the COVID-19 pandemic, the importance for social and economic development of strong and effective public institutions has been further reinforced. Further research will be needed to identify the factors behind the wide variations in infection and mortality rates across countries. It is already clear, however, that solidarity, and not just coercive control, played a role in those cases where the virus has been brought under control. As in previous pandemics, the vectors of transmission of the SARS-CoV-2 virus are largely social: they include poor sanitation, sub-standard housing, and informal work. They are also institutional: countries with a state which is not just well resourced, but also trusted to operate in the public interest, have been at a comparative advantage during the crisis. In the post-pandemic world, we can expect these issues to be high on the agenda of policy makers. As Lee notes, even more than the financial crisis, the COVID emergency has created "momentum to develop a more active role for the U.S. government in facilitating economic development for the majority of the American population, allowing for the proposed legal and institutional approaches to be addressed in this context." Thus, we find ourselves at a momentous juncture; out of the mismanagement of the COVID crisis, there is the potential for a new age of reform.

These are the issues at stake in the development of "law and development" as a field of research, and they could hardly be more important for the well-being of nations and ultimately for global security. With Lee's contribution, we have the analytical framework—as he puts it, the general theory of law and development—that we need to tackle these urgent questions.

Simon Deakin
Professor of Law
University of Cambridge
April 2021

Preface

This new edition, which builds on the previous edition of this book, is a continuing effort to form and expand scholarship in law and development. The second edition adds a new part, "Law and Development Analysis," comprised of five new chapters, including Property Rights and Economic Development (Chapter 8), Political Governance, Law, and Economic Development (Chapter 9), Legal Frameworks for Business Transactions and Economic Development (Chapter 10), State Industrial Promotion (Chapter 11), and International Legal Frameworks: Trade and Development (Chapter 12). These new chapters are adapted from my previous works as relevant to the theme of the new edition.

The new edition analyzes the impact of law, legal frameworks, and institutions in specific areas covered by the new chapters. These areas are chosen for their particular importance to economic development: the recognition of property rights, for example, has long been considered the cornerstone of economic development and needs to be examined in the context of law and development. Political governance has also been regarded as closely relevant to the promotion of economic progress. Freedom of contract and free business enterprise are both known to set a crucial foundation for the proliferation of economic activities and development. The role of the state in industrial promotion has been debated for decades and is relevant to explaining the success of newly industrialized countries. International trade has also been essential for economic development, and its legal framework has significant implications for the promotion of economic development policies.

The new chapters discuss pertinent issues in each of these areas and assess "conventional wisdom," such as the protection of property rights as a pathway to economic development (Chapter 8) and "good governance" as a necessary precondition to economic development (Chapter 9) critically in light of new arguments advocating alternative views. The new chapters also introduce new theories and novel approaches, such as the "New General Theory of Economic Development," in the context of state industrial promotion (Chapter 11) and pro-development reform proposals for international trade law under the auspices of the World Trade Organization (Chapter 12). With the publication of this new edition, I continue to proceed with the hope that this book will enhance law and development studies and facilitate law reform projects on the ground. The world has been suffering from the COVID-19 pandemic since January 2020, resulting in unprecedented economic difficulties in many places. Perhaps the call for new approaches for economic development and pro-development regulatory frameworks is stronger than ever.

Y.S. Lee
June 2021

Preface to the first edition

Law and development, an area of inquiry on the interrelationship between law and economic and social progress, has existed in the form of scholarship and considered relevant to law reform projects on the field for several decades. Yet it remains unfamiliar to many legal scholars, lawyers, students, and policy makers. Likewise, law and development has not been advanced as a robust academic field nor improved law reform projects by offering an effective analytical framework on the impact of law on development. This book, largely adapted from my previous works, attempts to build solid law and development scholarship and to make the latter more useful to development efforts on the ground. This book offers an account of both theory and practice in law and development, which I hope to be helpful to a wide range of audience, including students, scholars, policy makers, and professionals in related fields, and all others with an interest in the important interrelationship between law and development.

Law is relevant to development. Although law alone cannot create successful development, it can facilitate or inhibit development by influencing actors in the economy and society. As such, it is important to understand how law impacts development (law and development in "theory") and how it has been used to facilitate the latter (law and development in "practice"). Also, the concept of development, particularly economic development, has been used primarily in association with developing countries, rather than developed ones, but the changing economic conditions in recent decades, such as the widening income gaps among individual citizens and regions within developed countries, stagnant economic growth deepening economic polarization, and an institutional incapacity to deal with these issues, render this concept, as well as legal and institutional approaches, relevant to the assessment of the economic problems in developed countries. This will extend the application of law and development beyond developing countries, and this book, based on my previous works, demonstrates that the law and development approach can also be applied to address economic problems in developed countries, such as the United States.

This book also advocates for the development of the Analytical Law and Development Model (ADM) and explains how the ADM could be developed. The ADM is an analytical legislative reference to be developed in several key areas to facilitate economic development, empirically from successful development cases in recent decades. These areas include legal system, property rights (including intellectual property rights), political governance, the regulatory framework for business transactions, state industrial promotion, public health and the environment, taxation, corporate governance, competition law, banking and financing, labor, corruption, the criminalization of economic offenses, compliance and enforcement, and the international legal framework (*i.e.*, international economic law and international development law). The ADM will be an analytical device that applies the elements of the general theory of law and development, that are presented in this book, such as the organization of law, legal frameworks, and institutions (LFIs) and the adaptation to socioeconomic conditions, and assesses the impact of LFIs on economic development.

This book is the beginning of the path toward a more complete treatise on law and development. Building on the analysis of the present edition, future editions will include a more detailed account of law and economic development, as well as law and social development, in specific legal areas including those listed above. It is my hope that the present and future editions of this book will enhance law and development studies and facilitate law reform projects on the ground.

Y.S. Lee
May 2018

Acknowledgments

The publication of the new edition is owed to dedicated support from colleagues, research assistants, and many other individuals, all of whom cannot be listed in this limited space. I am grateful to my family for their continuing support for my work and their kind understanding when I had to set aside many hours to work on this book, away from family engagements. I am indebted to several leading scholars, including Professors Simon Deakin, Frank Upham, David Trubek, Noah Feldman, Hans-Bernd Schäfer, Faizel Ismail, Salim Farrar, Alex Lee, and Philipp Dann, for insightful comments and encouragements. I am thankful to my student research assistants, Andrew Smith, John Claeys, Thomas Oliver Flint, Skyler Martin, Monica Vu, Kedric Ross, and Kelly McGrath, for their research and editorial assistance. I am also grateful to Georgia State University for providing research support for this book. I am very appreciative of Routledge for its decision to proceed with this new edition. This edition would not have been possible without the excellent work of its editorial staff and the production team.

Acknowledgments from the first edition

This book would not have been possible without the valuable assistance of many individuals. I am grateful to my family, particularly my wife, Dr. Hye Seong Mun, for her enduring support for my academic endeavors. I am also indebted to Professors Simon Deakin, Philipp Dann, Ada Ordor, and Ambassador Faizel Ismail for their insightful comments on this book. I thank my student assistants, Mr. Jae Pil Kang, Ms. Marcela Melichar Suassuna, Mr. Justin Chase, Ms. Annelie Ellen Stallings, and Ms. Wei-An Wang, for their hard work. I am grateful to Routledge for deciding to publish this book and to its staff for working tirelessly to bring this book into the world. I also appreciate all the other individuals whose names could not be listed in this limited space but whose support and contribution have nevertheless been indispensable.

Abbreviations

ACWL	Advisory Centre on WTO Law
AD	Anti-Dumping
ADF	Agreement on Development Facilitation
ADM	Analytical Law and Development Model
ADP Agreement	Agreement on Implementation of Article VI of the GATT 1994 (WTO)
ASGISA	Accelerated and Shared Growth Initiative for South Africa (South Africa)
BBBEE	Broad-Based Black Economic Empowerment (South Africa)
BGB	Bürgerliches Gesetzbuch (Germany)
B.I.S.D.	Basic Instruments and Selected Documents
CBA	Cost/Benefit Analysis
CBO	Congressional Budget Office (United States)
CDF	Comprehensive Development Framework (World Bank)
CDP	Committee for Development
CPI	Corruption Perceptions Index
CVD	Countervailing Duty
DBS	Development Bank of Singapore
DDA	Doha Development Agenda
DFS	Development-Facilitation Subsidy
DFQF	Duty-Free, Quota-Free
DFT	Development-Facilitation Tariff
DPLG	Department of Provincial and Local Government (South Africa)
DSB	Dispute Settlement Body (WTO)
DSU	Dispute Settlement Understanding
EBA	"Everything But Arms"
EDA	Economic Development Administration (United States)
EDB	Economic Development Board (Singapore)
EDC	Economic Development Council
EDD	Department of Economic Development (South Africa)
EPB	Economic Planning Board (South Korea)
EU	European Union

FATCA	Foreign Account Tax Compliance Act (United States)
FDIs	Foreign Direct Investments
FPPRs	Formal Private Property Rights
FRED	Federal Reserve Economic Data (United States)
FTA	Free Trade Agreement
GATS	General Agreement on Trade in Services
GATT	General Agreement on Tariffs and Trade
GDP	Gross Domestic Product
GEAR	Growth, Employment, and Redistribution Strategy (South Africa)
GMS	Greater Mekong Subregion (Cambodia, Yunnan Province and Guangxi Zhuang Autonomous Region of China, Laos, Myanmar, Thailand, and Viet Nam)
GNI	Gross National Income
GPA	Agreement on Government Procurement (WTO)
GTAP	Global Trade Analysis Project
HDI	Human Development Index
IDB	Industrial Development Bureau (Taiwan)
IDL	International Development Law
IIAs	International Investment Agreements
I.L.M.	International Legal Materials
IMF	International Monetary Fund
IPRs	Intellectual Property Rights
IT	Information Technology
ITF	Innovation Technology Fund (Hong Kong)
KDI	Korea Development Institute
KITA	Korea International Trade Association
KOTRA	Korea Trade Promotion Corporation
L&D	Law and Development
LDI	The Law and Development Institute
LDR	Law and Development Review
LDRN	Law and Development Research Network
LDCs	Least Developed Countries
LED	Local Economic Development (South Africa)
LFIs	Law, Legal frameworks, and Institutions
LLSV	Raphael La Porta, Florencio Lopez-de-Silanes, Andrei Shleifer, and Robert Vishny
LSA	The Law and Society Association
MDGs	Millennium Development Goals
MENA	The Middle East and North Africa region
MFN Principle	Most-Favored-Nation Principle
MITI	Ministry of International Trade and Industry (Japan)
MNEs	Multinational Enterprises
NDE	New Development Economics
NDP	National Development Plan (South Africa)

NGO	Nongovernmental Organization
NICs	Newly Industrialized Countries
NPC	National Planning Commission (South Africa)
OAS	Organization of American States
OECD	Organisation for Economic Co-operation and Development
OHADA	Organization for the Harmonization of Business Law in Africa
PCCA	Prevention and Combating of Corruption Act (South Africa)
PWEDA	Public Works and Economic Development Act (United States)
R&D	Research and Development
RDP	Reconstruction and Development Programme (South Africa)
RIA	Regulatory Impact Analysis
RIS	Regional Innovation Strategies (United States)
RTAs	Regional Trade Agreements
RTD	The Right to Development
S&D Treatment	Special and Differential Treatment
SA	Agreement on Safeguards (WTO)
SBIR Program	Small Business Innovation Research Program (United States)
SCI	Strategic Computing Initiative (United States)
SCM Agreement	Agreement on Subsidies and Countervailing Measures (WTO)
SDGs	Sustainable Development Goals
SEC	Securities and Exchange Commission (United States)
SEI	Statute for Encouragement of Investment (Taiwan)
SUI	Statute for Upgrading Industries (Taiwan)
TAA	Trade Adjustment Assistance (United States)
TFA	Agreement on Trade Facilitation (WTO)
TRIMs	Trade-Related Investment Measures
TRIPS Agreement	Agreement on Trade-Related Aspects of Intellectual Property (WTO)
UCC	Uniform Commercial Code (United States)
UETA	Uniform Electronic Transactions Act (United States)
U.N.	United Nations
UNCITRAL	United Nations Commission on International Trade Law
UNCTAD	United Nations Conference on Trade and Development
UNESCO	United Nations Educational, Scientific, and Cultural Organization
UNDP	United Nations Development Programme
UN-OHRLLS	The United Nations Office of the High Representative for the Least Developed Countries, Landlocked Developing Countries and Small Island Developing States

U.N.T.S.	United Nations Treaty Series
U.S.	United States of America
USAID	United States Agency for International Development
USDA	United States Department of Agriculture
USITC	United States International Trade Commission
U.S.T.	United States Treaties and Other International Agreements
USTR	United States Trade Representative
WTO	World Trade Organization

Part I

Law and development in theory

1 Introduction

What is law and development?

1.1 Interrelationship between law and development

"Law and Development" is an area of inquiry on the interrelationship between law and development. In practice, this term, which is unfamiliar to many, refers to various studies, analytical approaches, and practical projects that concern the general or specific aspects of this interrelationship. This broad description reflects heterogeneous characteristics, diverse tendencies, and the rather amorphous nature of the discipline,[1] but such a general description is not particularly useful to those who want to understand exactly "what law and development is"; thus, more specific accounts of the constituent concepts in law and development and their applications are necessary. The introduction aims to answer the question of "what law and development is" by offering some explanation of its constituent concepts and the background of its development.

Broadly speaking, there are three perspectives on the relationship between law and development. The first perspective postulates that law[2] is merely a vehicle through which a chosen policy is implemented to achieve "development," however it is defined.[3] For example, if a government adopts an economic development policy to improve the use of land (*e.g.*, increase its productivity) by securing landowners' exclusive property rights to the land and adopts a law setting up a land registry that records such rights, the law that is adopted to protect and enforce these rights through land registration is merely a vehicle to carry out the government's development policy, and the particular law is not a subject of

---

1 Reflecting on the indeterminate and heterogeneous characteristics of the discipline, Scott Newton commented that law and development:

> does not appear to possess a particular normative armature or notable thematic consistency or much of a unifying logic or set of organizing principles. The most one can say is that the disciplinary range of L&D is constituted by the aggregate of studies pursued by its self-identifying adherents.

Scott Newton, "The Dialectics of Law and Development," *in* David M. Trubek and Alvaro Santos (eds.), *The New Law and Economic Development* (New York: Cambridge University Press, 2006), at 177.

2 The concept of "law" is further elaborated upon in Section 1.2, *infra*.

3 For further discussion of the concept of "development," see discussion *infra* Section 1.3.

DOI: 10.4324/9781003090175-2

an independent analysis. What is of substantive significance is the policy itself (in this case, one that grants exclusive property rights through land registry), not its vehicle (a law that has been adopted to implement the policy). The traditional economic analysis adopts this approach and assumes that whatever policy has been adopted will be implemented on the ground. The analytical focus is on the policy that the law advances (*e.g.*, whether the law guarantees private property rights or restricts them), and researchers examine the consequence of its implementation without performing a separate analysis as to whether the device, such as law, that has been adopted to implement the policy will be effective.

The second perspective is that law, as well as the policy that it advances, is relevant to development, justifying a separate analysis for law. Thus, one may attempt to analyze the mechanisms by which law impacts development (the policy being a part of these mechanisms). From this perspective, law is not just a vehicle to implement a policy, and laws that promote an identical policy may have varied impacts on development depending on relevant elements such as regulatory design, regulatory compliance, and quality of implementation.[4] For example, laws that require the establishment of a land registry have had different effects on land registration and the protection of property rights from one place to another where relevant social and economic consequences vary significantly; in some places, such laws have effectively enabled land registration and secured exclusive property rights for landowners, while in some other places it has not, instead causing substantial social and political disruptions.[5] The analytical focus is the impact of law and the relevant elements, such as institutions and socioeconomic conditions,[6] and it is not assumed that law successfully implements the policy that it purports to advance.

The third perspective posits that the existence of rational law or a governance system based on law ("the rule of law") constitutes an element of development, regardless of its specific impact on the economy and society. Under this approach, the rule of law is itself a development objective,[7] and law is no longer merely a means to achieve other developmental objectives, such as economic growth and industrial development. The rule of law has been emphasized since the 1980s in the context of neoliberalism; under this approach, law is seen as a neutral device used to secure individual freedom and to place restraints on state intervention in the economy.[8] The rule of law has been recognized as a development goal

---

4 Yong-Shik Lee, "A General Theory of Law and Development" (2017) 50(3) *Cornell International Law Journal* 415–472.

5 Frank Upham, "The Paradoxical Roles of Property Rights in Growth and Development" (2015) 8(1) *Law and Development Review* 253–269. See also Frank Upham, *The Great Property Fallacy* (New York: Cambridge University Press, 2018).

6 Lee (2017), *supra* note 4.

7 There are varied concepts of the rule of law, and scholars have pointed out its imprecise nature. For further discussion, see Alvaro Santos, "The World Bank's Uses of the 'Rule of Law' Promise in Economic Development," *in The New Law and Economic Development, supra* note 1, at 253–300.

8 Neoliberalism is a dominant political-economic ideology that emerged in the 1980s, which discourages positive government interventions in the economy and promotes free market approaches, including privatization and trade liberalization. Neoliberalism is based on the

set by national development agencies and intergovernmental organizations. For example, the United Nations' Sustainable Development Goals (SDGs) include the rule of law among the targets under their 17 economic and social development goals to be achieved by 2030.[9]

Among these perspectives, this book subscribes to the second approach for the following reasons. The first perspective, one that views law merely as a device for policy implementation and not as a subject of independent analysis, disregards the importance of law as a determinant of the success of policy implementation. One cannot assume that a policy will always be successfully implemented, as such is not the case on the ground; law is an essential component for the successful implementation of a policy, which necessitates an independent assessment, as advocated by the second perspective. As to the third approach emphasizing the rule of law,[10] the latter can be identified as a development objective, as demonstrated by the inclusion of the rule of law among the SDGs' development targets, although its imprecise nature generates an argument as to its scope, substantive standards, and procedural requirements.[11] If one is to accept the rule of law as a development objective, law becomes both an end and means (of achieving other development objectives, such as economic development) as long as the latter is not overlooked. Thus, the rule of law and its role need to be analyzed concerning the other development objectives. This means that the current emphasis on the rule of law does not preclude the adoption of the second approach.

Law and development, as an area of study, should also be distinguished from other (related) areas of studies such as "law and economics" and "law and society." Law and economics tends to focus on the microeconomic analysis of law, assessing the economic efficiency of law.[12] Law and development also examines economic issues in the context of development but focuses more on macroeconomic issues

---

"Washington Consensus," which refers to a set of policies representing the lowest common denominator of policy advice being advanced by Washington-based institutions, such as fiscal discipline, a redirection of public expenditure priorities toward areas offering both high economic returns and the potential to improve income distribution (such as primary healthcare, primary education, and infrastructure), tax reform to lower marginal rates and broadening the tax base, interest rate liberalization, a competitive exchange rate, trade liberalization, liberalization of inflows of foreign direct investment, privatization, deregulation (to abolish barriers to entry and exit), and protection of property rights. John Williamson, "What Washington Means by Policy Reform," *in* John Williamson (ed.), *Latin American Readjustment: How Much Has Happened* (Washington, D.C.: Peterson Institute for International Economics, 1990).

9 Goal 16 of the Sustainable Development Goals (SDGs) is the promotion of peaceful and inclusive societies for sustainable development, the provision of access to justice for all, and building effective, accountable institutions at all levels. There are ten targets to achieve this goal, including 16.3 that aims to "promote the rule of law at the national and international levels and ensure equal access to justice for all." United Nations, *Sustainable Development Goals*, available online at: www.un.org/sustainabledevelopment/sustainable-development-goals/; https://perma.cc/HQ6H-JJNQ.

10 *Supra* note 7 (for a reference on the varied concepts of the rule of law).

11 *Supra* note 9 (for a reference on the inclusion of the rule of law as a target among the SDGs).

12 Richard Posner provided excellent coverage of law and economics. Richard Posner, *Economic Analysis of Law* (7th ed., New York: Aspen Publishers, 2007).

such as economic growth and income distribution. Also, law and development addresses social progress issues, which is not a primary subject of law and economics but would be included in the ambit of law and society.[13] Law and society examines the impact of law on society more broadly but without a focus on development issues. In today's world, where development has become one of the most important international agendas, as demonstrated by major global initiatives such as the SDGs, there is a need for a discipline that focuses on the important interrelationship between law and development. Law and development, as a separate field of study, will serve this interest.

1.2 "Law" and associated concepts[14]

Law is a pillar concept of law and development; thus, it is essential to clarify the concept of "law" in the context of law and development. This section also discusses two other key concepts associated with law: "legal frameworks" and "institutions." "Law" is defined generally as a "body of rules of action or conduct prescribed by controlling authority, and having binding legal force"[15] or "a specific rule or a set of rules binding on the members of a society."[16] Examples of law include constitutions and statutes adopted by legislatures, regulations adopted by administrative agencies, and ordinances adopted by municipalities. In the law and development context, "law" may be broader than the term's usual conception based on formalistic characteristics. For example, binding judicial precedents are referred to as "law" (case law) in common law countries, such as the United States and Britain, even if such precedents are not formally considered "law" in civil law jurisdictions, such as France and Germany.[17] However, as long as judicial precedents are followed with *de facto* binding force, they are considered "law" for law and development studies in both common law and civil law countries. Scholars have recognized the existence and force of norms other than legislation

---

13 To promote studies in law and society, an international association, "The Law and Society Association" (LSA), was organized in 1964. Such an international academic association does not exist for law and development, which shows a weaker status as an academic field. More details about the LSA and activities in law and society are available online at: www.lawandsociety.org/. The Law and Development Institute (LDI, www.lawanddevelopment.net) and presently the only peer-reviewed academic journal in the field, *Law and Development Review* (LDR, www.degruyter.com/ldr), have been founded to promote law and development studies.

14 This section is adapted from Lee (2017), *supra* note 4, part I, section B, at 423–428.

15 Henry Campbell Black, *Black's Law Dictionary* (6th ed., St. Paul, MN: West Publishing Co., 1990), at 884.

16 Yong-Shik Lee, "Call for a New Analytical Model for Law and Development" (2015) 8(1) *Law and Development Review* 1–67, at 2, note 3.

17 "Common law" refers to the legal system that originated in England based on binding judicial precedents which has been adopted in many of the former British colonies and territories, including the United States, Canada, India, Australia, and New Zealand. "Civil law" is the legal system that originated in Roman law which is now prevalent in Continental Europe, Latin America, and East and Southeast Asia, and is based on formally legislated "codes."

and case law.[18] For law and development studies, "law" also includes some of these norms or informal rules, referred to as "customary law," that are consistently observed with an *opinio juris*.[19]

There is a question as to whether informal norms that practically bind the members of a society, but are not necessarily observed with an *opinio juris*, should be considered "law" in the context of law and development. An example of such an informal norm is the "administrative guidance"[20] adopted by Korean and Japanese governments for businesses and industries during periods of economic development. Administrative guidance was consistently followed, even though it was not formally a "law" or recognized as such by the public (*i.e.*, no *opinio juris*), because giving such guidance was considered a legitimate role of the government in their local political and social cultures. There is a suggestion that "law" should be understood more broadly, including the basic form of communal normative ordering (*i.e.*, informal norms followed by a particular community) regardless of the presence of *opinio juris*.[21] If this broader definition should be adopted, practices such as administrative guidance and all fundamental social norms will be included in the ambit of "law" in the context of law and development. However, this expansive definition blurs the distinction between law and non-legal orders.[22]

Another concept that is closely relevant to the discussion of law in the context of law and development is "legal frameworks." This concept refers to the frameworks in which law is organized, such as regulatory structures and legal systems (*i.e.*, common law or civil law legal systems). Legal frameworks affect the impact of law. For example, the impact of a law may vary depending on whether it is implemented as a stand-alone statute with its own monitoring and enforcement

18 For further discussion of informal norms regulating private transactions, see Stewart Macaulay, "Non-Contractual Relations in Business: A Preliminary Study" (1963) 28 *American Sociological Review* 55–67; Robert Ellickson, *Order Without Law: How Neighbors Settle Disputes* (Cambridge, MA: Harvard University Press, 1997); Lisa Bernstein, "Opting Out of the Legal System: Extralegal Contractual Relations in the Diamond Industry" (1992) 21(1) *Journal of Legal Studies* 115–157.

19 The existence of a customary law may be confirmed by a judicial decision. For further discussion of customary law, see Amanda Perreau-Saussine and James B. Murphy, *The Nature of Customary Law: Legal, Historical and Philosophical Perspectives* (New York: Cambridge University Press, 2009). Customary law includes religious codes, such as Sharia law (Islamic Law), adopted and enforced by most Muslim-majority countries. See, *e.g.*, Salim Farrar and Ghena Krayem, *Accommodating Muslims under Common Law: A Comparative Analysis* (Abington: Routledge, 2016).

20 "Haeng-Jung Ji-Do" (in Korean) or "Gyo-Sei Shi-Do" (in Japanese).

21 See, *e.g.*, Garrett Barden and Tim Murphy, *Law and Justice in Community* (New York: Oxford University Press, 2010), at 8–10.

22 In any case, the dividing line between law and non-legal orders is by no means clear. For instance, whether a particular informal norm is observed with an *opinio juris* could be a matter of debate. See also Tim Murphy, "Living Law, Normative Pluralism, and Analytic Jurisprudence" (2012) 3(1) *Jurisprudence* 177–210. Law and non-state legal forms, regardless of whether they are recognized by a state, are treated as relevant factors that together constitute the present reality of complex normative orders. See also Franz von Benda-Beckmann, "Legal Pluralism and Social Justice in Economic and Political Development" (2001) 32(1) *Institute of Development Studies Bulletin* 46–56, at 53.

mechanisms or as a part of a regulation subject to the control of a higher-level statute.[23] Legal frameworks may also present challenges for the adoption of laws that originated in another jurisdiction. Scholars have indicated that an adopted law's operative terms may reference legal norms and concepts used in the originating legal system but not in the adopting jurisdiction.[24] For example, the adoption of a new statute referencing "fiduciary duty" or "constructive trust," which are legal concepts developed through cases in common law jurisdictions, could pose considerable difficulty in its interpretation and application in a civil law jurisdiction without a similar legal development.[25]

Scholars have identified legal systems with different underlying ideologies and cultural traits. According to Paul Mahoney, the ideologies underlying English common law promote individual liberty and freedom from government intervention, while those underlying French civil law promote collective rights and greater government activism, leading to different development outcomes (*i.e.*, common law countries show on average higher economic growth rates over time).[26] This finding, however, does not seem to explain the most successful development cases since the Second World War, including South Korea ("Korea"),[27] Taiwan, Hong Kong, Singapore (the Newly Industrialized Countries or "NICs"),[28] Spain,

23 The works by La Porta and others have also emphasized the importance of legal frameworks. Raphael La Porta, Florencio Lopez-de-Silanes, Andrei Shleifer, and Robert Vishny (LLSV), "Law and Finance" (1998) 106(6) *Journal of Political Economy* 1113–1155. They argued that legal origin, such as common law or civil law legal origins, explains cross-country differences in financial development, and tried to demonstrate that a country's development in the financial market and its laws on property rights, shareholder rights, and creditor rights are affected by its legal origin. See also LLSV, "Investor Protection and Corporate Governance" (2000) 58 *Journal of Financial Economics* 3–27 and LLSV, "Investor Protection and Corporate Valuation" (2002) 5(3) *Journal of Finance* 1147–1170. Their conclusion that common law is superior to civil law in financial development reveals certain gaps and has been criticized as attributing the cited differences in economic performance among those countries to legal origin, when in fact these differences were likely attributable to other factors, such as differences in macroeconomic policies. See Kenneth Dam, *The Law-Growth Nexus: The Rule of Law and Economic Development* (Washington, D.C.: Brookings, 2006), at 31–49 and Frank Cross, "Law and Economic Growth" (2001) 80(7) *Texas Law Review* 1737–1775.
24 Katharina Pistor, "The Standardization of Law and Its Effect on Developing Economies" (2002) 50(1) *American Journal of Comparative Law* 97–134.
25 Hideki Kanda and Curtis J. Milhaupt, "Re-Examining Legal Transplants: The Director's Fiduciary Duty in Japanese Corporate Law" (2003) 51(4) *American Journal of Comparative Law* 887–901.
26 Paul Mahoney, "The Common Law and Economic Growth: Hayek Might be Right" (2001) 30(2) *Journal of Legal Studies* 503–525.
27 "South Korea" and "Korea" are used interchangeably without distinction throughout this book, and both refer to the Republic of Korea (*c.f.*, "North Korea" referring to Democratic People's Republic of Korea).
28 The NICs have achieved unprecedented economic development over the course of three decades; between 1961 and 1996, Korea increased its gross domestic product (GDP) by an average of 8.75 percent per annum, Hong Kong by 7.61 percent, Taiwan by 8.64 percent, and Singapore by 8.61 percent (calculated with real GDP figures at constant 2005 national prices), while the world's average annual GDP increase and the annual GDP increase of the low- and middle-income countries for the corresponding period were 3.85 and 4.39 percent, respectively. Robert C. Feenstra, Robert Inklaar, and Marcel P. Timmer, *Penn World Table Version 8.1* (April 13, 2015), available online at: www.rug.nl/ggdc/productivity/pwt/pwt-releases/pwt8.1; https://perma.cc/AUP9-FPZC

Chile,[29] and, more recently, China. Among them, only Hong Kong and Singapore are classified as common law systems. Mahoney's research also disregarded variances among common law countries and exaggerated the claimed differences between common law and civil law countries. For example, Singapore, a common law country, showed strong government initiatives and activism in its economic development process.[30] Chile, which maintained a civil law system, promoted liberal policies emphasizing individual liberty and freedom in both political and economic areas after the authoritarian rule of Pinochet ended in 1990. If there is any relevance between the legal system and development, it is that a civil law system based on state-sponsored codes appears to be more adoptable than a common law system. Consequently, except for countries formerly under British rule, most countries have adopted a civil law system.

Lastly, "institutions" are also conceptually relevant to the law and development discourse. The term "institutions," in the context of law and development, refers to organizations, norms, and practices related to the adoption, implementation, and enforcement of law.[31] The impact of law cannot be assessed separately from relevant institutions. For example, the adoption of a statute that imposes a criminal penalty for corruption would not be very effective if essential institutions that enforce it, such as an effective prosecutorial service or an independent judiciary, were absent. In addition, laws that attempt to establish formal private property rights ("FPPRs") to enhance economic efficiency by securing citizens' legal rights to their property may not be effective without the implementation of key

and World Bank, *GDP Growth (Annual %)*, available online at: https://data.worldbank.org/indicator/NY.GDP.MKTP.KD.ZG; https://perma.cc/ZRJ4-VEV5. GDP, defined as "an aggregate measure of production equal to the sum of the gross values added of all resident institutional units engaged in production (plus any taxes, and minus any subsidies, on products not included in the value of their outputs)," is commonly used to measure the economic output of a whole country or region. OECD, *Gross Domestic Product (GDP)*, available online at: http://stats.oecd.org/glossary/detail.asp?ID=1163; https://perma.cc/SE6A-2B8Q. "Real GDP" refers to GDP figures adjusted by inflation (calculated in fixed currency value). Economic indicators in "real" terms, such as "real growth" and "real consumption," are also adjusted by inflation.

29 Both Spain and Chile were in a state of economic deprivation by the time the Second World War ended. Spain achieved rapid economic development under General Franco beginning in the 1960s ("the Spanish Miracle"), and Chile beginning in the mid-1980s under the rule of Pinochet who, despite the atrocities that he committed, paved the way for the country's economic prosperity by undertaking economic reforms during his regime. As a result of successful economic development, both countries achieved high-income country status as classified by the World Bank (see *infra* note 45) and elective democracy under the rule of law after the authoritarian regimes of Franco and Pinochet, which ended in 1975 and 1990, respectively.

30 For a summary of the evolution of the industrial policies of Singapore and the other successful East Asian developing countries, see Mari Pangestu, "Industrial Policy and Developing Countries," *in* Bernard Hoekman, Aaditya Mattoo, and Philip English (eds.), *Development, Trade, and the WTO: A Handbook* (Washington, D.C.: World Bank Publications, 2002), at 153.

31 Douglass North defined "institutions" more broadly, to mean "the humanly devised constraints that structure political, economic and social interaction" which "consist of both informal constraints (sanctions, taboos, customs, traditions, and codes of conduct), and formal rules (constitutions, laws, property rights)." Douglass C. North, "Institutions" (1991) 5(1) *Journal of Economic Perspectives* 97–112, at 97.

institutional elements that support FPPRs, such as an affordable and reliable land registration system operated by non-corrupt and capable government officials.[32]

Institutions have gained a great deal of attention for their role in development. In the 1970s, scholars criticized that ethnocentric assumptions about the role of institutions, such as the judiciary, ignored local realities and denied the field a functional theory.[33] Douglass North, a Nobel laureate, emphasized the importance of institutions in the context of economic development.[34] Other scholars have argued that the quality of the institutions that administer law, rather than the law *per se*, is more relevant to development.[35] Institutions, particularly those sanctioned by the state,[36] have always been at the center of law and development studies, and there is a rising consensus that getting the right institutions is key to success.[37] The difficulty, however, is that there is little guidance as to *which* institutions are important[38]

---

32 For further discussion of FPPRs, see Guangdong Xu, "Property Rights, Law, and Economic Development" (2013) 6(1) *Law and Development Review* 117–142.

33 David M. Trubek and Marc Galanter, "Scholars in Self-Estrangement: Some Reflections on the Crisis in Law and Development Studies in the United States" (1974) *Wisconsin Law Review* 1062–1103, at 1078–1079.

34 Douglass C. North, *Institutions, Institutional Change and Economic Performance* (Cambridge: Cambridge University Press, 1990). Comparing the United States' success with its constitution and the lack of success Latin American countries had with their constitutions that were inspired by the United States, North also argued that the institutions that were previously in place affect the path that an economy takes in the future ("path dependency"). North (1991), *supra* note 31, at 110–111. According to North, institutions provide the incentive structure that directs economic and political growth. Douglass C. North, "Big-Bang Transformations of Economic Systems: An Introductory Note" (2000) 156(1) *Journal of Institutional and Theoretical Economics* 3–8, at 5. The evolution of that structure determines whether economies grow, stagnate, or decline. North (1991), *ibid.*, at 97.

35 Kevin Davis and Michael J. Trebilcock, "Legal Reforms and Development" (2001) 22(1) *Third World Quarterly* 21–36.

36 For the meaning of a "state," see *infra* note 243.

37 Several studies discuss the role of institutions for economic development. Based on empirical evidence, Frank Cross concluded that the necessity of legal institutions for economic growth is unquestionable. Cross (2001), *supra* note 23. Kenneth Dam also considered legal institutions to be important for economic development. Dam (2006), *supra* note 23, at 230–231. Additional empirical cross-country research acknowledges the importance of institutions for development. Daniel Kaufmann *et al.*, "Governance Matters," *World Bank Policy Research Working Papers*, no. 2196 (1999) and Dani Rodrik, Arvind Subramanian, and Francesco Trebbi, "Institutions Rule: The Primacy of Institutions over Geography and Integration in Economic Development" (2004) 9(2) *Journal of Economic Growth* 131–165.

38 Some scholars have advocated a "cluster of institutions" that are important to encourage growth, such as constraints on government expropriation, an independent judiciary, property rights enforcement, and institutions providing equal access to education and civil liberties. Daron Acemoglu, Simon Johnson, and James A. Robinson, "The Colonial Origins of Comparative Development: An Empirical Investigation" (2001) 91(5) *American Economic Review* 1369–1401, at 1371–1372. By contrast, others have observed that institutions such as the independent judiciary and formal property rights are not essential to successful economic growth. Richard A. Posner, "Creating a Legal Framework for Economic Development" (1998) 13(1) *World Bank Observer* 1–11, at 2; Upham (2015), *supra* note 5. Dani Rodrik enumerated five market-supporting

and *how* to develop such institutions under varying socioeconomic conditions affecting them.[39]

1.3 The question of development[40]

1.3.1 Definition and substance

"Development" is the other pillar concept of law and development. There is no universally adopted definition of development,[41] but in the context of law and development, it can be defined as "a progressive transformation of the economy and society"[42] or "economic or social progress."[43] However, this definition invites a circular debate, as there is no clear consensus as to what constitutes economic and social progress.[44] The first part of this section addresses this inquiry, followed

institutions, including property rights, regulatory institutions, institutions for macroeconomic sta-
bilization, institutions for social insurance, and institutions of conflict management. Dani Rodrik,
"Institutions for High-Quality Growth: What They Are and How to Acquire Them" (2000) 35(3)
Studies in Comparative International Development 3–31, at 6–10.

39 Rodrik *et al.* (2004), *supra* note 37, at 157–158. Cross-country statistical analyses done by scholars
such as Kevin Davis demonstrate causal relationships between variables measuring characteristics
of legal institutions and those measuring development levels. Kevin Davis, "What Can the Rule of
Law Variable Tell Us about Rule of Law Reforms?" (2004) 26 *Michigan Journal of International
Law* 141–161. A conclusion is drawn from this study that the development of legal institutions
induces economic development. However, even if this conclusion were to be accepted, the question
remains whether the necessary institutional development will be feasible at all under particular
socioeconomic conditions on the ground in the developing countries, which may not be conducive
to such development.

40 This section is adapted from Lee (2017), *supra* note 4, part II, at 428–435.

41 Noting this uncertainty, former U.S. representative to the United Nations Human Rights Council
Michael Novak said in 1981, "The concept of 'development' is itself in need of development ..."
A comment cited in Stephen Marks, "The Human Right to Development: Between Rhetoric and
Reality" (2004) 17 *Harvard Human Rights Journal* 137–168, at 148.

42 Trubek and Galanter considered development to mean "progressive social, political, and economic
changes in developing countries." Trubek and Galanter (1974), *supra* note 33, at 1062, note
1. The terms used in my definition, "a progressive transformation of [...] society" and "social
progress," encompass progressive political changes. Thus, the term, "social development," also
includes progressive changes of a political nature ("political development").

43 Under this definition, social development of a non-economic nature, such as an improvement in
gender equality, as well as economic development without concurrent social progress, would be
embraced in the notion of "development."

44 Thus, Philipp Dann suggested another approach to keep the notion of development open and
understand it as a political process in which concrete steps and goals are negotiated and agreed
upon. Philipp Dann, *The Law of Development Cooperation* (Cambridge: Cambridge University
Press, 2013), at 125. For critical reviews of "development" as an international initiative, see
Arturo Escobar, *Encountering Development: The Making and Unmaking of the Third World*
(Princeton, NJ: Princeton University Press, 2011); Sundhya Pahuja, *Decolonising International
Law: Development, Economic Growth and the Politics of Universality* (Cambridge: Cambridge
University Press, 2011); Balakrishnan Rajagopal, *International Law from Below: Development,
Social Movements and Third World Resistance* (Cambridge: Cambridge University Press, 2003).

by an examination of how both economic and social progress can be incorporated into a coherent theory of law and development. Additionally, the changing economic conditions in developed countries render the concept of "development" and the law and development approach applicable to economic issues in developed countries as well as developing ones. The latter part of the section discusses this point.

The substance of "development" and its focus have changed over time. In the 1950s and 1960s, development primarily meant economic growth or improvement in national income, supporting poverty relief efforts in developing countries[45] and endeavors to reduce economic gaps between developed and developing countries.[46] The concept of development has become more holistic since then, emphasizing non-economic values that are believed to enhance human life, such as political participation, right to property, gender equality, access to a clean and safe environment, and the rule of law,[47] as key elements of development.[48]

This holistic view of development became triumphant and won popular support when the 1998 Nobel laureate Amartya Sen advocated "development as freedom," meaning that "development" should comprise political freedom, economic choice, and protection from abject poverty.[49] Before Sen's work, the United Nations Development Programme (UNDP) had introduced the concept of "human development,"[50] which was in line with the holistic view

---

45 The dichotomy between developed and developing countries is not always clear, but the former are normally understood as high-income countries with advanced economic, technological, and industrial capacities. For the income classifications of countries, the World Bank defines, as of November 2020, low-income economies as those with a gross national income (GNI) per capita of $1,035 or less; lower middle-income economies, a GNI per capita between $1,036 and $4,045; upper middle-income economies, a GNI per capita between $4,046 and $12,535; high-income economies, a GNI per capita of $12,536 or more. World Bank, *Data: Country and Lending Groups*, available online at: http://data.worldbank.org/about/country-and-lending-groups; https://perma.cc/X9A6-FRYK. Developed countries are also members of the Organisation for Economic Co-operation and Development (OECD), although not all of the OECD countries may fit the cited description of developed countries. Many also view that the practice of elective democracy and the rule of law are essential qualifications for "developed countries."

46 Ruth E. Gordon and Jon H. Sylvester, "Deconstructing Development" (2004) 22(1) *Wisconsin International Law Journal* 1–98, at 9–10. See also David M. Trubek, "The 'Rule of Law' in Development Assistance: Past, Present, and Future," *in The New Law and Economic Development, supra* note 1, at 75.

47 For a discussion of the rule of law, see Santos (2006), *supra* note 7, at 256–266 and Brian Tamanaha, *On the Rule of Law: History, Politics, Theory* (Cambridge: Cambridge University Press, 2004).

48 Gordon and Sylvester (2004), *supra* note 46, at 13. The holistic view of development includes some of the social rights that are also relevant to enhance the economic and technological capacity of society, such as access to education, in the ambit of development.

49 Amartya Sen, *Development as Freedom* (New York: Oxford University Press, 1999). See also Kerry Rittich, "The Future of Law and Development: Second Generation Reforms and the Incorporation of the Social," *in The New Law and Economic Development, supra* note 1, at 208.

50 United Nations Development Programme (UNDP), *What Is Human Development?* available online at: http://hdr.undp.org/en/content/what-human-development; https://perma.cc/2PD3-8XZL.

of development. The UNDP clarified that "human development" consists of elements that directly "enhance human abilities," such as a "long and healthy life, knowledge, [and] decent standard of living," and those that create "conditions for human development," such as participation in "political and community life, environmental sustainability, human security and rights, and gender equality."[51] The World Bank's Comprehensive Development Framework (CDF)[52] and the SDGs[53] promoted by the United Nations also encompass this holistic view of development.

The holistic view, although noble in its aspirations, presents some difficulties, as reflected in the criticism raised by Bhupinder Chimni that Sen fails to adequately address the social constraints that inhibit the realization of the holistic goals of development ("development as freedom").[54] There are also economic constraints; to promote non-economic values, such as the rule of law, a society needs trained legal professionals, an efficient court system, and a reliable enforcement mechanism, all of which require considerable economic and technical resources. Access to a clean and safe environment and education also requires economic resources. Thus, without economic development, which enables a developing country to secure necessary economic resources to promote non-economic values, the effective promotion of these values as constituent elements of development may not be realistic. This explains why many places in poverty that fail to achieve economic development also have not met social development goals.

To achieve development goals effectively, one may have to set priorities among the constituent elements of development. It would be particularly difficult for developing countries without sufficient resources to promote all of their economic and social development goals simultaneously with equal focus and strength. The successful East Asian countries ("NICs")[55] prioritized economic development. One may characterize this path as "development without freedom,"[56] but the people of these countries secured political freedom, in addition to greater economic capacity and higher income, by the 1990s, after they achieved economic development and secured sufficient resources to meet social development goals,

---

51 *Ibid.*
52 The CDF accommodates the "social, structural, and human" side of development, such as health, education, and gender equality, human rights, good governance, and the rule of law, as well as economic growth. James D. Wolfensohn, *Comprehensive Development Framework* (February 9, 2000), available online at: http://documents1.worldbank.org/curated/en/208631583185352 783/pdf/The-comprehensive-development-framework.pdf; https://perma.cc/D57N-6Y7X. See also World Bank, *Comprehensive Development Framework: Meeting the Promise?* (September 17, 2001), available online at: http://documents1.worldbank.org/curated/en/593291468779076 728/pdf/303650CDF0meeting0the0promise.pdf; https://perma.cc/L4HJ-CFW5.
53 For further information on the SDGs, see *supra* note 9.
54 Bhupinder Chimni, "The Sen Conception of Development and Contemporary International Law Discourse: Some Parallels" (2008) 1(1) *Law and Development Review* 1–22.
55 For a discussion of the successful development of the NICs, see *supra* note 28.
56 Songok Han Thornton and William H. Thornton, *Development Without Freedom: The Politics of Asian Globalization* (Abington: Routledge, 2008).

including more equitable and democratic political participation based on the rule of law.[57]

The need for prioritization among varied development goals does not mean that non-economic values should be excluded from the notion of development or de-emphasized. Instead, it means that one should, as a practical matter, consider the resource constraints that developing countries face. Developing countries need to have the opportunity to focus on what they need most, so that they may secure the necessary resources to promote non-economic values. The holistic view of development creates multiple development goals and necessitates their sequencing to account for resource constraints. Such prioritization and sequencing will be consistent with the objectives of sustainable development,[58] as the advocated approach allows developing countries to secure the resources necessary to achieve the SDGs.

1.3.2 Economic and social development

Despite the noted importance of economic development, economic development and social development are not completely separate and, in fact, influence each other. The varied distributive effect of economic development among different groups of populations may raise social issues. For instance, economic development based on industrial promotion and exports would benefit those in the manufacturing and export sectors more than subsistence farmers in rural areas, creating economic gaps between urban and rural areas and raising social issues such as the desertion of rural communities by youths and migration to cities. Social progress may also influence economic development. For example, improved gender equality in workplaces, which is considered social progress in many places, can motivate increased female participation in productive economic activities, which, in turn, contributes to overall economic growth.[59]

Given this interrelatedness between economic and social development, is the priority for economic development justified? One may find justification in the compelling contemporary need to overcome the prevalent poverty around the world affecting a majority of the world's population. According to a World Bank report, as of 2017, 9.2 percent of the world population lived on less than US$ 1.90 a day, and nearly a quarter of the world population under US$ 3.20 a day.[60]

---

57 Kerry Rittich also observed that the most outstanding examples of both economic growth and social progress can be found in the NICs. Rittich (2006), *supra* note 49, at 239.
58 *Supra* note 9 (for a reference on the objectives of the SDGs).
59 Rittich (2006), *supra* note 49, at 207, 216 and World Bank, "Engendering Development—Through Gender Equality in Rights, Resources and Voice," *World Bank Policy Research Report* (2001), at 2, available online at: http://documents.worldbank.org/curated/en/51291146832 7401785/pdf/multi-page.pdf; https://perma.cc/TL3T-QHCX.
60 World Bank, *PovcalNet*, available online at: http://iresearch.worldbank.org/PovcalNet/povDupl icateWB.aspx; https://perma.cc/Q8GU-2PQF. Two seminal books in law and development also focus on economic development. See Trubek and Santos (2006), *supra* note 1 and Dam (2006), *supra* note 23.

The only permanent solution to the prevalent poverty issue is successful economic development, which creates an economy that provides economic resources that can bring the majority of populations out of poverty. As discussed in Section 1.2, prioritization and sequencing will also enable developing countries to resolve resource constraints to pursue non-economic development goals effectively.[61] The need for prioritization and sequencing, however, does not mean that the social agenda should always be set aside for economic development. The agenda can be included where it is relevant to promote economic development, as discussed above, or where it can be co-promoted without critical resource implications, regardless of whether it enhances economic development.

The non-economic values that comprise social development raise complex and multifaceted issues with divergent and often irreconcilable views as to their substance, characterization, constituent elements, and enforceability. Despite the existence of values and priorities claimed as "universal," such as fundamental human rights of a political and civil nature, what is viewed as political and social progress is a much broader question that often lacks cross-cultural consensus.[62] For example, one may or may not agree that the legalization of marriages between individuals of the same sex represents social progress.[63] One's subjective value system and preferences of a cultural and ideological nature would be determinative of this question.

As a result, the development of objective analytical criteria for social progress is extremely complex and controversial. There could also be a question as to what constitutes economic development. Nonetheless, the general concept of economic development, which denotes the process of the structural transformation of an economy from one based primarily on the production of primary products (*i.e.*, a product consumed in its unprocessed state), generating low levels of income, to another based on modern industries, generating higher levels of income for the majority of the population, is more widely accepted than any criteria to identify social development.[64] As for social

---

61 See also World Bank, *The World Bank and Human Rights: The Role of the World Bank* (Washington, D.C.: World Bank, 1998), at 5–10 for a discussion of the importance of economic development for the enhancement of human rights.

62 Lee (2015), *supra* note 16, at 4.

63 A U.S. Supreme Court decision legalized marriage between individuals of the same sex ("same-sex marriage") by requiring all States to issue a marriage license to same-sex couples. *Obergefell v. Hodges*, 135 S. Ct. 2584 (2015). However, a majority of countries had not legally recognized same-sex marriage by then.

64 There is, however, no consensus on the measurement of economic development, and no measure captures all the elements of economic development. Subject to this limitation, a possible measure of economic development in a given period is the rate of growth in GDP in the corresponding period. Measuring economic development by a change in GDP may appear to focus on the economic output aspect of economic development too much. There are more comprehensive indexes, such as the human development index (HDI). However, indicators such as HDI measure non-economic elements such as life expectancy, in addition to economic ones, and will thus not be appropriate to measure economic development. In addition, HDI and other similar indexes also tend to correlate with GDP per capita although they include measurement of non-economic aspects of development.

development,[65] most of the controversy centers on the question of its identification; *i.e.*, what should be classified as social progress, as demonstrated by the example cited above. This question is not prone to an objective assessment based on a set of criteria agreeable across different cultures and ideologies.

In this approach, one does not presume or attempt to prescribe what *has to be* considered "social progress" everywhere. The existence of diverse positions and viewpoints, however, does not preclude an observation or criticism that what is advocated as social progress in one place may not be consistent with what is considered to be a universal human right, as determined by relevant international conventions, such as the Universal Declaration of Human Rights (adopted in 1948), the International Covenant on Civil and Political Rights (1966), and the International Covenant on Economic, Social and Cultural Rights (1966). However, the consideration of human rights does not automatically inform what should be considered "social progress" everywhere. The determination of social progress is essentially a value judgment, which is not a majority rule. As observed by a commentator, the adopted approach is essentially descriptive and analytical rather than normative and prescriptive.[66]

1.3.3 Expansion of the concept of development

The concept of "development," which is defined as a progressive transformation of the economy and society, has been traditionally associated with developing countries.[67] However, its transformative nature may render the concept also applicable to economic problems in developed countries to the extent that economic and social transformation and the accompanying changes in law are required to address them. Such application may not be an orthodox approach, but the economic environment faced by many developed countries today may justify this extension of the concept;[68] the neoliberal economic shifts,[69] which have taken place in many developed countries, such as the United States and Britain since the 1980s, have created substantial income gaps among citizens

---

65 "Social development" or "social progress" could be defined as the transformation of a society that fulfills a particular value or a set of values shared by the majority of a society; however, as discussed above, these values are not identical across societies with varied cultural and ideological orientations.

66 William H. J. Hubbard, "Yong-Shik Lee, 'Call for a New Analytical Model for Law and Development': A Comment" (2015) 8(2) *Law and Development Review* 271–276, at 273–274.

67 See *supra* note 45 (for an explanation of the distinction between "developing" and "developed" countries).

68 Thus, the concept of economic development applicable to developed countries, whose economies are based on modern industries, rather than the production of primary products, can be redefined as "the process of progressive transformation of an economy, leading to higher productivity and increases in income for the majority of the population." This redefinition does not reference the structural transformation of an economy from one based primarily on the production of primary products to another based on modern industries, applicable to developing countries.

69 For a discussion of the neoliberal approach, see *supra* note 8.

and regions within developed countries.[70] The widening income gaps and the resulting poverty have led to significant political consequences, such as Britain's referendum outcome to exit the European Union (EU) in 2016 and the unexpected results of the U.S. presidential election in the same year.[71] Thus, the concept of "development" may be relevant to citizens with lower incomes as well as regions in relative economic backwardness within developed countries.[72]

Additionally, the structural issues in the economies of developed countries today, such as persistently low economic growth accompanied by significant unemployment and the institutional incapacity to deal with these issues, are not only cyclical economic issues that were once considered a normality in developed economies but also resemble the chronic problems of the developing world.[73] As such, there is a rising necessity for new analytical approaches, such as the legal and institutional approaches (*i.e.*, the law and development approach) that are used to deal with economic problems in developing countries and facilitate economic development therein.[74] Chapter 6 illustrates how the law and development approach could be adopted to address the economic problems in the United States.

The question of development also turns on political will; *i.e.*, whether the national leaderships of developed countries will have the political will to reduce the economic gaps existing in their countries and use their political capital for this purpose, at the risk of instigating resistance and losing support from the economic establishment and more prosperous regions that would have to fund this effort. This represents a potential tension between those pushing for more economic equality across the nation and the political and economic establishment in society, who may not stand to benefit from assisting the economically depressed regions. The latter's financial resources and political influence can put considerable pressure on governments promoting a development agenda, although

---

70 The OECD observed increasing wage gaps and household income inequality in a large majority of OECD countries. OECD, *Divided We Stand: Why Inequality Keeps Rising* (OECD Publishing, 2011). For example, according to the U.S. Census Bureau, New Orleans and Detroit are among the most impoverished major cities in the United States, with 27.8 percent and 39.3 percent of their populations living below a poverty line of US$ 24,008 for a family of four, respectively, as of 2014. Both cities also suffer from high rates of crime and low rates of formal education.

71 John Harris, "If You Have Got Money, You Vote In … If You Haven't, You Vote Out," *The Guardian*, June 24, 2016, and Trip Gabriel, "How Erie Went Red: The Economy Sank, and Trump Rose," *The New York Times*, November 12, 2016, www.nytimes.com/2016/11/13/us/politics/pennsylvania-trump-votes.html; https://perma.cc/AB25-Z4ZB.

72 Reflecting this reality, various national, regional, and local governments in developed countries have set up offices to foster "economic development." Examples include the Economic Development Administration (EDA) established under the United States Department of Commerce, the Georgia Department of Economic Development in the State of Georgia, USA, and the Office of Economic Development in the City of New Orleans.

73 Mohamed A. El-Erian, "Why Advanced Economies Need to Learn from Developing Nations," *Bloomberg View*, July 11, 2016.

74 *Ibid.*

the unexpected political outcomes in developed countries, such as the outcome of the 2016 presidential election in the United States and Britain's referendum result to exit the EU, may have affected the weakening of such pressure.[75]

The potential applicability of the law and development approach in developed countries will substantially expand the scope of law and development and its utility beyond addressing development issues in developing countries.[76] However, in expanding the law and development approach to developed countries, there is also a question as to whether the promoted approach would be consistent with the political and legal traditions of individual developed countries. For example, in the United States, the federal government traditionally has not engaged with local economic issues, except those caused by natural catastrophes and other types of emergencies,[77] nor has it traditionally provided economic support targeting economically depressed regions, as regional economic issues are left to be handled by regional and local governments.[78] The problem with this approach is that regional and local governments often lack resources to implement development-facilitating laws that provide sufficient incentives for investment and employment generation.[79] Also, a substantial portion of the general public advocating "small

---

75 For a further observation on this point, see *supra* note 71.

76 Thus, the general theory of law and development ("the general theory"), discussed in Chapter 3, offers an analytical framework to examine the effectiveness of relevant laws in developed countries, as well as developing ones, with references made to their legal frameworks, institutional arrangements, and socioeconomic conditions, in dealing with the cited economic issues faced by developed countries today. For example, we can adopt the general theory to examine the effectiveness of "jobs growth acts" in developed countries in creating jobs for low-income groups and reducing income gaps within these countries. See, *e.g.*, Jobs and Growth Act of 2012, S.C. 2012, c. 31 (Canada) and Humphrey-Hawkins Full Employment Act of 1978, 15 U.S.C. §§ 3101–3152 (expired in 2000) (United States).

77 For example, the U.S. federal government supported $110.6 billion in aid for relief, recovery, and rebuilding efforts in the Gulf Coast of Louisiana following Hurricane Katrina. United States Department of State, *Hurricane Katrina: What Government Is Doing*, available online at: https://2009-2017.state.gov/documents/organization/150082.pdf; https://perma.cc/N7TX-DES7. The U.S. government also expects to spend US$ 5 trillion in economic relief packages for COVID-19. Ben Winck, *The $5 Trillion in Pandemic-era Stimulus Is More Than Triple Great Recession-era Aid—and Suggests a Permanent Shift in the Way Congress Spends*, Business Insider (May 10, 2021), available online at: www.businessinsider.com/stimulus-package-pandemic-surpass-great-recession-fiscal-plans-recovery-2021-3; https://perma.cc/PE2X-93SR. By contrast, a relatively modest amount, US$ 350 million of federal aid, was spent for the bankrupt city of Detroit. Peter Harkness, "Detroit and New Orleans Have More in Common Than Most Think," *Governing* (January 2016), available online at: www.governing.com/archive/gov-detroit-new-orleans-resilience.html; https://perma.cc/ZV3P-33AD.

78 This is generally the case except for small-scale support for "economically distressed areas" provided by the EDA under the authority of the Public Works and Economic Development Act of 1965 (PWEDA), as amended, 42 U.S.C. § 3161 *et seq.* In Fiscal Year 2018, the EDA supported 692 development projects for a total grant of US$ 381 million, averaging around $550,000 per project. Economic Development Administration, *2018 Annual Report* (2019), available online at: www.eda.gov/files/annual-reports/fy2018/EDA-FY2018-Annual-Report-full.pdf; https://perma.cc/T9WS-R3FE.

79 Local and regional governments may provide incentives in the form of tax reduction or exemptions, but the finances of many regional and local governments may not be strong enough to afford

government" in developed countries may not support the idea of the government taking up an active role in economic development by spending public resources. Thus, this also involves the question of the appropriate role of the state in the economy, which is the subject of an on-going debate.[80]

meaningful tax relief and other concessions in lieu of direct subsidy payments. See Lucy Dadayan and Donald J. Boyd, *By the Numbers: 2016: Another Lackluster Year for State Tax Revenue* (Rockefeller Institute of Government) (May 2017), available online at: http://rockinst.org/wp-content/uplo ads/2018/02/2017-05-08-By-numbers-brief-no9-1.pdf; https://perma.cc/DQ5A-ESBZ.

80 See Joseph Stiglitz, "Globalization and the Economic Role of the State in the New Millennium" (2003) 12(1) *Industrial and Corporate Change* 3–26; George J. Stigler and Paul A. Samuelson, "A Dialogue on the Proper Role of the State," *University of Chicago Graduate School of Business Selected Papers*, no. 7 (1968); Peter J. Boettke and Peter T. Leeson, *The Economic Role of the State* (Aldershot: Edward Elgar, 2015).

2 Evolution of law and development

2.1 Law and development "movements"[81]

The idea that law is relevant to economic and social progress is not new. Adam Smith opined that "the imperfection of the law and the uncertainty in its application" was a factor that retarded commerce.[82] Max Weber, a lauded sociologist and philosopher of the late nineteenth and the early twentieth centuries, explained the importance of "rational" law in the economy and society.[83] Friedrich Hayek, another prominent philosopher and economist of the twentieth century, also discussed relevant legal concepts to support liberty as the cornerstone of wealth and growth.[84] The term "law and development" emerged and gained significance after the Second World War, when a group of scholars, practitioners, private foundations, and aid agencies in developed countries made efforts to transplant laws and legal practices from developed countries, particularly the United States, to assist in the economic and social progress of developing countries in the Third World.[85]

Modernization theory, which developed in the 1950s and 1960s, influenced these initial efforts, which are collectively referred to as the first "law and development movement."[86] Scholars who advanced this theory, such as Walt Rostow, argued that the modernization (development) of the Third World would be accomplished by the diffusion of capital, institutions, and values from the First World.[87] "Modern law" was believed to be the "functional prerequisite of an

---

81 This section is adapted from Lee (2017), *supra* note 4, part I, section A, at 420–423. The law and development movements are also referenced as distinct "moments" in law and development. David M. Trubek and Alvaro Santos, "Introduction: The Third Moment in Law and Development Theory and the Emergence of a New Critical Practice," *in The New Law and Economic Development, supra* note 1, at 1–18.

82 Adam Smith, *Lectures on Jurisprudence* (New York: Oxford University Press, 1978), at 528.

83 Max Weber, *Law in Economy and Society* (translated by Max Rheinstein) (New York: Simon and Schuster, 1954).

84 For Hayek's discussion on law, liberty, and economic growth, see Friedrich Hayek, *Law, Legislation, and Liberty*, vols. 1–3 (Chicago: University of Chicago Press, 1979).

85 See David M. Trubek, "The 'Rule of Law' in Development Assistance: Past, Present, and Future," *in The New Law and Economic Development, supra* note 1, at 74–75.

86 *Ibid.*, at 74–81.

87 Kevin Davis and Michael J. Trebilcock, "The Relationship between Law and Development: Optimists versus Skeptics" (2008) 56(4) *American Journal of Comparative Law* 895–946, at 900.

DOI: 10.4324/9781003090175-3

industrial economy";[88] law was seen as "a force which can be molded and manipulated to alter human behavior and achieve development."[89] Despite its laudable objective, the first law and development movement was largely unsuccessful. According to Trubek and Galanter, the ethnocentric assumptions about the nature and role of law, its relationship to social change, and the role of certain institutions (*e.g.*, judiciary) ignored local realities, in turn denying the field a functional theory that could be institutionalized.[90] Consequently, reformers faced considerable difficulty in implementing laws and legal practices adopted from developed countries, including reform of legal education, in developing countries where key socioeconomic conditions,[91] which were essential to their successful implementation, did not exist (such as lack of legal academic tradition amenable to the adoption of American law school-style education in the case of educational reform). Their absence was either overlooked or ignored.[92]

Law and development was resuscitated in the 1980s and 1990s after the fall of the Soviet bloc, with the proliferation of neoliberal[93] law reform projects that sought to reduce state intervention in the economy by promoting privatization and deregulation of the economy.[94] This second law and development movement (or the "Second Moment in law and development")[95] was substantially larger in scale and impact than the first, with significant effects on development projects and policies around the world.[96] The outcome of the second law and development movement was mixed at best, failing to result in successful development for most of the developing world.[97] Moreover, some of these reforms caused serious economic difficulties around the world, as demonstrated by the devastating economic outcome of the market-shock therapy in Russia, the economic emergency experienced by many Latin American countries adopting neoliberal policy prescriptions in the 1980s, and the serious economic recession in Asian

---

88 David M. Trubek, "Toward a Social Theory of Law: An Essay on the Study of Law and Development" (1972) 82(1) *Yale Law Journal* 1–50, at 6.

89 Elliot M. Berg, "Law and Development: A Review of the Literature and a Critique of 'Scholar in Self-Estrangement' " (1977) 25(2) *American Journal of Comparative Law* 492–530, at 505–506.

90 Trubek and Galanter (1974), *supra* note 33.

91 A series of presumptions or "pillars" on which the first law and development movement proceeded, such as a cultural reform and transplantation strategy, an *ad hoc* approach to reform based on simplistic theoretical assumptions, faith in spillovers from the economy to democracy and human rights, and a development strategy that stressed state-led import substitution, collapsed by the 1970s. See Trubek (2006), *supra* note 85, at 78–81.

92 Trubek and Galanter (1974), *supra* note 33.

93 The neoliberal approach is based on neoclassical economics, which emerged in the late nineteenth century and reaffirmed, against Marxism, that the market promotes economic efficiency and fair social distribution. Neoliberalism, which became a dominant political-economic ideology in the 1980s, discouraged positive government intervention in the economy and promoted free market approaches, including privatization and trade liberalization.

94 Trubek and Santos (2006), *supra* note 81, at 3.

95 *Ibid.*

96 *Ibid.*

97 *Ibid.*, at 6–7.

countries which resulted from the neoliberal measures imposed by international financial institutions to address their financial crisis in the 1990s.[98] The problems of the subsequent neoliberal movement of the 1980s paralleled those associated with the first law and development movement in that both presumed a set of conditions which did not exist on the ground for the operations of market and law, such as the (erroneous) premise that legal order applies, interprets, and changes "universalistic rules."[99] These conditions were nevertheless presumed when a set of prescriptions were imposed on developing countries in the context of development projects, and because of the unrealistic presumptions, the outcome was an eventual failure in both cases.

The reformers' ideological drive, which predominated the funding selection, implementation, and evaluation of development and law reform projects, was another cause for their failure.[100] The neoliberal position, as expressed by the Washington Consensus,[101] significantly affected development project funding from the aid agencies of major developed countries, as well as international financial institutions. While some of the most successful development experiences after the Second World War exhibited a policy path that was substantially different from this neoliberal stance, development projects did not incorporate lessons of such successes,[102] even after a substantial number of the projects that followed the neoliberal logic did not deliver their promised outcomes.

Law and development has been undergoing a period of reflection and new approaches, referred to as the "third moment," since the late 1990s.[103] Critical legal studies, postcolonial studies, and the Third World Approaches to International Law (TWAIL) formed an important academic context for this reflection.[104] Scholars noted that the new movement included a mix of different ideas for development policy, such as a new emphasis on market failures and the necessity of compensatory interventions, and the redefinition of "development" as a concept that exceeded merely economic growth to include notions of "human freedom."[105] They also acknowledged that a new form of development

---

98 These failures demonstrated that "markets do not create the conditions for their own success." *Ibid.* For further discussion of the Asian financial crisis, see also Hider A. Khan, *Global Markets and Financial Crises in Asia* (New York: Palgrave Macmillan, 2004).

99 See Trubek and Galanter (1974), *supra* note 33, at 1070–1080.

100 Santos (2006), *supra* note 7, at 296–297.

101 For a discussion of the Washington Consensus, see *supra* note 8.

102 Certain East Asian countries, such as Korea, Taiwan, Singapore, and, more recently, China, have achieved remarkable economic development, rising from a state of poverty to that of developed economies, by adopting strong state-driven industrial policies and through state involvement in the economy; however, these lessons were not incorporated in the development projects by international development agencies, such as the World Bank. For an account of the success of East Asian economies and the role of the state, see Yong-Shik Lee, *Reclaiming Development in the World Trading System* (2nd ed., Cambridge: Cambridge University Press, 2016), at 14–32, 301–333.

103 Trubek and Santos (2006), *supra* note 81, at 7–9.

104 See *supra* note 44 (for a reference on the critiques and their works).

105 Trubek and Santos (2006), *supra* note 81, at 7–8.

doctrine was emerging, which accepted the use of law not only to create and protect markets but also to curb market excess, support the social, and provide direct relief to the poor.[106] Supporting a more holistic view of development,[107] the new development doctrine incorporated a range of non-market values as the objectives of development. For example, law (or the rule of law) has become a development objective itself, not just a means to achieve other development objectives, which was how it was perceived in the two preceding movements.[108] Another notable development in this period is that major intergovernmental organizations, including the United Nations, initiated global efforts to eradicate poverty, such as the Millennium Development Goals (MDGs: 2000–2015)[109] and the subsequent Sustainable Development Goals (SDGs: 2015–2030).[110] As noted in Chapter 1, the SDGs include the rule of law among their targets under 17 economic and social development goals to be achieved by 2030.[111]

2.2 Evolution of law and development studies[112]

This section examines the evolution of law and development studies over the last four decades since the seminal publication of "Scholars in Self-Estrangement,"[113] which analyzed the growth of law and development as an area of inquiry in the United States in the 1950s and 1960s and assessed why law and development studies faced a crisis by the early 1970s.[114] Since then, scholars have addressed issues of law and development, but a theoretical framework and consistent methodology were not developed until recently. The following discussion provides summaries of academic literature[115] categorized by relevant topics

---

106 *Ibid.* Philipp Dann opined that another discussion is also central, namely about global governance, global administrative law, and the question of how to manage the world (or in the narrower development policy world, the discussions about aid effectiveness). In his view, the institutional dimension of how development interventions are actually organized has a central impact on development itself (correspondence on file with the author).

107 For an explanation of the holistic view, see discussion *supra* Section 1.3.1.

108 David Kennedy, "The 'Rule of Law,' Political Choices, and Development Common Sense," *in The New Law and Economic Development, supra* note 1, at 156–157.

109 For further details of the achievement of the MDGs, see United Nations, *The Millennium Development Goals Report 2015* (2015), available online at: www.un.org/millenniumgoals/ 2015_MDG_Report/pdf/MDG%202015%20rev%20(July%201).pdf; https://perma.cc/ 23WM-CXF5.

110 For further information on the SDGs, see United Nations, *Sustainable Development Goals, supra* note 9.

111 *Ibid.*, SDG Goal 16: "Promote just, peaceful and inclusive societies."

112 This section is adapted from Lee (2015), *supra* note 16, section 2.1, at 10–24.

113 Trubek and Galanter (1974), *supra* note 33.

114 In contrast, a parallel movement based on "law and economics," which examines the economic efficiency of law, did not face this type of crisis within academia.

115 For another review of the field, see Davis and Trebilcock (2008), *supra* note 87. See also David M. Trubek, "Law and Development 50 Years On," *University of Wisconsin Legal Studies Research Paper*, no. 1212 (2012), available online at: http://ssrn.com/abstract=2161899, accessed January 7, 2021.

in law and development, followed by a short assessment of the path forward in Section 2.3.

2.2.1 A field in "crisis"

"Scholars in Self-Estrangement" accounted that law and development, starting as development assistance activities of the United States after the Second World War,[116] was a reflection of how Washington believed its systems could help the Third World to develop. As discussed in Section 2.1, the first law and development movement was not successful, and scholars came to realize that the gaps caused by ethnocentric assumptions and ignorance about the nature and role of law, its relationship to social change, and the role of certain institutions such as the judiciary ignored local realities and prevented law and development projects from realizing their objectives.[117] This led to a moral dilemma among scholars, subsequently called a "crisis" in the field, and resulted in the movement's demise.[118]

Jon Merryman explored further into the movement's failure.[119] He observed that because the legal assistance lacked any theoretical backing, it became a direct export of American legislation, and he made a suggestion that a more appropriate name and perspective for the field would be "comparative law and social change," which implies that law and development should not just be a direct transfer of laws from developed countries but needs to be an analytical process, allowing subsequent adjustment of those laws to fit the local conditions.[120] James Gardner argued that the fundamental failure of the law and development movement was the lack of understanding of the multiple roles of law in diverse processes of social change and individual choice.[121] Building from this assessment, Nobuyuki Yasuda also suggested that it may be desirable in the long term to integrate or at least coordinate regional laws and policies on the basis that reflects regional rather than Western traditions.[122]

Brian Tamanaha subsequently observed that law and development's "irrelevance" as a field lies in the fact that its proponents were too keen on results, as well as in the belief of social scientists that they could objectively solve the multifaceted problems faced by any society.[123] Yet, they consistently failed to

---

116 Trubek and Galanter (1974), *supra* note 33.
117 *Ibid.*
118 *Ibid.*
119 Jon Henry Merryman, "Comparative Law and Social Change: On the Origins, Style, Decline & Revival of the Law and Development Movement" (1977) 25 *American Journal of Comparative Law* 457–483.
120 *Ibid.*
121 James Gardner, *Legal Imperialism: American Lawyers and Foreign Aid in Latin America* (Madison: University of Wisconsin Press, 1980).
122 Nobuyuki Yasuda, "Law and Development in ASEAN Countries" (1993) 10(2) *ASEAN Economic Bulletin* 144–154.
123 Brian Tamanaha, "The Lessons of Law-and-Development Studies" (1995) 89(2) *American Journal of International Law* 470–486.

understand the entire spectrum of issues faced by developing countries that need to be addressed in a successful law and development program.[124] Tamanaha opined that while law may be essential for development and political reforms, law and development scholars should simultaneously place more emphasis on local situations.[125] Maxwell Chibundu considered this issue in the African context[126] and reached the same conclusion; Chibundu concluded that the law and development movement must not only learn from past mistakes but also about its imperfections as a standard,[127] which indicates the necessity to improve the standard by developing an analytical framework to meet the need.

2.2.2 Law and development in neoliberalism: the rule of law

The 1980s saw the fall of communism in Eastern Europe and the rise of neoliberalism represented by the "Washington Consensus."[128] International financial and development institutions, based on the Washington Consensus, provided large amounts of financial support for development projects. With these changes, the law and development movement found a new lease on life and new avenues to approach its objectives.[129] An important line of inquiry in this period was the rule of law. Thomas Carothers evaluated the rule of law experience, cautioning renewed optimism while promoting a repackaged law and development formulation.[130] He attributed the reemerging interest in the rule of law to the pressures stemming from globalization and surmised that the real challenge lies in nurturing internal pressure to implement the rule of law. Richard Posner, after examining the failures of legal transplants in generating development, was convinced that it is the quality of specific laws as opposed to the quality of the judiciary and legal structures that can deliver development because the former is easier to apply in developing countries where weak legal training and limited economic resources render the application of complex and abstract standards associated with the latter more difficult.[131] He also emphasized the necessity of contract and property laws for economic growth.[132]

124 *Ibid.*
125 *Ibid.*
126 Maxwell Chibundu, "Law in Development: On Tapping, Gourding and Serving Palm-Wine" (1997) 29(2) *Case Western Reserve Journal of International Law* 167–261.
127 Chibundu also argued that since law represents the collective interactions and social constraints on the individual, it should be concerned not only with the physical necessities of the population but their ideological and social aspirations as well. *Ibid.*
128 For further discussion of the Washington Consensus, see *supra* note 8.
129 Thus, some scholars call this development the second law and development movement. See discussion *supra* Section 2.1.
130 Thomas Carothers, "The Rule of Law Revival," *Foreign Affairs* (March/April 1998), available online at: www.foreignaffairs.com/articles/53809/thomas-carothers/the-rule-of-law-revival; https://perma.cc/G4DN-GVWN.
131 Posner (1998), *supra* note 38.
132 *Ibid.*

In furthering the exploration of the rule of law, Rachel Belton placed definitions of the rule of law under two headings: (i) those focusing on the ends that the rule of law is intended to serve within society (such as upholding law and order or providing predictable and efficient judgments), and (ii) those that highlight the institutional attributes considered necessary to actuate the rule of law (such as comprehensive laws, well-functioning courts, and trained law enforcement agencies).[133] For practical and historical reasons, legal scholars and philosophers have favored the former definition, while practitioners of the rule of law development programs have tended to use the latter.

Stressing the rule of law issue in analyzing whether formal contracts are necessary for economic growth, Michael Trebilcock and Jing Leng concluded that at low levels of development, informal methods of contract enforcement could substitute for formal enforcement.[134] According to Trebilcock and Leng, even the absence of strict adherence to the rule of law could result in economic growth,[135] which implies that the formal rule of law may not be essential for economic development, at least in the initial stages of economic development. Frank Upham also found that the rule of law orthodoxy ignores evidence that the formalistic rule of law, as advocated by the World Bank and other donors, does not exist in the developed world and that attempting to transplant a set of institutions and legal rules into developing countries without attention to the local, indigenous contexts would be counterproductive and undermine preexisting local mechanisms for dealing with issues such as property ownership and conflict resolution.[136]

The characterization and understanding of the rule of law concept has also been a point of discussion: Simon Chesterman noted that nearly universal support for the rule of law, found at both the international and national levels, is only possible because of widely divergent views of what it means in practice.[137] However, this pluralism, while it may not pose a problem when existing simultaneously at national levels, needs to be reassessed in the international context.[138] In this vein, Chesterman proposed a core definition of the rule of law as a political ideal and argued that its applicability to the international level would depend on that ideal being seen as a means rather than an end or as serving a function rather than defining a status.[139] It has been observed that the promotion of the rule of law

133 Rachel Kleinfeld Belton, "Competing Definitions of the Rule of Law: Implications for Practitioners," *Carnegie Papers, Rule of Law Series* (2005), available online at: http://carnegieendowment.org/files/CP55.Belton.FINAL.pdf; https://perma.cc/2PRN-PQLX.

134 Michael J. Trebilcock and Jing Leng, "The Role of Formal Contract Law and Enforcement in Economic Development" (2006) 92 *Virginia Law Review* 1517–1580.

135 *Ibid.*

136 Frank Upham, "Mythmaking in the Rule of Law Orthodoxy," *Carnegie Papers, Rule of Law Series* (2005), available online at: http://carnegieendowment.org/files/wp30.pdf; https://perma.cc/AT6P-WUVW.

137 Simon Chesterman, "An International Rule of Law?" (2008) 56(2) *American Journal of Comparative Law* 331–361.

138 *Ibid.*

139 *Ibid.*

and good governance have delivered neither the improved rule of law nor the improved governance envisioned.[140] While the causes of these alleged failures may not be entirely clear, promoting the rule of law without sufficient understanding of the local conditions could have been a reason.[141]

Finally, on the rule of law, scholars have observed the increasing role that intergovernmental organizations play in international and transnational law-making, some in ways that were not anticipated by their constituent charters (as demonstrated by the World Bank's intervention, in its capacity as an institutional lender, in the governance of otherwise sovereign borrowing countries).[142] According to this observation, the increased role has been achieved by the expansion of the institutional mandate, employing a specific constitutional hermeneutic grounded in the balancing of institutional teleology with charter constraints.[143] Some scholars reference the emerging rules applying to development projects, including those which resulted from the expansion of the institutional mandate of the intergovernmental organizations, as the law of development cooperation, and argue that it has become a fundamental influence on the development and implementation of development projects in Africa, Latin America, and elsewhere.[144] Additionally, international economic law, including the legal frameworks for international trade under the auspices of the World Trade Organization (WTO), largely based on the neoliberal logic, also has a substantial impact on economic development by setting legal parameters on a wide range of development policies affecting trade and investment.[145]

2.2.3 Law and development in neoliberalism: financial assistance and financial markets

In addition to the rule of law, another focal point of the neoliberal development initiative was financial assistance, spearheaded by the World Bank, providing financial support for general development projects, and by the International Monetary Fund (IMF), for developing countries in financial distress. Carol Rose explored the renewed interest in law and development as a consequence of increased financial assistance to states by international financial institutions.[146] Rose used Vietnam

---

140 Thomas McInerney, "Law and Development as Democratic Practice" (2007) 37 *Vanderbilt Journal of Transnational Law* 935–969.

141 For example, the rule of law reforms that took place in Mexico for 20 years starting in the 1980s were met with mixed results. See Robert Kossick, "The Rule of Law and Development in Mexico" (2004) 21 *Arizona Journal of International and Comparative Law* 715–834.

142 Dimitri Van Den Meerssche, "The Evolving Mandate of the World Bank: How Constitutional Hermeneutics Shaped the Concept and Practice of Rule of Law Reform" (2017) 10(1) *Law and Development Review* 89–118.

143 *Ibid.*

144 Dann (2013), *supra* note 44.

145 For example, WTO rules prohibit member states from adopting export subsidies (subsidies contingent upon exportation), which was a key development policy of successful developing countries in the past. See *infra* note 802. See also Lee (2016), *supra* note 102.

146 Carol Rose, "The 'New' Law and Development Movement in the Post-Cold War Era: A Vietnam Case Study" (1998) 32 *Law and Society Review* 93–140.

as a case study to demonstrate a move away from the idea of legal transplants that was at the core of the first law and development movement.[147] She outlined that Vietnam acceded to legal cooperation but only incorporated legal developments within certain sectors and with no influence on the political setup (perhaps mirroring China).[148] Rose emphasized that the main challenge of the law and development movement was to protect against elites' attempts to leverage law and development as a means of legitimizing policy changes that make no provision to mitigate against the adverse impacts of a market economy.[149]

Others investigated the role of investor rights in financial development, corporate governance, and bankruptcy. According to a study by Stijn Claessens and Leora Klapper, a higher rate of bankruptcies is observed in countries with stronger creditor rights and judicial efficiency.[150] Katharina Pistor and Chenggang Xu opined that jump-starting stock markets in transitional economies had proved difficult, largely because these countries lacked effective legal governance structures and faced severe information problems.[151] Yet, not all financial markets failed because of a lackluster structural climate. Using China's initial stock market development as a case study, Pistor and Xu suggested that in certain circumstances, administrative governance can successfully substitute for formal legal governance.[152] As for the role of foreign investment in development, Jonas Bergstein's work on Uruguay concluded that there needs to be a two-pronged approach to investment and development[153]: first, steps should be taken to develop social and human capital to take advantage of the inward investments, and second, investment and economic policy should be aimed at maximizing the jurisdiction's attractiveness to investors in a competitive global marketplace.[154] A difficult task will be to balance the economic and social cost of such maximization against the actual benefit expected from the investment. This balancing may involve substantial regulatory adjustment.

Amy Chua addressed the problem of financial inequality and highlighted the problems caused by the deep ethnic divisions that exist within many developing countries, pointing out that the problems this poses to the law and development program are often overlooked.[155] Most significantly, when markets favor a certain ethnic group, often a different group is favored by democracy.[156] This creates

---

147   See discussion *supra* Section 2.1.
148   Rose (1998), *supra* note 146.
149   *Ibid.*
150   Stijn Claessens and Leora Klapper, "Bankruptcy Around the World: Explanations of Its Relative Use" (2005) 7(1) *American Law and Economics Review* 253–283.
151   Katharina Pistor and Chenggang Xu, "Governing Stock Markets in Transition Economies: Lessons from China" (2005) 7(1) *American Law and Economics Review* 184–210.
152   *Ibid.*
153   Jonas Bergstein, "Foreign Investment in Uruguay: A Law and Development Perspective" (1989) 20(2) *University of Miami Inter-American Law Review* 359–392.
154   *Ibid.*
155   Amy Chua, "Markets, Democracy, and Ethnicity: Toward a New Paradigm for Law and Development" (1998) 108(1) *Yale Law Journal* 1–107.
156   *Ibid.*

an obvious tension between majoritarian interests and the interests of those who produce the wealth required to improve a country's economic prospects.[157] This analysis can be applied to a broader class issue in a society where the interest of the state and those in the elite class, which may promote the long-term economic prosperity through maximizing resources for productive investments, does not align with others (perhaps in relative poverty) who may want immediate disbursement of the available resources through welfare spending and other means, even if the latter choice would reduce resources available for long-term investment. This conflict implies that a democratic choice may not always be most efficient for economic development, justifying, at least in part, the authoritarian economic governance of some East Asian countries during their rapid economic development from the 1960s through the 1980s.[158]

In the late 1990s, a group of scholars including Raphael La Porta, Florencio Lopez-de-Silanes, Andrei Shleifer, and Robert Vishny (collectively, "LLSV") conducted comparative studies and argued that legal origin helps to explain cross-country differences in financial development.[159] LLSV tried to demonstrate that the country's development in the financial market and its laws on property rights, shareholder rights, and creditor rights are affected by its legal origins, including, for example, common law or civil law legal origins.[160] Their work concluded that common law is superior in the development of a financial market. LLSV argued,

> The economic consequences of legal origins are pervasive. Compared to French civil law, common law is associated with (a) better investor protection, which in turn is associated with improved financial development, better access to finance, and higher ownership dispersion, (b) lighter government ownership and regulation, which are in turn associated with less corruption, better functioning labor markets, and smaller unofficial economies, and (c) less formalized and more independent judicial systems, which are in turn associated with more secure property rights and better contract enforcement.[161]

LLSV's works significantly influenced academia as well as development programs[162] and brought attention to institutions in the context of development studies. However, criticism has been raised that the gaps cited by LLSV in economic performance among those countries may not be attributed to differences in the legal origin at all; the convergence of common law and civil law systems

---

157 *Ibid.*
158 See *supra* note 28 (for a reference on the successful development of the East Asian countries).
159 LLSV (1998), *supra* note 23.
160 For an explanation of "common law" and "civil law," *supra* note 17. See also LLSV (2000), *supra* note 23 and LLSV (2002), *supra* note 23.
161 LLSV, "The Economic Consequences of Legal Origins" (2008) 46(2) *Journal of Economic Literature* 285–332, at 298.
162 LLSV's work is known to have influenced the World Bank in its development-support programs such as "Doing Business" and other specific development programs in developing countries.

largely muted the alleged effect of the distinct system,[163] and there is no convincing correlation between legal origin and economic growth, as there may have been another cause such as a difference in macroeconomic policy initiatives.[164] Simon Deakin also pointed out the limits of the legal origin theory as based on limited data and concluded that it is premature to use it as a basis for policy initiatives.[165]

2.2.4 State institutions

State institutions have always been at the center of law and development, whether they have been addressed from the perspective of developmental states[166] in the first law and development wave, which underscored the positive role of the state for development, or from the subsequent neoliberal perspective, which focused on limiting state involvement in the economy and encouraged privatization and deregulation.[167] Addressing state institutions, Frank Cross concluded, based on empirical evidence, that the necessity of legal institutions for economic growth is unquestionable, but further comparative legal research would be necessary to ascertain which institutions are most suitable for this purpose.[168] Davis and Trebilcock pointed out that it is the quality of the institutions that administer law and not the law *per se* that offers a chance for development,[169] which contrasts with Posner's earlier emphasis on specific law over institutions.[170]

Law, legal frameworks, and institutions (LFIs) affect one another and cannot be considered in isolation; thus, it is doubtful that the relative importance can somehow be assigned to one over another where LFIs are constituent

163 Frank Cross, "Identifying the Virtues of the Common Law" (2007) 15(1) *Supreme Court Economic Review* 21–59.
164 See Giuseppe Maggio, Alessandro Romano, and Angela Troisi, "The Legal Origin of Income Inequality" (2014) 7(1) *Law and Development Review* 1–22 and Dam (2006), *supra* note 23, at 39.
165 Simon Deakin, "Legal Origin, Juridical Form and Industrialisation in Historical Perspective: The Case of the Employment Contract and the Joint-Stock Company" (2008) 4(7) *Comparative Research in Law and Political Economy* 1–39. Joel Trachtman also commented that the LLSV and related literature was flawed because of the problems with the legal system specifications and the misplaced causation.
166 A "developmental state" is a sovereign state that assumes the key role for economic development and "creates [economic development] plans, relocate[s] surplus, combat[s] resistance, invest[s] and manage[s] key sectors, and control[s] foreign capital." Trubek and Santos (2006), *supra* note 81, at 8.
167 See *supra* note 8 (for a discussion of the neoliberal prescriptions). In addition to state institutions, intergovernmental institutions, such as the World Bank, play an important role in development by shaping how development projects are designed, implemented, and controlled at the international level. See also discussion *supra* Section 2.2.2 (for the increasing role that intergovernmental organizations play in international and transnational law-making).
168 Cross (2001), *supra* note 23. See also *supra* note 38 (for the types of institutions that are necessary to promote economic growth).
169 Davis and Trebilcock (2001), *supra* note 35.
170 Posner (1998), *supra* note 38.

parts of an amalgam, which by combination formulates a regulatory system. As discussed above, the same law can have a very different impact on development, depending upon the makeup of the institution that administers and enforces the law.[171] However, it is also the case that the same institution may have different impacts on development depending upon the law that the institution is assigned to administer and which organizes and supports the institution. Likewise, legal frameworks in which a law is organized to take effect are also relevant.[172]

The importance of state institutions has also been highlighted in the context of the successful economic development experience in East Asia.[173] Analyzing the role of law in the economic development of Korea, Y.H. Jung found that the pervasive and paternalistic influence of the state, rather than law, was vital for Korea's economic development.[174] According to Jung, the function served by law was limited in that there were fewer courts, lawyers, and institutions promoting Western-style legal learning during the development periods of Korea from the 1960s to the 1980s.[175] However, while the state played a key role for economic development in Korea, it is not conclusive that the fewer legal institutions, as argued by Jung, are necessarily indicative of lesser importance of law during the development of Korea: all of the major state development policies were meticulously legislated during the development era[176] and executed by legal means. Thus, there is sufficient scope for considering the role of law in Korean economic development in conjunction with its institutional arrangements.[177] As indicated by Joseph Stiglitz and Sergio Godoy, the state carried out a vital role of mediating the synergy between the old structures and new forms, as necessitated by development, and may not have necessarily downplayed the role of law.[178] John Ohnesorge also observed that given the indisputable success of economic and social development in Northeast Asia, it would be impossible to justify excluding

---

171 See discussion *supra* Section 1.2.

172 *Ibid.*

173 See *supra* note 28 (for a reference on the successful development of the East Asian countries).

174 Y.H. Jung, "How Did Law Matter for Korean Economic Development? Evidence From 1970s," paper prepared for the Korean Economic Association Conference (June 2012).

175 *Ibid.*

176 Legislation in Korea for economic development has been compiled in multivolume works with the support of the Korean government and Korea Development Institute (KDI). See Duol Kim (ed.), *History of Economic Laws in Korea: From Liberation to Present*, vols. 1–4 (Seoul: Haenam Publishing Co., 2011).

177 Professor Simon Deakin of the University of Cambridge also opined that non-legal mechanisms, such as corruption and authoritarianism, may support small numbers bargaining, but they cannot sustain impersonal, large-scale exchanges over long time periods. He observed that, in China, the limits of the mechanisms of guanxi (informal personal relations), on the one hand, and state power, on the other hand, are becoming clear. Hans-Bernd Schäfer also agreed that there are alternative, non-legal institutions, such as informal and bureaucratic methods of investor protection by social and political control, which might lead to investor protection and growth, but only for a limited time (correspondences on file with the author).

178 Sergio Godoy and Joseph Stiglitz, "Growth, Initial Conditions, Law and Speed of Privatization in Transition Countries: 11 Years Later," *National Bureau of Economic Research Working Paper*, no. 11992 (2006).

Northeast Asia, including Korea, from the center of law and development studies and emphasized the importance of studying their legal systems in the context of law and development.[179]

Mariana Prado added a new dimension in the discussion of state institutions by addressing the possibility of "institutional bypass" as a new way of development reform.[180] Prado observed that the results from the large-scale development assistance for institutional reforms had ranged from mixed to disappointing and identified successful institutional reforms that had a common feature: they bypassed dysfunctional institutions instead of trying to fix them, as most failed reforms did, and created a new institution in which efficiency and functionality would be the norm.[181] Institutional bypass is a noteworthy idea that can provide a breakthrough when institutional reform is resisted by those who have vested interests in maintaining the status quo. Yet, there would be a limit to the bypass method depending upon the role of the institution subject to reform. If the institution's primary role is policy-making, an institutional bypass would not be feasible because then institutional bypass may create multiple decision-makers who may render conflicting decisions. Additionally, the problems of the duplicity of spending scarce financial resources and limited manpower in developing countries could also be a ground for objection to the bypass method.

Finally, the role of state institutions in development is closely intertwined with the role of the state in economic development. As further discussed in Chapter 11, pro-development state institutions, such as government agencies devoted to the development and implementation of economic development policies, financial institutions set up under state mandate to facilitate national development, and state-supported entities designed to promote international trade and investment, have all played important developmental roles in successful developing countries.[182] Even in countries where the state does not play such a leading role in development, institutions that need to be protected and promoted

---

179 John Ohnesorge, "Developing Development Theory: Law and Development Orthodoxies and the Northeast Asian Experience" (2006) 28(2) *University of Pennsylvania Journal of International Economic Law* 219–307.

180 Mariana Prado, "Institutional Bypass: An Alternative for Development Reform" (April 19, 2011), text available online at: http://papers.ssrn.com/sol3/papers.cfm?abstract_id=1815442; https://perma.cc/ANR4-K8BS.

181 *Ibid.* An example of an institutional bypass that Prado introduced is a bureaucratic reform in Brazil called Poupatempo ("Saving Time"). *Id.*, at 3. In 1997, the government of the state of Sao Paulo created a one-stop shop for bureaucratic services that had been offered at multiple service points, offices of the federal, state, and, in some cases, local administration. *Id.* For convenience and faster service, Poupatempo became the main provider of governmental services within the state shortly after its creation. *Id.*

182 The dynamics between state institutions and economic development trajectory may be understood under the notion of "state capitalism." See Yong-Shik Lee, "State Capitalism and the Law," *in* Geoffrey Wood (ed.), *Oxford Handbook of State Capitalism and The Firm* (Oxford: Oxford University Press, forthcoming 2022), available online at: https://papers.ssrn.com/sol3/papers.cfm?abstract_id=3368065; https://perma.cc/G5L4-M3DM.

by the state, such as institutions for the protection of property rights and contract enforcement, are considered to be relevant to development. A study concludes that open access to economic organizations and activities in the absence of the necessary institutions in the areas of property rights protection, contract enforcement, the financial market, the rule of law, and human resources accumulation does not lead to long-term economic growth.[183]

2.2.5 Emphasis on economic development and neoinstitutional approaches

Chapter 1 emphasized the importance of economic development among development agendas.[184] Two major law and development publications also show the focus on economic development: one compiled by David Trubek and Alvaro Santos, titled "The New Law and Economic Development: A Critical Appraisal,"[185] and the other by Kenneth Dam, "The Law-Growth Nexus."[186] The former book analyzed the law and development movements since the 1950s and explored a new, "third" law and development moment that appeared to be forming.[187] Several leading scholars, including David Trubek, Duncan Kennedy, David Kennedy, Scott Newton, Kerry Rittich, and Alvaro Santos, discussed their views on relevant topics such as the rule of law in development assistance, the dynamics, and interrelations among the rule of law, political choice, and development, incorporation of the social, as well as the World Bank's uses of the rule of law promise in economic development.[188] Although the authors did not share the same view about the nature and objective of the third movement, they agreed that a new moment in law and development, which was distinctive from the previous two, was emerging.[189] Some of the authors also seemed to acknowledge the limited impact that law and institutions may have on economic development; Santos, for example, cited evidence to suggest that an efficient judiciary and clearly defined formal property rights are often of limited relevance to entrepreneurs in developing countries.[190]

Kenneth Dam discussed the role of law and institutions for economic development in general, as well as in the context of specific areas such as contracts, property, land, the judiciary, and the financial sector.[191] Based on the preceding works on institutions, such as North's influential book, "Institutions, Institutional Change, and Economic Performance,"[192] Dam sought to explain why legal institutions are

---

183　See Guanghua Yu, "Open Access Order and Interconnected Institutions in Brazil: A Challenge" (2018) 12(1) *Law and Development Review* 1–40.
184　See discussion *supra* Section 1.3.
185　Trubek and Santos (2006), *supra* note 1.
186　Dam (2006), *supra* note 23.
187　For a description of the first and the second moments, see *supra* Section 2.1.
188　Trubek and Santos (2006), *supra* note 1.
189　*Ibid.*, at 7–8.
190　*Ibid.*, at 253–300.
191　Dam (2006), *supra* note 23.
192　North (1990), *supra* note 34.

important to economic development and identify what aspects of law are particularly important.[193] Dam emphasized the consequences of the new institutional economics ("neoinstitutional economics") for legal reform and laid out the policy implications and policy means for maintaining the new focus on legal institutions as a major factor for economic development.[194] Dam also examined the preconceptions about the role that different legal systems play in economic development, proceeding on the presumption that the rule of law is important to economic development, which contrasts with Santos' view that it may have (at least in the context of the judiciary and property rights) limited relevance.[195]

Finally, a note needs to be made on the development of neoinstitutional economics, the academic foundation for the current focus on institutions, including the works of LLSV on legal origin, in the context of financial development, and the emerging consensus that institutions are the key element for development. As the term "institutional" signifies, neoinstitutional economics analyzes various institutions, including legal and social norms and rules, which underlie economic activities.[196] The term, "neoinstitutional economics" is to distinguish itself from institutional economics of the prewar period, which was advanced by scholars such as Thorstein Veblen and John Commons[197] and from neoclassical economics that forms mainstream economics focusing on economic concepts rather than organizations.[198]

The forerunners of neoinstitutional economics are two great sociologists and philosophers, Max Weber and Friedrich Hayek. Weber explained the relevance of culture to economic growth in his seminal work, "The Protestant Ethic and the Spirit of Capitalism,"[199] and the role of law in the economy and society in "Law in Economy and Society."[200] As discussed above, Hayek's works, "The Constitution of Liberty"[201] and "Law, Legislation, and Liberty,"[202] focused on relevant legal concepts to support liberty as the cornerstone of wealth and growth. His point that liberty forms an essential basis of wealth and growth was subsequently challenged by scholars such as Ha-Joon Chang[203] and contrasted by the process

---

193 Dam (2006), *supra* note 23, at 6.

194 *Ibid.*

195 *Ibid.*

196 Malcolm Rutherford, "Institutional Economics: Then and Now" (2001) 15(3) *Journal of Economic Perspectives* 173–194.

197 See Thorstein Veblen, *The Theory of the Leisure Class: An Economic Study of Institutions* (New York: Palgrave Macmillan, 1915) and John R. Commons, *Institutional Economics* (New York: Palgrave Macmillan, 1934).

198 Dam (2006), *supra* note 23, at 1–2.

199 Max Weber, *The Protestant Ethic and the Spirit of Capitalism* (New York: Charles Scribner, 1958).

200 Weber (1954), *supra* note 83.

201 Friedrich Hayek, *The Constitution of Liberty* (Chicago: University of Chicago Press, 1960).

202 Hayek (1979), *supra* note 84.

203 Ha-Joon Chang, *Kicking Away the Ladder: Development Strategy in Historical Perspective* (London: Anthem Press, 2002), chapter 3, at 69–124. Chang, through empirical studies, concluded that democracy is an outcome of economic development, rather than a cause. *Ibid.*

of the unprecedented success in economic development by East Asian countries that allowed limited civil liberty under authoritarian regimes.[204]

Ronald Coase and Douglass North, two Nobel laureates, are directly associated with the development of neoinstitutional economics. Coase analyzed the significance of transaction costs and property rights for the institutional structure and functioning of an economy.[205] North used history to illustrate the economic and institutional factors that contribute to economic development.[206] Several scholars have also performed an institutional analysis in the context of economic development: Dani Rodrik analyzed different forms that institutional solutions take, concluding that institutional function does not determine the institutional form and that there is no single institutional prescription for economic development.[207] Masohiko Aoki expanded the scope of neoinstitutional economics to include private sector organizations, emphasizing the state of equilibrium that is achieved through the interplay among various institutions over time.[208] Tilmur Kuran studied the role that the traditional institutions of the Middle East, including Islamic economic institutions, played in its political development.[209] As part of institutional studies, informal contracting and transaction costs have received attention among academics.[210] The concept of institutional approach has also been important in the study of international economic law, and a group of scholars, including myself, have analyzed the significance of the regulatory framework and the institutional makeup in the current trade regime for economic development.[211]

204 Those East Asian countries, including Korea, Taiwan, and Singapore, and, more recently, China, adopted authoritarian rule with limited civil liberty but nevertheless achieved unprecedented economic development since the 1960s (China from the 1980s).

205 Ronald H. Coase, "The Nature of the Firm" (1937) 4(16) *Economica* 386–405 and Ronald H. Coase, "The Problem of Social Cost" (1960) 3 *Journal of Law and Economics* 1–44.

206 North (1990), *supra* note 34.

207 Rodrik (2000), *supra* note 38 and Dani Rodrik, "Introduction: What Do We Learn from Country Narratives?" *in* Dani Rodrik (ed.), *In Search of Prosperity: Analytic Narratives on Economic Growth* (Princeton, NJ: Princeton University Press, 2005), at 1–19.

208 Masohiko Aoki, *Information, Corporate Governance, and Institutional Diversity* (New York: Oxford University Press, 2000) and Masohiko Aoki, *Toward a Comparative Institutional Analysis* (Cambridge, MA: MIT Press, 2001). Aoki uses evolutionary game theory to model institutions.

209 Timur Kuran, "The Scale of Entrepreneurship in Middle Eastern History: Inhibitive Roles of Islamic Institutions," *in* William J. Baumol, David S. Landes, and Joel Mokyr (eds.), *Entrepreneurs and Entrepreneurship in Economic History* (Princeton, NJ: Princeton University Press, 2010), at 62–87.

210 See Ronald J. Gilson, Charles Sable, and Robert Scott, "Braiding: The Interaction of Formal and Informal Contracting in Theory, Practice and Doctrine" (2010) 110(6) *Columbia Law Review* 1377–1447. Steven Tadelis and Oliver Williamson, "Transaction Cost Economics," *in* Robert Gibbons and Johnson Roberts (eds.), *The Handbook of Organizational Economics* (Princeton, NJ: Princeton University Press, 2013), at 159–190.

211 Yong-Shik Lee *et al.* (eds.), *Law and Development Perspective on International Trade Law* (Cambridge: Cambridge University Press, 2011) and Lee (2016), *supra* note 102.

2.3 The path forward[212]

Several conclusions may be drawn from law and development movements and studies over the last five decades. These are perhaps best summarized by Trubek, with his pithy identification of three major threads.[213] First, law and development did not properly develop as an academic field. Second, the results from the implementation of law and development projects were mixed and suffered from an insufficient quantity of case studies to isolate "what works and what doesn't." Third, there was a theoretical tension between the push for strong state involvement and more laissez-faire regulatory approaches.[214] Especially troublesome was what to make of the success found in East Asia.[215] Trubek highlights the lack of consensus on both hurdles faced and ideal policies to pursue in the law and development field.[216] Whether it is the basic scholarship approach taken toward law and development,[217] the differences in methods and conclusions between lawyers and economists, or the lack of communication between those who look at the full range of law and development issues and those with a more "silo" mentality, there is certainly no lack of internal conflict. While there may be positive aspects to more narrowly focused studies, their benefits may be outweighed by the deleterious effects accompanying field fragmentation.[218] According to Trubek's assessment, the path forward is anything but certain.[219]

However, there has also been a resurgence of optimism regarding the role of legal reforms in promoting development based upon a cross-country statistical analysis that indicates causal relationships between variables measuring characteristics of legal institutions and those measuring development levels.[220] Nonetheless, the basis of this optimism is limited in that many of the variables used to measure respect for the rule of law and enforcement of property rights and contracts do not isolate information capable of shedding light upon the potential impact of legal reforms.[221] Many scholars doubt the wisdom of investing more resources in the law and development mission when questions about its efficacy remain.[222] Davis and Trebilcock, in their review of law and development studies, concluded that none of the preeminent scholars in the field can assure that adherence to law would lead to development.[223] Despite these concerns,

212 This section is adapted from Lee (2015), *supra* note 16, section 2.2, at 25–27.
213 Trubek (2012), *supra* note 115.
214 See also David Kennedy, "The 'Rule of Law,' Political Choices, and Development Common Sense," in *The New Law and Economic Development*, *supra* note 1, at 95–137.
215 Trubek (2012), *supra* note 115.
216 *Ibid.*
217 Trubek sub-divides these scholarship approaches into skepticism, criticism, and optimism, respectively. *Ibid.*
218 *Ibid.*
219 *Ibid.*
220 Davis (2004), *supra* note 39.
221 *Ibid.*
222 Davis and Trebilcock (2008), *supra* note 87.
223 *Ibid.*

they still see law and development as a worthwhile pursuit, highlighting what has become an almost standard suite of advice: institutions may be a necessary precursor, but local cultures, history, and institutional traditions do play a significant role in successful development.[224]

Despite the cited uncertainties and ambiguities inherent in the field, there is a growing interest in law and development, first spurred by the neoliberal movement in the 1980s and then more recently by the countries that have achieved successful economic development in recent decades and now wish to share their development experience with other developing countries.[225] A vibrant discussion (even if it entails serious disagreements) and increased specialization are strong indicators that the academic space of law and development has a renewed lease. However, it is unclear whether past mistakes can be leveraged into future success stories. As was the case with the first law and development movement,[226] the second law and development movement, driven by neoliberalism since the 1980s, repeated the same mistake by adhering to a set of presumptions, such as that an economy runs and grows optimally with minimal governmental regulations, without due regard to the local conditions and variables which determine the adoptability of laws and institutions in recipient countries and, ultimately, their success. The burgeoning "rule of law" movement, such as the post-2015 development agenda,[227] will be destined to meet the same failure if it should disregard the local needs and socio-economic conditions on the ground.

As observed in Section 2.2, the recurring theme in the past and current literature is that local context is important, but the extent to which it affects the successful adoption and implementation of LFIs for development need to be further clarified. Scholars have also tried to demonstrate the effect of law and/or institutions in some of the areas relevant to development, such as property and financial development, with divergent conclusions, but the field requires a new direction to be aided by an adequate analytical framework and working methodology. If these conditions are fulfilled, there will be strong chances for law and development to be developed as a viable academic field as well as an effective means of achieving development. Chapter 3 introduces the general theory of law and development to provide such an analytical framework.

---

224 *Ibid.*
225 Some of the successful developing countries, such as China and Korea, have expanded their budget for international aid and development substantially. In addition, the Korean government announced that it would promote "law exports," meaning that it would introduce advanced Korean laws and legal frameworks to developing countries in their areas of need. Newsis, "Minister of Legislation (Announces) Exports of Advanced Korean Legal Systems" (in Korean), *Joongang Daily News* (April 16, 2013), available online at: http://article.joins.com/news/article/article.asp?total_id=11247168&ctg=1203; https://perma.cc/B464-5FXC.
226 See discussion *supra* Section 2.1.
227 United Nations, *High-level Event of the General Assembly on the Contributions of Human Rights and the Rule of Law in the Post-2015 Development Agenda* (June 9–10, 2014), available online at: https://sustainabledevelopment.un.org/index.php?page=view&type=13&nr=719&menu=35; https://perma.cc/EBR4-XURM.

3 General theory of law and development

3.1 Introduction: scope and necessity[228]

Law has become the framework and vocabulary for constructing and debating development policies,[229] but law and development is underdeveloped as an academic field despite decades of research.[230] As discussed in Chapter 2,[231] there is a need for a theoretical framework that systematically explains dynamics among law, institutions, and the existing political, social, and economic conditions. To meet this need, I have developed the general theory of law and development ("the general theory").[232] The general theory is comprised of two parts: the first part of the general theory sets the disciplinary parameters of law and development by clarifying the constituent concepts of "law" and "development," and Sections 1.2 and 1.3 discuss this part of the theory. This chapter explains the second part, which examines the causal relationship between law and development through "the regulatory impact mechanisms," *i.e.*, the mechanisms by which law impacts development, with references made to institutional frameworks and socioeconomic conditions.[233]

The clarification of the regulatory impact mechanisms is not only an academic exercise to establish law and development as a coherent and viable academic field, but it also has important practical implications; international financial institutions and aid agencies have sponsored many law reform projects with development objectives,[234] such as economic growth through privatization and deregulation of the economy. However, these projects were developed and implemented without

---

228 This chapter is adapted from Lee (2017), *supra* note 4, part III, at 435–456.
229 Development policies since the 1990s have been conceived and constructed in the notion of legal rights. See Kennedy (2006), *supra* note 214.
230 For a review of law and development scholarship, see *supra* Section 2.2.
231 See discussion *supra* Section 2.3.
232 It is described as a "general" theory as it sets the general parameters of the discipline by defining the constituent concepts of "law" and "development" and explains the general mechanisms by which law impacts development.
233 Socioeconomic conditions refer to a range of social, political, economic, and cultural conditions that are essential to the successful operation of law.
234 The World Bank is known to have embarked on over 600 such projects by 2004. Rittich (2006), *supra* note 49, at 221.

DOI: 10.4324/9781003090175-4

a solid understanding of how law impacts development in different institutional, economic, social, and political contexts.[235] As a result, many of the laws and legal practices that were transplanted or adopted through law reform projects did not operate successfully in host countries or deliver their anticipated outcomes.[236] The clarification of these causal mechanisms between law and development in the context of local socioeconomic conditions will assist reformers in improving the effectiveness of law reform projects through better regulatory design and implementation.[237]

These regulatory impact mechanisms are comprised of three categorical elements: "regulatory design," "regulatory compliance," and "quality of implementation," as well as additional sub-elements, summarized below. These elements are conceptually distinct for the most part but are interrelated and influence one another. The first element of the regulatory impact mechanisms, "regulatory design," concerns how optimally law is designed to achieve its regulatory objectives.[238] This assessment can be complex, and regulatory design is analyzed in the following three categories (sub-elements): anticipated policy outcome; organization of law, legal frameworks, and institutions ("LFIs"); and adaptation to socioeconomic conditions, as further explained in the subsequent section.[239] The second element of the mechanisms, "regulatory compliance," refers to the conduct of the general public in complying with law.[240] Law would not be effective without compliance by those who are subject to its application. The analysis of regulatory compliance entails the assessment of two sub-elements: general regulatory compliance, which refers to the overall level of compliance with law in a given jurisdiction, and specific regulatory compliance, which pertains to the strength of public compliance with a particular law.[241] The third and final element of the mechanisms is "quality of implementation."[242] It assesses the degree to which a state[243] meets the requirements

---

235 Tim Lindsey, *Law Reform in Developing and Transitional States* (New York: Routledge, 2006).

236 See Davis and Trebilcock (2008), *supra* note 87, at 916 and Santos (2006), *supra* note 7, at 254. Alan Watson also discussed the problem associated with the legal transplant. Alan Watson, "Legal Change: Sources of Law and Legal Change" (1983) 131(5) *University of Pennsylvania Law Review* 1121–1157, at 1146–1147.

237 In this respect, the general theory would be necessary to solve "the problem of knowledge" as indicated by Thomas Carothers. Thomas Carothers, "The Problem of Knowledge," *in* Thomas Carothers (ed.), *Promoting the Rule of Law Abroad: In Search of Knowledge* (Washington, D.C.: Carnegie Endowment for International Peace, 2006), at 16.

238 Law is designed in the process of legislation or, in the cases of customary law and case law, by evolution and adaptation (and in the process of its identification). For further discussion, see *infra* Section 3.2.

239 For further discussion of the three sub-elements, see *infra* Section 3.2.

240 See *infra* Section 3.3.1.

241 *Ibid.*

242 See *infra* Section 3.3.2.

243 A state refers to an organized political community directed by a sovereign government with control over a defined territory. For the purpose of this book, the concept of "state" includes both formal state, which is recognized by other states under international law, and *de facto* state, which may not be formally recognized but functions as one by the recognition and support of

of law and undertakes the mandates under the latter to fulfill its objectives.[244] A state implements law through legislation, judicial decisions, and administrative actions. This implementation, when it poses political challenges, also requires a degree of political will. Thus, two outstanding factors, state capacity and political will, determine the quality of implementation. The discussion of each element and sub-element inevitably entails a degree of abstract discourse. The following sections attempt to clarify relevant points with examples. The empirical application of the general theory in Part II will also assist in clarifying the conceptual aspects of the theoretical elements.

3.2 Regulatory impact mechanisms: regulatory design

The first analytical step in assessing regulatory impact is the analysis of law's design (regulatory design) concerning a particular development objective, such as economic growth. An effective impact analysis would require clarification and predetermination of a specific development objective; a reviewer may consider an analysis to be inappropriate if the latter focuses on an objective that the reviewer does not consider essentially important for development. For example, for those who value income distribution more than economic growth as a development objective, an analysis focusing on economic growth may not be appropriate. Thus, the controversy surrounding the appropriateness of the analysis will be lessened if an analytical task clarifies at the outset a development objective to be focused on. With a clear development objective to be assessed, the analysis of regulatory design begins with the examination of anticipated policy outcomes, the first of the three sub-elements as introduced above.

3.2.1 Anticipated policy outcome

Law, whether it is designed by legislation (*e.g.*, statute) or has evolved gradually over time (*e.g.*, customary law and case law), exhibits a policy or policies, which form regulatory objectives.[245] For example, a statute that requires the removal of customs tariffs on products imported from other countries, as a result of a free trade agreement (FTA) between the importing and exporting countries, advances the policies of increasing trade between them and contributing to the economic

---

its constituent members. For further discussion of the recognition of states in international law, see Hersch Lauterpacht, "Recognition of States in International Law" (1944) 53(3) *Yale Law Journal* 385–458.

244 See *infra* Section 3.3.2.

245 Legislation may have multiple objectives, all of which may not necessarily be agreed upon by all legislators or be consistent with one another. Even so, most legislators, if not all, could agree on the main purpose of a particular piece of legislation. Customary law and common law are also evolved over a period of time to deliver a policy outcome to meet the changing needs of society. See also C. R. M. Dlamini, "The Role of Customary Law in Meeting Social Needs" (1991) *Acta Juridica* 71–85.

growth of the participating countries.[246] Additional examples include the policy of improving gender equality in society through the enactment of a statute that prohibits gender-based discrimination in workplaces. In the case of customary law and case law, a regulatory objective is also "found" in the process of identifying relevant rules. A judicial court in the United States may identify a common law rule that denies damages for ameliorative waste (an improvement to an estate that changes its character), for instance, advancing the policy of encouraging improvements on land and economic development.[247]

Anticipated policy outcomes are the specific outcomes that are anticipated as a result of the implementation of such policies. In the first example, the increase in trade and economic growth would be the anticipated policy outcome,[248] and, in the subsequent examples, the improvement of gender equality and the increased improvements on land would be the anticipated policy outcomes. The explicit regulatory objectives stated in laws do not always identify anticipated policy outcomes, nor does the legislature otherwise make them clear.[249] Regardless of pronounced regulatory objectives, an objective assessment identifies policy outcomes, often aided by the methods of social sciences as further discussed below. A study has indicated that laws may cause a variety of transformations (anticipated policy outcomes) beyond their explicit purposes (regulatory objectives).[250]

The anticipated policy outcome is analyzed with references made to the theories and analytics of relevant social sciences, which, depending on the type of development objective pursued, may include economics, sociology, political science, anthropology, and development studies. Reference is also made to their methodologies,[251] including those adopted in the Regulatory Impact Analysis

---

246 See, *e.g.*, United States International Trade Commission (USITC), *U.S.–Korea Free Trade Agreement: Potential Economy-Wide and Selected Sectoral Effects* (2007), Investigation No. TA-2104–24, USITC Publication 3949, available online at: www.usitc.gov/publications/pub3949. pdf; https://perma.cc/H69M-PSMN.

247 See, *e.g.*, *Melms v. Pabst Brewing Co.*, 79 N.W. 738 (1899). For further discussion, see Thomas W. Merrill, "Melms v. Pabst Brewing Co. and the Doctrine of Waste in American Property Law" (2011) 94(4) *Marquette Law Review* 1055–1094.

248 Following the implementation of the United States–Korea Free Trade Agreement, trade between the United States and Korea increased by $23.5 billion between 2011 and 2015. United States Trade Representative (USTR), *Fact Sheet: Four Year Snapshot: The U.S.–Korea Free Trade Agreement* (March 2016), available online at: https://ustr.gov/about-us/policy-offi ces/press-office/fact-sheets/2016/March/Four-Year-Snapshot-KORUS; https://perma.cc/ 8RXL-8A7L.

249 Rittich (2006), *supra* note 49, at 212–213.

250 *Ibid.*, at 216.

251 Those methodologies include statistical and econometrical methods. The latter often adopts a regression analysis, which is a statistical process for estimating the relationships among independent and dependent variables. For further discussion, see David A. Freedman, *Statistical Models: Theory and Practice* (New York: Cambridge University Press, 2005) and A. Deaton, "Data and Econometric Tools for Development Analysis," *in* J. Behrman and T. N. Srinivasan (eds.), *Handbook of Development Economics*, vol. 3 (New York: North-Holland, 1995), at 1785–1882.

(RIA).[252] In adopting a social science analysis, consideration should be given to its imprecise nature; since social sciences address human behavior, which involves a degree of uncertainty and unpredictability, an analysis of a possible policy outcome aided by social sciences is inexact, and one needs to interpret its outcome broadly.[253] This imprecise nature is also compounded by multiple layers of causation. This means that a law may affect development, which in turn may also affect the law, as discussed later in this section, creating an additional layer of causation and so on. Thus, the impact is not linear but circular, which is another reason for the inexact nature of such an analysis.

In the case of economic development, an assessment will analyze whether the anticipated outcome of the policy is likely to increase economic productivity and, thus, achieve economic growth objectives or other economic development objectives, or, conversely, whether it would have an adverse effect or no effect at all. Economics is the most relevant social science discipline, subject to its inherent limitations, as discussed above. The assessment will adopt economic theories and analytics to evaluate the outcome. Additionally, the assessment will reference other social science research if such research is relevant to the particular economic development objective. For example, if improved income distribution is a key development objective, the assessment will reference relevant sociological and political science research and theories to the extent that they inform how

252 An RIA is a process for identifying and assessing the expected effects of regulatory proposals, and it adopts relevant analytical methods such as benefit/cost analysis. For further discussion, see OECD, *Introductory Handbook for Undertaking Regulatory Impact Analysis (RIA)*, Version 1.0, October 2008, at 3, available online at: www.oecd.org/gov/regulatory-policy/44789472.pdf; https://perma.cc/8JN7-NNSW. For further discussion of RIA, see generally Robert W. Hahn, Jason K. Burnett, Yee-Ho I. Chan, Elizabeth A. Mader, and Petrea R. Moyle, "Assessing Regulatory Impact Analyses: The Failure of Agencies to Comply with Executive Order 12,866" (2000) 23(3) *Harvard Journal of Law and Public Policy* 859–877; Thomas O. McGarity, "Regulatory Analysis and Regulatory Reform" (1987) 65(7) *Texas Law Review* 1243–1333; Claudio M. Radaelli, "The Diffusion of Regulatory Impact Analysis: Best Practice or Lesson-Drawing?" (2004) 43(5) *European Journal of Political Research* 723–747; Jacopo Torriti and Ragnar E. Lofstedt, "The First Five Years of the EU Impact Assessment System: A Risk Economics Perspective on Gaps between Rationale and Practice" (2012) 15(2) *Journal of Risk Research* 169–186.

253 For example, using the Global Trade Analysis Project (GTAP) model, the USITC estimated that trade between the United States and Korea would increase after the implementation of the U.S.–Korea FTA. Specifically, the USITC estimated that merchandise exports to Korea would increase by US$ 9.7 billion to 10.9 billion once the FTA was fully implemented, merchandise imports from Korea would increase by US$ 6.4 billion to 6.9 billion, reducing the U.S. trade deficit against Korea by US$ 2.8 billion to 4.5 billion. See USITC (2007), *supra* note 246, at xvii. With the implementation of the FTA in March 2012, U.S.–Korea trade indeed increased by US$ 12 billion between 2011 and 2015; however, the U.S. trade deficit with Korea did not decrease as estimated, but actually increased by US$ 14.4 billion between 2011 and 2016, showing the inexact nature of the earlier assessment. See USTR, *2017 Trade Policy Agenda* and *2016 Annual Report*, available online at: https://ustr.gov/sites/default/files/files/reports/2017/AnnualReport/Chapter%20III%20-%20Bilateral%20Trade%20Agreements.pdf; https://perma.cc/L9JU-GCVN.

the suggested law would or would not produce a policy outcome that achieves a better income distribution in society.

There is no clear consensus as to what policy leads to successful economic development and no agreement as to what the appropriate role of the state in the economy should be. Economists emphasized the role of the state in economic development in the 1950s and the 1960s,[254] but this emphasis on the state receded in the 1970s.[255] The neoliberal approach,[256] which favors economic policies that reduce state involvement in the economy and enhance the market (*i.e.*, the private sector), such as the policies of privatization and trade liberalization, became prevalent in the 1980s.[257] Chile's successful economic development in recent decades,[258] founded on its liberal economic policies, could support the neoliberal argument.[259] By contrast, the countries that achieved the most successful economic development, such as the newly industrialized countries (NICs), adopted extensive state-led development policies,[260] which were at odds with the neoliberal prescriptions.[261]

---

254 Development economists, such as Rosenstein-Rodan, Mandelbaum, Lewis, Rostow, Kuznets, Gerschenkron, Hirschman, and Kindleberger, advocated the state-led development strategy as key to development, although they did not exactly agree on how the state should lead economic growth. For example, Rosenstein-Rodan supported the "big push," which is a coordinated investment program across the board ("balanced growth theory"). By contrast, Hirschman advocated a policy of promoting a few key sectors with strong linkages to other sectors ("unbalanced growth theory"). Paul Krugman, *The Rise and Fall of Development Economics*, available online at: http://web.mit.edu/krugman/www/dishpan.html; https://perma.cc/H6KW-VJEZ. See also Pranab Bardhan, "Economics of Development and the Development of Economics" (1993) 7(2) *The Journal of Economic Perspectives* 129–142. This period of "development economics" coincides with the first law and development movement. For a discussion of the first law and development movement, see *supra* Section 2.1.
255 See Newton (2006), *supra* note 1, at 182.
256 For an explanation of the neoliberal approach, see *supra* note 93.
257 Williamson (1990), *supra* note 8.
258 For a discussion of Chile's economic development, see *supra* note 29.
259 This observation, however, is subject to the criticism that nearly all major sectors of the Chilean economy owe their existence to state intervention under the Pinochet regime. See James M. Cypher, "Is Chile a Neoliberal Success?" *Dollars & Sense: Real World Economics* (September–October 2004), available online at: http://dollarsandsense.org/archives/2004/0904cypher.html; https://perma.cc/R65K-HDDY. See also Ronald J. Gilson and Curtis J. Milhaupt, "Economically Benevolent Dictators: Lessons for Developing Democracies" (2011) 59(1) *American Journal of Comparative Law* 227–288.
260 State-led development refers to the development approach adopted by a developmental state. (For a definition of a developmental state, see *supra* note 166.) Perhaps an exception among the NICs is Hong Kong, which is known to have adopted a laissez-faire economic policy with minimal government involvement. In contrast, Schenk suggested that this perception was a myth; Catherine Schenk argued that the government subsidized industry indirectly through public housing, which restrained a rise in the cost of living that would have threatened Hong Kong's labor-cost advantage in manufacturing. Catherine Schenk, "Economic History of Hong Kong," *EH.Net Encyclopedia* (March 16, 2008), available online at: http://eh.net/encyclopedia/economic-history-of-hong-kong/; https://perma.cc/WV5J-6MJ4.
261 For a discussion of the successful economic development of the NICs, see *supra* note 28.

This divergence of views and the outcomes of these dissimilar development policies may render the analysis of the anticipated policy outcome on economic development complex and challenging. For example, a question may arise as to the anticipated policy outcome of a law that mandates government support of particular industries and their exports through subsidy grants and tax breaks. Those who subscribe to a neoliberal policy stance are likely to oppose this law due to the potential economic inefficiencies associated with government distribution of resources. Conversely, those who advocate for state-led industrial development policies are likely to support the law as necessary to stimulate industrial development and economic growth.

The NICs' successful adoption of state-led policies suggests that active government involvement in industrial promotion, accompanied by export promotion to overcome the constraints of small domestic markets, could be effective in the early stages of economic development[262] if the government, devoted to development, has political leadership and institutional strength. From a neoliberal point of view, a government "selecting" industries to receive support by way of public funding may appear to invite economic inefficiency and corruption.[263] However, in a developing country where the underdeveloped private sector may only have limited capacity to acquire information and capital, absent a working financial market, the role of government is essential. Supporting this point, a leading scholar has observed that industrial restructuring rarely takes place without significant government assistance.[264]

As the NICs' economies successfully developed and became more complex and divergent in the 1980s and onward, with their private sectors acquiring the institutional capacity to more efficiently undertake much of the role previously assumed by the state, they shifted policies, reducing government control of the economy and increasing private-sector autonomy.[265] One could describe this type

---

262 The early stages of economic development, which should be distinguished from Rostow's five stages of economic growth, refers to the initial state of economic development with the characteristics of over-dependency on primary industries (non-manufacturing industries), low-level industrialization, and low per-capita income, as compared to the later stages of economic development, referring to the more advanced economic state with sustained economic growth, industrialization, and higher (mid-level) per-capita income. There is no universally recognized cutoff line between the early stages of economic development and more advanced stages. In the early stages of development, there is generally a surplus of unskilled labor and a shortage of skilled labor and capital, which necessitates importation of the latter. As economic development progresses, the stock of unskilled labor diminishes, and those of skilled labor and capital rise, resulting in increases in the price (wage) of the former and decreases in the prices of the latter.

263 The public choice theory and the rent-seeking idea associated with government failures, adopted by the neoliberal policy analysis, would lead to this conclusion.

264 See Dani Rodrik, "Industrial Policy for the Twenty-First Century," *John F. Kennedy School of Government, Harvard University Faculty Research Working Papers Series*, RWP04–047 (2004), at 15, available online at: https://drodrik.scholar.harvard.edu/files/dani-rodrik/files/industrial-policy-twenty-first-century.pdf; https://perma.cc/5ZUD-XBUC.

265 Katharina Pistor and Philip A. Wellons, *The Role of Law and Legal Institutions in Asian Economic Development, 1960–1995* (New York: Oxford University Press, 1999).

of economic development process as a "marriage between state and market,"[266] in which the state assumes the role of a "developmental state"[267] in the early stages of economic development, manages the economy, develops economic development plans, and directs investments for key sectors. Under this policy, despite the key role of the state, market performance of the promoted industries, particularly in export markets, was the benchmark of success, and private sector autonomy increased over time.

In sum, socioeconomic conditions, such as the stage of economic development and the institutional strength of the government relative to that of the contemporary private sector, influence policy outcomes that law is anticipated to deliver in the context of development. As noted above, a law focusing on the state's facilitation of development can be more effective in the early stages of economic development, when the relative capability and institutional strength of the government is superior to those of the underdeveloped private sector.[268] By contrast, a law focusing on privatization and deregulation could be more effective in the later stages of economic development when the private sector has acquired institutional strength and experiences, as demonstrated by the successful policy transition in the NICs.[269] Economists have also begun to recognize the complementary roles of the state and the market, providing support for this type of policy.[270]

---

266 Lee (2016), *supra* note 102, at 305–309. Several scholars, including Dani Rodrik, Charles Sabel, Sanjay Reddy, and Ricardo Hausmann, have emphasized the importance of public–private partnerships to developing strategies and making investment choices for economic development. See also Trubek (2012), *supra* note 115, at 6.

267 *Supra* note 166 (for an explanation of the developmental state).

268 It may not be the case that the state is more capable than the private sector in the countries during the early stages of economic development. Multinational enterprises running businesses in these countries could also be effective, but their contributions to the economic development of the host countries could be limited due to potential inconsistencies between their (global) corporate interests and the long-term development interests of the host countries.

269 Pistor and Wellons (1999), *supra* note 265, at 110–111.

270 Michael J. Trebilcock observed a changing trend in development economics. Trebilcock stated,

> [b]y the late 1990s, the consensus in development economics had shifted dramatically. The Washington Consensus was agreed to have often been a failure … A more promising approach is represented by the New Development Economics (NDE) which eschews truisms such as "getting institutions right" and represents a break with big-picture paradigms that advance one-size-fits-all solutions … [d]rawing on the neoclassical paradigm, it recognizes that markets are not nearly as inefficient as the early structuralists believed; rather the fundamental principle of rational responses to incentives continues to organize economic behavior. Further, with the rise of the New Institutional Economics [which emphasizes legal institutions as a major factor for economic development], the distinction between government and markets has become blurred—each operating via similar fundamental mechanisms. As such, NDE advocates a complementary role for governments and markets, finding both to be susceptible to failures in coordination, imperfect information, and agency problems.

Michael J. Trebilcock, "Between Theories of Trade and Development: The Future of the World Trading System" (2015) 16(1) *Journal of World Investment & Trade* 122–140, at 128–129.

3.2.2 *Organization of Law, Legal Frameworks, and Institutions (LFIs)*

The organization and dynamics among LFIs is the second sub-element determining the effectiveness of regulatory design. Law may not be effective absent a suitable legal framework and an effective institutional arrangement. For example, a statute that aims to promote economic activities by protecting formal private property rights (FPPRs) with a criminal sanction for a violation may not be very effective without an effective institutional arrangement enforcing them, such as a working police force and an efficient and fair prosecution system. As to legal frameworks, one that imposes stringent requirements for the amendment of statutes, thereby making timely regulatory modifications difficult, may reduce their overall regulatory effectiveness on development under changing socioeconomic conditions. The impact of law cannot be considered in isolation from the legal framework in which it is organized and the institutions by which it is adopted and implemented, justifying the use of the term "LFIs" as an inseparable amalgam.[271] The inseparable nature of LFIs explains why many law reform projects promoting an identical set of laws (*e.g.*, those promoting deregulation) have had a limited and inconsistent impact where reformers fail to give due consideration to applicable legal frameworks and institutional arrangements in the design and implementation of these projects.[272]

In the inter-dynamics among the constituent elements of LFIs, the adoption of law also affects relevant legal frameworks and institutions just as it is affected by the latter. For example, a law that mandates additional funding and personnel to an institution that administers the law, such as a government agency in charge, may increase that institution's capacity to implement the law, provided that the government can secure funding and personnel as the law mandates. The increase in legislation in common law countries has diminished the distinctions in the legal system (legal framework) between common law and civil law countries. The logical consistency and policy compatibility among laws within a legal system also affect the effectiveness of the system as a whole.

An optimal regulatory design, which increases synergies among LFIs and their overall effectiveness, will strengthen the regulatory impact on development. By contrast, an ineffective regulatory design will lack supportive synergies and even create conflicts among the constituent elements of LFIs. For example, the enactment of a statute empowering the government to expropriate private land without due process and adequate compensation may not produce synergies with the institutions already in place to protect FPPRs and the other laws in the legal system that aim to do the same. This type of conflict may occur when a law is enacted without due consideration of applicable legal frameworks and institutional arrangements. In particular, consideration should be given to relevant details such as whether there is any potential inconsistency between the

---

271 Lee (2015), *supra* note 16, at 8.
272 See, *e.g.*, *supra* note 235.

promoted law and the existing legal frameworks and institutions, how legislation should be translated into administrative rulemaking, and how and where in the legislation government discretion should be lodged.[273] The Analytical Law and Development Model (ADM), which is discussed in Chapter 7, also aids with the assessment of the organization of LFIs in the context of economic development.[274]

3.2.3 Adaptability to socioeconomic conditions

Law may not be effective if it does not conform to the socioeconomic conditions on the ground,[275] and law's adaptability to socioeconomic conditions is the third sub-element determining the effectiveness of regulatory design. Socioeconomic conditions are a range of social, political, economic, and cultural conditions that are essential to the successful operation of law, including social or religious norms that may or may not support the law. For example, legislation that authorizes the charging of an interest rate by financial institutions to grow the financial industry and facilitate economic development would not be effective where the majority of the population observes a religious code prohibiting it.[276]

The following example further illustrates the importance of socioeconomic conditions. Several developing countries, including Vietnam, Cambodia, Myanmar, and Bangladesh, have shown interest in adopting certain Korean laws, including the *Code of Ethics for Government Officials* and the *Information Disclosure Act*, to improve their governance.[277] The success of this legal adoption would depend on whether the cited laws could operate effectively under the different legal frameworks, institutions, and socioeconomic conditions in those countries.[278] These developing countries may not have strong internal monitoring and surveillance systems within their governments to detect and deal with any improper conduct of public officials and may lack effective infrastructures for accessing and disclosing information promptly, which would impede the implementation of those laws. Thus, successful implementation requires reinforcement of the necessary socioeconomic conditions, including competent personnel,

---

273 Kennedy (2006), *supra* note 214, at 104.

274 See discussion *infra* Chapter 7.

275 Practitioners and advisors have cautioned against neglecting these differences on the ground. See, *e.g.*, Thomas W. Waelde and James L. Gunderson, "Legislative Reform in Transition Economies: Western Transplants: A Short-Cut to Social Market Economy Status?" (1994) 43(2) *The International Comparative Law Quarterly* 347–378, at 349.

276 The Qur'an characterizes charging interest as unfair, as implied by the use of an Arabic word "zulm" meaning oppression or exploitation. The Qur'an, 2:279. Thus, "Islamic banking," a banking practice compliant with the rules of Sharia law, has been developed. For further discussion of Islamic banking, see generally A. Abdul Raheem, *Islamic Banking: Principles, Practices and Performance* (New Delhi: New Century Publications, 2013). See also, Aida Othman, "Islamic Finance: Facing the Pandemic, Shaping the Future," *in* Salim Farrar and Paul Subramaniam (eds.), *Law and Justice in Malaysia 2020 and Beyond* (Thomson Reuters, 2021), 203–212.

277 Lee (2015), *supra* note 16, at 29.

278 *Ibid.*

technical expertise, financial resources, and cultural and political acceptance of their regulatory objectives.

The foregoing examples demonstrate the importance of identifying socio-economic conditions for the assessment of the regulatory impact on development. The essential socioeconomic conditions may vary depending on the particular law to be implemented. They may include economic conditions such as financial resources, the applicable stages of economic development,[279] technical expertise, political and social support, administrative capacity, and/ or cultural and religious acceptance of the particular law.[280] This is a broad categorization, and assessment of socioeconomic conditions relevant to the successful operation of a specific law may require more detailed identification.[281] To perform this task, it would be essential to secure the participation of local experts in the analysis, as they have detailed knowledge of socioeconomic conditions on the ground.[282]

The need for the adaptation of law to socioeconomic conditions on the ground also explains the impact development has on law. Development changes socioeconomic conditions and creates regulatory gaps because of these changes. States and societies then attempt to fill this regulatory gap ("regulatory adjustment") and reinforce regulatory support for development ("regulatory reinforcement"), which, in turn, causes changes to law. For example, the development of information technology and internet-based commercial transactions necessitated rules that address issues arising from increased online transactions, such as the validity of electronic signatures. In the United States, 47 States,[283] the District of Columbia, Puerto Rico, and the U.S. Virgin Islands adopted the Uniform Electronic Transactions Act (UETA) in 1999 to harmonize state laws concerning the retention of paper records and the validity of electronic signatures.[284]

The growth of the financial industry may also call for the establishment of an institution that oversees the conduct of players in the financial markets, such as

---

279 *Supra* note 262 (for an explanation of stages of economic development).

280 Some of the cited socioeconomic conditions, such as administrative capacity, may conceptually overlap with certain constitutive elements of quality of implementation, such as state capacity (see *infra* Section 3.3.2). Some other socioeconomic conditions, such as cultural and religious acceptance, may also affect regulatory compliance (see *infra* Section 3.3.1). As discussed above, the elements of the regulatory impact mechanisms (*i.e.*, regulatory design, regulatory compliance, and quality of implementation) are interrelated and influence one another. As relevant to socioeconomic conditions, Richard Posner also opined that precisely written rules, rather than institutions, such as a working judiciary, that are expensive to develop, or abstract legal standards that require a sophisticated legal technique to apply, are more conducive to economic development in developing countries with limited economic resources and weak legal traditions. See Posner (1998), *supra* note 38, at 2–10.

281 The development of the ADM, discussed in Chapter 7, will also require the assessment of key socioeconomic conditions for the successful implementation of LFIs.

282 Posner (1998), *supra* note 38, at 5–6 (adopting foreign laws).

283 See *infra* note 595 ("States" with a capital "S" denotes the constituent States of the United States).

284 Uniform Electronic Transactions Act (1999).

banks and companies listed in the stock markets, to prevent the disruption of the financial system and protect the general public from misleading and fraudulent practices. In the United States, the development of the financial industry in the early twentieth century necessitated the enactment of the Securities Act of 1934, which established the Securities and Exchange Commission ("SEC").[285] The SEC monitors the securities industry and enforces laws and rules governing the latter, *e.g.*, requiring the disclosure of certain information by companies listed in the securities markets.[286]

The foregoing analysis of regulatory design is also applicable beyond law and development and explains regulatory impact, generally. For example, France has enacted a law that bans face covering in public places, including those worn by practicing Muslims, such as the burka and the niqab.[287] The stated regulatory objectives are the enhancement of public security and facilitation of minimal social interactions by prohibiting the concealment of the face in public places, and these objectives are not directly related to development.

When analyzed through the lens of regulatory design, the anticipated policy outcomes include enhancing public security by facilitating the identification of a suspect individual, although the law's positive effect on the minimal social interactions would be more controversial. The law is also supported by the effective organization of legal frameworks and institutions: the law is in the form of legitimate statutory enactment that is effective throughout France (effective legal framework) and supported by the enforcement of police and public prosecution that effectively impose a penalty for a violation (effective institution).

The law raises further issues with its adaptability to socioeconomic conditions. Even if the actual number of the Muslim population in France who partake in full face covering may not be large, millions of Muslims and non-Muslims in French society, nevertheless, support the freedom to engage in this religious practice, resulting in a conflict and division in French society.[288] The law's adaptability to the socioeconomic conditions on the ground (*i.e.*, incompatibility to the religious practice and belief) is weakened due to this conflict, diminishing the effectiveness of its regulatory design and regulatory impact. The application of the regulatory design analysis reveals the weakness of the French law, as demonstrated by widespread resistance to the law.[289]

---

285   Securities Act of 1934, 15 U.S.C. §§ 1–16.
286   *Ibid.*
287   Loi 2010–1192 du 11 octobre 2010 interdisant la dissimulation du visage dans l'espace public [Law 2010–1192 of October 11, 2010, banning the covering of one's face in public].
288   See Edward Cody, "Tensions Flare in France over Veil Ban," *Washington Post*, August 9, 2012, available online at: www.washingtonpost.com/world/tensions-flare-in-france-over-veil-ban/2012/08/08/67b56fc2-e150-11e1-98e7-89d659f9c106_story.html?utm_term= .2a15a15b3dea; https://perma.cc/3R4E-5U9Q.
289   *Ibid.*

3.3 Regulatory compliance and quality of implementation

This section discusses the second and the third elements of the regulatory impact mechanisms, "regulatory compliance" and "quality of implementation," respectively. Their sub-elements are also analyzed under each sub-section.

3.3.1 Regulatory compliance

Regulatory compliance, the second element of the regulatory impact mechanisms, refers to compliance with law by those who are subject to the application of law. This section also examines the factors influencing regulatory compliance, some of which are associated with historical, economic, cultural, and political conditions that may be largely immune to top-down attempts at reform[290] and some others associated more directly with state action, such as regulatory enforcement.

Regulatory compliance in the context of law and development does not mean only the absence of rule violations but also the knowledge of law and participation in the processes mandated by law. For example, judicial reform would not be as effective where only a small minority of a population uses the court for dispute resolution.[291] Strong regulatory compliance is an essential precondition to the success of law reform, and a reform that does not consider regulatory compliance may end up a hollow declaration without any real impact. For this reason, regulatory compliance is one of the key elements in determining regulatory impact on development.

Regulatory compliance can be classified into general regulatory compliance, which refers to the general level of regulatory compliance in a given jurisdiction, and specific regulatory compliance, which pertains to the strength of public compliance with a particular law. In a place where general regulatory compliance is not strong, regulatory impact on development may generally be weak. Even in a society where general regulatory compliance is strong, however, a particular law may still have weak compliance or even resistance when it does not conform to the socioeconomic conditions prevailing on the ground. The subsequent discussion examines both general regulatory compliance and specific regulatory compliance.

---

290 Davis and Trebilcock (2008), *supra* note 87, at 920.
291 This lack of use may be a result of limited access to the court due to the cost of litigation; an absence of the knowledge required to use the court; the physical remoteness of the court; or cultural reasons, *i.e.*, residents may prefer to use informal, traditional venues to resolve disputes. Thus, a study indicated the necessity to engage customary dispute resolution processes in developing countries. See Paul Zwier, "Human Rights for Women in Liberia (and West Africa): Integrating Formal and Informal Rule of Law Reforms through the Carter Center's Community Justice Advisor Project" (2017) 10(2) *Law and Development Review* 187–235.

(a) General regulatory compliance

Several elements affect general regulatory compliance.[292] First, legal culture is relevant. Legal culture is defined as "those characteristics present in a legal system, reflecting the common history, traditions, outlook and approach of that system"[293] that may be "reflected in the actions or behaviors of the actors, institutions, and even of the substance of the system."[294] Legal culture, which may vary significantly according to the country and the jurisdiction, is said to exist "not because of regulation of substantive law, but as a result of the collective response and actions of those participants in the legal system."[295] Legal culture affects general regulatory compliance by influencing how the public perceives law and the degree to which they comply with it.

Second, public knowledge and understanding of law influence general regulatory compliance. The public would be more inclined to comply with law in general if they believe, based on their knowledge and appreciation of law, that compliance is in the interest of their communities, families, and themselves.[296] Public education and their confidence in the government,[297] which develops and implements law, are also essential. Because the government is in charge of developing and administering most laws, except customary law, compliance would be less likely where the public does not trust that the government develops and implements law to serve the public interest. Thus, it is not surprising to see weak regulatory compliance in failing states where public confidence in the government is weak. This observation does not necessarily mean that public confidence exactly correlates with the level of regulatory compliance. As indicated by the axiom, "an unjust law is nonetheless a law," there is a degree of morality and duty attached to obeying the law, regardless of its content and/or the government that administers it. Thus, it goes back to the question of the legal culture in place.

Yet another element that affects general regulatory compliance is the general quality of law, including its design and implementation. Well-designed and effectively implemented laws that fulfill the needs of the public and fit the socioeconomic conditions are more likely to command strong compliance and active participation by the public. Well-designed and implemented LFIs have been spread and complied with beyond their original jurisdictions. For example,

---

292 H. L. A. Hart also considered that regulatory compliance ("allegiance to the system") might be based on various elements, such as "calculations of long-term self-interest; disinterested interest in others; an unreflecting inherited or traditional attitude; or the mere wish to do as others do." H. L. A. Hart, *The Concept of Law* (2nd ed., New York: Oxford University Press, 1994), at 203.

293 Colin B. Picker, "International Trade and Development Law: A Legal Cultural Critique" (2011) 4(2) *Law and Development Review* 43–71, at 46.

294 *Ibid.*

295 *Ibid.*

296 For a relevant discussion, see Michael Ilg, "Profit, Persuasion, and Fidelity: Why People Follow the Rule of Law" (2017) 10(2) *Law and Development Review* 275–303.

297 Simon Deakin has described this as the "legitimacy of government" (correspondence on file with the author).

the highly developed Roman law not only laid the foundation for the Roman Empire, but it remained a working reference for the development of modern law in Europe and beyond, centuries after Rome itself perished.[298] In addition, a vast number of countries in Asia, Africa, and North America have adopted the modern civil law system, developed by France and Germany, and the common law system, by England. Additionally, many countries around the world have adopted and referenced the institutions of the British parliamentary government system and the American presidential system as the standard forms of modern democratic government. These examples illustrate the importance of regulatory design and implementation to induce compliance.

Lastly, the strength of regulatory enforcement also affects general regulatory compliance. The likelihood of regulatory compliance increases where a violation is sanctioned with a real penalty, including financial and penal ones, as a result of regulatory enforcement. Therefore, enforcement induces compliance with a threat of a penalty, and enforcement is also an evaluative criterion for determining the level of the rule of law.[299] Enforcement also requires considerable resources and capacity on the part of the state; efficient monitoring, policing, and the appropriate execution of penalties can be issues for developing countries that lack sufficient personnel, financial resources, and technical expertise. Thus, the enforcement issue goes to the question of state capacity, which will be discussed in Section 3.3.2.

(b) Specific regulatory compliance

Specific regulatory compliance is associated with the resource constraints that inevitably compel governments to prioritize laws for enforcement. Laws supported by a stronger political will are more likely to be enforced as a priority and, in turn, result in stronger compliance.[300] Some laws may not have real enforcement by a state when an external force compels the state to adopt them. For example, where a state is required to legislate a system of "good governance" as a condition for

---

298   For further discussion of Roman law, see generally Adolf Berger, *Encyclopedic Dictionary of Roman Law* (Philadelphia: The American Philosophical Society, 1953) and H. F. Jolowicz, *Historical Introduction to the Study of Roman Law* (3rd ed., Holmes Beach, FL: Gaunt, 1996). See also Henry Sumner Maine, *Ancient Law: Its Connection with the Early History of Society, and Its Relation to Modern Ideas* (New York: Henry Holt and Company, 1861), at 75–78.

299   See World Justice Project, *Rule of Law Index* (2020), available online at: https://worldjustice project.org/sites/default/files/documents/WJP-ROLI-2020-Online_0.pdf; https://perma. cc/XU6Z-AE6S. For further discussion of compliance theories and relevant literature review, see Julien Étienne, "La Conformation Des Gouvernes. Une revue de la littérature théorique" (2010) 60(3) *Revue Française de Science Politique* 493–517, English version available online at: www. cairn-int.info/article-E_RFSP_603_0493--compliance-theories.htm?contenu=article, accessed January 18, 2021.

300   Jodi L. Short, "The Politics of Regulatory Enforcement and Compliance: Theorizing and Operationalizing Political Influences," *Regulation and Governance* (December 12, 2019), available online at: https://onlinelibrary.wiley.com/doi/full/10.1111/rego.12291, accessed March 5, 2021.

receiving a loan from an international financial institution,[301] the state may be reluctant to devote resources and personnel to enforce the imposed system if it does not agree on the need for such a system but accepts it to obtain the loan. In this case, the donor development agency could try to ensure enforcement by threatening to discontinue the loan or requiring early repayment upon failure. An interesting question arises as to whether the public will comply with laws that a state adopts, perhaps reluctantly, for a condition imposed externally. The answer depends on whether the public would see the "imposed" laws as justified upon the laws' satisfaction of their needs or those of the state, although the public generally may not favor this type of external intervention, viewing it as an encroachment on national sovereignty (and their national pride), regardless of its specific content.[302]

Another key element determining specific regulatory compliance is the consistency between a particular law and the socioeconomic conditions on the ground. Any conflict should be weighed against the regulatory benefit, as perceived by the public, in adopting the law. In the case of the French law banning face coverings in public places,[303] French female Muslims under the religious practice of wearing the burka or the niqab may not be inclined to comply with the law, unless they considered the claimed benefits of improved communication through facial recognition and enhanced public security, coupled with the benefit of avoiding the penalty for a violation and potential persecution by non-Muslims who oppose anyone wearing them, to outweigh the conflict with their religious practice.

Specific regulatory compliance can also be classified as "passive compliance" and "active compliance." Passive compliance refers to a minimal level of compliance with the requirements of law, primarily to avoid a penalty for a violation. Active compliance refers to the type of compliance that exceeds fulfilling the minimum requirements, seeking to assist the state in meeting a regulatory objective by actively participating in the process mandated by law, often with encouragement to others to do the same. A voluntary public campaign against the use of illegally imported products, in compliance with customs law and industrial policy to promote domestic production, is an example. One can expect active compliance when the population identifies the regulatory objective to be in their own interest. In successful developing countries, governments secured active compliance for development-facilitating laws, because the general public considered the regulatory objective of these laws—economic development—as fulfilling their own interest in escaping from poverty.

Finally, a nation could be divided concerning specific regulatory compliance with a particular law, because the law may result in a net benefit for one group

---

301 For a discussion of the emphasis on "good governance" by the international financial institutions, see Rittich (2006), *supra* note 49, at 210. See also Wolfowitz (2006), *infra* note 1029.

302 For a discussion of the symbolic effects of law, see John Griffiths, "Do Laws Have Symbolic Effects?" *in* Nicolle Zeegers, Willem Witteveen, and Bart van Klink (eds.), *Social and Symbolic Effects of Legislation under the Rule of Law* (The Edwin Mellen Press, 2005), at 147–161.

303 *Supra* note 287 (for the citation of the relevant French law).

in a population and simultaneously cause a net loss for another. For example, traders would generally welcome a free trade agreement ("FTA"), as FTAs lower trade barriers, such as customs tariffs, and reduce traders' transaction costs. For this reason, traders would have an interest in complying with a law necessary for the adoption of the FTA, such as a statute implementing the FTA. In contrast, domestic producers competing with the imported products and domestic laborers whose jobs might be adversely affected by the imports may well oppose the FTA and the domestic law implementing it, as the FTA lowers the cost of imports, thereby making competing domestic products less competitive in the domestic market. To improve specific regulatory compliance in the presence of a conflict of interests among different groups, a government will endeavor to devise the implementation of law in such a way as to reduce the perceived loss and provide compensation to the losing groups.[304] However, the government may not always be "neutral" in this divide, and its ideological orientations and political preferences affect the divide and its outcome. For example, a government supporting free trade would try to find a way to legislate for the FTA despite the perceived loss to a population group.

3.3.2 *Quality of implementation*

(a) *Definition and importance*

The quality of implementation, which includes regulatory enforcement, is the third and final element of the regulatory impact mechanisms. Implementation refers to the act of a state meeting the requirements of law and undertaking mandates under the terms of law to fulfill its objectives. For example, to implement a statute that prohibits gender discrimination in workplaces, the state will have to monitor its application in workplaces, review suspect discrimination cases, and impose penalties for violations under the terms of the statute. It is the quality of implementation that determines the effectiveness of law, and it is measured by the extent to which a state meets the requirements set forth by the terms of law and fulfills the mandates under these terms, including its enforcement and monitoring terms. Cases of violations (particularly those not responded to by the state), omissions, and incomplete implementation on the part of the state count against the quality of implementation. Factors such as corruption and incapacity of the state adversely affect implementation.

For example, a law that requires the removal of customs tariffs on imports would not be as effective if customs officials at the border undermined the law by requiring an informal payment equivalent to a certain percentage of the value of an imported product as a condition for passing it through customs. Perceived

---

304 In the cited FTA example, Trade Adjustment Assistance (TAA) Programs under the Trade Expansion Act of 1962 and as defined further under the Trade Act of 1974 serve this purpose. 19 U.S.C. §§ 1911–1920 and §§ 2341–2356.

difficulty in the implementation of the WTO Agreement on Trade-Related Aspects of Intellectual Property (TRIPS Agreement)[305] in the least developed countries (LDCs)[306] is another example of such implementation issues. According to a study, the cost of implementing the TRIPS Agreement, including investments in buildings, equipment, and training, was US$ 150 million in the 1990s; this amount would have represented an entire year's development budget for many LDCs at the time.[307] In this circumstance, implementing TRIPS obligations in LDCs would be difficult due to a lack of financial resources.

A question arises as to whether a state is the only entity that implements law. For example, customary law and common law exist without the state act of legislation. As for common law, it is a state (the court) that "finds" its existence, identifies its terms, and enforces them. Thus, it can be said that the role of a state is essential in the implementation of common law. As for customary law, to the extent that it exists by voluntary recognition and compliance among the general public, it may not require state implementation. The state may also be called on to recognize its existence and enforce customary law where there is a dispute, so the state has an implementation role for customary law.[308] A state may also delegate some of its roles to another entity in the implementation of law, likely under its own monitoring and supervision.[309]

Finally, the other two elements of the regulatory impact mechanisms discussed in the preceding sections, regulatory design and regulatory compliance, also affect the quality of implementation. Laws that are well designed, congruent with socioeconomic conditions (including other social norms), and commanding strong compliance are more likely to be implemented effectively than those that are not. In addition, the two external factors, state capacity and political will, have a determinative impact on the quality of implementation, as further discussed below.

---

305 See Agreement on Trade-Related Aspects of Intellectual Property Rights, April 15, 1994, *Marrakesh Agreement Establishing the World Trade Organization* (WTO Agreement), Annex 1C, 1869 U.N.T.S. 299, 33 I.L.M. 1197 (1994).

306 LDCs are low-income countries designated by the United Nations. There are currently 47 LDCs, and the list is reviewed every three years by the Committee for Development (CDP). For identification of criteria for the LDCs, see United Nations, *LDC Identification Criteria & Indicators*, available online at: www.un.org/development/desa/dpad/least-developed-country-category/ldc-criteria.html; https://perma.cc/8S66-MZDL.

307 J. Michael Finger, "The WTO's Special Burden on Less Developed Countries" (2000) 19(3) *Cato Journal* 425–437, at 435.

308 Traditional community forums, rather than state courts, may hear and adjudicate claims based on customary law, as is the case in many underdeveloped regions. See Zwier (2017), *supra* note 291.

309 A state delegates its role of implementation when, for example, it contracts with a private company to operate a correctional facility. A commentator also observed a trend of the "third sectorization of law and policy" in which numerous non-state, non-market civil organizations such as voluntary associations, nongovernmental organizations (NGOs), and religious groups become independent sources of normative authority. See Rittich (2006), *supra* note 49, at 223.

(b) State capacity

As discussed, the state[310] implements laws relevant to development through legislation, judicial decisions, and administrative actions. Thus, the state must have the
due capacity to implement law. State capacity includes its financial, technological,
and administrative capabilities,[311] including internal controls against corruption,
to implement laws and fulfill regulatory objectives.

State capacity is essential to the implementation of law regardless of the ideological orientation of the development policies. Even in a development model in
which the role of the private sector is predominant, the state still has an important role in the functioning of the market economy. For example, freedom of
contract[312] is necessary for the market economy to operate. Therefore, a state
advocating for the market must enforce contracts in an appropriate legal framework ("contract law") that ensures the rights and obligations of the parties to the
contract. The recognition and enforcement of contractual rights through legislation, judicial decisions, and administrative actions are essentially state activities.
The market economy cannot successfully function if the state lacks capacity in one
or more of these areas.[313]

Developing countries often lack sufficient financial, technological, and administrative resources to implement all of their laws effectively. Thus, the question
arises as to how a developing country with limited resources could secure state
capacity to implement the laws necessary for development. Arguably, wealth may
not necessarily be a precondition to the development of high-quality laws and
institutions (*e.g.*, personnel costs are lower in developing countries).[314] Successful
East Asian countries found at least a partial answer to the question in their cultural tradition. They derived considerable state capacity from well-educated public
officials and efficient government bureaucracies. Despite financial constraints
(*i.e.*, modest government salaries), they were able to recruit elite public officials

---

310 For a definition of "state," see *supra* note 243.

311 These capabilities characterizing state capacity, such as administrative capability, may overlap with
     socioeconomic conditions, discussed in Section 3.2.3 (see *supra* note 280), although socioeco-
     nomic conditions are a broader concept and not identical to state capacity. Thus, an analysis of
     relevant socioeconomic conditions may also indicate state capacity and aid in the assessment of
     this third category (quality of implementation) that is more specific to the state.

312 Freedom of contract refers to the freedom of individuals and legal persons (legally recognized
     entities), including corporations, to form contracts and determine contractual terms. Freedom
     of contract is essential to the free market economy. David Bernstein, "Freedom of Contract," *in*
     David S. Tanenhaus (ed.), *Encyclopedia of the Supreme Court of the United States*, vol. 2 (Palgrave
     Macmillan Reference, 2008), at 263–266.

313 This explains the initial failure and economic confusion after the unprepared privatization in
     the former Soviet countries after the fall of communism in the 1980s where the state lacked the
     capacity to implement LFIs necessary for the market economy. For a discussion of the economic
     difficulty faced by the former Soviet countries, see William W. Hogan, "Economic Reforms in
     the Sovereign States of the Former Soviet Union," *Brookings Papers on Economic Activity*, no. 2
     (1991), available online at: www.brookings.edu/wp-content/uploads/1991/06/1991b_bpea_
     hogan.pdf; https://perma.cc/NZF9-JM8K.

314 Davis and Trebilcock (2008), *supra* note 87, at 922–923.

because their Confucian tradition encouraged elite, educated individuals to seek government positions with the notion that it is an honor to serve the state as a government official.[315] As a result, these countries were able to recruit and deploy highly disciplined and devoted officials to develop and administer law.[316]

State capacity was also a determinative factor for other countries that accomplished economic development. Germany achieved remarkable economic development in the late nineteenth century when Otto von Bismarck adopted state-led developmental policies, aided by substantially increased state capacity as a result of Germany's unification.[317] A similar development took place in the United States when President Lincoln led the Union to victory in the Civil War and stopped the Southern States' secession from the Union (an outcome that would have weakened the state capacity of the United States), followed by North-based industrialization and trade protection for industrial development.[318] Generals Franco and Pinochet also implemented strong state-backed economic reforms in Spain and Chile, respectively, which paved the path for their economic development, notwithstanding the authoritarian and repressive nature of their regimes.[319] By contrast, weak states in Africa and Latin America[320] could not successfully implement the LFIs needed for economic development for much of the twentieth century.[321]

---

315 For a discussion of the Confucian tradition in East Asia, see generally Wei-Ming Tu, *Confucian Traditions in East Asian Modernity* (Cambridge, MA: Harvard University Press, 1996).

316 See generally Roy Hofheinz, Jr. and Kent E. Calder, *The East Asia Edge: Why an Entire Region Is Overtaking the West in Technology, Exports and Management* (New York: Basic Books, 1982); Lucian W. Pye, *Asian Power and Politics: The Cultural Dimensions of Authority* (Cambridge, MA: The Belknap Press, 1985); Peter L. Berger and Hsin-Huang Michael Hsiao, *In Search of an East Asian Development Model* (Piscataway, NJ: Transaction Publishers, 1988).

317 See Otto Pflanze, *Bismarck and the Development of Germany, Volume II: The Period of Consolidation, 1871–1880* (Princeton, NJ: Princeton University Press, 1990), at 67–92, 207–245.

318 Henry Clay, Abraham Lincoln's early mentor, is known to have advocated the "American System" of trade protection in opposition to what he called the "British System" of free trade, which, he argued, was part of the British imperialist system that consigned the United States to the role of primary product exporter. See P. Conkin, *Prophets of Prosperity: America's First Political Economists* (Bloomington: Indiana University Press, 1980), at 302.

319 These policies included the 1959 Spanish Stabilization Plan and Pinochet's market-oriented reforms deliberated in 1973–1975 and implemented afterward. Leandro Prados de la Escosura, Joan Rosés, and Isabel Sanz Villarroya, "Stabilisation and Growth under Dictatorships: Lessons from Franco's Spain," *VOX: CEPR's Policy Portal* (March 22, 2010), available online at: http://voxeu.org/article/stabilisation-and-growth-under-dictatorships-new-lessons-franco-s-spain; https://perma.cc/Y2EU-VS78 and Robert A. Packenham and William Ratliff, "What Pinochet Did for Chile," *Hoover Digest* (January 30, 2007), available online at: www.hoover.org/research/what-pinochet-did-chile; https://perma.cc/CJ6K-LXVC.

320 For further discussion on weak states, see Robert Rotberg, "Failed States, Collapsed States, Weak States: Causes and Indicators," *in* Robert Rotberg (ed.), *State Failure and State Weakness in a Time of Terror* (Cambridge: World Peace Foundation, 2003) and Susan E. Rice and Stewart Patrick, "Index of State Weakness in the Developing World," *Brookings Institution* (February 26, 2008), available online at: www.brookings.edu/wp-content/uploads/2016/06/02_weak_states_index.pdf; https://perma.cc/K2EV-AMXS.

321 However, state capacity should not be confused with the state's ability and willingness to use or abuse its power. A state being "weak," lacking the cited key capacities to meet its development objectives, does not mean that it is completely powerless. Some of the weak states, as listed in the

State capacity is an overarching factor that is not only essential to the implementation of law but also influences the two other elements of the regulatory impact mechanisms, regulatory design and regulatory compliance. The state's evaluative and analytical capacity influences regulatory design, particularly legislation. Its capacity to enforce and raise public confidence in law influences regulatory compliance, as discussed in Section 3.3.1. Despite this overarching influence, state capacity alone does not determine the regulatory impact on development. Although states with sufficient analytical capacity are more likely to make laws, for example, with a better regulatory design than states without such capacity, there are numerous cases in which poorly designed laws, as a result of political compromise or other reasons, are implemented in states that otherwise have high capacities.[322] Likewise, regulatory compliance may also be affected by state capacity, but it is not necessarily controlled by the latter, particularly when a major segment of the general public does not support the objective of the law proposed by the state due to political, economic, cultural, or religious grounds.[323]

(c) Political will

Political will is another essential element affecting the implementation of law. In the context of regulatory implementation, political will is defined as the commitment and devotion of a country's political leadership to the implementation of law.[324] Political will, concerning law and development, should be distinguished from a mere interest in development facilitation, which the leadership of almost every developing country would have, given the state of their economies. Political will is more than a mere interest, which may be demonstrated by the continued implementation of consistent development policies for an extended

Index of State Weakness in the Developing World, were known to use brutal force against their own populations, including torture and summary executions. Rice and Patrick (2008), *ibid.* For another account of the mismatch between "state power" and "state capacity" (in the context of transnational law enforcement), see Mariano-Florentino Cuéllar, "The Mismatch between State Power and State Capacity in Transnational Law Enforcement" (2004) 22(1) *Berkeley Journal of International Law* 15–58.

322 See, *e.g.*, Frank Holmes, "FATCA: Good Intentions, Poor Design," *U.S. Global Investors* (June 25, 2014), available online at: www.usfunds.com/investor-library/frank-talk/fatca-good-intentions-bad-execution/#.V-28rIKQL3g; https://perma.cc/N5W3-S6D3.

323 See, *e.g.*, Cody (2012), *supra* note 288 (reporting religion-based public resistance to the French law that prohibits the use of facial coverings in public places). A study highlighted the importance of state capacity to regulatory impact concerning crime control. The study concluded that the suppression of sexual and gender-based violence had not been very effective in Liberia where the government enacted laws that substantially increased penalties for these crimes, but the state lacked the capacity to implement these laws effectively, due to an absence of resources to supply sufficient police force, prosecutorial services, and courts to monitor, prosecute, convict, and punish offenders. Zwier (2017) *supra* note 291. The weak state capacity, prevalent in developing countries, resulted in a poor regulatory impact. Rotberg (2003), *supra* note 320.

324 See Lori Ann Post, Amber N. W. Raile, and Eric D. Raile, "Defining Political Will" (2010) 38(4) *Politics and Policy* 653–676 (for a discussion of defining "political will" in various contexts).

period and the allocation of substantial political and economic capital. Lack of political will can result in ineffective laws, regardless of state capacity, where the government expects political challenges against the implementation of such laws and is reluctant to implement or enforce them to avoid any adverse political ramifications. By contrast, sustained political will instills consistency in regulatory implementation and enforcement.[325]

After the Second World War, many successful developing countries achieved economic development under authoritarian regimes, such as the East Asian countries from the 1960s to the 1980s (China since the 1980s), Spain in the 1960s and the 1970s, and Chile in the 1970s and the 1980s.[326] The success of these countries often hinged on the decision to save available resources for future investments, as opposed to immediate consumption. For example, the Korean government, which controlled commercial banks until the 1980s, did not make bank loans available for home mortgages so that the available capital could be used for long-term productive pursuits, such as building factories and social infrastructures. While this was an essential investment for the future that led to the world's highest sustained economic growth for over three decades, this type of policy is nevertheless unpopular to the general public, who are then compelled to save much of their income for many years to purchase homes.[327] Elective democracy tends to cater to voters' immediate concerns rather than long-term strategic development plans that may require public sacrifice until the development potential materializes.[328]

The preceding observation does not necessarily lead to the conclusion that the political will necessary for sustained growth could never be generated in a democracy.[329] However, its deliberative and elective nature is likely to present considerable challenges when making a long-term development decision that may require voters to make an immediate sacrifice, particularly in the early stages of economic

---

325 Conversely, successful economic development and improved state capacity, such as increased financial resources, may also reinforce political will. Initial success can provide encouragement and motivation for the continuation of a successful development path, and improved state capacity, such as a larger government budget and development funds, as well as a larger staff, can generate better conditions under which to carry out the will.

326 For a discussion of the development of Spain under General Franco and of Chile under Pinochet, see *supra* note 29. The East Asian countries also had legendary political leaders devoted to national development, such as Park Jung Hee of Korea (1917–1979), Chang Kai-Shek of Taiwan (1885–1975), Lee Kuan Yew of Singapore (1923–2015), and Deng Xiaoping of China (1904–1997) (The last name precedes the first name in East Asia; the names of prominent Asian political leaders are listed in this order.)

327 See Dackeun Park and Changyong Rhee, "Saving, Growth, and Demographic Change in Korea" (2005) 19(3) *Journal of the Japanese International Economies* 394–413, at 394–95, 410.

328 See Adam Przeworski *et al.*, *Democracy and Development: Political Institutions and Well-Being in the World 1950–1990* (New York: Cambridge University Press, 2000), at 143.

329 For instance, India, which is considered a democracy, has shown substantial economic growth in recent decades. Democratized Chile also benefitted from the economic reforms completed during the authoritarian regime of Pinochet. For further discussion of Chile's development under the Pinochet regime, see *supra* note 259.

development when resources are limited and difficult choices have to be made.[330] Likewise, a change of regime, which is an inevitable outcome in elective democracies, can also lead to a change in development policy and even in development objectives. Some of these changes are for political reasons rather than for development, and they may be averse to the development interests, the fulfillment of which requires a sustained and consistent development policy over time. Realistically, some minimum degree of development may be necessary before a democratic system of governance operates efficiently and continues to promote development. A working democracy requires economic and social resources,[331] such as public education, access to information, and the rule of law, which may not be achievable without economic development in place.

The inherent difficulty with elective democracy does not mean that dictatorships or authoritarian regimes are the answer; these regimes also do not automatically generate political commitment and devotion to development. The political will necessary for development is not determined by the length of time that one is in power. Otherwise, many authoritarian regimes and dictatorships still existing would have made progress in development, but that is not the case. This reality presents a dilemma: although authoritarian leaders in successful developing countries have led their countries to decades of successful economic development, a system of dictatorship or authoritarian governance does not guarantee the appointment of a "good leader" with the requisite political will.[332] There is no political system that guarantees a leader who will uphold the political will for development, ready to resist popular demand for short-term economic gain to meet long-term development objectives. The cited systemic issues with elective democracies and the uncertainty characterizing authoritarian regimes are likely a reason that only a small number of countries achieved development successfully

---

330 It took several decades before democratic India could finally embark on sustained economic growth, whereas authoritarian NICs and China achieved much more rapid economic development.

331 Chang (2002), *supra* note 203, at 69–124.

332 A majority of successful developing countries with "benevolent" or "good" authoritarian leaders have been located in East Asia, where the prevailing Confucian tradition emphasized the duty of the elite to their state and people. Such tradition may have been a reason for the production of a higher ratio of leaders devoted to economic development compared to that in other regions in the world without such tradition. For a discussion of the Confucian tradition in East Asia, see Tu (1996), *supra* note 315. Another view has been raised that individuals and groups interested in predation, rather than development, are more likely to capture the government in countries with rich natural resource endowments from which they can easily appropriate large economic rents. See Richard M. Auty, "Natural Resource Endowment, the State, and Development Policy" (1997) 9(4) *Journal of International Development* 435–673, at 651. Note that none of the NICs were resource rich. Yet another difficulty in forging a united political will toward development could be associated with enduring divisions along ethnic, religious, linguistic, and economic lines within countries. The East Asian countries were relatively homogeneous in ethnicity and culture and did not suffer from the degree of contentious ethnic, religious, and cultural division experienced by many developing countries in other regions.

since the Second World War and became developed ones.[333] The question of political governance and development is revisited in Chapter 8.

The preceding discussion of the general theory of law and development is a response to the call for a working theory in the field of law and development; the general theory explores the "missing links" between law and development (*i.e.*, the mechanisms that explain the regulatory impact on development). The theory presents the three categorical elements: regulatory design, regulatory compliance, and quality of implementation, which together comprise the regulatory impact mechanisms.[334] As discussed above, none of these elements operate in isolation, but, instead, each one interacts with and influences one another. Based on this understanding, Part II examines how these interconnected elements explain the development processes on the ground.

333 Developing countries other than those cited above have also progressed economically. Countries such as Malaysia, Thailand, and Vietnam have progressed in recent decades, although they have not reached the developed country status yet. Certain European countries, such as Portugal, several regions of Italy, Greece, Poland, Hungary, Slovakia, Slovenia, and Ireland were also relatively poor (compared to the other Western European countries) but progressed. Despite all this progress, the vast majority of developing countries have not yet successfully progressed into developed economies.

334 Scholars may have known these elements implicitly, but it is necessary to formulate them in a theoretical framework to explain systematically the causal mechanisms between law and development. Regulatory impact (I_r) can be described as a function of regulatory design (D_r), regulatory compliance (C_r), and quality of implementation (Q_i): $I_r = f(D_r, C_r, Q_i)$. This chapter has also discussed the impact of development on law, *albeit* briefly, and advanced additional elements, such as "regulatory adjustment" and "regulatory reinforcement" to explain this impact. See discussion *supra* Section 3.2.3.

Part II

Law and development in practice

4 Law and development in South Korea

The first three chapters in Part II (Chapters 4–6) discuss law and development in practice, examining the role of law and institutions for economic and social development in specific countries such as South Korea, South Africa, and the United States, under the analytical framework introduced in the preceding Chapter 3 ("the general theory of law and development"). These chapters serve the following two objectives: to assess how law and institutions have affected development on the ground through empirical cases and examine how the general theory could be applied to explain specific development cases from the legal and institutional perspectives.

4.1 Introduction: a success story

This chapter explores the legal and institutional dimensions of one of the most successful cases of economic and social development in history: the development of South Korea ("Korea") from the early 1960s to the mid-1990s (Korea's "development period").[335] The economic policies that led to successful development in Korea have been studied extensively,[336] but fewer studies have analyzed

---

335 This chapter is developed from Lee (2017), *supra* note 4, part IV, at 456–468. Korea initiated its five-year economic development plans in 1962 and completed its seventh five-year plan in 1996. In this period, Korea increased its GDP by an average of 8.75 percent per annum, while the world's average annual GDP increase for the corresponding period was 3.85 percent. *Supra* note 28 (for a reference on GDP increases by the NICs including Korea).

336 See, *e.g.*, Alice H. Amsden, *Asia's Next Giant: Korea and Late Industrialization* (New York: Oxford University Press, 1992); Larry E. Westphal, "Industrial Policy in an Export Propelled Economy: Lessons from South Korea's Experience" (1990) 4(3) *Journal of Economic Perspectives* 41–59; Kwang-suk Kim and Joon-kyung Park, *Sources of Economic Growth in Korea: 1963–1981* (Seoul: Korea Development Institute, 1985); John Brohman, "Postwar Development in the Asian NICs: Does the Neoliberal Model Fit Reality?" (1996) 72(2) *Economic Geography* 107–130; A. O. Krueger, "Trade Policies in Developing Countries," *in* R. W. Jones and P. B. Kenen (eds.), *Handbook of International Economics*, vol. 1 (New York: North-Holland, 1984), at 519–569; T. N. Srinivasan, "Trade, Development, and Growth," *Princeton Essays in International Economics*, no. 225 (December 2001); G. K. Helleiner (ed.), *Trade Policy, Industrialization, and Development* (Oxford: Oxford University Press, 1992); World Bank, *The East Asian Miracle* (New York: Oxford University Press, 1993).

DOI: 10.4324/9781003090175-6

its legal and institutional dimensions.[337] This chapter attempts to fill this gap[338] by drawing some insights and lessons from the development case of Korea from legal and institutional perspectives.[339]

Korea's success in development has indeed been unprecedented. In 2018, Korea hosted the Winter Olympics. Witnessing the wonders that it displayed at the opening ceremony, such as the 1,218 flying Shooting Star drones used to create the images of an airborne snowboarder, a bird flapping its wings, and the iconic Olympic Rings lighting up the sky,[340] one may not easily recall its arduous past. This country, a mid-sized nation located in Northeast Asia between China and Japan,[341] has a long history as an independent country of over 5,000 years or so.[342] Korea has undergone significant tumult in recent history, however, as demonstrated by a period of brutal Japanese colonization (1910–1945), the division of the country into North and South Koreas (1945), and a devastating war between the two Koreas (the Korean War, 1950–1953) that nearly destroyed the nation.[343] Barely recovering from this destructive war, Korea was among the poorest countries in the world, with a very low per-capita income and underdeveloped industries with low productivity.[344]

Korea's economic status has radically changed since it embarked on a state-led, trade-based industrialization process in the early 1960s. Korea had much of the characteristics shared by many developing countries today, such as low per-capita

---

337 Lee (2017), *supra* note 4; Pistor and Wellons (1999), *supra* note 265; Ohnesorge (2006), *supra* note 179.

338 Scholars have indicated that there has not been a serious study of the role that law has played in the economic development in Northeast Asia, including Korea. Ohnesorge observed that:

> [g]iven their indisputable record of economic and social success, and given the fact that literature on Northeast Asian legal systems is widely available, the failure to place Northeast Asia at the core of law and development theorizing seems impossible to justify.

Ohnesorge (2006), *supra* note 179, at 224.

339 See also Yong-Shik Lee, "Law and Development: Lessons from South Korea" (2018) 11(2) *Law and Development Review* 433–465.

340 Meera Dolasia, "PyeongChang 2018 Winter Olympics Open with Intel's Spectacular Shooting Star Drones," *Dogonews*, February 12, 2018, available online at: www.dogonews.com/2018/2/12/pyeongchang-2018-winter-olympics-open-with-intels-spectacular-shooting-star-drones; https://perma.cc/79P4-VYYK.

341 In 1960, the Korean population was 25 million in a territory of 98,480 square kilometers (38,023 square miles). See Encyclopedia of the Nations, *Korea, South*, available online at: www.nationsencyclopedia.com/economies/Asia-and-the-Pacific/Korea-South.html; https://perma.cc/B8GC-5ZFW.

342 For a history of Korea, see Kyung Moon Hwang, *A History of Korea* (New York, Palgrave Macmillan, 2016); Michael J. Seth, *A History of Korea: From Antiquity to the Present* (Lanham, MD: Rowman & Littlefield Publishers, 2010); Carter J. Eckert and Ki-Baik Lee, *Korea Old and New: A History* (Seoul: Ilchokak Publishers, 1991).

343 *Ibid.*

344 In 1962, Korea's GNI per capita was a mere US$ 120, lower than most other developing countries in Asia, Africa, and Latin America at the time. See World Bank, *GNI per capita (current US$)*, available online at: https://data.worldbank.org/indicator/NY.GNP.PCAP.CD; https://perma.cc/SKQ7-PXTK.

income causing prevalent poverty, an economy relying heavily on primary, non-manufacturing industries, low levels of technology and entrepreneurship in society, insufficient capital, a poor endowment of natural resources, over-population in a relatively small territory, and internal political instability and external threats to its security.[345] Successfully overcoming these unfavorable conditions, Korea's economy progressed from one reliant on low-productive primary industries and characterized by absolute poverty in the 1960s to an advanced economy based on large industrial capacity, generating high per-capita income by the mid-1990s.[346] The Korean development process is unique because it exhibits all major stages of economic development in only three decades (which is substantially shorter than the periods of development for most other developed countries today) and has also shown successful social and political development from authoritarian rule to elective democracy based on the rule of law by the 1990s.

As explained at the outset, this chapter explores the legal and institutional dimensions of this successful development and applies the general theory to explain the impact that law and institutions had on Korea's successful development. Section 4.2 applies the first part of the general theory and identifies the applicable law and Korea's economic and social development objectives. From there, Section 4.2 applies the second part of the general theory, "the regulatory impact mechanisms," to the development process of Korea and examines each component of these mechanisms to assess the impact of law on Korea's development. Section 4.3 draws lessons from the Korean case.

4.2 Law, institutions, and development

4.2.1 Applicable law

The first part of the general theory sets the disciplinary parameters of law and development.[347] In the context of law and development, "law" includes both formal state law, such as statutes, and non-state law that is observed by the general public, sometimes over generations, referred to as customary law.[348] In the case of Korea, formal state law, particularly development-facilitating statutes, is the focus of analysis. There are two main reasons for this focus. First, Korea, being a civil law country,[349] meticulously codified legal rules into major

---

345 Lee (2016), *supra* note 102, at 18.
346 As a result of successful economic development, Korea's GNI increased to US$ 13,254 by 1996, which elevated Korea to the status of a high-income country as defined by the World Bank at that time, with income distribution better than some of the most advanced developed countries, including the United States. See World Bank, *supra* note 344. As to the latter point, Korea's Gini coefficient, which shows income distribution, was 0.28–0.29 in the 1990s, based on the disposable income, which was lower (*i.e.*, better income distribution) than most other countries, including the United States (0.34).
347 See discussion *supra* Section 3.1.
348 See discussion *supra* Section 1.2.
349 For an explanation of civil law and common law, see *supra* note 17.

"codes"[350] and statutes, leaving relatively less room for the role of customary law.[351] Secondly, the Korean government assumed the role of a developmental state[352] during its period of development, meaning that it played the key role in economic development, creating economic development plans, relocating surplus, combatting resistance, making investments, managing key sectors, and controlling foreign capital.[353] As further discussed below, the Korean government used formal state law, particularly statutes, as a device to empower the government to implement state-led development policies.

Despite the focus on formal state law, a question may arise as to the role of customary law in the development of Korea. A relevant example would be the "administrative guidance" cited in Chapter 1,[354] by which the governments of Korea and Japan issued non-binding advice to domestic businesses for the purpose of protecting public interest, targeting and limiting, for example, price hikes on consumer goods considered necessaries for the general public.[355] Administrative guidance is not formal state law, and there is no legal requirement for compliance therewith, but it was nonetheless consistently followed in Korea, to the extent that one may see it as *de facto* law or customary law. However, the general theory makes a distinction between law, including customary law, and other non-legal orders, and the dividing line is the existence of "*opinio juris.*"[356] There is a question as to whether *opinio juris* exists concerning administrative guidance, where the general public may not have necessarily considered such guidance as creating binding legal obligations, as evidenced by lawsuits challenging administrative guidance.[357] An alternative explanation for compliance could be that the general public recognized and respected the role of the state (and the practical power that the authoritarian government had on their businesses) during the period of Korea's economic development.

The strength of public compliance and participation in the development process and policies mandated by the government,[358] as well as the resulting

---

350 Korea's six major codes include the constitution, civil affairs, criminal affairs, civil procedure, criminal procedure, and public administration.
351 For a study of customary law in Korea, see Marie Seong-Hak Kim, "In the Name of Custom, Culture, and the Constitution: Korean Customary Law in Flux" (2013) 48(3) *Texas International Law Journal* 357–391.
352 For a concept of developmental state, see Chalmers Johnson, "The Developmental State: Odyssey of a Concept," *in* Meredith Woo-Cumings (ed.), *The Developmental State* (Ithaca, NY: Cornell University Press, 1999), at 32–60.
353 Trubek and Santos (2006), *supra* note 81, at 8.
354 See *supra* Section 1.2.
355 *Ibid.*
356 *Ibid.*
357 Kihyun Roh, "訴訟上における行政指導の権利救済の限界と克服方案 ― 日本での議論を中心に [Ways to Overcome the Limits on Judicial Remedy for Infringement of Rights by Administrative Guidance—Based on Discussions in Japan]" (2012) 15(2) *Inha Law Review* 85–116.
358 See *infra* Section 4.2.4.

success, are noteworthy and justify further analysis, whether or not the norms and practices created by this public compliance and participation amounted to customary law. However, these norms and practices have also changed as the Korean economy and society have undergone rapid development. For example, the amount of administrative guidance has been reduced since the 1990s, and the number of lawsuits challenging government measures has rapidly increased since then,[359] implying that these norms and practices may have been voluntary responses, rather than binding and lasting customary law, embraced by the general public in support of the state's role in economic development when the public felt it was needed to meet contemporary development objectives. This explains why public compliance with government rules and policies has weakened over time, as demonstrated by the increased number of legal challenges against government measures when members of the public perceived the role of the state to be of less importance in the national economy as Korea achieved its development objectives in the 1990s.

4.2.2 Economic and social development objectives

In Korea, development objectives have been clear since the beginning of its development era in the early 1960s. The focus was economic development to overcome serious poverty affecting the majority of the population. This was to be achieved by industrial development as the means to generate employment and income. Exports were considered essential for industrial development to overcome the constraints of the small domestic market; the total value of exports, as well as the share of exports in the country's gross domestic product (GDP), increased substantially (see Table 4.1).

Table 4.1 Export expansion and exports/GDP of Korea[360]

Year	Real GDP growth rate (percent)	Goods export values (USD billion)	Exports of goods and services/GDP (percent)
1962–1966	8.0	1	7.7
1967–1971	9.7	3	13.7
1972–1976	8.0	22	27.8
1977–1981	6.2	77	31.5
1982–1986	8.7	141	34.4
1987–1991	9.4	307	32.3
1992–1996	7.3	510	28.7

359 Korea National Statistical Office, E-National Statistical Index, *The Number of Administrative Lawsuits* (in Korean), available online at: www.index.go.kr/potal/main/EachDtlPageDetail. do?idx_cd=1724; https://perma.cc/X44R-CS7P. The number of administrative lawsuits (lawsuits against government measures) increased from 17,063 in 1997 to 36,799 in 2016.
360 Lee (2016), *supra* note 102, at 304, table 10.2a.

The five-year plans (see Table 4.2) developed and implemented by the Korean government from the early 1960s to the mid-1990s also illustrate specific development targets at the time.

Table 4.2 Five-year economic development plans, 1962–1996[361]

1st (1962–1966)	2nd (1967–1971)	3rd (1972–1976)
- Promote import-substitute industries - Build petroleum and fertilizer plants - Transition to export-oriented policy (1964)	- Expand export bases - Strengthen international competitiveness of light industries - Produce industrial raw materials - Introduce and adopt new technologies	- Promote heavy and chemical industries - Promote science and technology - Increase exports
4th (1977–1981)	**5th (1982–1986)**	**6th (1987–1991)**
- Attain the status of the world's major (advanced) economy - Rationalize industrial structure - Build key plants	- Promote best quality and precision in products - Export plant facilities - Support private enterprises to develop production technologies	- Promote world-class industries - Promote aviation industry - Expand overseas industrial investments
7th (1992–1996)		
- Enhance the competitiveness of corporations - Promote social equity and balanced development - Support internationalization and develop foundations for the unification of two Koreas		

More complex and controversial were Korea's social development objectives. Except for a brief period between April 1960 and May 1961, when there was a democratic regime born after the Civil Revolution of 1960 ("the April Revolution"),[362] the nation went through a period of authoritarian rule until the 1980s. It meant that the resources at the disposal of the state were to be devoted to the priorities of these regimes, and their priorities were economic development. The majority of the population, suffering from crushing poverty at the time, supported the government's drive for economic development, but the

---

361 "Challenging Moments in Korean History (2): Five-Year Economic Development Plans," *Korean Economy Daily*, August 2008.
362 *Supra* note 342 (for references on the history of Korea).

other non-economic development objectives, such as political democratization, were not completely set aside.

For much of Korea's developmental era (1962–1996), the primary social development objective was political democratization, as evidenced by both the April Revolution, a series of public demonstrations throughout the 1970s and 1980s, and the major public strife in June 1987 that led to a constitutional amendment and free presidential election later that year.[363] The authoritarian regimes throughout the 1960s and into the 1980s did not defy the notion of political democracy, at least in form (*i.e.*, there were public elections, although they were heavily influenced and to some extent controlled by the administration), but they put severe limits on civil liberty, including freedom of speech, to maintain control over populations. This oppressive control created continuous tension between the administrations and civil societies and resulted in public resistance seeking the restoration of civil liberty and political democratization.

Thus, it would be fair to say that the most important social development objective for Korea, political democratization, was promoted by non-state civil groups, such as students and liberals, until the 1980s, often in the face of violent suppression by the authoritarian regimes. The 1987 constitutional amendment, which provided for free presidential elections, paved the way for political democratization. Following the 1987 constitutional amendment, the process of political democratization progressed by the initiatives of the elected civil administrations in the 1990s. The rule of law was strengthened, and the judiciary became independent of the administration by the 1990s. As political democratization progressed, several other social development objectives, such as gender equality, environmental protection, and reduction of the identified gaps in economic opportunities between "haves" and "have-nots," have also been promoted, with legislative and institutional measures in place.[364]

4.2.3 Regulatory impact mechanisms—regulatory design

The remainder of this section applies the second part of the general theory, "the regulatory impact mechanisms," to explain the causal mechanisms by which law impacted development in Korea. As discussed in Chapter 3, the regulatory impact mechanisms are comprised of three conceptually distinct but interconnected categorical elements: "regulatory design," "regulatory compliance," and "quality of implementation."[365] Each of these elements includes additional sub-elements. This section applies them in sequence to the development process of Korea and assesses the impact that law had on Korea's development.[366] The first element of

---

363 *Ibid.*
364 For example, Korea enacted the Basic Law for the Progress of Women in 1995 to promote gender equality, and the government set up the Special Committee on Women under the president in 1998.
365 See discussion *supra* Section 3.1.
366 For a full account of the theory, see *supra* Chapter 3.

the regulatory impact mechanisms is "regulatory design," which analyzes how law is designed to achieve a development objective. As readers may recall from Chapter 3, there are three sub-elements, including anticipated policy outcome, organization of law, legal frameworks, and institutions (LFIs), and law's adaptation to socioeconomic conditions.[367] These three sub-elements collectively determine the effectiveness of regulatory design in Korea, as further discussed below.

(a) Anticipated policy outcome

Applying this analytical framework to Korea, the primary objective of Korea's development policies was the relief of extreme poverty for the majority of its population.[368] To meet this objective, sustainable income sources for the majority of the population had to be created, and the government strategy was to develop industries that would generate employment and income. The conditions of poverty resulted in insufficient purchasing power in the domestic market. To overcome these constraints, the government adopted export-led development policies[369] and prioritized developing manufacturing industries using inexpensive and efficient labor, which Korea had in abundance.

Statutes mandating state support for exports, such as the Act on Temporary Measures for the Grant of Export Subsidies (1961), the Export Promotion Act (1962) (replaced by the Trade Transactions Act of 1967), and the Regulation of Tax Reduction and Exemption Act (1965), served as the legal device by which these policies were implemented. These statutes authorized the government to grant tax reductions for the profits generated by exports, ensure timely payment of subsidies contingent upon exports ("export subsidies"), make priority allocation of scarce foreign reserves for the purchase of raw material to produce export products, and permit only those traders with export performance to engage in the lucrative import business.

The government also enacted several statutes mandating direct support for specific manufacturing industries, such as the Act on Temporary Measures for Textile Industrial Facilities (1967); the Acts facilitating the development of other specific industries, such as the Mechanical Industries (1967), Shipbuilding Industries (1967), Electronic Industries (1969), Petrochemical Industries (1970), and Steel Industries (1970); the Act on Refining Service of Non-Ferrous Metals (1971); and the Act on Promotion of the Modernization of Textile Industries (1979).[370] These statutes authorized the government to adopt measures of support for

---

367 See discussion *supra* Section 3.2.

368 See discussion *supra* Section 4.2.2.

369 Empirical studies concluded that exports lead to economic growth under certain conditions and that export promotion policies are effective in increasing exports. See M. Michaely, "Exports and Growth" (1977) 4(1) *Journal of Development Economics* 49–53; Woosik Jung and K. Lee, "The Effectiveness of Export Promotion Policies: The Case of Korea" (1986) 122 *Weltwirtschaftliches Archiv* 340–357; Ran Koh and Jai Sheen Mah, "The Effect of Export Composition on Economic Growth: The Case of Korea" (2013) 47(1) *Journal of Developing Areas* 171–179.

370 See Kim (ed.) (2011), *supra* note 176, vol. 1, at 216–227.

the designated industries, including tax incentives; loans whose terms, such as interest rates, were more favorable than the prevailing commercial terms (*i.e.*, "policy loans"); subsidy grants; tariff rebates and import control; and overseas loan guarantees. Government support was provided to businesses on a conditional basis; in return for such support, businesses were required to show market performance.[371]

Korea's state-led development policies would have found support from contemporary development economists, such as Rosenstein-Rodan, Mandelbaum, Lewis, Rostow, Kuznets, Gerschenkron, Hirschman, and Kindleberger, all of whom advocated the state-led development strategy as key to development.[372] However, Korea implemented development policies without a strong prospect of success; the government did not have sufficient financial and industrial resources to implement these policies. The United States, the primary aid provider for Korea at the time, was also initially pessimistic about Korea's development policies for being too "socialistic."[373] The Korean government played a key role in economic development initiatives, a fact well demonstrated by the aforementioned Five-Year Economic Development Plans that the government developed and implemented from 1962 to 1996. As seen above, the plans stipulated specific economic development and industrial promotion goals, including economic growth and export promotion targets for each of the five-year periods.

The government also coordinated private sector activities and supported those that were consistent with its development goals. The government achieved this through its control of bank loans and its ability to provide subsidies.[374] These policy loans and subsidies had distributive effects in favor of producers who complied with the government policies, and the government allocated resources to those industries that were considered at the time to have the strongest potential for growth of the economy, resulting in the high economic growth in the 1960s and the 1970s. The government also used other measures of support, including tax incentives, favorable exchange rates (to promote exports), and a flexible import tariff regime (supporting exporters and suppressing imports that compete with rising domestic industries). The government also engaged extensively in public education campaigns to induce social support for economic development.[375]

Korean development policies are also characterized by substantial flexibility and adaptability. The government set its export promotion and industrial development goals in accordance with the available resources, technology, and industrial experiences at the time. In the 1960s, when Korea lacked capital and technology

---

371 Sung-Hee Jwa, *A General Theory of Economic Development Towards a Capitalist Manifesto* (Cheltenham: Edward Elgar, 2017), at 83.

372 For further discussion of development economics, see *supra* note 254.

373 Jong Suk Lee, "The Launching of Economic Development Plan (The Half Century of Korean Economy)," *E Daily*, May 5, 2005 (in Korean).

374 Lee (2016), *supra* note 102, at 305–309.

375 *Ibid.*, at 305–313. In addition to this policy, other factors, such as prewar industrial experience, land reform, the rise of national firms, administrative quality, and precision in policy targeting, are known to have contributed to this success. Amsden (1992), *supra* note 336.

resources, the government focused on labor-intensive industries that did not require large amounts of capital or technological resources, such as textile and clothing manufacturing, and endeavored to export these products to generate income. The industrial experience, the accumulation of capital, and technological development during the initial period of successful economic development enabled Korea to transition into more advanced and potentially more profitable industries, such as heavy and chemical industries in the 1970s and electronics in the 1980s.[376]

The government-supported industries were required to show market performance, particularly in export markets, to receive continuing support from the government.[377] Strong performers were rewarded with government support, and weak performers were let go. It was essentially this partnership between the private sector and the government that resulted in unprecedented success in economic development for Korea.[378] The innovation and industrial efforts of the private sector, as well as government support, created world-class Korean industrial brand names, such as Hyundai and Samsung. This market focus is different from a socialist planned economy favored by dependency theorists.[379] This approach is similar to those adopted by other newly industrialized countries (NICs), including Taiwan and Singapore. China subsequently adopted this controlled market approach (*i.e.*, use of the market under a government incentive structure) when it initiated market-oriented reforms in 1978 in the name of "the socialist market economy."[380]

A policy shift began in the 1980s; after two decades of successful economic development, Korea became a middle-income country with a robust private sector, and its economy matured into a technology-based one. There were legislative shifts to meet this change, reducing government control of the economy and supporting the private sector with increased capacity rather than specific industries. This policy change was demonstrated by replacing the aforementioned statutes providing industry-specific support with the Manufacturing Industry Development Act in 1986,[381] granting more selective assistance to industries based on a need to improve their efficiency by restructuring or reorganization.[382]

After three-and-a-half decades of successful economic development, the anticipated policy outcomes—economic growth, industrial development, and

---

376 Lee (2016), *supra* note 102, at 303–305.
377 Jwa (2017), *supra* note 371.
378 However, this partnership has been weakened in Korea since the late 1990s; large corporations ("Chaebols") have continued to grow, but their growth has not been translated into the growth of the national economy, employment, and household income, as was seen from the 1960s to the 1980s.
379 Charles K. Wilber and Kenneth P. Jameson (eds.), *Socialist Models of Development* (Oxford: Pergamon, 1982).
380 For further discussion of the socialist market economy, see Osman Suliman (ed.), *China's Transition to a Socialist Market Economy* (West Port, CT: Praeger, 1998).
381 This statute was, in turn, replaced by the 1999 Industrial Development Act. See Kim (ed.) (2011), *supra* note 176, at 225.
382 *Ibid.*, at 222–227.

poverty relief—became a reality for Korea. The magnitude of success was evident in several economic indicators; when the Korean government implemented the first Five-Year Economic Development Plan in 1962, its gross national income (GNI) per capita[383] was US$ 120,[384] among the lowest in the world, with the majority of its population suffering from poverty. Korea's unemployment rate also decreased from an estimated 35 percent in 1961 down to 5.2 percent in 1980 (and 2.4 percent in 1990).[385] When Korea's seventh and final Five-Year Economic Development Plan was completed in 1996, the country ranked among the world's most advanced, developed countries, with affluent economies and world-class industries.[386] Korea became a high-income country as classified by the World Bank, with its GNI per capita reaching US$ 13,040 in 1996,[387] a major industrial power, and a leading trader.[388]

After a long period of unprecedented economic growth and prosperity, Korea faced an abrupt change of economic condition in 1997, and the analysis of the anticipated policy outcome also explains this change. Korea faced a critical shortage of foreign exchanges following the collapses of major conglomerates and the loss of confidence of foreign lenders, leading to the 1997 financial crisis. The government was unable to resolve this crisis, and it requested a bailout from the International Monetary Fund (IMF). In return for the requested bailout, the IMF demanded neoliberal changes in policies and law—to reduce the role of the state in the economy—at a decidedly more rapid pace than the government had been implementing since the 1980s. Korea was left with no other choice and accepted this demand to avoid a national default. The problem was that the policy outcome the demanded changes attempted to deliver, such as balancing the financial market through increases in interest rates, was not consistent with the decades of economic management and practices in Korea; a large number of firms had operated with short-term loans on a rolling basis. Thus, the IMF "prescriptions" caused over 3,000 companies to fail and millions to lose jobs. The demanded policy changes also reduced investments and lowered economic growth, which never recovered to pre-crisis levels.[389]

---

383 GNI per capita is used to measure the average income level of citizens in a country.
384 World Bank, *GNI per capita (current US$)*, *supra* note 344. According to the Bank of Korea, Korea's GNI per capita in 1962 (nominal US$) was even lower, at US$ 91. Bank of Korea, *Economic Statistics System*, available online at: http://ecos.bok.or.kr/, accessed October 12, 2020.
385 Korea National Statistical Office, *Statistical Assessment of Changes in Korea's Economy and Society for the Past 60 Years* (August 2008) (in Korean), available online at: https://web.arch ive.org/web/20140219065908/http://kostat.go.kr/portal/korea/kor_nw/2/1/index. board?bmode=download&bSeq=&aSeq=60300&ord=1, accessed January 13, 2021.
386 As a result of successful economic development, the Korean economy grew at the remarkable rate of 8.75 percent on average per annum from 1991 to 1996.
387 World Bank, *GNI per capita (current US$)*, *supra* note 344.
388 Korea joined the ranks of the other advanced countries in Europe and North America at the OECD in 1996.
389 For further discussion of the financial crisis in Korea and in other Asian countries in the 1990s, see Khan (2004), *supra* note 98.

(b) Organization of LFIs

The effectiveness of regulatory design is also determined by the organization of LFIs. In Korea, the flexibility of legal frameworks enabled the timely enactment of the development-facilitating statutes cited above. The major codes in Korea's civil law system,[390] with their elaborate legal structures and embedded legal principles, were not easily amenable to revision, so the government set up a separate legal apparatus outside its codes by enacting several separate statutes that were not directly controlled by its major codes. This approach enabled expedient legislation and timely amendments to implement specific development policies without having to undertake the potentially time-consuming process of revising its codes. The provisions of these statutes took precedence over any inconsistent provision in any other earlier statute, including the codes, except the constitution.

Effective institutional support was another key feature during Korea's development process; effective institutions supported the implementation of the development-facilitating laws legislated under the flexible legal frameworks. The government set up a number of development-supporting institutions, both within the government and on the outside. The most important one was the Economic Planning Board (EPB), which was established within the central government in 1961 to be the control center for the development and implementation of development policies.[391] The EPB, until its merger with the Ministry of Finance in 1994, coordinated and instructed other government departments on policy measures for economic development over the span of three decades, with authority over personnel appointment and budget allocation.[392] The government also set up financial institutions to support economic development, including the Korea Development Bank, which provided loans for select industries, and the Korea Export–Import Bank, which provided export credit.[393] Korea also established trade-support organizations, such as the Korea Trade Promotion Corporation (KOTRA) and the Korea International Trade Association (KITA). KOTRA provided support for export companies, including access to overseas market information and business networks, and KITA promoted the interests of Korean traders and provided trade information to its members.[394]

(c) Adaptation to socioeconomic conditions

The third sub-element determining the effectiveness of regulatory design is the adaptation of law to changing socioeconomic conditions. As economic

---

390 *Supra* note 350 (for a list of the major "codes").
391 Lee (2016), *supra* note 102, at 313. Taiwan's Industrial Development Bureau (IDB) and Japan's Ministry of International Trade and Industry (MITI) undertook similar roles within the government.
392 *Ibid.*
393 *Ibid.*, at 307–308.
394 *Ibid.*, at 312.

development progressed in Korea, its socioeconomic conditions, such as available economic and technological resources and the capacity of the private sector, have also changed. To meet these changes, the government repealed the statutes mandating support for specific industries, as discussed earlier. The government endeavored to ensure that the development-facilitating statutes were up to date and remained effective by monitoring their implementation and operation and making amendments to increase their adaptability to the changing socioeconomic conditions. For example, the government reviewed 2,790 statutes and made 288 adjustments from 1977 to 1979,[395] and in addition, the government made 604 statutory adjustments in the 1990s.[396] With a separate government ministry devoted to this work (the Ministry of Government Legislation), the government increased the adaptability of Korea's laws to its changing socioeconomic conditions and, ultimately, increased their effectiveness for development through consistent legislative monitoring and adjustment.[397] The ruling party supporting the government efforts maintained a majority in the Korean legislature until 1988, and this legislative control enabled the government to make timely legislative adjustments and new enactments.

Despite such government efforts to increase the adaptability of laws to socioeconomic conditions, Korean laws that aimed to protect certain social interests, such as protecting the integrity of the government from corruption, had not been very effective until the later stages of Korea's development.[398] It was because certain socioeconomic conditions on the ground did not support the laws; in the case of corruption, such adverse socioeconomic conditions included the cultural tradition that allowed and, to some extent, encouraged gift offering as a courtesy to authorities, such as government officials and schoolteachers. Economic and political factors (*e.g.*, low government salary and absence of regional government elections) also had an impact. (Such elections can work as a check against corrupt practices of the regional or local government.) The laws became more effective, and corruption was better controlled only after the gradual, decades-long evolution of these socioeconomic conditions, including growing public awareness of the social cost of corrupt behavior, higher government salary, and the introduction of regional government elections in the 1990s.[399] The successful implementation of a tougher anti-corruption law that imposes stringent guidelines for acceptable gifts to individuals in certain categories of positions (*e.g.*, no gift

---

395 Kim (ed.) (2011), *supra* note 176, at 15.

396 *Ibid.*, at 15–16.

397 *Ibid.*, at 16–17.

398 In 1995, Korea ranked 27 out of 41 countries (bottom 35 percent) in terms of the Corruption Perceptions Index (CPI) measured by Transparency International. Transparency International, *1995 TI Corruption Index*, available online at: www.transparency.org/files/content/tool/1995_CPI_EN.pdf; https://perma.cc/EG7D-WD8A.

399 As a result, Korea's CPI rank improved to 39 out of 180 in 2019 (top 22 percent). Transparency International, *Corruption Perceptions Index 2019*, available online at: www.transparency.org/en/cpi/2019/results/table; https://perma.cc/M236-9W5J.

over 50,000 won [approximately US$ 45] to government officials or teachers)[400] demonstrates the changed socioeconomic conditions in Korean society.[401]

As discussed above, a disparity may exist between laws that aim to achieve a development objective and relevant socioeconomic conditions, particularly when the law attempts to change current practices prevailing on the ground, which form a constituent part of the existing socioeconomic conditions, such as cultural practices. For example, in 1969, the Korean government enacted a law that regulated costly practices on "family rites" such as weddings and funerals in an attempt to simplify them, prevent economic waste, and reduce the economic burden on families when a majority of the population was still in poverty.[402] The law did not conform to contemporary socioeconomic conditions, including a traditional cultural emphasis on the importance of family rites and a popular preference for large, costly ceremonies.[403] This conflict between the law and the socioeconomic conditions led to low rates of compliance with the law and necessitated reinforcing the strength of the law, including its punishment terms for violations.[404] The prospect of success for such laws that do not conform to socioeconomic conditions, but are nevertheless necessary to achieve a development objective, hinges on the existence of consensus as to the necessity of regulatory reform on the part of the public and the political will on the part of the government, which is further discussed below.

4.2.4 Regulatory compliance

The second element of the regulatory impact mechanisms, "regulatory compliance," examines compliance with law by the general public. Law would not have an impact on development without due compliance by the general public. Regulatory compliance is categorized into two sub-elements: general regulatory compliance and specific regulatory compliance. General regulatory compliance examines the overall level of compliance with law in a given jurisdiction.[405] Social and political factors, such as legal culture in society and the public confidence in the state implementing law, influence general regulatory compliance.[406] Specific regulatory compliance pertains to the strength of compliance with a particular

---

400   Improper Solicitation and Graft Act of 2016.
401   The change reflects the consensus among the Korean public on the necessity of such regulatory reform to control corruption and create a more just and fair society. Soo Jin Park and Ji Min Shin, "One Year after the Implementation of Improper Solicitation and Graft Act," *The Hankyoreh*, September 25, 2017 (in Korean), available online at: www.hani.co.kr/arti/society/society_general/812409.html; https://perma.cc/2RC3-VQ45.
402   The Act on Family Rite of 1969 (amended in 1972).
403   Ae Ri Nam, *The Regulation on Family Rite*, National Archives of Korea (in Korean), available online at: http://theme.archives.go.kr/next/koreaOfRecord/homeRule.do; https://perma.cc/U4BV-PGLD.
404   *Ibid.*
405   See discussion *supra* Section 3.3.1(a).
406   *Ibid.*

law.[407] Regulatory compliance is also categorized into "active" and "passive" compliance, according to its strength, as further discussed below.

(a) General regulatory compliance

In 1996, toward the end of its successful development period, Korea achieved a percentile rank of 71.4 (0–100 scale) for the rule of law assessment by the World Bank.[408] Assuming its validity, this rating indicates a relatively high level of general regulatory compliance, without which the rule of law would not be feasible.[409] An explanation for the strength of regulatory compliance could be found in Korea's political and cultural tradition; according to the Confucian tradition shared by the Korean population, due compliance with state's policies and laws was considered one's duty because the state is responsible for the well-being of its subjects, and the citizens' compliance would be necessary for the state to meet this obligation. The citizens' duty to comply was reinforced by the colonial government of Japan (1910–1945) and subsequent authoritarian regimes, which imposed strict rules of law on the Korean population, with severe penalties for any violations. This compelled regulatory compliance, even if it may have only been passive compliance to avoid a penalty.

The remarkable achievement of the Korean government was that it was able to turn this passive compliance into active compliance for economic development by successfully aligning the interests of citizens with those of the state. Aided by the successful outcome of the initial development policies, the government was able to instill in Koreans a confidence that they could escape from poverty by trusting the government and complying with its laws and policies. Koreans actively complied with development-facilitating laws and policies, such as those which encouraged savings by offering high-interest rates and promoting strong work ethics, the latter of which was subsequently compensated by rising wages and increased employment.[410] Koreans' active compliance has been evidenced by the longest working hours[411] and the highest savings rate in the

---

407 See discussion *supra* Section 3.3.1(b).
408 Word Bank, *Worldwide Governance Indicators*, available online at: http://info.worldbank.org/governance/wgi/index.aspx#reports; https://perma.cc/48X8-KP2W.
409 See also World Justice Project, *Rule of Law Index* (2020), *supra* note 299. The Index adopts eight evaluative criteria, including constraints on government powers, order and security, absence of corruption, open government, fundamental rights, regulatory enforcement, civil justice, and criminal justice. *Ibid.*
410 Lee (2017), *supra* note 4, at 465–466.
411 In 1993, Korea's average annual working hours were as high as 2,656 hours. OECD, *Hours Worked*, OECD Data, available online at: https://data.oecd.org/emp/hours-worked.htm; https://perma.cc/4JRJ-4HJS. There is criticism that the long working hours are a result of the excessively competitive working environment for Korean laborers, but jobs were abundant due to rapid economic growth, as demonstrated by the low unemployment rate (*supra* note 385), and Koreans worked extra hours for additional pay and career opportunities.

world.[412] The illiteracy rate was also very low,[413] despite the prevalent poverty in the 1960s,[414] and this enabled Koreans to understand and comply with government policies and the requirements of law. Korea also achieved inclusive growth,[415] providing additional motivation for Koreans to comply with the development policies and laws promoted by the government, as they believed that the economic opportunity was open to every hard-working individual.

(b) Specific regulatory compliance

The development-facilitative nature of the cited statutes suggests that it would have been in the interest of the potential beneficiaries to comply with the terms of these statutes and receive the support mandated by them. As discussed above, the terms of the statutes granted direct support for exports and specific industries, such as tax benefits and grants, and stipulated the conditions to receive such support. The Korean government offered regulatory incentives and support, rather than penalties and compulsion, to motivate individuals and companies to comply with its development-facilitating laws and policies. Korea's major codes[416] also made an essential contribution to development, even if they did not provide direct support for industries, by protecting fundamental economic rights, such as freedom of contract and the right to property.[417] This legal protection encouraged Koreans to participate in economic activities pursuant to government policies and laws by offering legal guarantees for the individual right to the economic returns from one's own economic activities.

Koreans have shown regulatory compliance with development-facilitating laws, but the laws that the administration had enacted in the 1970s and 1980s to reinforce its political control over citizens by limiting their civil liberties were met with resistance. These laws included a series of constitutional amendments in 1972 (called the "October Restoration"), which concentrated political power in the president's hands and restricted fundamental civil rights, such as freedom of speech.[418] The subsequent "Emergency Measures" ("Kin-Keup-Jo-Chi"), applied under the amended constitution, further restrained citizens' political rights. The administration explained that the uncertain and unstable international

---

412   Korea's savings rate was as high as 34.0 percent in 1993. Daekeun Park and Changyong Rhee, "A Study on the Savings Rates in Korea: Synthetic Cohort Analysis," *Korea Institute of Public Finance Research Report* (May 1997).

413   The illiteracy rate in Korea was 4.1 percent in 1958. National Archives of Korea, *The Path That Hangul (Korean Alphabet) Walked On* (in Korean), available online at: http://theme.archives.go.kr/next/hangeulPolicy/business.do https://perma.cc/JQ4E-93ZS.

414   The high rate of literacy was influenced by the cultural emphasis on education and a solid public education system.

415   *Supra* note 346 (for Korea's Gini coefficient).

416   *Supra* note 350 (for a list of the major codes).

417   These rights are guaranteed under the constitution and civil code.

418   See Martin Hart-Landsberg, *The Rush to Development: Economic Change and Political Struggle in Korea* (Monthly Review Press, 1993).

environment of the 1970s—as illustrated, for example, by the withdrawal of the United States from Vietnam in 1973 and the subsequent communist victory of North Vietnam—necessitated these measures to protect the nation and promote economic development without setbacks,[419] but many Koreans did not approve of them and instead offered resistance under severe and often violent oppression by the administration.

The political discontent instigated a period of civil unrest and a series of public demonstrations, culminating in the eruption of the "Gwangju Movement for Democracy" in 1980 (or the "Gwangju Massacre" for the hundreds of casualties caused by the military action) shortly after the death of President Park Jung Hee and during the rise of the new military regime. Political strife and resistance against the authoritarian regime continued through the 1980s and led to the major civil resistance in June 1987 ("the June Resistance") and the eventual concession by the administration for another constitutional amendment, completed in the same year.[420] The 1987 constitutional amendment ("the 1987 system") included liberal reforms, democratic presidential elections by which citizens directly voted for president, and constitutional review by an independent constitutional court. These constitutional amendments and subsequent liberal regulatory reforms in the 1990s originated in civil resistance to the authoritarian regulatory system of the 1970s and 1980s and represented the achievement of important social development objectives in Korea, such as political democratization and the rule of law.

4.2.5 *Quality of implementation: state capacity and political will*

"Quality of implementation," which refers to the degree to which a state[421] meets the requirements of law and undertakes its mandates to fulfill regulatory objectives, is the third and final element of the regulatory impact mechanisms.[422] Law that is otherwise well designed and commanding strong compliance by the public would not have much impact on development if the state fails to properly implement them.[423] For example, laws that attempt to secure formal private property rights (FPPRs) would not be effective unless the state implements them by enforcing these laws and setting up an effective registration system for FPPRs with adequate capacity. State capacity, including its financial, technological, and administrative capabilities for the implementation of law, is a key determinant of the quality of implementation.[424] The implementation of law also requires a degree of political will, particularly when the implementation poses political challenges for reasons including a conflict of interests within a society and among

---

419 *Ibid.*
420 *Ibid.*
421 For a definition of state, see *supra* note 243.
422 See discussion *supra* Section 3.3.2.
423 *Ibid.*
424 *Ibid.*

different classes of the population. These two factors, state capacity and political will, determine the quality of implementation.[425]

In the Korean context, the role of the state has been essential in stimulating development, but some of the key resources constituting state capacity, such as financial resources, were not initially sufficient.[426] Korea had to manage and promote economic development with significant resource constraints, as illustrated by historical anecdotes and episodes about saving scarce resources, even at the top level; *e.g.*, President Park Jung Hee refused to use the air conditioner in his office to save electricity during the summer, except for occasions to meet foreign guests and kept a brick inside his toilet tank to conserve water.[427] Various austerity measures were widely adopted in the public and private sectors to save resources, and extensive public campaigns encouraging resource savings continued throughout the period of Korea's development.

Despite resource constraints, Korea secured state capacity from its manpower, government organization (*i.e.*, organizational strength), and administrative capabilities. For example, Korea had over 237,400 government officials among its population of 25 million in 1960.[428] Korea's traditional Confucian value upholding one's service to the government and the state, as well as the lack of employment opportunities in the private sector, enabled the government to recruit educated and talented individuals to its key posts, some of whom had academic training in North America and Europe.[429] They were able to develop economic development strategies and necessary LFIs, such as the development-facilitating statutes and institutions, including the EPB.

Korea's central and local administration, which had ancient origins, was efficient and well organized. Korea had long established a strong central administration with regional territorial reach since its first unification in the seventh century. In the early twentieth century, the Japanese colonial government in Korea also reinforced central and local administration, *albeit* for the purpose of exploitation. The administrative capacity of the Korean government further developed after its independence, and President Park Jung Hee, who rose to power by a military

---

425 *Ibid.*

426 In 1962, the national budget was 74 billion won, equivalent to US$ 290 million at the time and less than 20 percent of the net income of General Motors in the same year. See Economic Planning Board, *Government Budget Allocation in 1962*, BA0084326 [National Archives of Korea document call number] (1962) (in Korean).

427 Austerity measures were prevalent in the government, even in the 1990s when Korea had achieved economic development and joined the OECD. When I traveled to Geneva in the late 1990s to attend World Trade Organization (WTO) meetings as a member of the Korean delegation, the entire delegation had to use an inexpensive accommodation outside the City of Geneva to save money in the government travel budget.

428 The number increased to over 315,000 in 1965. See National Index System, *Annual Public Official Status*, available online at: www.index.go.kr/potal/main/EachDtlPageDetail.do?idx_cd=1016; https://perma.cc/8M59-QYMP.

429 Dr. Nam Duk Woo, a former Minister of EPB from 1974 to 1978, is a good example of Korea's elite bureaucrat. Dr. Woo, initially an academic with doctorate training in the United States, led Korea's economic success after joining the administration under Park.

coup in 1961, strengthened the administration by instilling military discipline and organizational strength in the government. By the time Korea embarked on the path for development in the early 1960s, it had a well-trained army of central and local administrators who effectively implemented and enforced development policies and laws.[430]

The leadership's political will to achieve economic development reinforced Korea's state capacity and made up for its weaker elements, such as insufficient financial and natural resources. The extent of this political will is well demonstrated by the "Extended Meetings for Export Promotion," in which President Park and a large number of government officials and private sector players discussed a range of issues about export promotion and sought solutions.[431] President Park held these monthly meetings for 14 years, from 1965 to 1979 until his death. These meetings, beyond their practical purpose of seeking solutions to problems associated with export promotion, consistently sent a political message to the nation that its top priority was the achievement of economic development through the implementation of export-led growth strategies.[432] This extraordinary political will enabled a sustained focus on the national development agenda for the entire period of Korea's development, and this sustained focus was the key reason for success.

There is a political explanation for the strength of the leadership's will for economic development. The legitimacy of the new administration was in question, as it had risen to power through a military coup, and the administration needed to win public approval and support by seeking to resolve the biggest problem then facing the Korean society, which was prevalent poverty.[433] The leadership's drive for economic development was also justified by Korea's national security situation. Communist North Korea, whose economic and military powers were superior to those of its southern counterpart until the early 1970s, was hostile to Korea and proclaimed its desire to "liberate" the entire Korean peninsula. Aid from the United States had been decreasing, and the United States considered withdrawing U.S. military forces from Korea after it failed in Vietnam in the 1970s. In the presence of these security issues, the administration felt a strong need to develop modern industries and a sustainable economy to build military forces to protect its security.[434] The majority of Koreans shared this desire to promote economic development to escape from crushing poverty and to secure

---

430 Korea was not free of the corruption of its government officials, similar to many other developing countries. The difference lied in the extent of corruption, rather than its existence, which was not extensive enough to overturn the successful process of development. The situation of corruption improved in Korea, as discussed above, when the government was able to offer public officials improved salaries as a result of economic development that improved the government budget. The process of democratization, which took place in the 1990s, also made public officials more accountable to the public and deterred corruption.

431 Lee (2016), *supra* note 102, at 313.

432 *Ibid.*

433 Hwang (2016), *supra* note 342 and Seth (2010), *supra* note 342.

434 *Ibid.*

economic and industrial resources necessary to protect their nation (a pressing need for the Koreans who had experienced the tragic Korean War waged by North Korea); thus, they supported the government development policies and laws for over three decades.[435]

The administration's political will focused on economic development until the 1980s, but the focus shifted to social development in the 1990s, while economic development continued. The 1992 election of the "civilian" president, Kim Young Sam, a long-time opposition leader, set a new direction and momentum. He initiated several law reforms and institutional changes to promote a democratic and transparent society; *e.g.*, to promote transparency in finance and banking, one such reform required all financial transactions to be undertaken only under authentic legal names on the confirmation of personal identity. He also sought to reduce government control of the economy and ordered the merger of the EPB, which had long been the government's control center of economic development, with the Ministry of Finance.[436] These reforms represented the political will to promote social development by building civil democracy and the rule of law in Korea, which was renewed by the subsequent elections of liberal presidents, such as Kim Dae Joong (1998–2003), a Nobel Peace Prize winner and a legendary freedom fighter in the 1970s and 1980s,[437] and Roh Moo Hyun (2003–2008), a civil rights lawyer who continued with liberal reforms during his presidency. During this period, economic growth also continued, *albeit* at lower rates than those for the preceding periods.[438]

4.3 Lessons from the Korean experience

There are lessons to be drawn from the successful development of Korea. The country was in a state of absolute poverty, facing substantial security threats and trauma from tragic incidents in its history, such as the Korean War, when

---

435 Based on this support, Park Jung Hee won presidential election three times since 1963 until he suspended the constitution in 1972.

436 The EPB was the control center of Korea's economic development since the 1960s. However, its authority in budget allocation and control over the adoption and the implementation of economic development policies created tension and rivalry with other government departments such as the Ministry of Finance. Its 1994 merger with the Ministry of Finance operated to resolve this issue and represented a change of economic paradigm in Korea to one that emphasizes the role of the private sector. However, an expert cited that reduced government oversight in the economy resulting from the dissolution of the EPB was a cause of the 1997 financial crisis. Tae Hee Lee, "Issues and Solutions at the Time of the IMF," *The Hankyoreh*, December 17, 1997, at 3 (in Korean).

437 President Kim Dae Joong continued with economic reforms that reduced government control in the economy and strengthened private sector autonomy, including neoliberal labor reform that relaxed the legal preconditions to dismissal. The International Monetary Fund (IMF) required these reforms as a condition for its bailout package for Korea. The package was imperative for Korea to recover from the 1997 financial crisis, but after the reforms, Korea's economic growth slowed down to approximately 4 percent per annum and never returned to pre-crisis levels.

438 *Ibid.*

it embarked on state-led development in the early 1960s. The economic and social conditions prevailing in this divided country, as of the early 1960s, were worse than those observed in many of the developing countries seen today, including some of the least developed countries. Despite the obstacles, Korea achieved historically unprecedented development from the 1960s to the mid-1990s, while only a few other countries achieved successful economic development and transformed into advanced economies during the same period. So, what set Korea apart from most of the developing world?

The preceding discussion provides some answers from the law and development perspectives. First, the laws adopted at the beginning of Korea's development period (*i.e.*, the early 1960s) enabled the government to provide effective support—in the form of subsidies and trade measures—to industrial development and trade expansion. This may be at odds with the neoliberal policy prescriptions that attempt to restrain government involvement in the economy, but in Korea, the state-led development policy was effective in the early stages of economic development where the private sector had been underdeveloped. Korea was different from the other socialist and non-socialist developing countries at the time in that even with the substantial state involvement in the economy, its laws focused on providing support to private enterprises based on their market performance, particularly in export markets. It adopted trade protection measures (*e.g.*, high tariffs) for much of its development period to protect infant domestic industries, but at the same time, it provided focused support to export activities.[439]

Second, there was a degree of flexibility and adaptability in Korean laws and development policies. Changes were made to the laws to provide support to changing key industries as Korea's economic and industrial development progressed and attained different industrial and technological capacities (*e.g.*, "light" industries in the 1960s, heavy and chemical industries in the 1970s, then electronics and other high-tech industries in the 1980s and 1990s). The industry-specific support legislation, which was conducive to promoting industries and economic development in the 1960s and the 1970s, was subsequently repealed and replaced with laws that provided industrial support on a more selective basis. This granted greater autonomy to the private sector and reduced government control in the economy as the private sector, with increasing capacities, assumed dominant roles in the economy. The flexible legal frameworks and consolidated political control of the legislature during the development period enabled timely changes in laws to meet the changing development needs.

Third, Korea developed a "web of institutions" for the promotion of economic development at every level of the government. The EPB, for example, operated as the nation's top agency for development planning and implementation. Other pro-development institutions existed at the central and regional levels, in the form of government and non-government entities, and within the country and

---

439 These state-led, export-based development policies have been adopted by other successful developing countries, such as Taiwan, Singapore, and, more recently, China.

abroad. KOTRA provides an illustrative example of one such institution, with its global network of offices geared toward assisting Korean companies engaged in trade and investment. As discussed above, the Korean legal frameworks, which allowed expedient on-point legislation and adjustments, increased the system's efficiency. The LFIs formed an inseparable amalgam that created highly productive synergies for the country's success.

Fourth, there was strong motivation on the part of the general public, industries, and businesses to work with the government and comply with its laws and development policies to escape from poverty through successful economic development. There was also strongly motivated political leadership, despite its authoritarian nature, which was committed to achieving economic development, lifting the country out of poverty, and setting its course on economic development. The strong compliance and political leadership devoted to economic development were sustained for over three decades until the country became an advanced economy with world-class industries and high per-capita income in the 1990s, and such sustainability and consistency were key reasons for the success.

The successful economic development also spurred democratization and the rule of law in Korea. The political struggles and demonstrations in the 1960s and the 1970s, primarily by liberal activists and students, were largely unsuccessful in changing the authoritarian rule. However, beginning in the 1980s, the general public, who then possessed significant economic resources as a result of economic development, strongly demanded constitutional reform mandating the direct public election of the president and called for regional government elections. The rule of law was also reinforced with the development of a fully independent judiciary, and a separate constitutional court was set up to conduct a constitutional review of laws. By the mid-1990s, Korea developed elective democracy based on the rule of law. This contrasts with the failure of social development in the countries that did not achieve economic development.

Lastly, the preceding discussions of the Korean case also enable us to address a key question that has been raised and debated for decades: "Does law matter for development?"[440] While classical thinkers such as Weber and Hayek advocated for the relevance and importance of formal, rational law that affords predictability in economic transactions[441] and protects civil liberty for economic prosperity,[442] the cases of successful development in Korea (and the other East Asian countries) seem to indicate otherwise and suggest that this may not be the case.[443] For

---

440 This question is whether or not law affects development, and it should be distinguished from one that inquires whether or not law should be considered to be an end itself or an objective of development. See discussion *supra* Section 1.1.

441 Weber (1954), *supra* note 83.

442 Hayek (1960), *supra* note 201.

443 Hayek considered that under the rule of law, individual decisions, rather than the government authority, guide the productive activity. See Friedrich Hayek, *The Road to Serfdom* (London: Routledge, 1944), at 80–96. The successful state-led development in East Asia was not consistent with this position. Kanishka Jayasuriya, "Introduction: A Framework for the Analysis of Legal Institutions in East Asia," *in* Kanishka Jayasuriya (ed.), *Law, Capitalism, and Power*

much of the development period, Korean laws did not guarantee full civil liberty but allowed authoritarian rule and substantial government control of the economy and society. The role of law or the importance of the rule of law for economic development may remain controversial[444] and seems to depend on other contingencies such as institutional frameworks, relevant capacities, and cultural orientations (*e.g.*, legal cultures), but there is less controversy on the point that development is not feasible without a degree of internal stability that provides for economic predictability.[445] Measures to secure and sustain such stability may include non-legal forms, particularly in the early stages of economic development, but they tend to be formalized into legal forms over time to secure consistency and transparency. Thus, law is important to the extent that it secures and sustains such stability and guides policies to be implemented throughout the process of development, and it is subject to local variances.[446] The successful development history of Korea validates this point.

in Asia (London: Routledge, 1999), at 7; Tom Ginsburg, "Does Law Matter for Economic Development? Evidence from East Asia" (2000) 34(3) *Law and Society Review* 829–856; Amanda Perry, "The Relationship between Legal Systems and Economic Development: Integrating Economic and Social Approaches" (2002) 29(2) *Journal of Law and Society* 282–307.

444 For a discussion of the rule of law and economic development, see Stephan Haggard and Lydia Tiede, "The Rule of Law and Economic Growth: Where Are We?" (2011) 39(5) *World Development* 673–685. The authors found that measures of property rights, checks on government, and corruption are correlated much less tightly with economic growth than is often thought. *Ibid.*, at 673.

445 Based on a survey of 113 countries for a period from 1950 to 1983, a study concluded that economic growth is negatively correlated with political instability. Alberto Alesina *et al.*, "Political Instability and Economic Growth," *National Bureau of Economic Research Working Paper*, no. 4173 (September 1992).

446 In addition, the operation of law may not be clearly separated from that of other mechanisms of state intervention. The earlier discussion emphasized the importance of legal frameworks and institutions and suggested "law, legal frameworks, and institutions" (LFIs) as an inseparable amalgam (see *supra* Section 3.2.2). For instance, "administrative guidance" adopted by Korea and Japan (see *supra* Sections 1.2 and 4.2.1) may not be strictly "law," but could this seemingly non-legal mechanism of state intervention be clearly separated from law or should it be considered part of LFIs that systematically affect the operation of law and are affected by the latter? In other words, it may not be feasible to assess the relative importance of law in isolation from other mechanisms of state intervention (and *vice versa*).

5 Law and development in South Africa

5.1 Introduction: the end of Apartheid but lackluster economic development?

South Africa is among the largest economies and the most advanced countries in the African continent.[447] The country has also achieved one of the most important and aspirational social developments in the twentieth century by ending "Apartheid" in 1991, a system of institutionalized racial segregation and discrimination implemented since 1948,[448] followed by the peaceful transition of power from the white minority to the black majority in 1994. Under the presidency of Nelson Mandela, a legendary freedom fighter in South Africa and the Nobel Peace Prize laureate in 1993, the government adopted measures to address decades of social injustice caused by systematic racial discrimination and to bring social reconciliation, all without persecution of the white minority previously in power.[449] The South African government also adopted policies to facilitate economic development, such as "the Reconstruction and Development Programme" (RDP) and "the Growth, Employment, and Redistribution Strategy" (GEAR).

Despite South Africa's towering social achievement, its economic development since the end of Apartheid has been described as "lackluster" due to sluggish growth, high unemployment, and alarming economic disparity among its citizens.[450] Although its economic performance, measured by gross national income (GNI)

---

447 According to the World Bank, South Africa's GDP was US$ 351.4 billion in 2019, the second largest after Nigeria's US$ 448.1 billion. World Bank, *GDP (Current US$)*, available online at: https://data.worldbank.org/indicator/NY.GDP.MKTP.CD; https://perma.cc/L3X3-WN3Y. South Africa is also widely recognized as one of the most technologically advanced countries in Africa. It has some of the top universities and research institutions in the region with global reputations, such as the University of Cape Town and University of Pretoria, and has made important discoveries in science and technology, as demonstrated by the achievements of South African scientists such as Aaron Klug, who received a Nobel laureate in chemistry in 1982.
448 For further discussion of Apartheid, see Saul Dubow, *Apartheid, 1948–1994* (Oxford: Oxford University Press, 2014).
449 Marisa Traniello, "Power-Sharing: Lessons from South Africa and Rwanda" (2007) 3(2) *International Public Policy Review* 28–43.
450 T. K. Pooe, "Law and Economic Development in South Africa: An Assessment through the General Theory of Law and Development" (2019) 12(2) *Law and Development Review* 377–401.

DOI: 10.4324/9781003090175-7

per capita and other economic indicators, may have been superior to many other African countries,[451] the rate of its economic progress for the past several decades shows contrast with more economically successful developing countries in the past, such as Korea.[452] The graph below illustrates this trend, depicting South Africa and Korea's relative changes in GNI per capita since the 1960s (Figure 5.1).

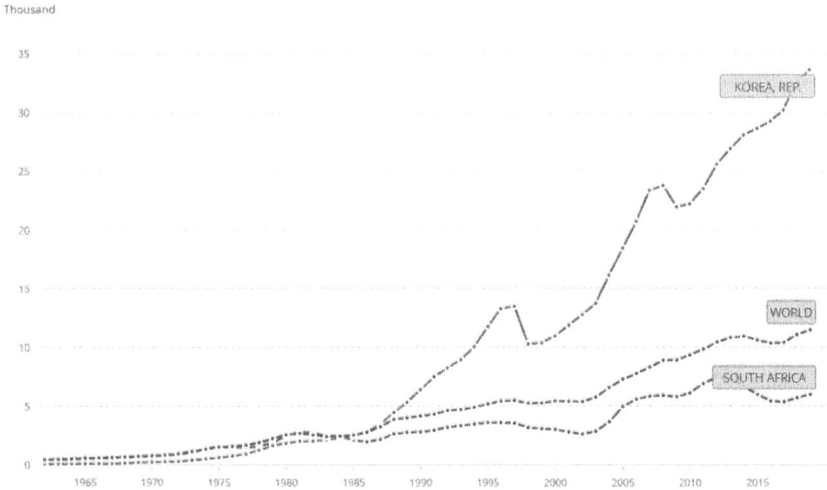

Figure 5.1 GNI per capita (Atlas Method, Current US$).[453]

In 1962, South Africa's GNI per capita was US$ 450 (slightly lower than the world average of US$ 480 but over three times higher than Korea's GNI per capita of US$ 120). In 1991, when Apartheid ended, the figures changed to US$ 3,210, 4,353, and 7,440 for South Africa, the world average, and Korea, respectively, with South Africa substantially behind. By 2019, the gap had grown much larger, with South Africa's GNI per capita at US$ 6,040, the world average at US$ 11,570, and Korea at US$ 33,720.[454] As to the unemployment rate, South Africa was at an alarming 28.5 percent in 2019, compared to the world average of 5.3 percent and Korea at 3.7 percent in the same year.[455] As estimated by the

---

451 For example, the average GNI per capita for the sub-Saharan African countries was US$ 1,550 in 2019, only 25.7 percent of South Africa's GNI per capita of US$ 6,040. World Bank, *GNI Per Capita, Atlas Method (Current US$)*, available online at: https://data.worldbank.org/indica tor/NY.GNP.PCAP.CD?locations=ZG-ZA; https://perma.cc/67CA-BYYD.

452 For a discussion of South Korea's economic development, see *supra* Chapter 4.

453 World Bank, *GNI Per Capita, Atlas Method (Current US$)*, available online at: https://data. worldbank.org/indicator/NY.GNP.PCAP.CD?locations=ZA-KR-1W; https://perma.cc/ TZU7-EQWM.

454 *Ibid.*

455 World Bank, *Unemployment, Total (% of Total Labor Force) (National Estimate)*, available online at: https://data.worldbank.org/indicator/SL.UEM.TOTL.NE.ZS?locations=KR-1W-ZA; https://perma.cc/Z2E5-RXYC.

Gini coefficient, South Africa's income inequality is far greater at 0.63 (2014) than Korea at 0.32 (2012).[456] In fact, South Africa's income inequality is among the highest in the world and is particularly stark along racial lines, justifying a comment that Apartheid may have ended in political terms but not in economic terms.[457]

Reported statistics support this observation; the average monthly salary of the white minority in South Africa (less than 10 percent of the South African population) was approximately 3.6 times higher than that of the black majority (over three quarters of the South African population) for a period between 2011 and 2015,[458] while the salary gap between male and female was much smaller; the average female salary was 30 percent lower than the male salary.[459] In addition to the salary gaps, unemployment rates also differ vastly along racial lines: as of 2019 (fourth quarter), 7.6 percent of white South Africans were unemployed, compared to 32.4 percent of the black majority.[460] There is also a significant disparity in access to education; as of 2018, 51.6 percent of blacks aged 22–25 completed at least Grade 12 (pre-college education), in comparison to 81.1 percent of whites in the same age group.[461] There is also a substantial gap in healthcare coverage between whites and blacks in South Africa.[462] This disparity indicates that the political liberalization achieved with the end of Apartheid has not been translated into economic improvements for the black majority, which is a reason for the sluggish economic growth of the whole economy. Economic problems also generate a negative social impact; indeed, lack of economic foundation for the majority of the population undermines the achievement of other social and economic development objectives.

This chapter reviews the economic and social development case of South Africa since the end of Apartheid from the legal and institutional perspectives. As in Chapter 4, the analysis adopts the general theory of law and development[463]

---

456 World Bank, *GINI Index (World Bank Estimate)*, available online at: https://data.worldb
ank.org/indicator/SI.POV.GINI?locations=ZA-KR; https://perma.cc/XZF9-HSYR. Data
converted into Gini coefficient.

457 Peter S. Goodman, "End of Apartheid in South Africa? Not in Economic Terms," *The New York
Times*, October 24, 2017, available online at: www.nytimes.com/2017/10/24/business/south-
africa-economy-apartheid.html; https://perma.cc/2EKB-MWCA.

458 Statistics South Africa, *Inequality Trends in South Africa: A Multidimensional Diagnostic of
Inequality, 2017*, Report-03-10-19 (November 14, 2019), at 61–62, available online at: www.
statssa.gov.za/publications/Report-03-10-19/Report-03-10-192017.pdf; https://perma.cc/
U9J6-MLA6.

459 *Ibid.*, at 62.

460 Statistics South Africa, *Quarterly Labor Force Survey* (Quarter 4: 2019), at 21–22, available online
at: www.statssa.gov.za/publications/P0211/P02114thQuarter2019.pdf; https://perma.cc/
6GB9-FKHD.

461 "Four Tables and Graphs You Should See Ahead of South Africa's Matric Results," *Business Tech*,
January 5, 2020, available online at: https://businesstech.co.za/news/government/363480/
4-tables-and-graphs-you-should-see-ahead-of-south-africas-matric-results/, accessed December
9, 2020.

462 Statistics South Africa (2019), *supra* note 458, at 81.

463 See *supra* Chapter 3.

and makes comparisons to the development approaches taken by Korea during its development period.[464] These two countries faced substantially different conditions, which should be considered in the analytical process; in the early 1960s, Korea started at a much lower economic point than South Africa, as demonstrated by its GNI per capita equivalent to only 27 percent of that of South Africa at that time.[465] Korea, unlike resource-rich South Africa, had a poor endowment of natural resources, had barely recovered from the devastating Korean War, lacked technology and capital, and was under constant security threat from North Korea.[466] South Africa did not have these adverse conditions but had to deal with other obstacles not faced by Korea, such as diverse racial groups with a history of violent confrontations and the negative legacy of Apartheid, which deeply divided the nation for generations. Despite these differences, the comparative analysis will help to identify the causes of the difference in development trajectory between the two countries.[467] The following section applies the general theory of law and development to analyze the development process in South Africa since the end of Apartheid.[468]

5.2 Economic and social development in South Africa

5.2.1 Preliminary considerations

(a) Development objectives

The RDP, adopted in 1994, was the first main policy framework to set forth development objectives for post-Apartheid South Africa.[469] The primary objective was to meet the "basic needs" of the formerly suppressed majority, followed by the development of human resources through education and training.[470] The subsequent White Paper on the RDP, issued in 1995, included five broad objectives: the creation of a strong, dynamic, and balanced economy; development of human resource capacity for all South Africans; assurance of no racial or gender discrimination in hiring, promotion, or training situations; development of a prosperous, balanced regional economy in Southern Africa; and democratization of the state and society.[471] The subsequent national development initiatives, such as the GEAR, included similar economic and social development objectives.

---

464 See *supra* Chapter 4.
465 World Bank, *supra* note 453.
466 See discussion *supra* Section 4.1.
467 World Bank, *supra* note 453.
468 Chapters 3 and 4 provide detailed accounts of the general theory and its summary, so they are not repeated here.
469 Joachim Wehner, "Development Strategies in Post-Apartheid South Africa" (2000) 35(2) *Afrika Spectrum* 183–192, at 183–184.
470 *Ibid.*, at 184.
471 South African History Online, *South Africa's Key Economic Policies Changes (1994–2013)*, available online at: www.sahistory.org.za/article/south-africa%E2%80%99s-key-economic-policies-changes-1994-2013; https://perma.cc/MJU4-NP3N.

The South African government experienced difficulty in meeting the development objectives in the 1990s; the South African currency, the Rand, collapsed in February 1996,[472] followed by sharp increases in unemployment. South Africa faced significant economic problems, including stagnant economic growth, high unemployment, and serious economic disparity among its citizens, as illustrated in Section 5.1. Reflecting on these economic issues, the government's development initiative announced in 2010, "New Growth Path," identified "mass joblessness, poverty, and inequality" as the core challenge.[473] The development objectives to address these core problems are comprised of economic growth, increased employment, and reduced economic disparity.

(b) Laws and institutions under analysis

South Africa has a "hybrid" or "mixed" legal system, based on several distinct legal traditions such as a common law system from the British, a civil law system inherited from the Dutch, and a customary law system originated in native African traditions.[474] All of these diverse legal traditions potentially affect the development process in South Africa and need to be considered. Enacted statutes and regulations, including the constitution, judicial precedents, and customary law with diverse origins, are the subjects of analysis; however, this chapter focuses primarily on South Africa's pronounced development initiatives, contemporary constitution and statutes, and institutional frameworks.

The South African government announced several development initiatives for the past two decades without setting up elaborate legal frameworks to support them;[475] thus, this section does not attempt to analyze relevant laws in separation from the pronounced development initiatives. Instead, it takes a broader approach, examining the development initiatives taken under the legal mandate of the government[476] and the institutional frameworks associated with them. In doing so, the subsequent discussion proceeds in the analytical sequence of the regulatory impact mechanisms, the second part of the general theory of law and development, comprised of three analytical elements and additional sub-elements, including "regulatory design," "regulatory compliance," and "quality of implementation."[477] Readers may refer to Chapter 3 for the relevant concepts of these elements and the sub-elements.[478]

472 Wehner (2000), *supra* note 469, at 185–186.
473 Republic of South Africa, *New Growth Path Framework* (November 23, 2010), at 3.
474 Chuma Himonga and Thandabantu Nhlapo (eds.), *African Customary Law: In South Africa: Post-Apartheid and Living Law Perspectives: Private Law* (Oxford: Oxford University Press, 2015).
475 By contrast, the Korean government set up a number of industry-specific development-facilitating acts to support its development initiatives in the early stages. See *supra* Section 4.2.3(a).
476 The South African Constitution authorizes the president to adopt national policies, including those designed to promote economic development. Constitution of the Republic of South Africa 1996 [assented to December 16, 1996], chapter 5, section 85, text available online at: www.justice.gov.za/legislation/constitution/saconstitution-web-eng.pdf; https://perma.cc/42SL-BDZ8.
477 See discussion *supra* Sections 3.2 and 3.3.
478 *Ibid.*

5.2.2 *Regulatory impact mechanisms—regulatory design*

(a) *Anticipated policy outcome*

The South African case has displayed gaps between the pronounced development objectives[479] and the actual policy outcomes that may not have been anticipated by the policy framers. Such gaps are not observed or have been minimized in successful developing countries such as Korea[480] but have been significant in South Africa. For example, the RDP successfully set up an extensive social welfare system that expanded healthcare coverage and offered free meals to 3.5–5 million schoolchildren.[481] The RDP also provided clean water, electricity, land (through land reform), and public works for millions of people.[482] These outcomes may have met some of the basic needs pronounced as objectives of the RDP,[483] but the RDP did not spur economic growth, which was another key development objective, and as a result, the RDP did not take root as a guiding developmental principle.[484]

The RDP was replaced by a macroeconomic policy framework named the GEAR strategy in 1996 to facilitate economic growth.[485] The GEAR stressed the need for high levels of sustained growth to be achieved through a competitive outward-oriented economy.[486] The GEAR set a target gross domestic product (GDP)[487] growth rate of 6 percent per annum and envisioned the creation of 400,000 jobs per annum by 2000.[488] The GEAR also set targets to achieve fiscal discipline and deficit reduction, financial stability, and the reduction of the inflation rate, as well as a reduction of exchange controls and tariffs.[489] Management of public finances improved under the GEAR, but the targets for job creation, private investment, and economic growth were not met; in 2000, South Africa reported a GDP growth rate of 4.2 percent, which was substantially below the target 6 percent mark and which fell further—to 2.7 percent—the following year.[490] The GEAR was replaced in 2005 by yet another development initiative, "the Accelerated and Shared Growth Initiative for South Africa" (ASGISA), with

---

479 See discussion *supra* Section 5.2.1.
480 See discussion *supra* Section 4.2.3(a).
481 South African History Online, *supra* note 471.
482 Tom Lodge (ed.), *Politics in South Africa: From Mandela to Mbeki* (Cape Town: David Philip, 2003), at 54–69.
483 See discussion *supra* Section 5.2.1.
484 South African History Online, *supra* note 471.
485 Wehner (2000), *supra* note 469, at 184–185.
486 *Ibid.*, at 185.
487 For an explanation of GDP, see *supra* note 28.
488 Wehner (2000), *supra* note 469, at 185.
489 *Ibid.*
490 World Bank, *GDP Growth (Annual %)—South Africa*, available online at: https://data. worldbank.org/indicator/NY.GDP.MKTP.KD.ZG?end=2019&locations=ZA&name_desc= false&start=1961; https://perma.cc/LMA4-EBHS.

policy objectives in poverty reduction and job growth. The ASGISA did not meet these policy objectives and was replaced, again, by "the New Growth Path" in 2010 with the initiation of the National Development Plan (NDP) in 2013.[491] The New Growth Path targeted the creation of five million jobs by 2020, but as of 2019, South Africa's unemployment rate increased from 24.7 percent in 2010 to 28.5 percent in 2019.[492] President Cyril Ramaphosa announced a new economic plan titled "South Africa's Economic Reconstruction and Recovery Plan" in October 2020.[493]

Throughout the periods of these various development initiatives, the targets for economic growth, poverty elimination, and unemployment reduction have been consistently missed, causing one development initiative to replace another without achieving development objectives. This outcome contrasts with the development process of Korea, as discussed in Chapter 4, by which a consistent development framework, such as the Five-Year Economic Development Plans, continued for over three decades, achieving development targets set for each period.[494] As mentioned earlier, Korea began at a much lower economic point than South Africa in the early 1960s but eradicated absolute poverty by the 1970s and developed into an economically advanced country with a high-level income for the majority of its population by the 1990s.[495] Today, the economic status of these two countries has completely been reversed; Korea's total GDP and GNI per capita are nearly five times higher than those of South Africa, which has a population greater than Korea by 4.6 million.

What caused this difference in development outcomes? Could the rather disappointing development policy outcomes in South Africa (*i.e.*, sluggish growth, high unemployment, and large economic disparity among its citizens) have been anticipated? A possible explanation is the lack of continuity in development initiatives; the initial RDP continued for less than two years, and the South African government introduced three other major national development initiatives, one replacing the other, for a period of two decades since 1996. These development initiatives are not markedly different from one from another, with all targeting economic growth, job increases, and reduction in the economic disparity, and encompassing social development objectives as initially laid down by the RDP. Yet, not a single national development initiative continued for over one decade before being concluded a failure and replaced by another, in contrast to the consistent development framework in Korea continued for over three decades. The periodical scrapping of national development initiatives and all the transition

---

491 The NDP aims to eliminate poverty and reduce inequality in South Africa by 2030. Wehner (2000), *supra* note 469, at 185.
492 World Bank, *supra* note 455.
493 Republic of South Africa, *President Cyril Ramaphosa: South Africa's Economic Reconstruction and Recovery Plan* (October 15, 2020), available online at: www.gov.za/speeches/president-cyril-ramaphosa-south-africa%E2%80%99s-economic-reconstruction-and-recovery-plan-15-oct, accessed December 9, 2020.
494 See discussion *supra* Chapter 4.
495 *Ibid.*

costs resulting from it could not have been conducive to achieving positive development outcomes.

Another point is that South African national development initiatives, such as the RDP (after the White Paper) and the GEAR, adopted the neoliberal economic stance, emphasizing fiscal discipline and the diminished role of the state in the economy (*i.e.*, the government was to create an enabling environment for private sector growth).[496] This stands in contrast to the state-led approach adopted by Korea, with the government actively facilitating industrial development and exports through statutory devices that provided measures to promote development, such as subsidies, tax incentives, policy loans, tariff rebates, and import control, as well as overseas loan guarantees to support domestic industries and exporters.[497] The New Growth Path, adopted in 2010, shows a more state-led developmental approach,[498] but as of 2019, this policy shift has not resulted in growth in the economy or reduction in unemployment.[499] By contrast, some other African countries that adopted state-led development approaches, such as Botswana, Rwanda, and Ethiopia, have achieved high-rate economic growth and generated improved incomes for their populations.[500]

When Apartheid was over, the South African government did not adopt active industrial development policies, such as those adopted by Korea and other successful developing countries, which would have facilitated industrial development and increased employment for the black majority. Instead, much of the economic resources and industries remained largely in the control of the white minority, with no significant improvement in participation of the black majority in South African industries and its economy, which would have been imperative to reduce unemployment and economic disparity. Schemes to improve black participation in the economy, such as the Black Economic Empowerment program (later the Broad-Based Black Economic Empowerment [BBBEE] program),[501] were introduced subsequently, but the initial efforts focused on the reallocation of assets rather than the systematic improvement of black participation in the economy, particularly through the enhancement of education and training. While successful negotiations for power-sharing between races in the political arena led to a peaceful transition to democracy in South Africa,[502] a lack of such

496 Wehner (2000), *supra* note 469, at 185.
497 See discussion *supra* Section 4.2.3(a).
498 Republic of South Africa, *New Growth Path Framework*, *supra* note 473.
499 World Bank, *supra* notes 447 and 455.
500 Botswana was known as Africa's most successful developmental state, increasing its GNI per capita from a mere US$ 70 in 1962 to US$ 7,660 in 2019. Rwanda and Ethiopia have also achieved substantial economic development in recent decades, raising their GNI per capita from US$ 210 in 2003 to US$ 820 in 2019 and from US$ 110 to US$ 850 in the same periods, respectively. World Bank, *GNI Per Capita, Atlas Method (Current US$)*, available online at: https://data. worldbank.org/indicator/NY.GNP.PCAP.CD?locations=BW-ET-RW-ZA; https://perma.cc/ DYX2-L7A3.
501 See *infra* note 525 (for a reference on the Broad-Based Black Economic Empowerment Act).
502 Traniello (2007), *supra* note 449.

arrangement and cooperation in the economic arena resulted in vast economic disparity along racial lines and sluggish economic development.

Attention should also be given to development initiatives at the local level; under the 1996 Constitutional framework, local governments have affirmative obligations to promote economic and social development, and significant efforts for economic development have also been made at the local level.[503] The Constitution and the subsequent 1998 White Paper on Local Government elevated the Local Economic Development (LED) Policy, which had also existed during Apartheid, to an obligatory mandate for all South African local authorities.[504] The Local Government Municipal Systems Act of 2000 stipulated a number of key LED functions and responsibilities, providing for the core principles, mechanisms, and processes that are necessary to enable municipalities to move progressively toward the social and economic improvement of local communities.[505] Despite these efforts, the LED has not played a significant role in achieving core development objectives, such as economic growth, poverty alleviation, and unemployment reduction. Without a proper understanding of their objectives, local authorities often could not facilitate LED activities, and it has been observed that years of LED practice in South Africa have served to reinforce geographical inequalities in economic and social development across the country.[506]

As to social development, the end of Apartheid marked the beginning of a new era, finally removing the institutionalized system of racial discrimination and the grave injustices associated with such a system, after decades of struggles led by inspiring leaders such as Nelson Mandela. The anticipated outcome of post-Apartheid social policies would, thus, be to contribute to the creation of an integrated society without racial or other forms of discrimination. The 1996 Constitution embodied this post-Apartheid ethos and spirit. Former Constitutional Court Deputy Chief Justice Dikgang Moseneke offers some insight into this embodiment as the guiding principle of South Africa's development. He stated:

> Our constitutional democracy was forged on the anvil of division, past injustice and economic inequity, but also on the hope for reconciliation, nation building and social cohesion. Notionally, our Constitution is premised on

503 The Constitution provides that:

> [a] municipality must (a) structure and manage its administration and budgeting and planning processes to give priority to the basic needs of the community, and to promote the social and economic development of the community; and (b) participate in national and provincial development programmes.

Constitution of the Republic of South Africa 1996, *supra* note 476, chapter 7, section 153.
504 Christian Rogerson, "Tracking Local Economic Development Policy and Practice in South Africa, 1994–2009" (2011) 22(2) *Urban Forum* 149–168, at 150.
505 *Ibid.*, at 151.
506 *Ibid.*, at 164–165.

the will of the people expressed in representative and participatory processes. It does not only establish its supremacy, rule of law and fundamental rights but also recites our collective convictions. It contains our joint and minimum ideological and normative choices of what a good society should be. It enjoins the state, all its organs, to take reasonable steps without undue delay to achieve that good society.[507]

The 1996 Constitution, with 243 provisions in 14 chapters, is one of the most complete and advanced embodiments of civil and human rights, including liberal socioeconomic rights, in the form of a constitution. Supporting this point, the late United States Supreme Court Justice Ruth Bader Ginsburg stated that "I would not look to the United States Constitution if I was drafting a constitution in 2012"[508] and recommended that Egyptians instead look to the South African Constitution.[509] The quality of the Constitution has also led other American scholars to admit that the appeal of the United States Constitution has waned and that states like South Africa have a more formidable and noteworthy constitution.[510] The 1996 Constitution is indeed lauded for its statement of the best ideals of the liberal ethos, accompanied by supportive constitutional rulings from the judiciary, such as one that found the government accountable for free housing and water provision to the poor.[511]

The celebrated South African Constitution, however, is not sufficient to fulfill social development objectives, many of which require economic capacity on the part of the state. For example, the constitutional protection of the rights to housing and water may offer a legal safeguard for these rights from potential adverse political choices made by the authorities, but such constitutional safeguard would not help if the responsible authorities do not have the economic capacity to provide them. The rights-based approach, without consideration of economic constraints, has its limits and needs to be complemented by policies and measures that would increase the state's capacity to fulfill those rights. The

---

507 Cited in Pooe (2019), *supra* note 450. Pooe also observes that the vision of the Constitution offered by the former Deputy Chief Justice expresses three key ideas concerning how South Africa as a country is envisioned: first, South Africa, despite being a state founded on the underdevelopment of the African majority, desires a political environment founded on non-retribution; second, notions such as reconciliation, nation building, and social cohesion are hallmarks of South Africa's constitution; and third, the fulfillment of these and other human rights-inspired concepts require necessary institutions to be set up by the government. *Ibid.*

508 Adam Liptak, "'We the People' Loses Appeal with People Around the World," *The New York Times*, February 6, 2012, available online at: www.nytimes.com/2012/02/07/us/we-the-people-loses-appeal-with-people-around-the-world.html; https://perma.cc/JLK5-77V7, cited in Pooe, *supra* note 450.

509 *Ibid.*

510 David S. Law and Mila Versteeg, "The Declining Influence of the United States Constitution" (2012) 87(3) *The New York University Law Review* 762–858, at 826–829, cited in Pooe, *supra* note 450.

511 *Government of the Republic of South Africa and Others v. Grootboom and Others* (October 4, 2000), ZACC 19, 2001 (1) SA 46 (CC), 2000 (11) BCLR 1169 (CC).

dilemma is, as discussed in Chapter 1, that economic constraints will create prac-tical difficulties for the authorities to implement all social development objectives simultaneously and with equal strength; prioritization and sequencing are inev-itable.[512] However, in this process, disagreement is bound to occur (as to what should be prioritized and done first), the resolution of which will require sub-stantial political leadership to persuade its constituencies with its vision and plans.

(b)   Organization of law, legal frameworks, and institutions (LFIs)

The effective and synergetic organization of LFIs is essential for the successful implementation of development policies.[513] As discussed in Chapter 4, Korea's development policies were supported by an optimal organization of LFIs, including development-facilitating laws, flexible legal frameworks, and effective institutions such as the Economic Planning Board (EPB).[514] In the case of South Africa, it is not clear whether such optimal organization could be found. For example, national development initiatives, including RDP, the GEAR, and the ASGISA, lacked an effective institutional apparatus to implement the devel-opment initiatives in coordination with relevant government departments and agencies, as well as local governments. The RDP Office, which was in charge of administering the RDP, did not function as a control center in the same vein as the EPB during Korea's development initiatives, and it was closed within two years of the RDP's launch. The GEAR, which replaced the RDP, advocated for a reduced government role in the economy and did not have an effective institu-tional apparatus for its implementation.

These national development initiatives also lacked supporting legal frameworks and development-facilitating laws, such as those facilitating specific industries in Korea during the 1960s and the 1970s or those supporting industrial restructuring in the 1980s, with policy devices including subsidies and tax benefits.[515] Absence of such legal apparatus meant that there was no strong industrial policy imple-mentation in South Africa. The Local Government Municipal Systems Act of 2000 supports and also obligates local governments to engage in LED activi-ties,[516] but the LED lacks institutional frameworks to ensure coordination and cooperation among local governments and also between the national and local governments to facilitate development at the local level, particularly where local governments lack capacity and require support from the central government. As a result, the respective role of each layer of government was not made clear in LED activities and sometimes overlapped with one another, making effective coordina-tion and implementation of LED projects difficult.[517]

---

512   See discussion *supra* Section 1.3.1.
513   See discussion *supra* Section 3.2.2.
514   See discussion *supra* Section 4.2.3(b).
515   *Ibid.*
516   Rogerson (2011), *supra* note 504, at 151.
517   *Ibid.*, at 154.

The Zuma administration set up the Department of Economic Development in 2009 and the National Planning Commission (NPC) in 2010, along with the launching of the New Growth Path, which was a new institutional development heading toward more of state-led developmental policy.[518] The mandate of the department is to

> coordinate the contributions of government departments, state entities and civil society to effect economic development; improve alignment between economic policies, plans of the state, its agencies, government's political and economic objectives and mandate; and promote government's goal of advancing economic development via the creation of decent work opportunities.[519]

The NPC aims to "develop a long-term vision and strategic plan for South Africa."[520] Given the divided mandate between these two institutions (one for coordination and the other for planning), coupled with modest budget and personnel,[521] neither the Department of Economic Development nor the NPC seems to have the institutional status and authority comparable to those granted to Korea's EPB which will be necessary to lead economic development initiatives coordinating the complex and often conflicting interests and agendas among different government departments and agencies, and between the government and private sector.[522] In addition, the resignation of President Zuma,[523] who launched the New Growth Path and set up those institutions, also cast uncertainty on the continuation of their institutional roles.

(c) *Adaptation to socioeconomic conditions*

The adaptability of development initiatives to the socioeconomic conditions on the ground is a factor that determines their effectiveness. Perhaps the most relevant socioeconomic condition would be the legacy of Apartheid, which deprived the majority of the population—the black majority—of capital, education, land, and industrial experience through decades of systematic exclusion and discrimination.[524] The question is raised as to whether South Africa's development

---

518 Republic of South Africa, *New Growth Path Framework, supra* note 473.

519 National Government of South Africa, *Department: Economic Development (EDD)*, available online at: https://nationalgovernment.co.za/units/view/13/Department-Economic-Deve lopment-EDD; https://perma.cc/F75D-VCHL.

520 National Planning Commission, available online at: www.nationalplanningcommission.org.za/ Pages/default.aspx; https://perma.cc/D2VQ-UZNE.

521 National Government of South Africa, *Department: Economic Development (EDD), supra* notes 519 and National Planning Commission, *ibid.*

522 See discussion *supra* Section 4.2.3.

523 Norimitsu Onishi, "Jacob Zuma Resigns as South Africa's President," *The New York Times*, February 14, 2018, available online at: www.nytimes.com/2018/02/14/world/africa/jacob-zuma-resigns-south-africa.html; https://perma.cc/Y8SV-BER7.

524 Dubow (2014), *supra* note 448.

initiatives have been designed and implemented corresponding to these socio-economic conditions faced by the black majority. For example, the economic growth target will not be met unless the black majority engages with economic production, and unemployment will not be reduced unless more of the black majority become employable through education and training. The significant economic disparity and poverty concentrated in the black majority cannot be reduced by social security provisions alone; greater economic opportunity must be made available to them.

In response to this problem, the BBBEE Act of 2003 seeks to improve the participation of the non-white majority[525] through asset redistribution with target ownership rates, increases in management control, skills development, enterprise and supplier development, and socioeconomic development.[526] The BBBEE is an affirmative intervention by the government to improve black participation in industries and the economy, but the number of beneficiaries under the BBBEE has been a small portion of the black majority (because the number of qualified blacks did not increase, substantially due to the problems in educational attainment); consequently, the program's economic impact has not proven to be significant.[527] Education and training are essential to increase economic participation and to reduce both unemployment and economic disparity, but the development initiatives have not successfully enhanced education and training for the black majority, as demonstrated by the record of weak educational attainment by blacks.[528] By contrast, Korea offered solid education and training for the majority of its population, even in the 1950s when they were undergoing absolute poverty; educational attainment formed an essential base for Korea's rapid development in the 1960s.[529]

The socioeconomic conditions are also relevant to the implementation of the LED. The following case illustrates issues with the LED's adaptation to the socioeconomic conditions on the ground. In 1999, the Department of Provincial and Local Government (DPLG) launched the LED Fund in the context of the government's overall poverty alleviation strategy.[530] The Fund was a major step for a project-based approach to LED practice across the country.[531] Under the

---

525   Broad-Based Black Empowerment Act of 2003 (Act No. 53, 2003), text available online at: www.environment.gov.za/sites/default/files/legislations/bbbee_act.pdf; https://perma.cc/GC99-LNL2. For the purpose of this Act, the beneficiary "black people" is a generic term which means "Africans, Coloureds and Indians." *Ibid.*, section 1.

526   Daron Acemoglu, Stephen Gelb, and James A. Robinson, *Black Economic Empowerment and Economic Performance in South Africa* (August 2007), available online at: www.treasury.gov.za/publications/other/growth/06-Procurement%20and%20BEE/02-BLACK%20ECONOMIC%20EMPOWERMENT%20AND%20ECONOMIC%20PERFORMANCE%20IN%20SO.pdf; https://perma.cc/UM53-L4J2.

527   *Ibid.* See also L. P. Bogopane, "Evaluation of Black Economic Empowerment (BEE) Policy Implementation in the Ngaka Modiri Molema District, North West Province, South Africa" (2013) 34(3) *Journal of Social Sciences* 277–288.

528   *Supra* note 461.

529   See discussion *supra* Section 4.2.4.

530   Rogerson (2011), *supra* note 504, at 157.

531   *Ibid.*

mandate of this Fund, municipalities were allowed to apply to DPLG for the funding of LED projects, such as cultural tourism initiatives, promotion of agro-processing, and development of business incubators or human resource programs.[532] However, this led to the proliferation of small, unsustainable projects, the majority of which closed after the end of project funding.[533] The flaw of this funding scheme was that the sustainability of LED projects after initial government funding was not properly assessed against relevant socioeconomic conditions in the relevant municipality, such as the possibility of attracting local or external financing and marketability leading to sustainable income generation.[534]

The examination of relevant socioeconomic conditions is also applicable to the assessment of the lauded South African Constitution in the context of law and development. While the Constitution is celebrated for the commendable statement of civil and human rights, including socioeconomic rights, the proclamation of these rights in the Constitution alone would not secure, for South Africans, the enjoyment of these rights as discussed above. In other words, if the socioeconomic conditions on the ground, such as the availability of public funding resources, do not allow the facilitation of some of these rights, such as free housing, then the Constitution will not only be ineffective concerning the realization of these rights but also counter-effective; this approach could induce people, particularly those at an economic disadvantage, to believe that they can secure these rights by simply demanding them as a right, instead of seeking ways to secure them in their self-reliant efforts, while the socioeconomic conditions would not permit the government to provide them. An alternative approach would be to underscore the importance of economic development as a necessary means to secure socioeconomic rights, with a clarification that socioeconomic rights could only be secured where relevant resources were available.

5.2.3 Regulatory compliance

As discussed in Chapter 3, laws and policies would not be effective without active compliance by those subject to these laws and policies.[535] This sub-section examines the level of compliance with the development initiatives in South Africa, beginning with the general regulatory compliance, which refers to the overall level of regulatory compliance in a given jurisdiction.[536]

---

532 *Ibid.*, at 157–158.
533 *Ibid.*, at 158.
534 By contrast, Korea's Saemaul Undong (SU or "New Village Movement"), a rural development movement that was designed to encourage the spirit of self-help took a different approach; the government provided funding for SU projects, but the government support was made contingent upon the continuing performance of projects; *i.e.*, non-performing projects did not receive funding, while performing projects received incentives. For further discussion of the movement, see Asian Development Bank, *The Saemaul Undong Movement in the Republic of Korea* (2012), available online at: www.adb.org/sites/default/files/publication/29881/saemaul-undong-movement-korea.pdf; https://perma.cc/9WJD-P7LM.
535 See discussion *supra* Section 3.3.1.
536 *Ibid.*

(a) General regulatory compliance

The legacy of Apartheid has had a profound impact on South African society.[537] The oppressive Apartheid laws,[538] requiring racial segregation and discrimination, sought to control the conduct of South Africans with severe penalties for violation, including imprisonment under harsh conditions.[539] Many resisted these laws, despite penalties, but others complied with the laws; such compliance would have been passive, rather than active, to avoid harsh penalties for violation. The white minority regime continued for an extended period, since the colonial era of the nineteenth century, and the regime's oppressive nature, particularly after the adoption of Apartheid, set the legal culture in society, which caused the black majority to respond to government policies and laws in passive compliance to avoid penalties for breach. This would be a concern for the implementation of development initiatives that require active, rather than passive, compliance for their successful implementation, as seen by the Korean example.[540]

Rule of law indexes allow an assessment of general regulatory compliance, as the rule of law would not be feasible without compliance. As of 2020, the Rule of Law Index by the World Justice Project ranks South Africa at 45th among 110 countries assessed, and the Rule of Law Indicator by the World Bank places South Africa at the percentile rank of 51.[541] In these indexes, South Africa ranks lower than the advanced countries in North America, Europe, and East Asia, but higher than most other developing countries in Africa and many others in Latin America and Asia. It is not clear whether the economic and political circumstances after the end of Apartheid support the proposition that regulatory compliance in South Africa has become more active. On the one hand, the democratization of the regime and the independent judiciary could have raised public confidence in the government that sets laws and policies, moving toward stronger general regulatory compliance. On the other hand, the slow progress of economic and social integration in South Africa and the resulting dissatisfaction among the black majority (and possibly others as well) could have also undermined it. In any event, the current assessment, including those afforded by the rule of law indexes and indicators, seems to indicate that general regulatory compliance is not of the level at which society in general disregards laws and policies advanced by the government; *i.e.*, laws and legal institutions are not regarded as meaningless and could be made effective in South Africa.

---

537 Dubow (2014), *supra* note 448.
538 For a chronological introduction of Apartheid laws, see South African History Online, *Apartheid Legislation 1850s–1970s*, available online at: www.sahistory.org.za/article/apartheid-legislation-1850s-1970s; https://perma.cc/VQ9M-VP47.
539 Dubow (2014), *supra* note 448.
540 See discussion *supra* Section 4.2.4(a).
541 World Justice Project, *Rule of Law Index* (2020), *supra* note 299 and World Bank, *World Governance Indicators* (dataset 2019), available online at: http://info.worldbank.org/governance/wgi/#reports; https://perma.cc/L682-PZK2.

(b) Specific regulatory compliance

Specific regulatory compliance in this analysis refers to the degree of compliance specifically with the development initiatives in South Africa. Chapter 4 explains Koreans' active compliance with the government development initiatives, driven by their strong motivation to escape from poverty and high level of confidence in the government for the initial success of the development initiatives.[542] A relevant question is whether South Africans have shown active compliance with the development initiatives. The constituencies of the national development initiatives could be classified into the black majority (including other non-white races) and the white minority retaining substantial control over South African industries and economic resources.[543] Thus, the development initiatives are unlikely to succeed without active compliance by both of these groups.

The extreme economic disparity existing in South Africa would not have induced active compliance with the development initiatives by both classes of South Africans for the following reasons. From the perspective of the white minority, already possessing substantial economic control with high levels of income and stable employment,[544] the questions of economic growth, unemployment issues, and economic disparity may not seem particularly relevant to their interests, at least as it relates to their immediate futures, and they have a vested interest in maintaining the status quo or minimizing any adverse change to their existing interests (*e.g.*, reallocation of their resources and income sources to the black majority). As a result, no strong incentive may exist for them to comply with the development initiatives that pursue these objectives, which may not be in their immediate interest.

It is also doubtful that major South African industries, largely controlled by the white minority, had a reason to comply actively with the government's development initiatives. This is because, unlike Korea, the South African government, adopting the neoliberal economic stance, did not offer incentives[545] to industries for complying with their development initiatives. It is also not clear whether

---

542 See discussion *supra* Section 4.2.4(a).

543 According to a report, the white minority constituted 68.9 percent of top management in all sectors as of 2016, while the black majority held only 14.3 percent of top management positions and directly owned only 3 percent of shares on the Johannesburg Stock Exchange. Thanti Mthanti, "Systemic Racism behind South Africa's Failure to Transform its Economy," *The Conversation* (January 31, 2018), available online at: https://theconversation.com/syste mic-racism-behind-south-africas-failure-to-transform-its-economy-71499; https://perma.cc/ 4R5J-N4NN.

544 Goodman (2017), *supra* note 457. Wehner observed,

> Although South Africa statistically falls into the group of middle-income countries, its income inequalities are amongst the most extreme in the world. The World Bank reports that 13% of the population live in "first world" conditions, and 53% in "third world" conditions, often lacking access to basic service such as electricity and running water.

Wehner (2000), *supra* note 469, at 183, note 1.

545 See discussion *supra* Section 4.2.3(a).

President Zuma's shift to the state-led developmentalism[546] offered strong incentives to the industries for active compliance. As for the black majority, the repeated failures of the national development initiatives, coupled with the frequent financial and personal scandals of the government officials, including the president,[547] would have undermined their confidence in the government and in the development initiatives that they tried to implement, leaving little incentive for them to show active compliance. It remains to be seen whether the legislated incentives such as BBBEE[548] will change the circumstance and enhance compliance for the future.

Compliance also has been an issue for the LED. The correct understanding and proper knowledge of laws and policies would be necessary for due compliance, but there has reportedly been a general lack of understanding of the LED at a local government level.[549] For example, an investigation of the state of LED, conducted in the province of Mpumalanga in 2002, revealed that municipal administrations were uncertain as to what LED meant, what they were supposed to do, and how they were supposed to organize it.[550] The lack of understanding and knowledge resulted in the undertaking of LED projects in a manner less consistent with the objectives of the LED, as demonstrated by poorly conceived business plans and LED projects submitted without any prior feasibility assessments.[551] In addition, beneficiaries of these projects were often not consulted in the process, which diminished their sense of ownership in the projects.[552] Without active compliance or a sense of project ownership, the outcome was a set of poorly managed projects that were dependent on external funds for their continued existence.[553]

5.2.4 Quality of implementation

(a) State capacity

As discussed in Chapter 3, the capacity of the state is essential for the implementation of laws and policies designed to achieve development.[554] Lack of state capacity, which is not unusual for developing countries with limited resources, was cited as a reason for difficulty with the implementation of the RDP;[555] the government experienced difficulties in the implementation of the RDP due to the

---

546 Republic of South Africa, *New Growth Path Framework, supra* note 473.

547 Onishi (2018), *supra* note 523.

548 See discussion *supra* Section 5.2.2.

549 Rogerson (2011), *supra* note 504, at 158.

550 *Ibid.*

551 *Ibid.*

552 *Ibid.*

553 *Ibid.*

554 See discussion *supra* Section 3.3.2(b).

555 South African History Online, *South Africa's Key Economic Policies Changes (1994–2013), supra* note 471.

fiscal constraints and lack of sufficiently skilled managers and administrators.[556] The government was not successful in building the necessary state capacity; it did not try to remedy the fiscal constraints by collecting new taxes, which would have been justified to rebuild a nation torn apart by Apartheid, but the government instead focused narrowly on fiscal prudence and revenue reallocation.[557] The LED also suffered from a lack of capacity on the part of local governments; as discussed in Section 5.2.3, local administrators did not have the capacity to understand the LED properly and undertake LED projects in compliance with the mandate and objectives of the LED.[558]

The circumstances of South Africa are in contrast to those of Korea, where the government had secured a solid body of able central and local administrators, ready to serve the nation and implement developmental laws and policies by the early 1960s.[559] Education and training are essential to generate qualified administrators. Unlike Korea in the 1960s, with a severely insufficient budget,[560] the South African government today has a sizable budget, which is the largest among all African countries (with a consolidated budget revenue of approximately US$ 105.4 billion for the 2020–2021 fiscal year)[561] to recruit and train administrators. The government may also actively explore additional sources to generate revenues that would be essential to build necessary state capacity. The projected budget deficit[562] and the rather narrow tax base (reportedly only 13 percent of the South African population paying income tax)[563] seem to require such an effort on the part of the government.

Corruption is another problem that adversely affects state capacity in South Africa. A report points out that "South Africa suffers from widespread corruption … It has a robust anti-corruption framework, but laws are inadequately enforced. Public procurement is particularly prone to corruption, and bribery thrives at the central government level."[564] The Corruption Perceptions Index (CPI) 2019 by Transparency International ranks South Africa at 70 out of 180 countries, which is better than most other African countries but weaker than the advanced countries in North America, Europe, and Asia.[565] The principal South African

---

556 *Ibid.*
557 *Ibid.*
558 See discussion *supra* Section 5.2.3.
559 See discussion *supra* Section 4.2.5.
560 *Supra* note 426 (for Korea's relevant budget figure).
561 Republic of South Africa (National Treasury), *Budget Review 2020*, available online at: www.treasury.gov.za/documents/national%20budget/2020/review/FullBR.pdf; https://perma.cc/CR2V-YV8E.
562 *Ibid.*
563 "This Is Who Is Paying South Africa's Tax," *Business Tech*, October 26, 2017, available online at: https://businesstech.co.za/news/finance/207631/this-is-who-is-paying-south-africas-tax/; https://perma.cc/6TYK-RLBX.
564 GAN Business Anti-Corruption Portal, *South Africa Corruption Report* (December 2015), available online at: www.business-anti-corruption.com/country-profiles/south-africa; https://perma.cc/3DRU-BD6X.
565 Transparency International (2017), *supra* note 399.

anti-corruption law is the Prevention and Combating of Corruption Act (PCCA),[566] which criminalizes corruption in public and private sectors, including attempted corruption, extortion, active and passive bribery, bribery of a foreign public official, as well as fraud and money laundering, and further obliges public officials to report corrupt activities.[567] Under the PCCA, it is also a criminal offense to provide any form of "gratification" to an official if it is not lawfully due, a provision that is stricter than anti-corruption laws in many other countries, which do not prevent the furnishment of gifts to a government official *per se*, particularly when the gift is of a modest value unconnected to any business affected by the official's power or discretion.[568]

Corruption is not unique to South Africa; corruption is also prevalent in other countries, including developed ones and successful developing countries, such as China.[569] Successful developing countries have achieved economic development despite the existence of corruption in their own countries; thus, corruption is not an absolute impediment to achieving development. Nonetheless, the extent of corruption needs to be controlled, lest it critically damage state capacity and overturn the development process. In the case of Korea, corruption was more effectively controlled when the government secured increased revenues as a result of successful economic development and was able to improve the pay for government officials and when government officials, particularly those at the local level, were checked by democratic devices such as regional and local elections.[570] The level of compensation for officials at both central and local levels needs to be set at adequate levels so that the incentive to engage in corrupt practices to meet a financial need is alleviated. The prevalence of corruption at the central government level in South Africa is particularly damaging to development interests because it sends the wrong signal throughout government, including among regional and local government officials who may be inclined to act per the precedents set by central government officials.

(b) Political will

Political will, which is defined in the context of law and development as the commitment and devotion of a country's political leadership to the implementation of law,[571] is essential for the implementation of developmental laws and policies. Since Nelson Mandela, every South African president pronounced development initiatives, but this does not necessarily reflect on the strength of political

---

566 Prevention and Combating of Corruption Act of 2004 (Act No. 12, 2004) [assented to April 27, 2004], text available online at: https://web.archive.org/web/20200422100231/www.just ice.gov.za/legislation/acts/2004-012.pdf; https://perma.cc/2KUF-AKML.

567 *Ibid.*

568 See, *e.g.*, Improper Solicitation and Graft Act of 2016 (Korea), *supra* note 400.

569 China's 2019 CPI rank (90th out of 180 countries) was even lower than South Africa's (70th). Transparency International (2019), *supra* note 399.

570 See discussion *supra* Section 4.2.3(c).

571 See discussion *supra* Section 3.3.2(c).

will, as the latter should be distinguished from a mere interest or an initiative in development facilitation.[572] As explained in Chapter 3, political will is not merely an interest in development; it is demonstrated by the continued implementation of consistent development policies for an extended period of time and allocation of substantial political and economic capital, as witnessed in Korea for over three decades.[573] In other successful developing countries in the past, such as Taiwan, Singapore, Chile, Spain, and, more recently, China, the leaders of these nations have also shown strong political will for development extending over the course of multiple decades.[574]

It is not clear whether the leaderships in South Africa have shown such long-enduring political will for development. Nelson Mandela was one of the most inspiring leaders of the twentieth century. During his presidency, however, his administration focused on political reconciliation and the immediate economic needs of the majority of the South African population. His government undertook the RDP to meet the latter interest but failed to develop the RDP into a long-term economic development initiative that South Africans could support.[575] The subsequent leadership also pronounced development initiatives, but there was a lack of focus on the part of the administrations, which often became tainted by financial and personal scandals, including one which eventually led to the resignation of President Zuma.[576] The government failed to exercise leadership and bring South Africans, including both the black majority and the white minority, to support their development initiatives, and the outcome was sluggish economic growth, widespread unemployment, and a significant economic disparity.

There is an innate difficulty in South Africa: unlike Korea, where the population is largely homogeneous in terms of ethnicity and culture, the South African government has to deal with a much more diverse population, comprised of multi-racial and multi-ethnic groups, with a history of social and political divisions and confrontations among them, caused by the legacy of Apartheid. In this type of situation, political leadership will have to tolerate and embrace the challenges associated with the diverse nature of the population, and it could be substantially more difficult to elicit unitary support for the government's development initiatives from such a diverse population characterized by economic disparity, conflicting interests, and potential mistrust (about the other racial or ethnic groups and the government). The Korean government did not face this problem in its development era—at least not to the extent experienced by South Africa—but even in Korea, when a full elective democracy was restored (with the terms for president limited to only five years) and when the economic gaps among its citizens widened after its financial crisis in the 1990s, the Korean people no

---

572   *Ibid.*
573   See discussion *supra* Section 4.2.5.
574   *Supra* note 326 (for a list of the leaders).
575   For a discussion of the RDP, see discussion *supra* Section 5.2.2.
576   Onishi (2018), *supra* note 523.

longer stood "united" to achieve their common interests in development, as they did during the previous development era.[577]

Despite the difficulty that the political circumstances present, it is still imperative for the South African leadership to renew strong political will for development if it is to improve its critical economic situation. The leadership needs to bring focus on development, clearly prioritizing the tasks that must be performed and others that can wait, reminding the population and the entire government (central and local) of the importance of economic development as a necessary condition to meet other social development objectives.[578] While political liberation took place by the peaceful transition of power in 1994, records indicate that social and economic integration is yet to be achieved.[579] Without this integration, with the black majority left behind in economic backwardness, it will not be possible for South Africa to meet economic development objectives and create a fair and just society, as envisioned by Nelson Mandela. The leadership will have to look for ways to achieve this integration, which in itself is also an important social development objective initially set by the RDP.[580]

5.3 Future prospects

The World Bank published a bleak forecast of South Africa's economic performance in 2018, a mere 1.1 percent growth for the year, which was substantially lower than the growth estimates of its competitors: 2.5 percent growth for Nigeria and 1.6 percent for Angola.[581] South Africa underperformed, failing to achieve even this modest mark: its growth rate in 2018 was 0.8 percent.[582] President Zuma, who was developmentally oriented, as demonstrated by setting up new developmental initiatives and institutions, such as the New Growth Path, Department of Economic Development, and Development Planning Commission, resigned from office for a personal scandal only a month after the publication of the World Bank report.[583] During the eight years of his presidency, despite the president's development initiatives, the South African economy continued to suffer from stagnant growth, high unemployment, and economic disparity. A new administration is

---

577 The regular change of administrations was accompanied by changes in economic policies to meet the interests of each administration's constituencies, and economic growth gradually waned. See *supra* Section 4.2. See also Yong-Shik Lee, "South Korean Economy at the Crossroads: Structure Issues under External Pressure—An Essay from a Law and Development Perspective" (2019) 12(3) *Law and Development Review* 865–885.

578 See *supra* Section 1.3.

579 Goodman (2017), *supra* note 457.

580 See discussion *supra* Section 5.2.1.

581 World Bank, *Global Economic Prospects* (January 2018), at 4, available online at: https://openkn owledge.worldbank.org/bitstream/handle/10986/28932/9781464811630.pdf?sequence= 16&isAllowed=y; https://perma.cc/767X-Q6RJ.

582 World Bank, *GDP Growth (Annual %)—South Africa*, available online at: https://data. worldbank.org/indicator/NY.GDP.MKTP.KD.ZG?end=2019&locations=ZA&name_desc= false&start=1961; https://perma.cc/LMA4-EBHS.

583 Onishi (2018), *supra* note 523.

in place under the leadership of Cyril Ramaphosa, but economic growth further plummeted to 0.15 percent in 2019.[584] It remains to be seen whether his new economic initiative, South Africa's Economic Reconstruction and Recovery Plan,[585] will reverse the downturn.

Despite the current predicaments, South Africa remains among the most advanced countries in Africa and has significant potential for development. The country is described as a middle-income country economically relying on mineral exports,[586] but this does not have to be the permanent designation for South Africa. With the most developed technology and productive capacity in the continent, a vast endowment of natural resources, fertile land, and a strong agricultural base, as well as deep and diverse cultural and academic traditions, successful economic development is by no means an impossible task for South Africa. What has been lacking is the focus and prioritization among economic and social development objectives, and the willingness of the leadership to deploy its political capital to drive focused and sustained economic development efforts. Reference should be made to the successful development cases, such as Korea, wherein the state assumed an active role in facilitating industrial development. The facilitation of industrial development, particularly in the manufacturing sector, has proven to be effective for creating employment, and this is an urgent economic task for South Africa.[587]

Laws and institutions play a pivotal role in the sustained implementation of development initiatives, as demonstrated by the case of Korea.[588] There is a need for development-facilitating laws to support development initiatives and for effective institutions to facilitate their implementation. Concerning the latter, consideration can be given to elevating the status of the current Department of Economic Development so that it can play a leadership role in the planning and execution of the development initiatives, coordinating with other government departments, agencies, and local governments for their effective implementation. Establishing such a control center for economic development, per the precedents in successful developing countries of the past, such as Korea, Taiwan, and Japan,[589] would be effective in bringing a focus on development. LED projects should be selected and supported on the basis of merit after due feasibility assessments and should also be adjusted and calibrated to work with the national development initiatives.

South Africa has achieved the most important social development in its history by abolishing Apartheid and undertaking a peaceful transition of power

---

584 World Bank, *supra* note 582.
585 *Supra* note 493.
586 Jan Cronje, "World Bank Predicts Just 1.1% GDP Growth for SA in 2018," *fin 24*, January 10, 2018, available online at: www.fin24.com/Economy/world-bank-predicts-just-11-gdp-growth-for-sa-in-2018-20180109; https://perma.cc/R2ZD-J58Z.
587 Republic of South Africa, *New Growth Path Framework, supra* note 473.
588 See *supra* Chapter 4.
589 See *supra* note 391 (for examples of the control centers within governments).

from the white minority to the black majority through their lauded power-sharing scheme.[590] This achievement was embodied in the widely celebrated 1996 Constitution setting forth a range of civil and human rights, including extensive socioeconomic rights, that are not stipulated in constitutions of some other advanced countries such as the United States. Given this background and legacy, it would be politically difficult for the government to avoid addressing various demands for these socioeconomic rights. Yet, as discussed earlier, the rights-based approach without consideration of economic restraints has its limits, and the government could lose focus and priority if it were to try to accommodate all these demands at the same time. It will thus be necessary for the nation's leadership to exercise the political will to bring focus on priority development objectives by persuading their constituencies of the need for prioritization and sequencing.[591]

The prospects for South African development depend on whether the country will achieve social and economic integration among majority and minority racial groups. As it stands, South Africa has two nations within its border, a first-world nation for a small minority of its population and a third-world one for the majority.[592] Every country has different economic classes within its border, but a division of this extreme extent, in a country still grappling with the traumatic legacy of Apartheid, cannot be sustained in the long run, and it is not conducive to long-term economic development. This means that it will be necessary for the political leadership to engage the white minority, who are still retaining much control over the economy, to cooperate with the proposed economic and social integration. The prospect for this cooperation is not necessarily dim; the white minority agreed to the political power transfer with the realization that in the modern world, a minor group of the population cannot control a nation permanently by putting the majority under systemic oppression and discrimination. Likewise, a modern economy cannot grow and prosper for long without the full participation of the majority of the population in industries and the economy. The current stagnant growth, high unemployment, and significant economic disparity are no more in the long-term interest of the white minority than in the interest of the black majority.

As discussed in Section 5.2, education and training are essential for the proposed social and economic integration. It will not be possible for the black majority to participate in the skilled professions offering higher levels of income without educational attainment. Both educational attainment and school facilities for the black majority are currently inadequate,[593] and it will be necessary for the central and local governments to increase investments in education. Successful economic development never occurred in places where public education was inadequate or the majority of the population did not receive education, and educational

---

590 Traniello (2007), *supra* note 449.
591 See discussion *supra* Section 5.2.4.
592 *Supra* note 544 (for a discussion of the economic disparity).
593 *Ibid.* See also *supra* note 461 (for a discussion of the weak educational attainment of blacks in South Africa).

attainment has to be facilitated as a priority for development initiatives. This is an area where the white minority with capital could assist by making investments, as a part of the proposed cooperation for social and economic integration. The LED could also focus on building educational facilities and increasing educational attainment for blacks at the local level. The prospects for South African development will be all the more promising when the majority of the population has proper educational attainment.

6 Application of the law and development approach in the United States

6.1 Introduction: beginning of an uncertain era?

As discussed in Chapter 1, the concept of development has traditionally been associated with developing countries. However, the changing economic realities for developed countries, such as regional economic disparities within developed countries, increasing income gaps among their citizens ("economic polarization"), and stagnant economic growth, which led to dramatic political outcomes such as the United Kingdom's referendum result to exit the European Union and the unexpected conclusion in the United States' 2016 presidential election, justify the application of the concept of development to address economic problems in developed countries, such as the United States. This chapter examines contemporary economic problems in the United States and applies the law and development approaches.[594]

The 2016 election of Donald Trump, a controversial businessman and political outsider, as the 45th President of the United States was an unexpected event marking the end of an era known for providing a degree of political and economic predictability and the beginning of an uncertain new age. The deteriorating economic conditions prevailing in many States[595] in the United States,[596] such as the decline of manufacturing industries, unemployment, and income losses, despite the overall wealth and economic prosperity of the United States, were a primary cause of this dramatic election outcome,[597] signaling the necessity of new approaches to tackle these root economic problems.

---

594 This chapter is adapted from the author's work, "Law and Economic Development in the United States: Toward a New Paradigm" (2019) 68(2) *Catholic University Law Review* 229–290, text available online at: https://papers.ssrn.com/sol3/papers.cfm?abstract_id=3168964; https://perma.cc/8RUH-J97F.

595 "State" with a capital "S" denotes a constituent "State" of the United States of America, as opposed to an independent sovereign state (with a lower case "s"), such as the United States.

596 The decline of the manufacturing industries in many regions of the United States, signified by the term, "Rust Belt," and the resulting loss of employment, income, and population caused substantial social discontent across the country. Yong-Shik Lee, "Trans-Pacific Partnership Agreement: A Commentary on Developing/Developed Country Divide and Social Considerations" (2017) 9(2) *Trade, Law and Development* 21–53, at 33–34.

597 Gabriel (2016), *supra* note 71.

DOI: 10.4324/9781003090175-8

The economic policies of the Trump administration, based on confrontational trade protections[598] and tax cuts primarily benefitting the wealthy,[599] have not resolved the economic problems faced by the United States. For an alternative approach, reference can be made to successful economic development cases; successful developing countries in the past, such as Korea, adopted legal and institutional approaches to stimulate economic development, generate higher incomes for the majority of their populations, and lift their populations out of poverty. As readers may recall from Chapter 4, the Korean government adopted a series of effective economic development policies, such as promoting coordination and cooperation between the public and private sectors. Additionally, the government granted subsidies and tax exemptions to the growing key industries that generated jobs and income for the Korean population and successfully endeavored to spur economic growth through enabling legislation and a range of institutions to support these policies.[600]

The present economic circumstances of the United States and those of Korea during its development period are vastly different, the former commanding the largest economic resources among all countries and the latter facing serious poverty and significant resource constraints. Despite these differences, the form of the legal and institutional approach adopted by successful developing countries in the past could still be referenced and employed, with necessary modifications, to provide focused support to industries and businesses that contribute to economic development and generate jobs and income for the population, particularly for those in economically disadvantaged regions and communities in the United States. Section 6.2 examines the economic problems in the United States and proposes legal and institutional approaches to address them.

6.2 Economic problems in the United States

6.2.1 *Regional economic disparity*

Regional variance in economic performance and income level is by no means unusual and is readily observed in every country, but such variance becomes a regional economic disparity with the potential to divide a country when economic gaps are deep and persistent. In the United States, such regional economic disparity is obvious. In 2019, the median household income ranged from US$ 24,725 to

---

598 For a discussion of the controversial trade policies and the subsequent trade disputes, see Yong-Shik Lee, "Three Wrongs Do Not Make a Right: The Conundrum of the U.S. Steel and Aluminum Tariffs" (2019) 18(3) *World Trade Review* 481–501.

599 John Harwood, "Trump's Tax Cut Isn't Giving the US Economy the Boost It Needs," *CNBC*, August 16, 2019, available online at: www.cnbc.com/2019/08/16/trumps-tax-cut-isnt-giving-the-us-economy-the-boost-it-needs.html; https://perma.cc/UYV4-D2S5.

600 See discussion *supra* Section 4.2.3. The Korean government set up effective institutions, such as the Economic Planning Board (EPB) and the Korea Trade Promotion Agency (KOTRA), with offices in a number of export markets around the world, to offer assistance with export activities of Korean companies by providing market information and trade networks. *Ibid.*

US$ 151,806 among 3,142 counties, with a national median of US$ 65,712[601] and unemployment rates ranging from 0.7 percent to 19.3 percent.[602] Figure 6.1 illustrates the large income gaps existing among the various counties, with the more affluent counties generally being located in the major population centers of the East and West Coasts, pockets in the West, and in the State of Texas; while the poorer counties are found in the rural South, Southeast, Southwest, and the Midwest.

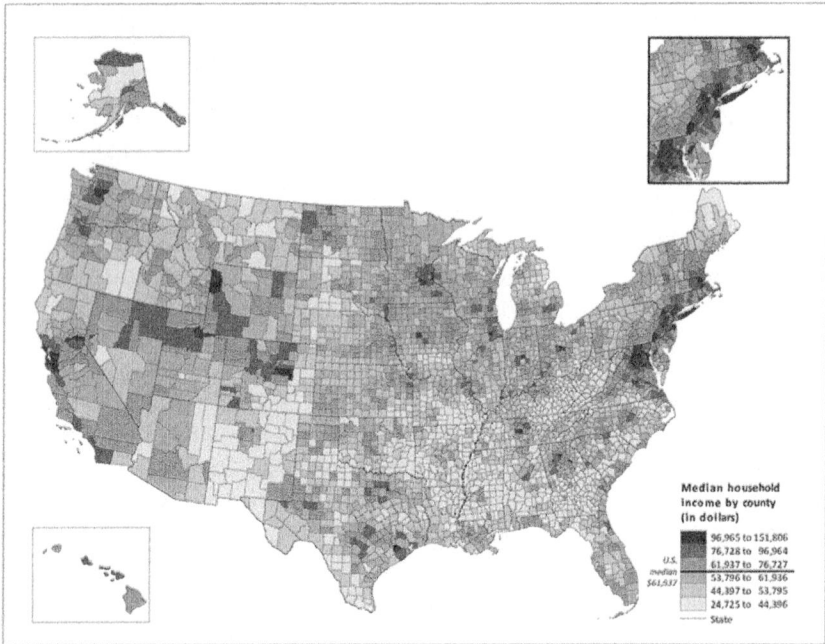

Figure 6.1 Median household income of the total population by county, 2019.[603]

601 See United States Census Bureau, *2019 Poverty and Median Household Income Estimates*, available online at: www2.census.gov/programs-surveys/saipe/datasets/2019/2019-state-and-county/est19all.xls; https://perma.cc/GC4D-BAT6.
602 United States Bureau of Labor Statistics, *Labor Force Data by County, 2019 Annual Averages*, available online at: www.bls.gov/lau/laucnty19.xlsx; https://perma.cc/QEU3-5AXN.
603 United States Census Bureau, *Median Household Income of the Total Population by County: 2019*, available online at: www.census.gov/content/dam/Census/library/visualizations/2020/demo/p30-08/f1-mp-19.pdf; https://perma.cc/ZJ6K-YS5V.

The regional economic disparity, as measured by the median household income, is significant; in the highest bracket, the median household income is over 240 percent of the national median, and in the lowest, it is below the poverty line.[604] According to a study by the United States Department of Agriculture (USDA), 11.2 percent of all counties (353 counties) in the United States are persistently poor. These counties have had 20 percent or more of their populations living in poverty over the last 30 years.[605] Poverty in the United States is regionally concentrated. The USDA study notes that "people living in poverty tend to be clustered in certain regions, counties, and neighborhoods rather than being spread evenly across the [n]ation."[606]

The geographic location of the respective wealthier and poorer counties and regions has not changed significantly over the years. A study concluded that counties consistently underperforming economically are primarily found in seven regions: the Northern Rockies, the Great Plains, the Rio Grande Valley, the Mississippi Delta, the Great Lakes, the Appalachian Mountains, and the Deep South.[607] Many of the counties marked as exhibiting lower household incomes on the above 2019 map are also located in the aforementioned regions and on the following 2002 map illustrating the median household income by county at the beginning of the century (Figure 6.2). The substantial similarities in the locations of the wealthier and poorer counties between these two maps demonstrate that persistent regional economic gaps, accompanying unemployment, and poverty exist in the United States.

604 United States Census Bureau, *supra* note 601. The "poverty thresholds" identified by the U.S. Census Bureau were $20,335 for a family of three and $26,172 for a family of four in 2019. United States Census Bureau, *Poverty Thresholds*, available online at: www.census.gov/data/tables/time-series/demo/income-poverty/historical-poverty-thresholds.html; https://perma.cc/7NCE-X972.

605 United States Department of Agriculture Economic Research Service, *Geography of Poverty*, available online at: https://web.archive.org/web/20180109092507/www.ers.usda.gov/top ics/rural-economy-population/rural-poverty-well-being/geography-of-poverty.aspx; https://perma.cc/N847-9UVR.

606 *Ibid.*

607 The study examined population change from 1970 to 2006, employment change from 1970 to 2006, wage change from 1970 to 2006, and average wages in 2006. If a county ranked in the bottom third in three out of the four categories, the county was identified as underperforming. Yoav Hagler, "Introduction: Identifying Underperforming Regions," *in* Petra Todorovich and Yoav Hagler (eds.), *America 2050: New Strategies for Regional Economic Development* (2009), at 7, available online at: https://s3.us-east-1.amazonaws.com/rpa-org/pdfs/2050-New-Strateg ies-for-Regional-Economic-Development.pdf; https://perma.cc/85SV-WGAJ.

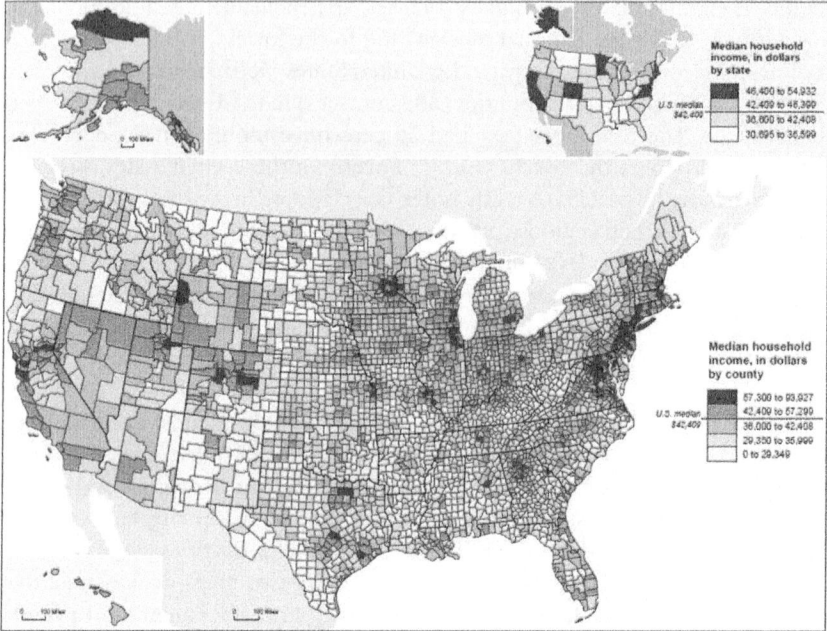

Figure 6.2 Median household income of the United States by county, 2002.[608]

The causes of this persistent regional economic disparity include geographical elements such as location (*e.g.*, access to ports and transportation links),[609] infrastructure,[610] the availability of human capital through educational attainment,[611] and natural amenities.[612] These elements have influenced the location of new industries generating employment and income, such as information technology (IT), biotechnology, and financial industries.[613] Uneven industrial development

---

608   See United States Census Bureau, *Small Area Income and Poverty Estimates,* available online at: www.census.gov/content/dam/Census/library/visualizations/2004/demo/2002-state-county-maps/med-hh-inc2002.pdf; https://perma.cc/S5BD-53XC.

609   A study identified geographical isolation as the primary cause of economic disparity within the United States. Junjie Wu and Munisamy Gopinath, "What Causes Spatial Variations in Economic Development in the United States?" (2008) 90(2) *American Journal of Agricultural Economics* 392–408, at 407. The study observed that areas that were farther away from metropolitan areas showed significantly lower labor demands, wages, housing prices, and demand for land development. *Id.,* at 404.

610   *Ibid.,* at 402.

611   Hagler (2009), *supra* note 607, at 14. The age composition of the population is also relevant. *Id.,* at 7.

612   Wu and Gopinath (2008), *supra* note 609, at 404.

613   Thus, these industries are concentrated in regions with the cited advantages, such as the East and West Coasts. Isolated rural areas in the Midwest and South have suffered from a lack of

and subsequent regional adaptation have also played a role in creating this disparity; once-powerful traditional manufacturing industries in the United States, such as the iron and steel industries, failed to adapt to the changing global economic environment, causing the sites of these industries to decline, as signified by the term "Rust Belt."[614]

The regional economic disparity creates a range of socioeconomic issues, including gaps in education, healthcare, and public safety; the loss of population in poorer regions; and social discontent, which can lead to political unrest.[615] Perhaps the most dramatic demonstration of such social discontent was the unexpected outcome of the 2016 U.S. presidential election. Donald Trump, who had been largely considered a political outsider, won the election against former U.S. Senator for New York and the U.S. Secretary of State Hillary Clinton, despite the overwhelming forecasts predicting a Clinton Presidency.[616] The Trump administration owed its victory, in no small part, to the economic discontent and growing public mistrust in the political establishment,[617] concentrated in the regions facing economic deprivation. Trump lost the 2020 presidential election to Joe Biden, but he still received the second largest popular vote in the history of U.S. presidential elections, second only to Biden. There is a significant correlation between the counties where Donald Trump won and the median household income pattern observed above, as depicted by the following map (counties marked in darker color tone—which tend to be wealthier counties—represent stronger support for then-Democratic presidential candidate Biden).

economic opportunities. See Hagler (2009), *supra* note 607. The poverty rate in the rural South (non-metro counties) reached 21.7 percent during 2011–2015. United States Department of Agriculture Economic Research Service, *supra* note 605.

614 "The Rust Belt" refers to the large area from the Great Lakes to the upper Midwest States, including western New York, Pennsylvania, West Virginia, Ohio, Indiana, parts of Michigan, northern Illinois, eastern Iowa, and southeastern Wisconsin. The term signifies the economic decline, deindustrialization, population loss, and urban decay caused by the decline of its once-prosperous manufacturing sector. This region has lost more than 1.2 million manufacturing jobs since 1990 and 2.2 million since 1970. Hagler (2009), *supra* note 607, at 9. However, not all of the traditional manufacturing sites have declined; for example, Chicago, New York, and Los Angeles also lost large numbers of traditional manufacturing jobs (548,185, 376,838, and 330,944, respectively), but these places were able to adapt and replace the declining industries with new ones that generated employment. *Id.*

615 According to the USDA's research,

the poor living in areas where poverty is prevalent face impediments beyond those of their individual circumstances. Concentrated poverty contributes to poor housing and health conditions, higher crime and school dropout rates, as well as employment dislocations. As a result, economic conditions in very poor areas can create limited opportunities for poor residents that become self-perpetuating.

United States Department of Agriculture Economic Research Service, *supra* note 605.

616 See John Slides, "A Comprehensive Average of Election Forecasts Points to a Decisive Clinton Victory," *Washington Post*, November 8, 2016.

617 See Gabriel (2016), *supra* note 71.

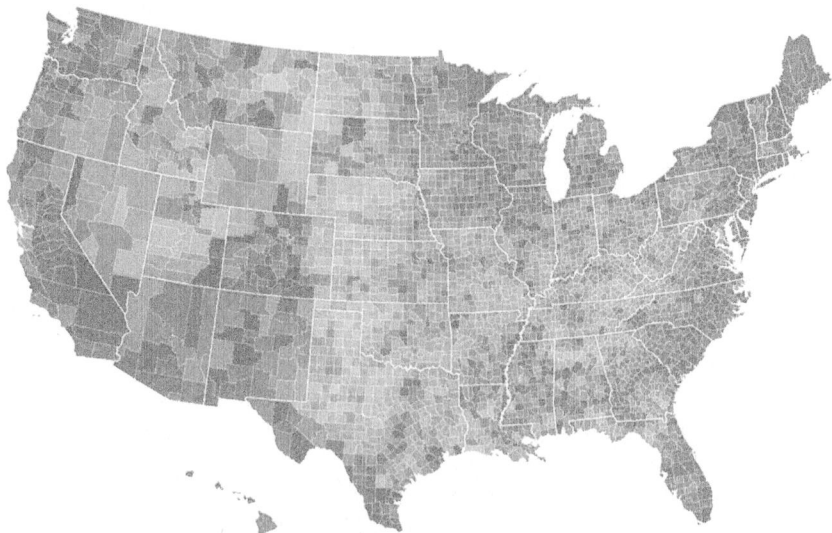

Figure 6.3 2020 U.S. presidential election result by county.[618]

Figure 6.3 illustrates the regional economic disparity reflected in the election outcome; the counties in regions identified as wealthier, such as the population centers along the East and West Coasts (colored darker on the map), voted for Biden, and those in the poorer regions, including the South, much of the Southwest and Southeast, and the Midwest, revealed the tendency to vote for Trump.[619] This could be characterized as a national divide in the country, where the regional economic disparity has become so significant as to affect the outcome of a national election. Given this divide, each group of counties and regions can be viewed as a country within a country, with vastly divergent income levels and economic capacities; the poorer counties and regions, analogous to "developing countries" in this sense, exist alongside developed ones on the world stage. Trump vowed to improve economic conditions for impoverished individuals and poorer regions, which were his support base,[620] and won the presidency in 2016 and the second largest popular vote in history in 2020; thus, the economic

---

618   Mitchell Thorson, Janie Haseman, and Carlie Procell, "Four Maps That Show How America Voted in the 2020 Election with Results by County, Number of Voters," *USA Today*, November 20, 2020, available at: www.usatoday.com/in-depth/graphics/2020/11/10/election-maps-2020-america-county-results-more-voters/6226197002/; https://perma.cc/93NV-M2XY.

619   Gabriel (2016), *supra* note 71.

620   Heather Long, "Trump Vows 25 Million Jobs, Most of Any President," *CNN Money*, January 20, 2017, available online at: https://money.cnn.com/2017/01/20/news/economy/donald-trump-jobs-wages/index.html; https://perma.cc/K5V9-QJWY.

improvement, or "economic development," of the poorer regions in the United States has acquired political tenancy.[621]

6.2.2 Structural issues in the economy

In addition to the regional economic disparity, there are significant structural issues in the U.S. economy, such as stagnant economic growth and economic polarization (*i.e.*, worsening income distribution), that necessitate adoption of the legal and institutional approaches.

(a) Economic growth

The U.S. economy has shown a steady decline in growth since the 1970s. Figure 6.4 illustrates the downward trend of real gross domestic product (GDP)[622] growth rates.

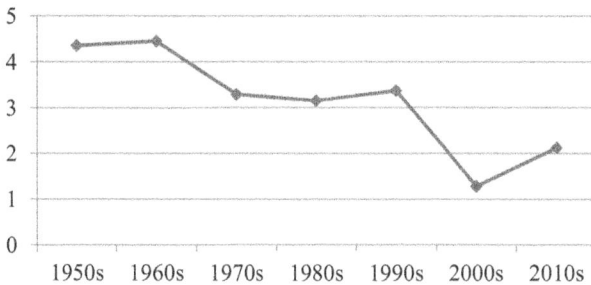

Figure 6.4 Average annual real GDP growth rates by decade (percentage).[623]

There is a long-term trend of steady decline, and the particularly low average real growth rate in the 2000s was due to the 2007–2008 financial crisis. This crisis led to a severe recession in the U.S. economy, sharply lowering real GDP growth rates, which had ranged from 4.33 to 3.13 percent between 2003 and 2005, down to –2.75 and 0.18 percent in 2008 and 2009, respectively.[624] Since then, growth has been stagnant, with the real GDP growth rate kept under 3 percent.[625]

---

621 The term, "economic development," is increasingly used in the context of developed country economies. Reflecting this trend, national, regional, and local governments in developed countries have set up offices to promote "economic development." Examples include the Economic Development Administration (EDA) under the United States Department of Commerce, the Department of Economic Development in the State of Georgia, and the Office of Economic Development in the City of New Orleans.

622 For an explanation of real GDP, see *supra* note 28.

623 Compiled from *US Real GDP Growth Rate by Year*, available online at: www.multpl.com/us-real-gdp-growth-rate/table/by-year; https://perma.cc/5YCY-DYQH, a table of annual percentage changes in U.S. Real GDP, chained 2012 dollars (inflation adjusted).

624 *Ibid.*

625 *Ibid.*

This stagnant growth affects employment. The employment/population ratio for males aged 25 to 44 has remained below 87 percent since 2010, as compared to a constant 90-plus percent until the 1970s,[626] and even declined to 76 percent in November 2020 for all persons aged 25 to 54, as compared to 81 percent in 1999–2000.[627] A study observes the weakened stability of the labor market in the United States;[628] until the end of the 1960s, the unemployment rate was relatively steady, averaging approximately 5–8 percent, depending on the economic cycle. After 1970, however, unemployment increased sharply during recessions.[629] The 2007–2008 recession was particularly severe, and prime-aged, male unemployment peaked at almost 20 percent, down only to 16.6 percent by 2014.[630] The employment rate has improved since then, but the recent COVID-19 pandemic has turned the tide again.[631]

What caused the stagnant growth in the United States? An important reason is the relative decline of U.S. industries since the 1970s. After the Second World War, U.S. industries enjoyed a dominant position in the world, but their dominance was challenged; first by European countries, such as Germany, as they recovered from the war and regained productive capacity; subsequently, by Japan and the newly industrialized countries (NICs), such as South Korea and Taiwan; and most recently by China, which has rapidly industrialized since the 1980s. Facing competition from the producers in these countries, U.S. producers lost many of their overseas and domestic consumers and many even relocated their production facilities overseas, seeking cheaper labor and consumer outlets, reducing, in turn, employment opportunities for U.S. workers. U.S. producers found strength in some of the new, technological industries, such as IT, biotechnology, and financial services, but are not enjoying a dominant position, as they once did with the traditional manufacturing industries during the postwar period, and they face strong challenges from abroad. Consistent with the economic stagnation, U.S. investment growth, which is measured by the non-residential fixed investment growth rate and the domestic net fixed investment/GDP ratio, has also been in a downward trend, as illustrated by Figures 6.5 and 6.6.

626 Edward Glaeser, "Secular Joblessness," *in* Coen Teulings and Richard Baldwin (eds.), *Secular Stagnation: Facts, Causes and Cures* (CEPR Press, 2014), at 70, available at: https://scholar.harv ard.edu/files/farhi/files/book_chapter_secular_stagnation_nov_2014_0.pdf; https://perma. cc/6ZC7-TRML.

627 Federal Reserve Economic Data (FRED), *Employment Rate: Aged 25–54: Males for the United States*, available online at: https://fred.stlouisfed.org/series/LREM25MAUSM156S, accessed January 3, 2021; Federal Reserve Economic Data (FRED), *Employment-Population Ratio—25– 54 Yrs.*, available online at: https://fred.stlouisfed.org/series/LNS12300060, accessed January 3, 2021.

628 Glaeser (2014), *supra* note 626, at 74.

629 *Ibid.*

630 *Ibid.*

631 United States Bureau of Labor Statistics, *Labor Force Statistics from the Current Population Survey* (last modified December 4, 2020), available online at: www.bls.gov/web/empsit/cpseea10.htm; https://perma.cc/7DLW-PFLA.

Figure 6.5 Non-residential fixed investment growth rate.[632]

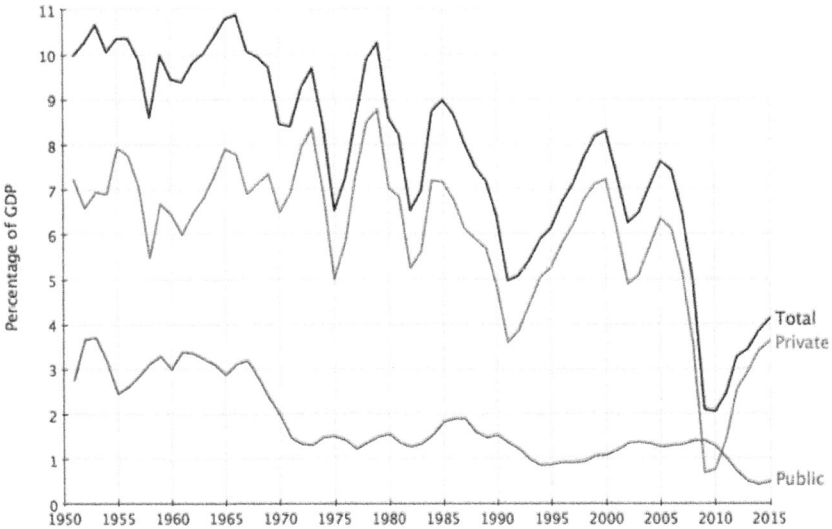

Figure 6.6 Domestic net fixed investment (percentage of GDP).[633]

632 Excerpted from Chris Matthews, "America's Investment Crisis Is Getting Worse," *Fortune Finance* (December 5, 2015), available online at: http://fortune.com/2015/12/02/corporate-investment-crisis/, accessed January 17, 2021. From 2015 to 2019, the growth rate fell further to 2.9 percent on average. Compiled from YCHARTS, *US Real Nonresidential Fixed Investment QoQ*, available online at: https://ycharts.com/indicators/us_change_in_real_nonresidential_f ixed_investment; https://perma.cc/B83K-PRPF.

633 Excerpted from AnEconomicSense.org, "How Fast Can GDP Grow? Not as Fast as Trump Says," *An Economic Sense* (August 1, 2017), available online at: https://aneconomicsense.org/2017/ 08/01/how-fast-can-gdp-grow-not-as-fast-as-trump-says/; https://perma.cc/D8UN-74VU.

(b) Economic polarization

Robert Gordon cites the inequality of income distribution as an impediment to the long-term economic growth of the United States.[634] He observes that the increasing share of the top 10 percent of the income distribution has deprived the middle class of income growth.[635] Since the 1970s, the real incomes[636] of households in the low- to middle-income groups have stagnated, whereas the real incomes of households in the highest income group have increased sharply since the 1970s. Upward mobility in the U.S. economy is declining, despite being active from the 1950s until the 1970s; since the turn of this century, polarization has mostly affected lower income groups.[637] The share of middle-income households has decreased from around 58 percent in 1970 to 47 percent in 2014, and the income share of the middle-income household from 47 percent in 1970 to 35 percent in 2014 (Figures 6.7–6.9).[638]

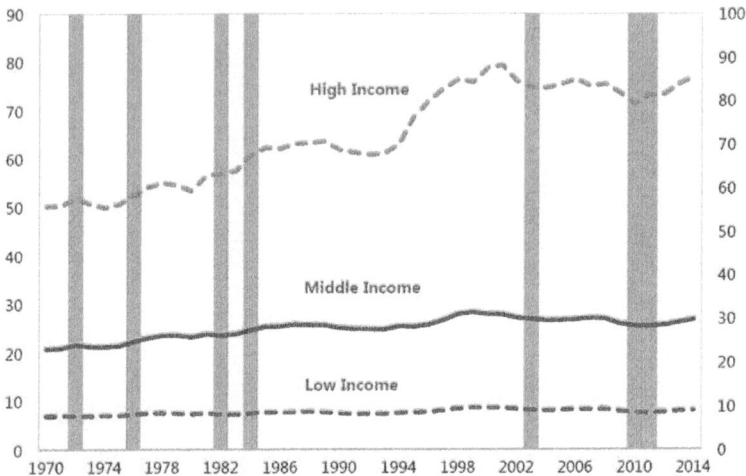

Figure 6.7 Average scaled household income, 1970–2014 (thousand 2005 US$).[639]

634   Robert J. Gordon, "The Turtle's Progress: Secular Stagnation Meets the Headwinds," *in Secular Stagnation: Facts, Causes and Cures, supra* note 626, at 51.
635   Teulings and Baldwin (2014), *supra* note 626, at 4.
636   For an explanation of economic indicators in "real terms," see *supra* note 28.
637   Ali Alichi, Kory Kantenga, and Juan Solé, "Income Polarization in the United States," *IMF Working Paper*, WP/16/121 (June 2016), at 5.
638   *Ibid.*, at 5–8. The low-income group is comprised of households with less than 50 percent of the median income; the middle-income group, households with 50–150 percent of median income; and the high-income group, households with more than 150 percent of median income. Household income is divided by its size using OECD's equivalence scale. *Ibid.*, note 6. According to another study, the income share of middle-income households fell from 62 percent in 1970 to 43 percent in 2018. Pew Research Center, *Trends in Income and Wealth Inequality* (January 9, 2020), available online at: www.pewsocialtrends.org/2020/01/09/trends-in-income-and-wealth-inequality/#fnref-27657-5; https://perma.cc/SLX7-V49M. The middle-income group is categorized differently in this study: it includes households with annual incomes that are two- thirds to double the median family income after incomes have been adjusted for household size and the local cost of living. *Id.*
639   Alichi, Kantenga, and Solé (2016), *supra* note 637, at 4.

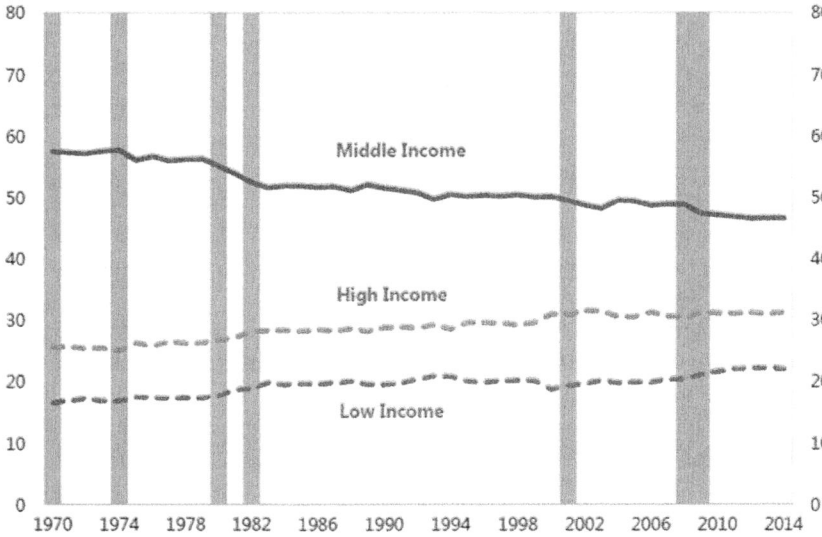

Figure 6.8 Number of households by income group, 1970–2014 (percentage).[640]

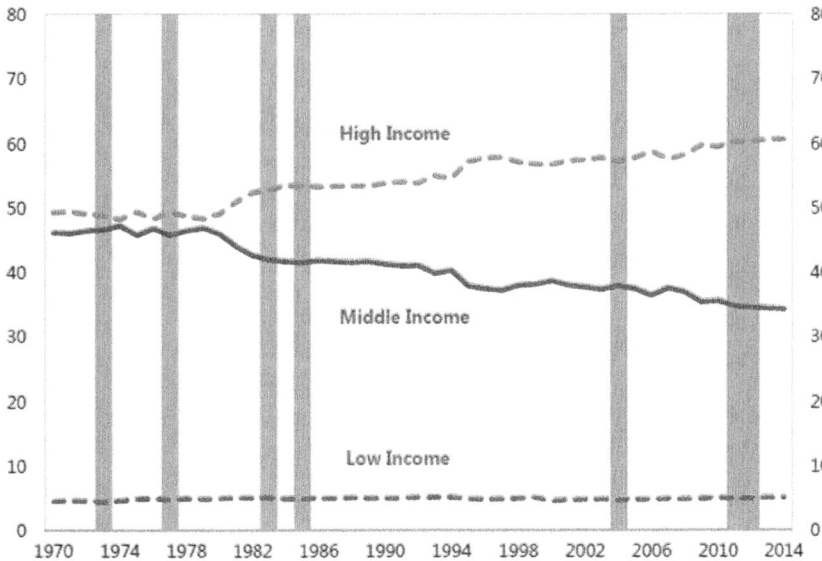

Figure 6.9 Income shares by income group, 1970–2014 (percentage).[641]

640 *Ibid.*, at 5.
641 *Ibid.*, at 8.

The polarization has continued in a deteriorating trend; while more middle-income households rose into the high-income group than fell to the low-income group during 1970–2000, that trend is now reversed since 2000; only 0.25 percent of households have moved up to the high-income group compared to 3.25 percent of the middle-income households who have moved down to the low-income group.[642] With the stagnation of income growth for middle- and low-income groups, the majority of U.S. households have experienced sluggish income growth since the 1970s.

Economic polarization presents a significant structural problem in the economy, as it lowers the level of real consumption for the whole economy, which in turn suppresses economic growth.[643] This is because low- and middle-income households spend a larger share of their income, compared to high-income household spending, to meet their cost of living ("higher propensity to consume"). Therefore, the stagnant income growth in these two income groups and the shrinking middle-income households means weakening consumption, which further explains stagnant economic growth over the years.

6.2.3 Call for a new approach

Regional economic disparity and structural issues in the U.S. economy, characterized by stagnant growth and economic polarization, are major economic impediments that call for a new approach—one which addresses the actual causes of such impediments. As discussed in the previous sections, the causes of regional economic disparity, stagnant growth, and economic polarization include insufficient education and training, particularly for those on the lower end of the economic ladder; lack of infrastructure, isolating many areas from economic centers; income inequality, weakening the aggregate demand level; the downward trend for investment growth; stagnant population growth, eroding the consumer base and supply of labor for the future; excessive debts owed by the public, suppressing consumption;[644] and changes in technology, reducing the need for labor.[645]

These causes are diverse, multifaceted, and interconnected. There are legal and institutional frameworks in place to promote economic development, but they have proven to be insufficient. For example, the Public Works and Economic Development Act (PWEDA) authorizes the provision of federal grants, loans, and other types of assistance to support businesses in economically distressed

---

642 *Ibid.*, at 5.

643 *Ibid.*, at 2.

644 United Nations, "Low Growth with Limited Policy Options? Secular Stagnation—Causes, Consequences and Cures," *Development Issues*, no. 9 (March 1, 2017), at 3, available online at: www.un.org/development/desa/dpad/wp-content/uploads/sites/45/publication/dsp_policy_09.pdf; https://perma.cc/U43H-5P83.

645 Yong-Shik Lee, "Sung-Hee Jwa, A General Theory of Economic Development: Towards a Capitalist Manifesto—A Critical Review" (2017) 10(2) *Law and Development Review* 643–657, at 653–654.

areas[646] for job creation and economic growth.[647] The Economic Development Administration (EDA), established under the authority of PWEDA, is currently the only federal agency focused exclusively on economic development.[648] The EDA works with local economic development officials and provides grants for relatively small-scale development projects,[649] including public works in economically distressed areas, regional innovation strategies, partnership planning, economic and trade adjustment assistance, and research and evaluation programs.[650]

As a small agency under the Department of Commerce, the EDA's mandate is limited, and it does not have the institutional status, authority, or budget to address the cited causes of the United States' economic problems; it is incapable of coordinating effectively with federal, State, local, and private actors on a scale that is necessary to tackle the causes of economic problems at the national level. Other federal government departments and agencies, such as the Department of Agriculture and the International Trade Administration under the Department of Commerce, also have programs to assist agricultural and industrial producers, but their jurisdiction is limited to specific areas, without the authority to address causes of the economic problems across the board.

To address these causes effectively, there is a need for stronger and more comprehensive institutional and legal frameworks targeting them and focusing on economic development. The purpose of such frameworks is to facilitate effective cooperation and coordination across the different levels of government and between the government and private sector. The necessity of adopting this new approach arises from the failures in such coordination and cooperation. For example, the federal effort to establish an efficient trucking network was impeded by individual States' attempts to impose their own regulations.[651] The federal government tried to strike down varied State regulations and set a uniform standard in the trucking industry by applying Supreme Court decisions, but State

646 Sections 301(a)(1) and 301(a)(2) of PWEDA provide that an area is economically distressed if it has a per capita income of 80 percent or less of the national average or an unemployment rate that is, for the most recent 24-month period for which data are available, at least 1 percent greater than the national average unemployment rate. 42 U.S.C. § 3161. An area that does not meet the criteria in section 301(a)(1) or 301(a)(2) of PWEDA may still be considered economically distressed if it meets the special need criteria under 301(a)(3) of PWEDA. *Id.*

647 Public Works and Economic Development Act of 1965 (PWEDA), as amended, 42 U.S.C. § 3121 *et. seq.*

648 *Ibid. C.f.,* the Appalachian Regional Commission is established at the regional level under the authority of the Appalachian Redevelopment Act of 1965 to facilitate economic growth in the economically depressed Appalachian region. 40 U.S.C. § 14101 *et. seq.*

649 In 2018, the per-project grant ranged from $2,000 to $7,110,012, and EDA supported 692 projects for a total of US$ 381 million in grant funding, averaging around $550,000 per project. Economic Development Administration (2019), *supra* note 78.

650 Economic Development Administration, *EDA Fiscal Year 2017 Budget Request At-A-Glance: Supporting 21st Century Economic Development,* available online at: www.eda.gov/pdf/EDA-FY-2017-Budget-Fact-Sheet_FINAL.pdf; https://perma.cc/2V7L-PEQQ. See also Economic Development Administration (2019), *ibid.*

651 Thomas W. Hazlett, "Is Federal Preemption Efficient in Cellular Phone Regulation?" (2003) 56(1) *Federal Communications Law Journal* 155–238, at 186–187.

governments continued to impose their own rules by interpreting these decisions narrowly.[652] This conflict continued until Congress subsequently enacted laws governing the trucking industry nationwide.[653]

Another example shows a conflict between federal and several State governments on one side and local governments on the other: the federal and State governments have endorsed fracking, a new technology adopted to extract oil or gas.[654] This technology is reinvigorating manufacturing investment, but such endorsement has faced intense opposition from local governments on environmental grounds.[655] Yet another example shows a lack of coordination between the public and private sectors: problems with real estate developments operating under the "Public-Private Partnership" model in Minnesota, New Jersey, New York, Pennsylvania, and Washington, D.C., have failed due to a lack of well-calculated coordination between public and private interests.[656] Disagreements may ensue among the federal, State, and local governments and between the public and private sectors, and the absence of effective mechanisms for their resolution is not conducive to economic development;[657] the consequences of these failures in coordination and cooperation have been enduring regional economic disparity, stagnant growth, and widening economic polarization for decades.

6.3 Applying the legal and institutional approaches in the United States

This section, drawing from the experiences of successful developing countries in the past, such as the NICs, discusses the applicability of the proposed legal and institutional approaches in the United States. These developing countries successfully lifted their economies from poverty to prosperity within a single generation, achieving the highest economic growth and the most successful economic development in history.[658] The legal and institutional approaches adopted by these countries present a useful reference model not only for other developing countries seeking success in economic development but also for developed ones today, such as the United States, experiencing stagnant growth and economic polarization.

---

652 *Ibid.*
653 *Ibid.*
654 David B. Spence, "The Political Economy of Local Vetoes" (2014) 93(2) *Texas Law Review* 351–413, at 355–357.
655 *Ibid.*
656 See Marc Scribner, "The Limitations of Public-Private Partnerships: Recent Lessons from the Surface Transportation and Real Estate Sectors," *Issue Analysis* (Competitive Enterprise Institute) (January 2011), at 15–22.
657 Such failure of coordination has also been demonstrated in the context of the recent COVID-19 pandemic. See Yong-Shik Lee, *Managing COVID-19: Legal and Institutional Issues* (November 6, 2020), available online at: https://papers.ssrn.com/sol3/papers.cfm?abstract_id=3724655, accessed December 10, 2020.
658 See *supra* note 28 (for a discussion of the NICs' successful economic development).

Among the NICs, the case of Korea is particularly helpful because it shows not only how a successful developing country maintained a high level of economic growth for over three decades but also how it was able to break out of a period of stagnation and achieve sustained economic growth. Chapter 4 accounts in detail Korea's economic achievement under arduous conditions. The country achieved one of the most successful and inclusive economic growths in history,[659] ending a period of stagnation that began in the late 1950s.[660] The study of the legal and institutional dimensions of this transformation may shed light on the legal and institutional approaches that could be adopted, despite the large differences between the two countries, to sunset the current economic stagnation, bridge the regional economic gaps, and reduce the economic polarization prevalent in the United States. As in Chapters 4 and 5, the remainder of this chapter also applies the general theory of law and development to address economic issues in the United States.

The preceding discussion has established the development objectives of the United States as bridging regional economic disparity, stimulating economic growth, and reducing economic polarization.[661] The types of law under analysis would be legislation, including statutes and regulations, and judicial precedents that are binding as law in a common law country such as the United States.[662] This section moves to the second part of the theory, "the regulatory impact mechanisms," comprised of three categorical elements: "regulatory design," "regulatory compliance," and "quality of implementation."[663]

6.3.1 Applying the general theory of law and development: regulatory design

This sub-section begins with the first element of the regulatory impact mechanisms, "regulatory design," which evaluates how optimally law is designed to achieve its regulatory objectives.[664] As discussed in Chapter 3, the assessment of regulatory design, a potentially complex task, is performed by examining three sub-elements: anticipated policy outcome; organization of law, legal frameworks, and institutions (LFIs); and adaptation to socioeconomic conditions.[665]

---

659 *Ibid.* Between 1961 and 1996, Korea increased its GDP by an average of 8.75 percent per annum. See also discussion *supra* Section 4.1.

660 With substantial U.S. aid, the Korean economy recovered from the destruction of war in the 1950s, but economic stagnation began when the United States started to reduce its aid to Korea in 1958. Korea's economy grew at a rate of 3.49 percent in 1958, but its growth rate fell to 1.63 percent in 1959 and shrank further to a mere 1.18 percent the following year. Calculated from Federal Reserve Economic Data (FRED), *Real GDP at Constant National Prices for Republic of Korea*, available online at: https://fred.stlouisfed.org/series/RGDPNAKRA666N RUG, accessed January 3, 2021.

661 See discussion *supra* Section 6.2.

662 For an explanation of common law countries, see *supra* note 17.

663 See *supra* Sections 3.2 and 3.3.

664 *Ibid.*

665 *Ibid.*

(a) Anticipated policy outcome

The first sub-element of regulatory design, "anticipated policy outcome," refers to the policy outcome that law is expected to deliver.[666] For the United States, the policy objectives will concern the economic problems that have been identified in the preceding discussion: regional economic disparity, stagnant economic growth, and deepening economic polarization. Just as Korea designed laws to meet its economic needs at the time (*i.e.*, industrial development and export promotion),[667] a similar approach could be adopted in the United States, including the enactment of laws addressing the causes of these problems. For example, the earlier discussion identified several causes of persistent regional economic disparity, including location (*e.g.*, access to ports and transportation links), infrastructure, the availability of human capital through educational attainment, and natural amenities.[668]

To address these causes, the government may adopt statutes that mandate government support to develop the necessary infrastructure, improve public education in economically distressed regions, and promote the establishment and expansion of businesses in those same regions. PWEDA has provided for some of these supports, including the facilitation of businesses in these areas,[669] but its operational scale is thus far inadequately small.[670] Specific support measures may vary and include subsidy grants, loans, and tax exemptions.[671] Consideration should be given to the appropriate level of government at which this task should be undertaken. Given the potentially large budgetary requirement for these types of projects and the limited financial capacity of State and local governments,[672] the federal government would have to assume primary responsibility,[673] but State and

666 Law exhibits a policy or policies forming regulatory objectives. *Ibid.*

667 See *supra* Section 4.2.3(a) (for examples of development-facilitating statutes).

668 See *supra* Section 6.2.1.

669 *Supra* note 649 (for a reference on the projects supported under PWEDA).

670 *Ibid.* An empirical study concluded that the overall magnitude of the EDA program's effect on changes in income growth rates was insignificant. Randolph Martin and Robert Graham, "The Impact of Economic Development Administration Programs: Some Empirical Evidence" (1980) 62(1) *The Review of Economics and Statistics* 52–62, at 62. Public investment in economically depressed areas or isolated rural areas needs to be increased. Other studies indicated that the employment impacts of public works projects in these areas were relatively large and that federal economic development programs helped rural communities to sustain, grow, and create new businesses, diversifying their economies. Richard Barrows and Daniel Bromley, "Employment Impacts of the Economic Development Administration's Public Works Program," (1975) 57(1) *American Journal of Agricultural Economics* 46–54, at 53 and Anne Berblinger, "Federal Aid for Rural Economic Development," (1993) 529(1) *The Annals of the American Academy of Political and Social Science* 155–163.

671 These were also the primary means used to support individual industries and promote exports in Korea in the process of its economic development. See *supra* Section 4.2.3(a). PWEDA authorizes grants and loans for development projects.

672 For a discussion on the insufficient State budgets, see Lucy Dadayan and Donald J. Boyd (2017), *supra* note 79.

673 Thus, this is distinguished from the approach taken by PWEDA, which stipulates that "economic development is an inherently local process, the Federal Government should work in partnership

local governments, as well as the private sector, should participate in this process. The primary responsibility of the federal government does not preclude State and local governments from setting up their own laws and institutions to meet their economic development objectives within the bounds of their available resources, provided that there is intergovernmental coordination and cooperation. The subsequent discussion examines the necessity of coordination and cooperation among different levels of government and the institutional frameworks required for this task.

Improving the regional economic disparity will have a positive impact on overall economic development, but the legal and institutional approaches could also be adopted to stimulate economic development at the national level. In Korea, the government supported the development of specific industries and exports, but given the technological and financial capacities of U.S. industries, this type of support is unlikely to be necessary.[674] Instead, legislative support can focus on identifying and promoting innovations that facilitate technological and operational transformation, enhancing productivity and competition, and generating employment and higher levels of income, particularly in the areas where private investment is insufficient.[675] The legislation may also provide a set of criteria to identify qualified innovations and stipulate the types of government support that can be offered to promote such innovations.[676] As further discussed in Chapter 11,[677] the Stevenson-Wydler Technology Innovation Act of 1980[678] is an example of such an effort—one which could be reinforced to promote economic development across the board.

The justification for government support for development-facilitating innovations is that innovators consistently tend to be undercompensated for their innovations because others may benefit from such innovations through

---

...” 42 U.S.C. § 3121(a)(4). Economic development is a national, regional, and local process, not just a local process, and the federal government should assume primary responsibility, particularly when the economy is stagnant across the nation over a long period.

674 In the 1980s, as the economy was being successfully developed, Korea also shifted legislative focus from promoting specific industries to supporting the then-robust private sector as a whole and granting assistance to industries on a more selective basis where there was a need to improve their efficiency by restructuring or reorganization. See *supra* Section 4.2.3(a).

675 The EDA has offered the regional innovation strategies (RIS) program to promote economic development projects that spur entrepreneurship and innovation, but the allocated budget for this program has been small (US$ 21 million in 2018). Economic Development Administration (2019), *supra* note 78.

676 There are several questions that must be addressed before innovation-supporting legislation could be devised. What specific activities qualify as innovations worthy of publicly funded support? How can the outcomes of such identified innovation be reliably estimated? What are the most effective means of government support? What measures should be taken to ensure that government "support" does not interfere or overlap with the private sector's own innovative efforts and to avoid waste of public resources? Should every qualified innovator be the beneficiary of government support or should there be limitations? This potentially very complex task will require much of the government's analytical and investigative resources.

677 See discussion *infra* Section 11.4.2.

678 Stevenson-Wydler Technology Innovation Act of 1980, 15 U.S.C. §§ 3710–3753.

learning and sharing without necessarily paying for their full value ("positive externalities").[679] As this could de-incentivize innovators and hamper innovation, the government has a legitimate interest in supporting innovators in their endeavors to undertake innovations successfully for the interest of economic development. Priority could be given to new and smaller enterprises that, through government support, can grow to challenge market monopolies and enhance competition.[680] The government may also support or directly engage in innovative research that could lead to technological transformation for economic development.[681]

Additionally, to promote economic growth in the United States, it is necessary to counter consistently falling public and private investments (see Figures 6.5 and 6.6), as the decline in investments is responsible for stagnant growth. The legal and institutional approaches are also relevant in this area; for instance, consideration could be given to legislation that requires monitoring of investments, allocation of resources for key public investments essential to economic development (*e.g.*, transportation, communication, and education infrastructures), and facilitation of private investments in the key areas by offering appropriate incentives (*e.g.*, tax benefits and subsidies).

Finally, laws that promote certain social development objectives may also be relevant to economic development. For example, laws that protect gender equality and the rights of minorities in workplaces also contribute to economic growth by motivating more women and minorities to participate in productive pursuits.[682] Laws that facilitate education and training, particularly for those at the lower end of the socioeconomic ladder, and laws that reduce the high costs of necessities for the middle class, such as increasing healthcare and college education costs (including debt repayments), will assist with economic development efforts. So will laws that reinforce taxation on the highest income brackets, which will counter and overturn economic polarization. Lastly, laws that support immigration and protect immigrants will compensate for the dwindling population

---

679 Jwa (2017), *supra* note 371, at 30–34.
680 The Small Business Innovation Development Act of 1982 (codified at 15 U.S.C. § 638) set up small business innovation research (SBIR) programs to assist small businesses with innovations. For a further discussion, see discussion *infra* Section 11.4.2.
681 The National Artificial Intelligence Research and Development Strategic Plan, funded by the federal government, would be an example of this type of research support. National Science and Technology Council, *The National Artificial Intelligence Research and Development Strategic Plan* (October 2016), available online at: www.nitrd.gov/PUBS/national_ai_rd_strategic_plan. pdf; https://perma.cc/V49Y-94FW. The Bayh-Dole Act of 1980 also encourages innovation by permitting federal contractors to acquire ownership of inventions made with federal funding. 35 U.S.C. §§ 200–212.
682 See European Institute for Gender Equality, *Economic Benefits of Gender Equality in the European Union: Report on the Empirical Application of the Model* (2017), available online at: http:// eige.europa.eu/sites/default/files/documents/mh0217174enn_web.pdf; https://perma.cc/ S3MV-EEJ8; Sarah Treuhaft and David Madland, *Prosperity 2050: Is Equity the Superior Growth Model?* (Center for American Progress, April 2011), available online at: https://cdn.americanp rogress.org/wp-content/uploads/issues/2011/04/pdf/prosperity_2050.pdf; https://perma. cc/UZT4-W5YL.

growth rate, which is cited as a cause of stagnant growth because of its erosive effect on the consumer base and the supply of labor for the future.[683]

(b) Organization of LFIs

The second sub-element of regulatory design is the organization of LFIs.[684] As discussed earlier, synergetic coordination among LFIs is essential to effective legal and institutional approaches.[685] In Korea, the development-facilitating laws[686] were supported by effective institutions. For example, the Korean government set up the Economic Planning Board (EPB) within the central government in 1961.[687] The EPB crafted economic development plans and coordinated and instructed other government departments on a wide range of policy measures related to economic development.[688] The EPB, like Taiwan's Industrial Development Bureau (IDB) and Japan's Ministry of International Trade and Industry (MITI), was a control center for Korea's industrial policy and economic development. In addition to the EPB, the Korean government also set up several other institutions, including Korea Trade Promotion Corporation (KOTRA), as discussed above, an agency designed to collect and disseminate economic and trade information to assist with Korean businesses.[689]

Some of these institutional functionaries, such as those that facilitate coordination and cooperation among government departments and offices, can also be adopted by the United States. Lack of coordination and cooperation among the different levels of government (*e.g.*, federal, State, and local) and between the public and private sectors has proven to impede economic projects.[690] As discussed earlier, the EDA, as an agency subordinate to the Department of Commerce, has not enjoyed the status and authority over intergovernmental coordination that the EPB wielded in Korea.[691]

Thus, the establishment of an EPB-type control center at the federal level of government, charged with the roles of overseeing coordination and ensuring cooperation among the relevant federal, State, and local governments in the formulation and implementation of economic development policies, would enhance the overall effectiveness of those same policies. This type of central coordination institution, which could be provisionally titled, "Economic Development

683   Gordon (2014), *supra* note 634, at 47–50.
684   See *supra* Section 3.2.2.
685   *Ibid.*
686   See *supra* Section 4.2.3(a) (for examples of development-facilitating laws).
687   See *supra* Section 4.2.3(b).
688   *Ibid.* The head of the EPB, who, as a deputy prime minister, enjoyed budgetary and personnel authority over other government departments and agencies. This status and authority enabled the EPB to coordinate and instruct the various government departments and agencies effectively in the implementation of economic development policies. The EPB led the economic development of Korea until its merger with the Ministry of Finance in 1994. See also *supra* note 436.
689   See *supra* Section 4.2.3(b).
690   *Supra* notes 651, 654, and 656 (for examples of failed coordination).
691   *Supra* note 688 (for the status and the authority of the EPB).

Council" or "EDC," may also be open to the participation of the private sector and invite inputs from relevant private sector players in the development and implementation of policies.[692] Consideration should also be given to the mandatory appointment of certain private sector personnel, such as industry representatives, in the EDC's decision-making body.

Given the complexity of the U.S. economy and the strength of its private sector, the EDC could not be expected to develop Korean-style "economic development plans," with specific target growth rates and industrial promotion goals.[693] The primary role of the EDC would include the development of long-term economic strategies, facilitation of intergovernmental and public–private sector coordination, and identification of the focus areas in which such coordination and cooperation will be essential. A KOTRA-type agency that collects and disseminates business and trade information would also be useful, particularly for businesses in economically depressed regions, with limited resources and information. These agencies can also cooperate with the existing State or local offices for economic development.[694]

(c) *Adaptation to socioeconomic conditions*

The third and final sub-element of regulatory design is law's adaption to socioeconomic conditions. As discussed earlier, law may not be effective if it does not conform to social, political, economic, and cultural conditions (socioeconomic conditions) essential to the successful operation of law, including social or religious norms.[695] In the context of the United States, the proposal for the new legal and institutional approaches may run counter to some of its socioeconomic conditions, such as the ideologies and established practices in the United States. First, those subscribing to the traditional liberal or neoliberal economic stance[696] may disagree that the issues such as regional economic disparity, stagnant growth, and economic polarization are problems that require remedial

---

692 At the federal level, the EDC should be granted independent status from the other departments and agencies as well as the mandate to coordinate and cooperate with them. Such departments include the Department of Commerce, the Department of Finance, the Department of Agriculture, and the Department of State (for development policies with international ramifications).

693 See *supra* Section 4.2.2.

694 These offices include the existing State and local economic development agencies. For an overview of their activities, see Norton Francis, "What Do State Economic Development Agencies Do?" *Economic Development Strategies Information Brief* 6 (Urban Institute) (July 2016), available online at: www.urban.org/sites/default/files/publication/83141/2000880-What-Do-State-Economic-Development-Agencies-Do.pdf; https://perma.cc/4MJB-JPED.

695 See *supra* Section 3.2.3.

696 *Supra* note 93 (for an explanation of the neoliberal economic stance). There were substantial federal initiatives, such as President Lyndon Johnson's agenda for the Great Society, the "New Deal" under President Roosevelt, and the Hamiltonian economic program of the eighteenth century, to improve the economy and foster industries, but the neoliberal policy stance, represented by the Washington Consensus, which emphasized individual autonomy and discouraged government interventions in the economy, became dominant since the 1980s.

measures. From this perspective, differences in economic performances and income levels among regions and individuals are natural consequences of competition in a free market economy and not a problem that justifies government intervention. Second, as to the stagnant economic growth, a study has concluded that the time for rapid economic growth in the United States has passed,[697] and now the economy faces "secular stagnation," which is a new normal state in today's economy.[698]

Third, there is a deeper cultural characteristic embedded in the American ethos that may not be consistent with this proposal. In a culture that emphasizes and values individual autonomy, the economic well-being of an individual rests primarily on his or her own effort and responsibility, not government aid in hard cash or regulatory support. The government is expected to protect individual political and economic liberties and secure fair market rules (*e.g.*, punishing a disseminator of fraudulent information on the stock market) but not to intervene in the economy and use its regulatory power to meet economic growth targets. From this perspective, the establishment of new legal and institutional frameworks focusing on economic development might be seen as an unconventional attempt to play a role that is not consistent with the traditional American expectations of government.[699]

However, public trust and confidence in the ethos and traditional policy recommendations of the establishment have weakened since the 2007–2008 financial crisis. Many Americans seem to realize that regional economic disparity, stagnant growth, and economic polarization have created obstacles to the extent that it is no longer possible for most, if not all, individuals to improve their economic well-being solely on their own efforts without systematic assistance from the government, whichever it might be. The adverse economic effect of the financial crisis and the economic hardship caused by the recent COVID-19 pandemic[700] have created momentum to develop a more active role for the U.S. government in facilitating economic development for the majority of the American population, allowing for the proposed legal and institutional approaches to be addressed in this context.

697 Robert J. Gordon, *The Rise and Fall of American Growth: The U.S. Standard of Living since the Civil War* (Princeton, NJ: Princeton University Press, 2016).

698 United Nations (2017), *supra* note 644.

699 The enactment of PWEDA and the establishment of the EDA do not deviate from these traditional expectations in that they only offer small-scale assistance for economically distressed areas with a modest budget. See *supra* note 650.

700 Congressional Budget Office (CBO) estimated in May 2020 that the gross domestic product (GDP) would be $3.9 trillion lower over the 2020–2021 period than the same year's January estimates. Congressional Budget Office, *Letter to Honorable Nancy Pelosi* (June 9, 2020), available online at: www.cbo.gov/system/files/2020-06/56395-CBO-Pelosi-Letter.pdf; https://perma.cc/E8FL-JB7H.

6.3.2 *Regulatory compliance and quality of implementation*

This sub-section addresses the second and third elements of the regulatory impact mechanisms under the general theory, "regulatory compliance" and "quality of implementation,"[701] in the economic context of the United States.

(a) *Regulatory compliance*

The second element, "regulatory compliance," refers to "compliance with law by those who are subject to the application of law."[702] For the United States, a country that is an ardent advocate of the rule of law around the world, the level of regulatory compliance is generally high, as demonstrated by its high rankings in the rule of law indexes (21st among 128 countries under the Rule of Law Index 2020 by the World Justice Project and 89.9 percentile under the Rule of Law Indicator 2020 by the World Bank)[703]—as the rule of law would not be feasible without regulatory compliance.

Despite the high level of general regulatory compliance, there is no assurance that Americans would show active compliance with the laws and policies to be adopted pursuant to the new approaches, as Koreans did during the development era. As discussed in the previous sub-section, a majority of Americans may approve the government mandate to change the economy to work for the majority of working Americans, in light of the systemic economic problems that cannot be overcome solely by individual efforts;[704] however, a substantial number of Americans are, for ideological or practical reasons, likely to remain skeptical of the government playing a more active and direct role in economic development. The refusal by Louisiana's governor to accept the State's share of a federal stimulus bill, offered in the aftermath of the 2008 financial crisis, demonstrates this sentiment.[705]

The strength of public support and compliance will depend on the initial success of the new approaches, as seen by the contrasting outcomes in Korea and South Africa.[706] If the proposed approaches yield successful economic growth, accompanying innovations and job creations, show improvements in economically depressed areas, and reduce economic polarization, then the skepticism and

---

701 See *supra* Sections 3.3.1 and 3.3.2.

702 See *supra* Section 3.3.1.

703 *Supra* note 541 (for rule of law indexes).

704 See discussion *supra* Section 6.2.3.

705 See "Jindal Rejects La.'s Stimulus Share," *The Washington Times*, February 21, 2009, available online at: www.washingtontimes.com/news/2009/feb/21/lousiana-gov-rejects-states-stimulus-share; https://perma.cc/FER7-ZUNP. States' recent refusal to expand Medicaid, for which the federal government takes up most of the cost, could be another example. Kaiser Family Foundation, *Status of State Medicaid Expansion Decisions: Interactive Map* (November 2, 2020), available online at: www.kff.org/medicaid/issue-brief/status-of-state-medicaid-expansion-decisions-interactive-map/; https://perma.cc/S2KW-8S5B.

706 See discussion *supra* Sections 4.2.4(b) and 5.2.3(b).

objections to the extended role of the government in economic development could be turned into active support and compliance, as witnessed in Korea during its successful development.[707] Given the federal structure of the United States and the traditions of local governance, it would be important to have active participation from State and local governments, as well as the private sector in the development and implementation of economic development policies and laws.

(b) Quality of implementation

The quality of implementation, which is the third and final element of the regulatory impact mechanisms, refers to the act of a state meeting the requirements of law and undertaking mandates under the terms of law to fulfill its objectives.[708] Since it is a state that implements law, "state capacity" and "political will" are two essential elements determining the quality of implementation.[709] State capacity refers to the financial, technological, and administrative capabilities of the state, including internal controls against corruption, to implement laws and fulfill regulatory objectives.[710] Political will, in the context of implementation, can be defined as the commitment and devotion of a country's political leadership to the implementation of law.[711]

The U.S. government has at its disposal the largest state capacity of all nations in terms of financial, technological, and administrative capabilities. The government may also draw upon the world's largest pool of private sector experts in most areas. Significant intellectual, technological, and financial resources may indeed be necessary to develop the economic development policies and devise the laws that have been discussed above.[712] Their implementation, including monitoring, coordination, and enforcement, will also require a substantial amount of resources, and the United States has better state capabilities than any other country to meet these needs.

What could be more of an issue in the United States than state capacity is political will. As discussed earlier, the proposed legal and institutional approaches would entail the extended role of the federal government in developing, coordinating, and implementing economic development policies. Those who advocate State and local autonomy may not support this extended role of the federal government in the economy.[713] Private sector players, particularly major multinational enterprises (MNEs), may not welcome such a government initiative, which could be perceived as an encroachment upon their business sphere (*e.g.,*

---

707 See discussion *supra* Section 4.2.4(b).
708 See *supra* Section 3.3.2.
709 *Ibid.*
710 *Ibid.*
711 *Ibid.*
712 Section 6.3.1(a) and *supra* note 676 (for a discussion of difficulties associated with such legislation).
713 *Supra* note 705 (for an example of State resistance to the federal initiative).

allocation of public resources as support for other qualified innovators). The preceding discussion has emphasized the necessity of engaging State and local governments as well as the private sector in the development and implementation of economic development policies and laws in the United States, and it is indeed up to the national political leadership and their political will to overcome potential challenges and turn initial dissenters into supporters.

6.3.3 Toward a new paradigm?

This chapter makes a bold attempt to propose new legal and institutional approaches (those adopted by the successful developing countries) to address chronic economic problems in the largest and among the most advanced economies in the world. The idea may seem provocative at the outset, but the rationale of the proposal corresponds to the economic reality on the ground. The magnitude of the problem requires direct involvement of the federal government which has due financial capacity. Given the federal structure, the federal, State, and local governments should be working in close partnership toward solving them. The policy initiatives of the former Trump administration to protect trade, infringing upon the rules of international trade under the World Trade Organization (WTO),[714] did not revive the U.S. economy but instead undermined consumer interests and the position of U.S. exporters, without resulting in job increases or economic growth.

The proposal instead suggests legal and institutional approaches that would enable more active engagement of the federal government with coordination and cooperation among the different layers of government and between the public and private sectors. Currently, different levels of government fragmentally pursue economic development without effective coordination mechanisms in place. As seen above, the current federal legal and institutional frameworks, such as PWEDA and the EDA, are inadequately small in their operational scale to meet the challenge.[715] The private sector in the United States is among the most robust and sophisticated in the world, but prosperous corporations have not offered a solution to the chronic economic problems in the United States, namely regional economic disparity, stagnant growth, and economic polarization. As seen in the earlier section, these problems are not being relieved but have worsened over the years.[716] This calls for a new approach and a new paradigm.

The proposed legal and institutional approaches are arguably this new paradigm. At the core of these approaches lies the development of a legal and institutional framework for economic coordination among the federal, State, and local governments and between the public and private sectors. This paradigm allows the government, as well as the private sector, to make strategic investments for innovation and long-term growth. This approach has been successful elsewhere;

---

714 See Lee (2019), *supra* note 598.
715 See discussion *supra* Sections 6.2.3 and 6.3.1(a). See also *supra* notes 649 and 650.
716 See discussion *supra* Section 6.2.3.

the economic achievements of successful developing countries, such as the NICs, owe more to the successful coordination function of the government and investment for innovation than anything else, including economic planning *per se* and state control over industries that have also been tried by many other (unsuccessful) developing countries. Countries succeeded in achieving economic development when they were also successful with this coordination and strategic investment. When they were not, efforts by the government and the private sector became fragmented and ineffectual, and they achieved little in economic development.[717] Should these new legal and institutional approaches be proven successful, it will expand the scope and applicability of law and development to all nations, not just developing ones.

---

717   The successful coordination in Korea and its failure in South Africa have produced very different development outcomes. See discussion *supra* Sections 4.2 and 5.2.

7 Law reform projects and Analytical Law and Development Model

7.1 Proliferation of law reform projects

7.1.1 Big business but questionable outcome

This chapter examines law reform projects and the Analytical Law and Development Model (ADM).[718] Since the 1980s, international financial institutions and aid agencies, such as the World Bank and the United States Agency for International Development (USAID), have sponsored a large number of law reform projects with development objectives such as economic growth through privatization and deregulation of the economy.[719] The law reform projects have included a wide range of law reform initiatives, for instance, to facilitate private sector growth, secure land rights (FPPRs), combat corruption, improve gender equality, and reform the judiciary ("judicial reform").[720] By the turn of the century, law reform projects had become big business; for example, the World Bank is known to have embarked on over 600 such projects by 2004 and spent billions of dollars on these projects.[721] These law reform projects have largely promoted neoliberal policy prescriptions, attempting to reduce state interference with the economy and reinforce the autonomy of the private sector.[722]

However, as discussed in Chapter 3, these projects were developed and implemented without a solid understanding of how law impacts development in different institutional, economic, social, and political contexts.[723] As a result, many of the laws and legal practices that were transplanted or adopted through law reform projects did not operate successfully in host countries or deliver their anticipated outcomes.[724] As illustrated in Chapter 2, some of these neoliberal reforms caused serious economic difficulties around the world in the 1980s

---

718 This chapter is developed from Lee (2015), *supra* note 16, section 3, at 27–52.
719 See discussions *supra* Sections 2.1 and 3.1.
720 See, *e.g.*, World Bank, *Initiatives in Justice Reform 1992–2012* (2012), available online at: http://documents.worldbank.org/curated/en/575811468175154113/pdf/707290WP0Full000Box370050B00PUBLIC0.pdf; https://perma.cc/CR77-N2WB.
721 Rittich (2006), *supra* note 49, at 221.
722 For a discussion of neoliberal policy prescriptions, see *supra* note 8.
723 See discussion *supra* Section 3.1. Lindsey (2006), *supra* note 235.
724 See discussion *supra* Section 2.1.

DOI: 10.4324/9781003090175-9

and 1990s, including the catastrophic economic outcomes of the market-shock therapy in Russia, the economic emergency experienced by many Latin American countries, and the serious economic recession in Asian countries which adopted neoliberal policy prescriptions imposed by international financial institutions to address their financial crises.[725] It is evident that "markets do not create the conditions for their own success,"[726] and law reform projects that proceed without this precaution are unlikely to succeed.[727]

The problems of the law reform projects paralleled the failures in the first law and development movement, as explained in Chapter 2, in that both proceeded with a set of hypothetical conditions for the operations of market and law, such as that the market promotes economic efficiency and overall economic welfare, and law needs to protect its functions, particularly from state interferences, and that legal order applies, interprets, and changes "universalistic rules."[728] As to the former, the economic success of the East Asian countries, which adopted market economies but implemented very different legal and institutional approaches from the liberal market prescriptions, allowing substantial state engagement in the economy, has demonstrated that such hypothetical presumptions are not always correct;[729] as to the latter, such universalistic rules do not seem to exist, not even in the West where it has been advocated. Law reform projects nevertheless proceeded with a set of unrealistic prescriptions that were imposed on developing countries, and the development effect of these projects was questionable without notable "success stories."[730]

The preceding discussions have shown that the legal and institutional developments in successful developing countries are different from the prescriptions on which law reform projects relied;[731] however, they hardly incorporated lessons from these successes[732] and did not seek to facilitate industrial development in developing countries through legal and institutional reforms. In other words, past law reform projects have not adopted the alternative approach successfully employed by the successful developing countries in the past.[733] All in all, the underlying policy directions that facilitate development, the specific ways in which legal discretion and constraints on government authorities should be lodged, and the factors that induce compliance and enable the effective implementation of laws and institutions were far from clear and uninformed by law and development studies, and law reform projects continued with the transplantation of "advanced" laws and institutions. These transplants could not take root

---

725 Trubek and Santos (2006), supra note 81, at 7.

726 *Ibid.*

727 For further discussion of the Asian financial crisis, see also Khan (2004), *supra* note 98.

728 See *supra* Section 2.1. Trubek and Galanter (1974), *supra* note 33, at 1072.

729 *Supra* note 8 (for an explanation of neoliberal policy prescriptions).

730 Santos (2006), *supra* note 7, at 295.

731 See discussion *supra* Section 3.2.1.

732 See also Ohnesorge (2006), *supra* note 179, at 224.

733 See discussion *supra* Section 3.2.1.

in many developing countries under very different socioeconomic conditions,[734] lacking the conditions essential to their successful adoption and implementation.

7.1.2 The ADM: a new approach

To improve the effectiveness of law reform projects on the ground, the general theory emphasizes the effective organization of law, legal frameworks, and institutions (LFIs) and the adaptability of law to the key socioeconomic conditions as essential components of "regulatory design," which has a determinant effect on the impact of law.[735] Thus, to improve the effectiveness of law reform projects, it would be helpful to devise an analytical legislative guide, which is to be developed from empirical studies of successful development cases, to determine an optimal set of LFIs and identify the key socioeconomic conditions for their successful implementation. This analytical guide may suggest an optimal set of LFIs in specific key areas[736] to promote economic development, with the identification and analysis of the socioeconomic conditions necessary for successful implementation. The proposed ADM is such an analytical guide. The following example shows the approach adopted by the ADM.

As readers may recall from a discussion in Chapter 3 (in the context of socioeconomic conditions) that the adoptability of select Korean laws, such as the *Code of Ethics for Government Officials* and the *Information Disclosure Act,*[737] in certain developing countries in Southeast Asia would depend on a set of legal frameworks, institutions, and socioeconomic conditions in place in the recipient countries. Thus, for the successful implementation of these laws, it would be necessary to identify and analyze the underlying conditions[738] which have enabled them to operate successfully in Korea, assess how those laws are expected to work under a different set of legal frameworks, institutions, and socioeconomic conditions in the recipient country, and determine what adjustments, if any, should be made to ensure effective implementation.

This process is potentially complex, for there may be a number of conditions pertinent to the successful implementation of laws, and it may not be feasible to identify and assess all of them. Nonetheless, the most important factors, which would determine failure or success of implementation, would have to be identified and analyzed. The recipient country will then be able to assess whether the identified key conditions also exist and determine how the missing or differing conditions on the ground, if any, would affect the implementation of the laws to be adopted. The recipient country may also consider whether it would be possible to create the institutions, legal frameworks, and the socioeconomic conditions essential for successful implementation in the recipient country and/

---

734 See Watson (1983), *supra* note 236, at 1146–1147 and Waelde and Gunderson (1994), *supra* note 275, at 349.

735 See discussion *supra* Sections 3.2.2 and 3.2.3.

736 See *infra* Section 7.3.

737 Newsis (2013), *supra* note 225.

738 The terms "underlying conditions," "factors," and "conditions" refer to the institutions, legal frameworks, and socioeconomic conditions essential for economic development.

or whether laws can be adjusted to enable their successful operation under the existing conditions of the recipient country.[739] The suggested ADM will, thus, be referential, not prescriptive, and will be distinctively different from the earlier approaches which did not give due consideration to the local conditions.[740]

7.2 Elements of the ADM

7.2.1 A dynamic analytical model

As discussed in Section 7.1.2, the adoptability of law depends on the existence of the conditions essential for successful implementation. Therefore, Cambodia, presently a U.N.-designated least developed country,[741] which was known to seek adoption of the cited Korean laws,[742] may find that the significant difference in underlying conditions makes these laws rather ineffective after its adoption;[743] the law would be more effective in Cambodia if it should fit the underlying socio-economic conditions in the country. Thus, it stands to reason that if the law as it was implemented in Korea on the subject decades ago could be identified, when Korea's economic and social circumstances may have been closer to those of Cambodia today, the former Korean law would likely be more effective in Cambodia than the laws applied in Korea today. This is because the underlying conditions in Cambodia would be closer to those in Korea when it underwent the earlier stages of economic development—a point in development that more closely aligns with the socioeconomic position of Cambodia today. For example, the level of financial and technological resources available for the government to implement the proposed law, such as those required to timely disclose requested information under the *Information Disclosure Act*, is likely to bear closer resemblance between countries going through similar stages of economic development than those in very different stages.

This suggests that the ADM needs to be dynamic, rather than static, if it is to be useful for developing countries; *i.e.*, the ADM should be able to present different sets of LFIs, adoptable in different stages of economic development.[744] It will be possible to develop such a model through empirical studies

739 This presumes that developing countries are aware of their own conditions relevant to the implementation of law and will be able to conduct their own analysis. Thus, it would be important to improve the developing countries' capacity to conduct law and development analysis. The enhanced capacity will assist developing countries with undertaking this analysis.

740 As discussed earlier, the first and second law and development movements did not focus on the conditions and realities on the ground of developing countries, which, in turn, hindered successful implementation of law reform projects.

741 For further discussion of least developed countries, see UN-OHRLLS website, available online at: http://unohrlls.org/docs/ohrlls/ldcs/Summary_LDC_Caucus_ethiopia.pdf; https://perma.cc/Z73V-6SQB.

742 Newsis (2013), *supra* note 225.

743 For example, insufficient resources, such as personnel, necessary for handling and processing such requests, may create difficulty for implementing the Information Disclosure Act effectively, assuming there exists political willingness to disclose the information in the first place.

744 For an explanation of different stages of economic development, see *supra* note 262.

of successful development cases, studying LFIs that have been successful in each stage of economic development. Korea, as well as other East Asian countries and economies such as Taiwan,[745] would be useful empirical cases for reference[746] due to their successful economic development in relatively recent decades, advancing from poor economies in the 1960s to affluent developed economies with world-class industries and advanced technologies by the 1990s. As discussed earlier, Korea went through all major stages of economic development in just three decades, implementing most of its development policies in legal forms;[747] thus, the Korean example will enable investigators to find legislative and institutional references for every stage of economic development in a relatively small, easily traceable time frame. The development cases of other countries, such as China and Brazil, could also be considered, but their cases may have limited applicability to many developing countries that do not have a comparable population and resource base and consequently have significantly different socioeconomic conditions.[748]

7.2.2 A two-step approach

Incorporating the preceding discussion, the ADM provides a two-step analytical framework, first on the LFIs that facilitate economic development as identified by the empirical studies of development cases (thus assisting with the identification of the optimal organization of LFIs discussed)[749] and then on the socioeconomic conditions that are essential for successful implementation.[750] As discussed, the ADM may propose different sets of LFIs for different stages of economic

---

745 See *supra* note 28 (for a reference on the successful development of Korea and Taiwan).

746 Successful economic development cases in other regions should also be considered: for example, Rwanda, which has developed its economy successfully for the past 20 years (economic growth averaged 7.5 percent over the decade to 2018 and per capita GDP growth at 5 percent annually), could also be studied as a case of success in the early stages of economic development. See World Bank, *Rwanda Overview*, available online at: www.worldbank.org/en/country/rwanda/overview; https://perma.cc/9QXL-LJVQ.

747 Kim (ed.) (2011), *supra* note 176. See *supra* Section 4.1.

748 Japan's development has also been studied by many, but its reference value for the ADM with respect to developing countries may be limited in that Japan was not a developing country when it progressed economically after the Second World War: Japan initiated economic development ("modernization") 150 years ago under a strong government mandate ("Meiji Restoration") and had already achieved high levels of economic and industrial development by the early twentieth century. Thus, Japan's "economic development" since the 1950s is not a case of economic development of a developing country, but that of economic recovery by an already developed country from the disasters of the Second World War, similar to the case of Germany. Nonetheless, Japan's economic and legal systems had a significant influence on the development of countries in East Asia, such as Korea and Taiwan.

749 See discussion *supra* Section 3.2.2. There will be potentially multiple sets of LFIs to be identified as helpful for economic development. As demonstrated by Dani Rodrik's work, successful economic development cases have shown that there is no single regulatory and institutional prescription for economic development. See Rodrik (2000), *supra* note 38 and Rodrik (2005), *supra* note 207.

750 See discussion *supra* Section 3.2.3.

development. The ADM may be used as a diagnostic and implementation tool for specific law reform efforts[751] as well as a scholarly enterprise to assess the organization of LFIs for economic development and the essential socioeconomic conditions, as outlined in the framework of the general theory.[752]

The following example demonstrates one possible use of the ADM in the former diagnostic/implementation mode. Suppose that a developing country is considering, perhaps from the aforementioned empirical case studies, legislative options between a set of contract law rules for the sale of goods which impose strict requirements for the formation and enforcement of a contract, including, for example, the precise description of a product to sell or buy, as well as precise price terms, quantity, and delivery terms,[753] and another set which relaxes those requirements and allows for the formation and enforcement of a contract with lesser terms, even without precise price terms, in the absence of which a "prevailing market price," among other standards, may apply.[754] Suppose also that the country is undergoing an early stage of economic development where parties to a contract typically have only limited legal sophistication and commercial experiences.

In the first analytical step described above, if the relevant empirical analysis indicates that the relaxed approach proves to be more efficient and conducive to promoting commercial transactions and economic development in the early stages of economic development[755] than the more rigid former approach would be, perhaps for the reason of limited legal sophistication and commercial experience, then the preliminary proposal will be to adopt the more relaxed set of contract law rules. This step will also require an examination of relevant legal frameworks and institutions that need to be in place to enforce contracts. Thus, if as a result of this examination, no effective court or its equivalent is found to enforce contracts, the proposed adoption of contract law would probably not be very useful. The second step goes beyond the analysis of LFIs and will look into other relevant socioeconomic contexts. Thus, if a majority of the population in that country does not normally engage in enforceable contracts, as a prevalent cultural practice, to sell goods, regardless of the existence of legal institutions such as courts, the proposed adoption of law will not be very effective due to the absence of the socioeconomic conditions necessary to support a formal contract system.

Consideration can be given, with the participation of local experts, to whether the population can be encouraged to use a contract for sales transactions (*i.e.*, adjusting socioeconomic conditions) or the proposed law can be revised to fit

---

751 Law reform efforts involve changes in LFIs (*i.e.*, reforming laws, legal frameworks, and/or institutions).

752 See discussion *supra* Sections 3.2.2 and 3.2.3.

753 This approach will be analogous to the requirements of common law contract. See E. Allen Farnsworth, *Contracts* (4th ed., New York: Aspen Publishers, 2004), chapters 2–6, at 43–410.

754 This relaxation was also adopted in commercial laws of many countries, such as the Uniform Commercial Code (Article 2) enacted by all of the States in the United States.

755 For an explanation of the early stages of economic development, *supra* note 262.

the transactional practice on the ground. For example, the law could waive a requirement that a contract must be in writing for enforcement. Additionally, adjustments of socioeconomic conditions and revision of the proposed law may be attempted at the same time for a better outcome. A cost/benefit analysis,[756] if conducted, may also reveal that the cost of adopting the law, including necessary adjustment of the socioeconomic conditions and/or revision of the law, outweighs the potential benefit, and the proposed adoption may not proceed further. In any event, the process of the ADM would be more effective with better chances of success than merely trying to transplant laws of an advanced country without consideration of the essential conditions on the ground.

The ADM may also be used to propose sets of LFIs conducive to economic development in specific key areas, including legal systems, property rights, legal frameworks for political governance, regulatory frameworks for business transactions, state industrial promotion, public health and the environment, taxation, corporate governance, competition law, protection of intellectual property rights (IPRs), banking and financing, labor, corruption, criminalization of economic offenses, compliance and enforcement, and international legal frameworks (*i.e.*, international economic law and international development law).[757] For this analysis, the ADM will first develop a common analytical framework applicable to all areas, such as one identifying common institutions that need to be in place regardless of the area, including, for example, effective state administration and judicial courts or an equivalent forum for dispute settlement, and then calibrate the framework to fit each of the specific areas, such as identifying a patent granting agency or its equivalent as an institution specifically necessary for IPRs.[758] As this is a necessary analytical step toward identifying suitable LFIs, it is effectively distinguished from the previous prescriptive attempts to transplant existing laws from advanced countries.

The second step involves determining the socioeconomic conditions essential for the successful implementation of the identified LFIs. The proposed development of the ADM will entail the repetition of this two-step analysis in each of the key areas, potentially developing separate ADMs for each of the areas. This analysis may be conducted in more than one economic scenario; for example, one for the early stages of economic development and another for more advanced stages, as LFIs tend to evolve through different stages of economic development.[759]

---

756 A cost/benefit analysis ("CBA") measures the benefit of the proposed regulation against its cost.

757 Dam provided analysis in some of these areas including legal systems, contracts, and the property and financial sectors. Dam (2006), *supra* note 23. Robert Cooter and Hans-Bernd Schäfer also addressed some of the key areas in their work, including property, contracts, finance and banking, corporations, and corruption. Robert Cooter and Hans-Bernd Schäfer, *Solomon's Knot: How Law Can End the Poverty of Nations* (Princeton, NJ: Princeton University Press, 2012).

758 See discussion *infra* Section 7.3.10.

759 For example, Korea shifted legislative focus from promoting specific key industries in the 1960s and 1970s to supporting the private sector as a whole, and provided assistance to industries on a more selective basis from the 1980s onward to meet a need to improve their efficiency through restructuring or reorganization. See *supra* Section 4.2.3(a).

This means that the analysis to be performed in the ADM would make different references in each scenario, one to the LFIs found in successful development cases in the early stages of economic development and the other to those found in the more advanced stages,[760] which may lead to the recommendation of different sets of LFIs for different stages of economic development.

To determine whether specific LFIs are expected to contribute to development, it would be necessary to develop an appropriate methodology to assess their impact on economic development. The general theory would be relevant: the ADM can be used to determine the optimal organization of LFIs and the socioeconomic conditions that support implementation, the constituent analytical sub-elements of regulatory design under the general theory. The other elements of the general theory, such as regulatory compliance and quality of implementation, in turn, can be adopted to assess the regulatory impact of the identified LFIs.[761] Discerning this impact will be a complex process that requires the elimination of various other factors, such as macroeconomic initiatives, which may have concurrently contributed to the economic changes in question.[762] As discussed in Chapter 3, the impact may not always be precisely quantifiable.[763] A set of varied techniques could also be adopted, including the methods used by the regulatory impact analysis (RIA), such as cost/benefit analysis (CBA).[764] The latter would be particularly relevant when the ADM is applied to address a specific development need because this method can help to determine whether the adoption of a particular law would be cost-efficient.[765]

The ADM aims to provide legislative guidance, again with the identification of necessary socioeconomic conditions, in specific key areas for economic development. The cited areas are not an exhaustive final list and remain open to future revision. Section 7.3 briefly introduces each of the key areas, highlighting their relevance to economic development, and discusses some of the pertinent questions and issues to be addressed by the ADM. Many of the questions have already been addressed by previous studies but are nonetheless discussed as the relevant starting place to develop the ADM.

---

760 For an explanation of more advanced stages, see *supra* note 262.

761 There are some overlaps between the general theory and the ADM; for example, compliance is one of these elements under the general theory and is also listed as an area for analysis under the ADM, along with enforcement. See *infra* Section 7.3.15.

762 This is the problem of "endogeneity," and there are econometric techniques to address the problem such as instrumental variable methods and propensity score methods. See Freedman (2005), *supra* note 251 and Judea Pearl, *Causality: Models, Reasoning, and Inference* (New York: Cambridge University Press, 2000), at 348–352.

763 See discussion *supra* Section 3.2.1.

764 For further discussion of the methodologies for the ADM, including feasible methodologies such as modeling techniques, see Lee (2015), *supra* note 16, section 4, at 54–58.

765 *Ibid.*

7.3 Areas for analysis under the ADM

7.3.1 Legal system and development

The legal system, which refers to a procedure or process for interpreting and enforcing the law, may have significant relevance to how law affects development, and the ADM seeks to clarify the impact of a given legal system on economic development. For example, for a system that places emphasis on codified statutes, such as a civil law system, the statutory framework would be a particularly important aspect of a legal device for development. The legal origin theory discussed in Chapter 2 explores how the legal system affects economic development.[766] However, in assessing the impact of a given legal system, close attention should be paid to the issue of causation so that the difference in development outcomes is not attributed to a difference in the legal origin where there may be another intervening factor, such as macroeconomic initiatives, which may neutralize the impact of the legal origin.[767] While differences in legal origins and legal systems exist, the trend of convergence among different systems should also be considered in the analysis.[768]

The ADM may analyze the effect of the legal system in a broader context. In the legal cultural context, certain forms of governmental communication and social norms may have *de facto* mandatory legal effect,[769] regardless of whether formally announced as law, and this should also be considered. For example, as discussed in Chapters 1 and 4, "administrative guidance" imposed by governments in Korea and Japan on businesses and industries during periods of economic development[770] was consistently followed, although it was not formally a "law" and did not mandate compliance by law. Compliance was nevertheless secured voluntarily because it was perceived in their local political and legal cultures as a legitimate role of the government to give such guidance.[771]

7.3.2 Property rights

Property rights have been advocated as an important prerequisite to economic development;[772] a legal right to property ownership motivates economic players

---

766 See discussion *supra* Section 2.2.3.
767 Dam concluded through analysis of relevant periods that Britain outperformed France economically from the 1970s to 1990s due to macroeconomic policy initiatives rather than any superiority of common law over French law. Dam (2006), *supra* note 23, at 39.
768 For example, in common law countries where judicial precedents form binding laws, new areas subject to regulation tend to be codified in statutes, and in civil law countries where all laws should be found in the form of written statutes in principle, judicial decisions from higher courts tend to form *de facto* binding precedents.
769 C. M. Chinkin, "The Challenge of Soft Law: Development and Change in International Law" (1989) 38(4) *International and Comparative Law Quarterly* 850–866, at 856.
770 See discussion *supra* Sections 1.2 and 4.2.1.
771 *Ibid.*
772 Dam (2006), *supra* note 23, at 129–133 and Cooter and Schäfer (2012), *supra* note 757, chapter 6, at 64–81. Hernando De Soto, *The Mystery of Capital: Why Capitalism Triumphs in the*

to engage in economic activities when these activities yield property interests, and this, in turn, contributes to economic development. All of the Organisation for Economic Co-operation and Development (OECD) countries today, which are economically advanced, protect individual property rights. At the same time, there are historical instances in which the absence of property rights did not necessarily result in economic stagnation but instead led to significant economic growth.[773] The ADM needs to identify and analyze the socioeconomic conditions that require property rights for economic development and those which enable economic growth without clearly defined property rights. Where property rights are deemed necessary to promote economic development, the institutional makeup and operational requirements to secure property rights—to the extent feasible given the particular stage of economic development—should also be examined.

Individual property rights also need to be balanced against the public interest, particularly in the context of expropriation for economic development purposes. As discussed in Chapter 8, it may be the case that in the early stages of economic development, when building social infrastructure, such as roads, is important, it would be essential to have laws that allow governments to expropriate private land for public interest under less stringent conditions than those prevailing in more advanced countries.[774] The requirements of government expropriation can be reinforced in the later stages of development when essential social infrastructure has already been built, generating a lesser need for expropriation, and appropriate compensation could more readily be made with additional resources retained as a result of economic development.[775] The ADM will also assess the manner and the extent to which individual property rights promote economic development, subject to relevant socioeconomic conditions, and examine the point of balance[776] between individual property rights and public interest in property.[777]

7.3.3 Legal framework for political governance

Political stability is an important precondition for economic development.[778] Although political stability cannot be created by laws alone, an effective legal framework for political governance, such as a constitution, can facilitate political stability.[779] As explained in Chapter 9, political stability is not synonymous

---

West and Fails Everywhere Else (New York: Basic Books, 2003). See also T. Beseley and M. Gothak, "Property Rights and Economic Development," *in* Dani Rodrik and M. R. Rosenzweig (eds.), *Handbook of Development Economics*, vol. 5 (New York: North-Holland, 2009), at 4525–4595.

773 Santos (2006), *supra* note 7, at 253–300. See also Xu (2013), *supra* note 32, at 117–142 and Upham (2018), *supra* note 5, at 88–98.

774 See discussion *infra* Section 8.4.2.

775 *Ibid.*

776 This "balance" will represent an optimal regulatory point to serve the interest of economic development in the given stage of economic development. It may also reflect a normative standard in the host country imposed by the local socioeconomic conditions on the ground.

777 See discussion *infra* Section 8.4.3.

778 *Supra* note 445 (for a study assessing the impact of political stability on economic development).

779 See discussion *infra* Section 9.4.

with democracy; while civil liberty has been considered a key ingredient for prosperity,[780] it has been historically observed that promotion of democracy, although an important value, does not necessarily lead to economic development.[781] Successful economic developments in Korea from the 1960s to the 1980s and in contemporary China show the importance of political stability, *albeit* with certain democratic deficits. The system of political governance that creates political stability may indeed differ from country to country, depending upon political needs, cultural priority, historical context, and popular aspirations,[782] and the ADM will have to consider these elements.

The ADM also needs to examine, based on local conditions and priorities, what form of political governance may bring political stability and what legal framework will be most conducive to creating political stability. As discussed earlier, some of the successful developing countries with authoritarian rule in the past have become democracies once they have achieved a degree of economic development.[783] Chapter 3 discusses the potential adverse impact that representative democracy could have on economic development.[784] Although authoritarian rule or dictatorship *per se* would also not be the answer, an argument could nevertheless be made that authoritarian rule with limited civil participation may have been justified in the early stages of economic development for its efficiency in mobilizing resources for economic development, as shown in the development cases of Korea and Taiwan; but as the economy develops and the capacity and role of civil society increases, the call for civil representation in governance increases as does the demand for democratic rule.[785] It remains to be seen whether other successful developing countries, such as China, will follow the same path.

7.3.4 Legal framework for business transactions

Freedom of contract[786] and laws that effectively enforce contracts have long been considered important for economic development.[787] On the other hand,

---

780   Hayek, *supra* notes 84 and 201. See also Jean-Marie Baland, Karl Ove Moene, and James A. Robinson, "Governance and Development," *in Handbook of Development Economics*, vol. 5, *supra* note 772, at 4597–4656.

781   Ha-Joon Chang observed that democracy tends to be an outcome, rather than a cause, of economic development. Chang (2002), *supra* note 203, chapter 3, at 69–124. See also discussion *infra* Section 9.3.2.

782   See discussion *infra* Section 9.2.2.

783   Both Korea and Taiwan achieved political democracy with full civil representation by the 1990s. See discussion *supra* Section 1.3.1.

784   See discussion *supra* Section 3.3.2(c).

785   See, *e.g.*, the political development process discussed in South Korea in *supra* Chapter 4.

786   For a discussion of freedom of contract, see *supra* note 312. Freedom of contract is considered the cornerstone of free market economies but may be restricted by public interest, such as interests associated with labor rights, minimum wages, and antitrust requirements. See Michael J. Trebilcock, *The Limits of Freedom of Contract* (Cambridge, MA: Harvard University Press, 1997).

787   Philip Keefer and Stephen Knack, "Why Don't Poor Countries Catch Up? A Cross-National Test of an Institutional Explanation" (1997) 35(3) *Economic Inquiry* 590–602, at 596. See also discussion *infra* Section 10.1.

Chapter 10 introduces an equally strong observation that formal contracts are not particularly relevant to business transactions and that the issues and difficulties arising from business transactions are often resolved informally, without reference to contractual terms.[788] Even if informal interactions and dealings are an important part of business transactions, the case may be that the existence of effective and enforceable contract law, in conjunction with effective legal frameworks and institutions, will be helpful to promote business transactions by creating predictability in remedies should "informal" recourse fail to work.[789] Thus, the ADM will identify LFIs that recognize the prevalent forms of contractual relations and provide an effective remedy for breach.

Freedom of contract may also need to be balanced against the public interest of protecting economically weaker parties and creating an equitable playing field in business relations where the parties have dissimilar bargaining powers.[790] For example, the rights of consumers in commercial relations, such as the commercial sale of goods and services, insurance products, and other financial transactions, need to be protected against more powerful corporate suppliers by mandatory rules overriding contractual terms inconsistent with this aim.[791] The government may also have to intervene in private contractual relations to meet the needs of economic development, such as cases of expropriation for infrastructure projects.[792] The ADM needs to examine this balance between freedom of contract and the public interest to determine when intervention is necessary, which may indeed be different for different stages of economic development, where the relative bargaining powers of the parties may change.[793] Beyond freedom of contract and the regulatory control of business transactions, the ADM may also address additional issues, including secured transactions, which allow asset holders to leverage otherwise economically unproductive assets.[794]

7.3.5 State industrial promotion

Economists have argued since the eighteenth century on the economic efficiency of government involvement in the economy.[795] As discussed in Chapter 11, while state-led development policies in some of the most successful development cases have been effective, as with Korea, Taiwan, Singapore, and, more recently, China,[796] many have long doubted the wisdom of government involvement in the

---

788 See discussion *infra* Section 10.2.2. Trebilcock and Leng (2006), *supra* note 134, and Gilson *et al.* (2010), *supra* note 210.
789 *Ibid.*
790 See discussion *infra* Section 10.3.2.
791 *Ibid.*
792 *Ibid.*
793 For instance, large corporations attaining significant economic and social influence in the process of successful economic development are in a superior bargaining position *vis-à-vis* individual consumers.
794 See discussion *infra* Section 10.4.
795 See discussion *infra* Section 11.2.
796 *Ibid.* See also discussion *supra* Section 3.2.1.

economy.[797] The doubts seem to have abated, however, after the financial crisis of the last decade, caused in substantial part by the absence of proper government regulation of dubious financial products.[798] Where the availability of information is limited and the financial market is imperfect (which are the inherent conditions of less-developed countries), the government can implement useful initiatives in productive industrial pursuits, as demonstrated in the cited successful development cases.[799] Adoption and management of industrial promotion policies are indeed a hallmark of developmental states.[800]

On the other hand, industrial promotion by the state, which might be useful in the early stages of economic development, may not be sustained indefinitely, and at some point, those industries promoted by the state would have to sustain themselves in the market environment without continuing government support.[801] State industrial promotion is also subject to international regulation today; the current regulatory framework for international trade (WTO legal disciplines) prohibits a range of government subsidies affecting international trade and also regulates other government measures affecting international trade, such as the imposition of tariffs, which has been used to promote domestic industries.[802] The ADM needs to clarify the conditions for successful state industrial promotion as well as the legal frameworks that enable the government to provide effective assistance to meet the development needs, which may vary in different stages of economic development.

7.3.6 Public healthcare and the environment

The provision of adequate public healthcare and a suitable natural environment are essential for successful economic development. Widespread disease and poor health caused by inadequate healthcare and an unhealthy environment are not conducive to sustaining the effective labor force essential for economic development, particularly in the early stages of development when the availability of

---

797 Lee (2016), *supra* note 102, Section 1.4, at 14–32. See also A. Harrison, "Trade, Foreign Investment, and Industrial Policy for Developing Countries," *in Handbook of Development Economics*, vol. 5, *supra* note 772, at 4039–4214.

798 For the causes of the financial crisis of 2008, see Stijn Claessens and Fabian Valencia (eds.), *Financial Crises: Causes, Consequences, and Policy Responses* (Washington, D.C.: International Monetary Fund, 2014) and Jeffrey Friedman (ed.), *What Caused the Financial Crisis* (Philadelphia: University of Pennsylvania Press, 2010).

799 Lee (2016), *supra* note 102, Section 1.4, at 14–32. See also discussion *infra* Section 11.2.

800 See *supra* note 166 (for a definition of a developmental state). See also discussion *infra* Section 11.3.

801 Thus, successful developing countries in the past reduced government control of their economies as their economies successfully developed. See discussion *supra* Section 3.2.1.

802 For instance, government subsidies contingent upon exportation and substitution of imports ("export subsidies" and "import substitution subsidies") are prohibited under the WTO Agreement on Subsidies and Countervailing Measures. Certain other subsidies affecting international trade are "actionable": *i.e.*, may invoke countervailing measures. For a detailed discussion, see Lee (2016), *supra* note 102, at 84–96. See also discussion *infra* Section 11.2.3.

capital and technology is limited, and production tends to rely on labor. The worldwide COVID-19 pandemic and the subsequent economic downturn have vividly demonstrated the importance of public health for economic development.[803] Where income levels are generally low, private healthcare tends to be more expensive than can be afforded by laborers, and some form of a public healthcare system, as mandated by law, is necessary to safeguard public health. It has further been demonstrated that the introduction of a public healthcare system had a significant and immediate effect on the dynamics of infant mortality and crude death rates, and those reductions have a positive effect on growth in per capita income.[804] On the other hand, maintaining an extensive public healthcare system is costly, and the ADM will have to undertake the difficult task of determining the regulatory balance between an ideal level of public healthcare provision and the available resources.

As for the environment, the promotion of manufacturing industries in the process of economic development may cause substantial pollution and other forms of environmental damage.[805] Conversely, however, repressing industrial activities that have adverse impacts on the environment may also harm the industrial promotion that the country may need for economic development. There is a substantial cost to protect the environment and prevent environmental damage, and the resource distribution will be a dilemma for developing countries where the available resources are limited. It will indeed pose a challenge to find an adequate regulatory balance, which may differ depending on the level of economic development and the resources available. The ADM will nevertheless need to perform this task. It has been observed that the countries that have achieved economic development have also shown a tendency to highlight the environmental issues and tighten the environmental requirements as their economies develop and their income levels rise.[806]

---

803 See World Bank, "The Global Economic Outlook During the COVID-19 Pandemic: A Changed World," *Who We Are/News*, June 8, 2020, available online at: www.worldbank.org/en/news/feature/2020/06/08/the-global-economic-outlook-during-the-covid-19-pandemic-a-changed-world; https://perma.cc/6244-VECZ.

804 Anthony Strittmatter and Uwe Sunde, "Health and Economic Development—Evidence from the Introduction of Public Health Care" (2013) 26(4) *Journal of Popular Economics* 1549–1584. See also G. Mwabu, "Health Economics for Low-Income Countries" *in* T. Paul Schultz and John Strauss (eds.), *Handbook of Development Economics*, vol. 4 (New York: North-Holland, 2008), at 3305–3374.

805 See Lixia Yang, Shaofeng Yuan, and Le Sun, "The Relationships between Economic Growth and Environmental Pollution Based on Time Series Data: An Empirical Study of Zhejiang Province" (2012) 7(1) *Journal of Cambridge Studies* 33–42.

806 Efforts have also been made to restore the environment that had been damaged as a result of industrial drive during the periods of economic development. A notable example is the successful restoration of "Cheonggyecheon" (Cheonggye River Stream) in the City of Seoul, Korea. The river stream, an 8.4 km-creek flowing west to east through downtown Seoul, was covered with concrete for over 20 years since the late 1950s for serious pollution created by the migration of people to the surrounding area after the Korean War. In 1976, a 5.6-km-long, 16-m-wide elevated highway was completed over the concrete-covered stream, and the area became an example of the successful economic development of Korea. In 2003, the Seoul Metropolitan

7.3.7 *Taxation*

Taxation has a considerable impact on development, as states affect specific economic activities through taxation. For instance, a higher tax on the consumption of specific products will discourage consumption as well as production of those products.[807] An indirect tax that is added to the price of goods and services across the board, such as value-added tax, may have an effect of encouraging savings and discouraging domestic consumption.[808] Higher taxes on real estate transactions may also discourage speculative real estate transactions; property prices, especially those in urban areas, tend to increase rapidly when the economy grows at a high rate, and such rapidly increasing prices attract a high volume of investment in real property. Speculative investments further raise property prices, which cause serious housing issues for workers relying upon fixed wages, and the governments of developing countries have responded by trying to restrain these speculative investments with high taxes.[809]

Taxation has been used to promote the activities that the government deems beneficial for economic development and to discourage those considered detrimental. For example, to promote export-driven economic development policies, some successful developing countries have adopted taxation that favors exports.[810]

Government initiated a US$ 900 million-environmental project to restore the stream, resulting in the successful recovery of the stream itself, the natural environment around the stream, and natural habitats in the area. For further details of the restoration project, see Peter G. Rowe (ed.), *A City and Its Stream: An Appraisal of Cheonggyecheon Restoration Project and Its Environs in Seoul, South Korea* (Harvard University Graduate School of Design, 2010). The Chinese government, with the resources that they now have as a result of successful economic development, is also making efforts to improve the environment, such as air quality, in major cities including Beijing and Shanghai. Liu Qin, "China's Five-Year Plan to Radically Tighten Air Pollution Targets," *Climate Home News*, November 3, 2016, available online at: www.climatechangenews.com/ 2016/03/11/chinas-five-year-plan-to-radically-tighten-air-pollution-targets/; https://perma. cc/M3GF-L3AA.

807 Nicholas Kaldor, "Taxation for Economic Development" (1963) 9(1) *The Journal of Modern African Studies* 7–23, at 17. See also E. Ahmad and N. Stern, "Taxation for Developing Countries," *in* Hollis Chenery and T. N. Srinivasan (eds.), *Handbook of Development Economics*, vol. 2 (New York: North-Holland, 1989), at 1005–1092.

808 A relevant study shows that taxing consumption rather than income generates more savings and leads to higher growth. See James Alm and Asmaa El-Ganainy, "Value-added Taxation and Consumption" (2013) 20(1) *International Tax and Public Finance* 105–128, at 124–126.

809 For example, the Korean government taxed profit generated by short-term sale of residential property at over 40 percent. National Tax Service, *Capital Gains Tax* (in Korean), available online at: https://web.archive.org/web/20200422103312/www.nts.go.kr/support/support_ 11.asp?cinfo_key=MINF5720100720165645; https://perma.cc/Z2AA-C9FN.

810 Customs-free export zones have been widely used by developing countries to encourage investment. There have been successful experiences across the Middle East and North Africa (MENA) region. See OECD, *Tax Incentives for Investment—A Global Perspective: Experiences in MENA and non-MENA Countries* (2007), at 10, available online at: www.oecd.org/mena/investment/38758855.pdf; https://perma.cc/ZKT3-XVV8. Duty drawbacks have also been used to encourage export and economic development. See Jai S. Mah, "Export Promotion Policies, Export Composition and Economic Development of Korea" (2011) 4(2) *Law and Development Review* 3–27, at 13.

In contrast, higher taxes (tariffs) have been imposed on imported products that are competing with domestic products, subject to the rules of international trade. The activities that are considered beneficial for economic development may change in different stages of economic development;[811] thus, the ADM needs to examine the modes of taxation that encourage new enterprises and productive pursuits in the given stages of economic development, as well as effective legal frameworks and institutional arrangements which enable such taxation.[812]

7.3.8 Corporate governance

The existence of business corporations that function effectively is considered an important precondition for economic development.[813] Corporate governance determines the manner in which a corporation functions and the effectiveness thereof. In the early stages of economic development, the system of corporate governance that enables corporate heads (often the founders of corporations) to make prompt decisions and readily mobilize resources that are available to the corporation may prove effective.[814] In the later stages of economic development, corporations become more diverse and complex in their activities and also attain substantial influence within society with the resources they possess and the economic opportunities they control (such as employment). Thus, a system of corporate governance that ensures transparency, protects the rights of shareholders, particularly those of smaller shareholders, and upholds corporate social responsibility would be important for sustainable development.[815] The ADM needs to identify LFIs that meet these changing needs.

A difficulty in the transition is that once corporate control is concentrated in the hands of a few, which may be disproportionate to their actual shares in the corporations,[816] and if the corporations are deemed successful, taking up a large portion of a developing national economy,[817] then there is a tendency to maintain the status quo; thus, creating a system that ensures transparency and protects the

---

811 For instance, taxation that continues to favor domestic products may become counterproductive when domestic products can compete with imported products, and competition with imported products has become necessary to improve economic efficiency.

812 See also Yariv Brauner and Miranda Stewart (eds.), *Taxation, Law and Development* (Cheltenham: Edward Elgar, 2013).

813 The majority of economic output has been produced by corporations in countries that have achieved economic development.

814 Charles P. Oman, "Corporate Governance and National Development," *OECD Development Centre Working Paper*, no. 180 (October 2001), at 13.

815 *Ibid.*, at 28. See also Archie B. Carroll, "A Three-Dimensional Conceptual Model of Corporate Social Performance" (1979) 4 *Academy of Management Review* 497–505.

816 Such control is attainable when law allows circular cross-shareholding among subsidiaries.

817 In Korea, the revenue of the ten largest "chaebols," or corporations, reached 84 percent of the country's entire GDP as of 2012. Cynthia Kim, "S. Korea Crackdown on Underground Economy Stokes Angst," *Bloomberg*, February 2, 2014, available online at: www.bloomberg.com/news/articles/2014-02-02/south-korea-s-crackdown-on-underground-economy-stokes-angst; https://perma.cc/H55Q-K2R4.

rights of small shareholders will become difficult. This means that, besides the issue of fairness associated with corporate governance concentrated in a small number of people, the corporate decisions to be made by a few could have a significant effect on the whole national economy.[818] Their decisions are likely to protect the interest of their corporations rather than that of the other smaller corporations and of the entire economy and may not be conducive to sustainable economic development.[819] Thus, the ADM also needs to examine, with references to the empirical cases, the LFIs, as well as the necessary socioeconomic conditions, which facilitate the needed transition in corporate governance.

7.3.9 Competition law

Competition law is another key area in which study needs to be undertaken in relation to economic development.[820] Anti-competitive behavior, which reduces market competition through means such as price fixing by collusion, dividing sales territories, and tying, has adverse impacts on consumer welfare and economic efficiency. Competition law aims to control such behavior. While strong competition law and its robust application may induce competition in the economy, the ADM will analyze the possible adverse development impacts in the early stages of economic development where allowance should be made for effective entrepreneurs to accumulate resources and profits without regulatory obstacles to achieve economies of scale for economic growth.[821]

This means that in the early stages of economic development, the enforcement of competition law may need to be modified in accordance with the need of the economy as a whole. However, *some* competition might still be necessary to avoid one entrepreneur taking complete control over a sector and attaining economically inefficient monopolistic control. The emergence of large corporate groups, as seen in the development cases of Korea,[822] may have a detrimental effect on competition, but those corporate groups with productive capacities and financial resources may also be useful to achieve the economies of scale, which is important for economic development, particularly in the early stages. Laws that ensure an adequate level of consumer protection will also be necessary, particularly where competition is limited by a small number of suppliers. In this vein, the ADM will examine the important role of consumer law in conjunction with competition law.

---

818   *Ibid.*
819   This has been demonstrated by the record-breaking profit increases for Chaebols in Korea since the early 2000s, while the national economic growth remained relatively stagnant.
820   For a recent study in the area, see Daniel Sokol, Thomas K. Cheng, and Ioannis Lianos (eds.), *Competition Law and Development* (Stanford: Stanford University Press, 2013).
821   Chaebols in Korea, such as Samsung and Hyundai, were allowed a degree of market control domestically so that they could secure revenue bases and increase their sizes to achieve economies of scale, which subsequently enabled them to compete internationally during the country's period of economic development.
822   *Ibid.*

7.3.10 *Protection of intellectual property rights*

The importance of IPRs has been highlighted in recent decades, particularly by developed countries with significant stakes in IPRs.[823] IPR protection has a double-edged impact on economic development. An effective IPR regime, which protects the rights of inventors and ensures financial returns for innovation, may have the effect of encouraging technological innovation and new creation, and this may be helpful for economic development. However, extensive IPR protection also presents obstacles for developing countries and start-up entrepreneurs in attaining new technology that is essential to promote economic development. Thus, it will be important for the ADM to find a regulatory balance between the need to protect IPRs and the need to facilitate new technological acquisition.

The balancing point may well be different according to the level of economic development due to the different benefit/cost ratio from IPR protection; in the early stages of economic development, inexpensive access to advanced technology may prove more beneficial for economic development than the gains from IPR protection.[824] IPR protection has been enforced through international regulatory frameworks such as the Trade-Related Aspects of Intellectual Property (TRIPS) Agreement. WTO member states, including developing country members, are required to protect IPRs, as stipulated in the TRIPS Agreement, through domestic legislation.[825] Questions have been raised as to the justification of imposing IPRs through the mechanism of international trade law.[826] The ADM could, subject to assessment, justify LFIs that impose a lower license fee or none at all, depending upon the level of economic development.

7.3.11 *Banking and financing*

The legal framework for banking and financing is essential for economic development, as it sets forth the regulatory apparatus for the accumulation and distribution of capital through various banking and financing devices, such as savings and loans.[827] The regulatory frameworks and practices in some of the successful developing countries in the past facilitated state control over banking and financing.[828] Through this control, the state maximized the use of available capital for industrial pursuit, with policy interest rates lower than market rates, and it also induced a

---

823 Lee (2016), *supra* note 102, Section 5.3, at 155–164.
824 *Ibid.*
825 *Ibid.*
826 *Ibid.*
827 See M. A. Kose, "Financial Globalization and Economic Policies," *in Handbook of Development Economics*, vol. 5, *supra* note 772, at 4283–4359.
828 For example, banking and financial industries in Korea were under the control of the government until the 1980s, and they were directed to provide loans to the industries, rather than individual consumers, to promote the economic development of Korea. Lee (2017), *supra* note 4, at 455.

high rate of savings by setting high interest rates and, in some cases, by restraining consumer loans such as home mortgage financing.[829]

However, some have criticized the practice as a cause for the East Asian financial crisis in the 1990s, as state control over banking and financing weakened the competitiveness of the sector and resulted in many non-performing loans.[830] "Liberalization" of the banking and financing sector has been emphasized since then,[831] but many of the liberalization prescriptions by the International Monetary Fund (IMF) also caused substantial disruptions and halted economic growth for years for the developing countries that accepted the prescriptions.[832] The ADM needs to clarify, based on research with historical references, the merits and shortcomings of the regulatory framework that allows state control over banking and financing in the early stages of economic development, as well as the adequate timing and sequence of necessary liberalization.

7.3.12 Labor law and development

Labor law, which sets forth the legal requirements of the security and conditions of employment, is an important determinant of labor mobility, which is relevant to economic development.[833] The World Bank, through its "Doing Business" project, recommends increasing flexibility in labor law to enhance economic development,[834] but it has been criticized that the suggested labor mobility is not essential for economic development.[835] The question of job security and labor protection goes beyond the economic agenda and directly affects political and social stability, and even those countries that are fully prepared to focus on economic development would not be able to entirely sacrifice labor protection just to enhance labor mobility at potentially high political and social costs.[836]

---

829 *Ibid.* See also *supra* Section 3.3.2(c) and Youngjoon Kwon and Yong-Shik Lee, "Legal Analysis of Traditional Leasehold in Korea (Chonsegwon) from Comparative Legal Perspective" (2012) 29(2) *Arizona Journal of International and Comparative Law* 263–286, at 282.

830 Giancarlo Corsetti, Paolo Pesenti, and Nouriel Roubini, "What Caused the Asian Currency and Financial Crisis? Part I: A Macroeconomic Overview," *National Bureau of Economic Research Working Paper*, no. 6833 (1998), available online at: www.nber.org/papers/w6833; https://perma.cc/J2P6-N4VS.

831 See Aparna Shivpuri Singh, "Banking and Financial System in GMS Countries, Its Relationship to Economic Development," *Policy Brief* (Hanoi Resource Center) (September 2007), available online at: http://cuts-international.org/HRC/pdf/PB-9-07.pdf; https://perma.cc/RS2G-9BFM.

832 See also Khan (2004), *supra* note 98.

833 See R. B. Freeman, "Labor Regulations, Unions, and Social Protection in Developing Countries: Market Distortions or Efficient Institutions?" *in Handbook of Development Economics*, vol. 5, *supra* note 772, at 4657–4702.

834 Alvaro Santos, "Labor Flexibility, Legal Reform and Economic Development" (2009) 50(1) *Virginia Journal of International Law* 43–106.

835 *Ibid.*

836 Lydia Fraile, "Lessons from Latin America's Neo-Liberal Experiment: An Overview of Labour and Social Policies since the 1980s" (2009) 148(3) *International Labour Review* 215–233. The author claims that a more balanced policy approach should be applied in Latin America to enjoy

In contrast, development history shows that successful developing countries have achieved high rates of economic growth without sacrificing labor protection.[837] An argument could be made that adequate job protection enhances the financial security among laborers and promotes productivity based on relative stability, provided that there exist prevalent work ethics and proper incentive for higher performance within the firm. The ADM will assess, through empirical studies, the relationship between labor protection/mobility and economic development as well as the other socioeconomic conditions that determine this relationship. The ADM also needs to analyze the cost of lowering labor protection against the gains from increasing labor mobility.[838]

7.3.13 Corruption and development

It is widely recognized that corruption is one of the most serious impediments to economic development in less-developed countries.[839] While corruption distorts economic decisions and interferes with efficient distribution of resources,[840] some of the most successful developing countries in the past, particularly in East Asia, achieved economic development notwithstanding the existence of significant corruption.[841] Complete elimination of corruption is unlikely to be attainable in most developing countries, but history has shown that economic development can be achieved *despite* the existence of corruption.[842] The ADM will explore

a more equitable growth path, such as raising the minimum wage, restoring industry-wide wage bargaining, regulating subcontracting, and stepping up labor inspection and enforcement. *Id.* Social insurance may also reduce the social cost associated with increasing labor market flexibility. Simon Deakin accounts that this was historically important in Western Europe and has become one of the mechanisms used to facilitate China's transition (correspondence on file with the author).

837 During the periods of economic growth, labor mobility, except migration from rural areas to urban centers, was relatively low in East Asian countries, such as Korea, Taiwan, and Japan, which all achieved high rates of economic growth.

838 Some of the economically successful countries, such as Japan, are known for having ensured long-term employment security during their respective periods of economic growth.

839 A study showed that corruption slows the rate of poverty reduction by reducing growth and increases income inequality. See Sanjeev Gupta, Hamid Davoodi, and Rosa Alonso-Terme, "Does Corruption Affect Income Inequality and Poverty?" (2001) 3(1) *Economics of Governance* 23–45, at 25. See also Daniel Kaufmann, "Rule of Law Matters: Unorthodoxy in Brief," *Brookings Report* (January 21, 2010), available online at: www.brookings.edu/research/reports/2010/01/21-governance-kaufmann; https://perma.cc/324Y-928D.

840 *Ibid.* See also Vito Tanzi, and Hamid Davoodi, "Corruption, Public Investment, and Growth," *in* Hirofumi Shibata and Toshihiro Ihori (eds.), *The Welfare State, Public Investment and Growth* (Springer, 1998), at 41–60; Arvind K. Jain, "Corruption: A Review" (2001) 15(1) *Journal of Economic Surveys* 71–121, at 93–94; R. Pande, "Understanding Political Corruption in Low Income Countries," *in Handbook of Development Economics*, vol. 4, *supra* note 804, at 3155–3184.

841 Vito Tanzi, "Corruption Around the World: Causes, Consequences, Scope and Cures" (1998) 45(4) *Staff Papers* (International Monetary Fund) 559–594, at 571. See also Susan Rose-Ackerman, "Corruption and Development," paper prepared for the Annual Bank Conference on Development Economies, Washington, D.C. (1997), at 40.

842 *Ibid.*

regulatory prescriptions to contain corruption to a level that will not undermine the economic development process as a whole.

The ADM also needs to analyze the socioeconomic conditions necessary for successful corruption control. The systematic reduction of discretion exercised by individual public officers may help to reduce corruption, but this needs to be measured against the potential loss of administrative efficiency, particularly in the early stages of economic development where the number of trained administrators is limited. Anti-corruption laws, accompanied by effective penal sanctions, are important to repress corruption. Likewise, the substance of effective anti-corruption laws and the process in which such laws take effect may be different depending upon the cultural practices and the social dynamics between the officials and the general public. The ADM needs to clarify, with historical references, the effective legal framework, as well as the underlying conditions, for corruption control. Successful economic development, which enables the government to increase the wages of public officials, as well as expansion of civil representation in governance, has contributed to reducing corruption.[843]

7.3.14 Criminalization and development

Most societies regulate offenses related to economic transactions, such as committing a fraudulent act causing financial damage to another. The most prevalent form of sanctions would be civil sanctions (*i.e.*, monetary damages through civil suits), but to prevent serious offenses which have a significant impact on the economy,[844] the state may also impose criminal sanction as a stronger form of penalty.[845] The scope of the economic offenses to be "criminalized" and the penal sanctions to be enforced will differ according to the local socioeconomic context; the degree of criminalization (*i.e.*, the degree to which these activities are made punishable by law) that will be tolerated by the society and the extent of the need that those economic offenses have to be dealt with criminal punishment, rather than civil sanction, will be different from society to society.[846]

843　See *supra* note 430 (in the case of Korea).

844　Economic-related crimes, such as money-laundering, damage financial institutions and reduce productivity in the economy by encouraging crime and corruption. Shawgat S. Kutubi, "Combating Money-Laundering by the Financial Institutions: An Analysis of Challenges and Efforts in Bangladesh" (2011) 1(2) *World Journal of Social Sciences* 36–51, at 36.

845　The use of penal sanctions for economic offenses is a controversial topic. Liberally oriented social scientists may support strict penal enforcement against economic violators while conservative groups appear less sanguine for criminal prosecution when the punishment of business offenders is debated. See Sanford H. Kadish, "Some Observations on the Use of Criminal Sanctions in Enforcing Economic Regulations" (1963) 30(3) *The University of Chicago Law Review* 423–449, at 424.

846　For instance, there is a trend toward criminalization of cartel conduct, and the evolution of criminal sanctions requires adaptation of agencies and practitioners to new processes and significant changes in judicial and public attitudes to the moral contemptibility of cartel conduct. See Julie Clarke, "The Increasing Criminalization of Economic Law—A Competition Law Perspective" (2012) 19(1) *Journal of Financial Crime* 76–98, at 88.

The ADM needs to measure, through empirical research, the effect of criminalization on preventing economic offenses. The ADM will also assess the impact that the criminalization of economic offenses has on economic development. Any beneficial effect should be measured against the social and economic cost of criminal investigations and proceedings on those offenses. Perhaps more importantly, excessive criminalization may cause entrepreneurs to act more conservatively to avoid possible criminal sanctions, and this may have a detrimental effect on economic development, particularly in the early stages of economic development. Finding an adequate balance will be a difficult task, and the point of the balance may vary not only by societies but also through different stages of economic development. The ADM will have to identify, from the perspective of economic development, the legal standard to define specific economic behaviors that ought to be dealt with through criminal penalties and how criminal law should be enforced against those offenses.

7.3.15 Compliance and enforcement

Compliance and enforcement have already been examined in the general theory of law and development,[847] but they may also be considered in the context of the ADM.[848] As discussed in Chapter 3, laws that are proposed to promote development will not be useful unless they are observed and enforced.[849] The degree of legal compliance and enforcement varies from one place to another,[850] and to secure the level of compliance and enforcement necessary to implement the laws, the ADM needs to analyze the legal and cultural context as well as the socioeconomic conditions and local priorities relevant to compliance and enforcement. The most effective means to secure compliance and enforcement, including institutional frameworks, need to be explored in consideration of these factors.

Voluntary compliance is more cost-efficient than enforcement and is, thus, preferable. As discussed in Chapter 3, governments are more likely to secure voluntary compliance when the public understands that it is in their interest to comply with law.[851] This requires systematic public education, and the effectiveness of such education will be, in turn, determined by the degree of general public confidence in the government.[852] Enforcement will be necessary in the absence of voluntary compliance. Consistent and effective enforcement is a difficult task, particularly for developing countries with limited financial resources and administrative control, and efforts need to be made to ensure that corruption does not lead to inconsistently selective enforcement of law, which will erode the public confidence essential to secure compliance. Prior rule of law studies and

---

847 See discussion *supra* Section 3.3.
848 See *supra* note 761 (for a note of the overlap).
849 See discussion *supra* Section 3.3.
850 World Justice Project, *Rule of Law Index* (2020), *supra* note 299.
851 See discussion *supra* Section 3.3.1.
852 *Ibid.*

reports addressed compliance and enforcement issues,[853] and the outcomes of those studies need to be analyzed.

7.3.16 International legal framework: international economic law and international development law

International legal frameworks, particularly the international legal framework for economic transactions ("international economic law") and international norms for development ("international development law"), are relevant to economic development. International economic law, including the rules of international trade under the auspices of the WTO and the rules of international monetary affairs under the IMF, binds the member countries of the WTO and the IMF, respectively, which include most developing countries, and regulates their conduct in international trade and monetary affairs. Expansion of international trade and adequate monetary management, including foreign-exchange reserve management,[854] are essential for economic development.[855] The ADM needs to analyze the rules that regulate government conduct on international trade and international monetary affairs, for they have direct impacts on the policies that can be adopted for economic development.[856]

As discussed in Chapter 12, a relevant debate endures as to whether international trade law should allow a degree of protectionism for developing countries to support their infant domestic industries for economic development or should instead promote open trade, as the current WTO regime does, as the latter ensures economic welfare and efficiency.[857] Despite popular belief, these two presumably opposing policies are not mutually exclusive, and as discussed in Chapters 3 and 4, the successful developing countries in East Asia adopted open trade policies, on the one hand, to expand exports and increase imports essential for their export industries, such as raw materials and machinery, and protectionism, on the other hand, to curtail imports, particularly consumer goods, that would compete with products from their infant domestic industries.[858] There has been further debate on the effectiveness

---

853 See, *e.g.*, World Justice Project, *Rule of Law Index* (2020), *supra* note 299. See also David H. Bayley, "Law Enforcement and the Rule of Law: Is There a Tradeoff?" (2002) 2(1) *Criminology and Public Policy* 133–154.

854 Foreign-exchange reserves refer to foreign-currency assets held by central banks and monetary authorities, and the reserves are necessary to pay for imports and service international loans. Lack of foreign-exchange reserves has caused financial crises in developing countries, and securing a sufficient level of foreign-exchange reserves is essential to maintain the monetary stability necessary for economic development. See Khan (2004), *supra* note 98.

855 Successful developing countries have achieved economic development through the expansion of international trade and increases in exports. Chapter 12, *infra*, examines the role of international trade in economic development. See also Lee (2016), *supra* note 102, Section 1.4, at 14–32.

856 See discussion *infra* Chapter 12. See also James Raymond Vreeland, *The IMF and Economic Development* (New York: Cambridge University Press, 2003); Lee (2016), *supra* note 102; Lee *et al.* (2011), *supra* note 211.

857 For the debate between open trade and trade protectionism as means for economic development, see Lee (2016), *supra* note 102, Section 1.4, at 14–32.

858 See discussion *supra* Sections 3.2.1, 4.1, and 4.2. See also discussion *infra* Section 12.1.

of supporting infant industries for economic development.[859] Notwithstanding the debate, most of the countries that have achieved successful economic development protected domestic industries from foreign competition one way or another during the periods of their own economic development.[860] WTO legal disciplines allow certain regulatory exceptions to protect domestic industries, although the regulatory treatment does not seem to be sufficient to facilitate the economic development of developing countries.[861]

International development law (IDL) refers to a set of international norms for the promotion of development. The United Nations declared the right to development (RTD) to be a human right in 1984,[862] and it is recognized that the international community as a whole has a duty to promote economic development as reflected in the Millennium Development Goals (MDGs) promoted by the U.N. with an international mandate.[863] However, scholars have not reached a consensus as to whether the RTD is an enforceable legal right and what constitutes the substance of IDL. Many, particularly those from developed countries, tend to believe that IDL is a soft law at best, and its enforcement is either unfeasible or should not even be attempted.[864] Parallel to IDL, there has been a demand for "sustainable development,"[865] which has become a significant pressure on developing countries by requiring them to take measures to protect and preserve the environment for future generations.[866]

Regardless of whether IDL should be considered an enforceable legal right or a soft law, there is consensus in the international community that economic development needs to be fostered, particularly for the least developed countries as advocated in international development initiatives.[867] The ADM will take account of this and assist in developing LFIs which utilize international support

---

859　See discussion *infra* Section 11.2. See also Lee (2016), *supra* note 102, Section 1.4, at 14–32.

860　See discussion infra Section 11.3. See also Lee (2016), *ibid.*

861　See discussion *infra* Section 12.2. See also Lee (2016), *ibid.,* Sections 9.1 and 9.2, at 270–290.

862　United Nations, *Declaration on the Right to Development*, G.A. Res. 41/128, annex, 41 U.N. GAOR Supp. (No. 53) at 186, U.N. Doc. A/41/53 (December 4, 1986). The RTD was reaffirmed by the 1993 Vienna Declaration and Programme of Action.

863　United Nations (2015), *The Millennium Development Goals Report 2015, supra* note 109.

864　A study pointed out the difficulty in the enforcement of IDL in the context of RTD:

> The value of the concept of a right is that it creates entitlements, and the entitlements are easier to enforce if the contents and beneficiaries of the right are clearly specified. In the case of the right to development, it is not clear who are the right and duty bearers, equally vague is the content of the right.

Yash Ghai, "Whose Human Right to Development?" *Human Rights Unit Occasional Papers* (Commonwealth Secretariat) (November 1989), at 12.

865　See *supra* note 9 (for a discussion of sustainable development).

866　See Yong-Shik Lee, "Reflections on Sustainable Development: A Note on Current Development" (2019) 9 *KLRI Journal of Law and Legislation* 193–204.

867　See, *e.g.*, United Nations (2015), *The Millennium Development Goals Report 2015, supra* note 109; United Nations Conference on Trade and Development (UNCTAD), *Achieving the Sustainable Development Goals in the Least Developed Countries* (2018), available online at: https://unctad. org/system/files/official-document/aldc2018d4_en.pdf; https://perma.cc/8S49-2864.

for development, including laws that mandate advance planning and monitoring to ensure proper use of the resources provided by international development agencies for economic development.

In closing this chapter, a short concluding remark on the ADM is due. The ADM is an innovative new approach—an approach that represents a step away from the prescriptive approach of attempting to transplant "advanced laws" from developed countries. The prescriptive approach has proven to be ineffective in recipient countries with dissimilar socioeconomic conditions and different legal and institutional frameworks in place.[868] Extensive research needs to be conducted to develop the proposed ADM; the research will have to identify and analyze the LFIs of successful developing countries that have been found effective in bringing economic development in each of the key areas discussed above and the socioeconomic conditions essential for their implementation. The magnitude of this task will be substantial and could take many years to complete, but it will be a necessary endeavor to develop an analytical framework that will improve the effectiveness of law reform efforts on the ground.[869] A pragmatic approach, rather than one embedded in fixed ideologies,[870] will also be necessary for the successful undertaking of this task.

---

868 See discussion *supra* Section 7.2.
869 Given the magnitude of the task, interest and support from major development-related funding agencies and foundations, such as the World Bank, would greatly assist with this endeavor.
870 Examples may include rigid neoliberal approaches that advocate certain types of policies, such as deregulation and privatization, without due consideration of the economic realities on the ground, including different stages of economic development.

Part III

Law and development analysis

8 Property rights and economic development

The next five chapters in Part III, a new addition to this edition, provide an account of "law and development analysis" in several key areas relevant to economic development, including property rights (Chapter 8), political governance (Chapter 9), domestic legal frameworks for business transactions (Chapter 10), state industrial promotion (Chapter 11), and international legal frameworks (Chapter 12). The LFIs in these areas significantly impact economic development, and these chapters examine their effect on economic development.

8.1 Property rights and economic development: a controversy

This chapter examines the relationship between property rights and economic development.[871] It is widely accepted that property rights are a necessary condition for economic development.[872,873] Numerous leading scholars, such as Ronald Coase, Kenneth Dam, Robert Cooter, Hans-Bernd Schäfer, Hernando De Soto, Harold Demsetz, Douglass North, Timothy J. Besley, and Maitreesh Ghatak, have underscored the importance of property rights for economic development.[874] Property ownership is often seen as a stepping stone to building

---

871 This chapter is adapted from the author's article, "Property Rights and Economic Development" (2020) 14(1) *Review of Institution and Economics*, 25–64.

872 See *supra* note 68 (for the concept of economic development).

873 Ronald H. Coase (1960), *supra* note 205; Dam (2006), *supra* note 23, at 129–133; Cooter and Schäfer (2012), *supra* note 757 at 64–81; De Soto (2003), *supra* note 772; Harold Demsetz, "Toward a Theory of Property Rights" (1967) 57 *American Economic Review* 347–359; Douglass C. North, *Structure and Change in Economic History* (New York: Norton, 1981); Besley and Gothak (2009), *supra* note 772. For the concept of economic development, see *supra* note 68.

874 *Ibid*. However, Hans-Bernd Schäfer has criticized the term property rights as being imprecisely defined. He opines, "The concept of property rights has led to a change in the approach to the problem within the economic sciences and has led to the elimination of several inadmissible theoretical simplifications in economics. However, it has not remained without criticism. As a jurisprudential research term, "property right" is very unspecific. Thus, this concept does not distinguish between absolute and relative rights. The former protect the right holder against everyone, the latter only against certain persons, usually contractual partners. "Property Right" can therefore by no means be translated as "ownership." The concept does not distinguish between constitutional rights (*e.g.*, fundamental rights) and post-constitutional rights (*e.g.*,

DOI: 10.4324/9781003090175-11

personal wealth, and thus, the right to property ownership motivates economic players to engage in commercial, industrial, and business activities, when these activities yield property interests. This increased engagement of the economy, in turn, contributes to economic development. The validity of this proposition has empirical support. For example, all of the OECD countries today, which are economically advanced, protect individual property rights. Some of the countries that achieved the most successful development, such as South Korea, Taiwan, and Singapore,[875] also ensured legal protection of property rights during their respective periods of development (although they dispossessed some traditional landowners in the course of land reform and may have had weaker protection of intellectual property rights until the 1980s). The safeguarding of property rights has become a standard development policy prescription by intergovernmental development organizations and national development agencies.[876]

However, the reality for developing countries seems more complex, and there are historical instances in which the absence of property rights did not necessarily result in economic stagnation but instead led to significant economic growth and development.[877] Conflicting with the mainstream view that property rights are essential for economic development, economic development has occurred, in certain instances, by breaching the existing property rights (which Frank Upham called "creative destruction").[878] Reports also document a possible adverse impact of property rights, where such rights have impeded economic development and social peace rather than promoting them.[879] These conflicting accounts suggest that the socioeconomic conditions[880] under which property rights promote economic development and those under which economic growth occurs without clearly defined property rights vary and need to be identified.

Section 8.2 discusses the protection of formal private property rights (FPPRs). Section 8.3 examines the mainstream view as well as dissents and analyzes whether FPPRs are a prerequisite to economic development. Lastly, Section 8.4 examines the point of balance between individual property rights and public interest in property.[881] Individual rights to property need to be balanced against the public interest; for example, the government may limit FPPRs by permitting

patent law). Finally, it does not distinguish between public and private law restrictions on action or between mandatory and non-mandatory legal positions. This broad generalization implies that it is of limited use for further analyses" (correspondence on file with the author).

875 See *supra* note 28 (for a discussion of the rapid economic development of South Korea, Taiwan, and Singapore).

876 The World Bank, for instance, rates property rights and rule-based governance of each country. See World Bank, *CPIA Property Rights and Rule-Based Governance Rating*, available online at: https://data.worldbank.org/indicator/IQ.CPA.PROP.XQ; https://perma.cc/3QLT-XW9Y.

877 Santos (2006), *supra* note 7, at 253–300. See also Xu (2013), *supra* note 32, at 117–142 and Upham (2018), *supra* note 5, at 88–98.

878 Upham (2018), *supra* note 5, at 88–98.

879 Upham (2015), *supra* note 5, and Xu (2013), *supra* note 32, at 119.

880 See *supra* note 233 (for a definition of socioeconomic conditions).

881 This "balance" will represent the optimal regulatory point, at which the interest of economic development in the given stage of economic development will be best served. It may also reflect a normative standard in the host country, imposed by the local socioeconomic conditions.

expropriation for a public objective, including economic development. In the early stages of economic development,[882] when it is important to build critical social infrastructure, such as roads, it would be essential to have laws that allow governments to expropriate private land for public interest under less stringent conditions than those prevailing in more advanced countries. The requirements of government expropriation can be tightened in the later stages of development when building additional social infrastructure is less necessary and more resources, including those available for compensation, are available.

8.2 Protection of formal private property rights

8.2.1 Origin and development

This section examines, in the context of development, property rights—referring to the rights of an individual to property—those rights which an owner can defend against everyone and which consequently impose a duty on everyone to observe them, including the rights to own, possess, and dispose of property, guaranteed by law and enforced by the state.[883] These FPPRs are distinguished from collective or communal rights, which are recognized and enforced by custom and convention. Larissa Katz also explains that FPPRs are those that the state recognizes, defines, and enforces, emphasizing the role of the state.[884] FPPRs are protected and enforced in most countries today, including all OECD countries, *albeit* with some limitations.[885] Even in communist or socialist economies, economic reform often entailed expanding private property rights, although the government may not have formally denounced state ownership of property.[886] FPPRs are the backbone of a market economy, only limited by public policy such as expropriation for public interest.[887] In the legal order, FPPRs take up a premier position, as demonstrated by constitutional protections, major statutory protections (such as large sections containing property provisions found in various countries' civil codes), and a large body of judicial precedents (particularly in the common law system) that serves to recognize and protect FPPRs.[888]

---

882 See *supra* note 262 (for a discussion of the stages of economic development).

883 See also Xu (2013), *supra* note 32, at 118.

884 Larissa Katz, "Governing through Owners: How and Why Formal Private Property Rights Enhance State Power" (2012) 160 *University of Pennsylvania Law Review* 2029–2059, at 2033 note 12.

885 A few countries that remain communist or socialist economies place limits on private property rights. For example, North Korea does not grant its nationals full property rights, including the right to own real estate, although communist countries would enforce the property rights associated with movables, such as bicycles.

886 See Gang Taek Im and Sung Chul Kim, "Unofficial Undertaking of Property Rights in North Korea (in Korean)," Research Report 03–19, Korea Unification Research Institute (2003), available online at: http://repo.kinu.or.kr/bitstream/2015.oak/712/1/0000598245.pdf; https://perma.cc/EB9Q-2NA4.

887 See discussion *infra* Section 8.4.

888 Civil codes typically include large sections with provisions that recognize, classify, and protect FPPRs. For the judicial cases, see, *e.g.*, Joseph William Singer and Bethany R. Berger, *Property Law: Rules, Policies, and Practices* (Aspen Publisher, 2017).

FPPRs can be traced to ancient times: Roman law recognized private ownership of property;[889] in Ancient Egypt, private property ownership was prevalent to the point that even slaves were allowed to own property under certain circumstances.[890] In a state of open access where everyone shares resources and properties, private property rights cannot prevail. However, the development of commercial interest for individuals and competition among those commercial interests led to the organic development of FPPRs. For example, native tribes inhabiting Canada's Labrador Peninsula, who used to live and hunt on common property, developed a system of private hunting territories allocated to individual families in response to increased demand for fur by Europeans.[891] The families' rights to the allocated territories were exclusive, and they had the right to retaliate against trespassers.[892] Individual property rights have evolved in every major civilization, although the form, extent, and manner in which societies, and eventually states, recognized and enforced individual property rights have varied significantly; in some places, such as Europe and North America, private property rights have been "formalized" through legal stipulation and state enforcement.

FPPRs, as we understand them today, developed as an important element of both the civil law system in Europe and the common law system in England and, with the West's rise to global prominence, began to influence the rest of the world (although elements of FPPRs by that time already existed in many other parts of the world).[893] Douglass North and Robert Thomas attributed the rise of the Western world to the creation and development of effective private ownership.[894] Hernando De Soto also found that the inadequate protection of FPPRs was a cause of prevalent poverty and lack of economic development in the Third World.[895] He considered this inadequate protection a major impediment to accumulating capital, which is necessary for economic growth and prosperity:[896]

> [T]hey [those in developing countries] hold these resources in defective forms: houses built on land whose ownership rights are not adequately recorded, unincorporated businesses with undefined liability, industries

---

889 See Rafael Domingo, "The Law of Property in Ancient Roman Law" (June 2017), available online at: https://papers.ssrn.com/sol3/papers.cfm?abstract_id=2984869, accessed October 12, 2020.

890 "Egyptian Law," *Encyclopaedia Britannica*, available online at: www.britannica.com/topic/Egyptian-law; https://perma.cc/5TK9-8D48.

891 See James E. Krier, "Evolutionary Theory and the Origin of Property Rights" (2009) 95 *Cornell Law Review* 139–159, at 140.

892 *Ibid.*

893 See Domingo (2017), *supra* note 889.

894 Douglass C. North and Robert Paul Thomas, *The Rise of the Western World: A New Economic History* (New York: Cambridge University Press, 1973), cited in Xu (2013), *supra* note 32, at 118.

895 De Soto (2003), *supra* note 772. Frank Upham argued that De Soto also advocated for the destruction of the landowner's FPPRs by transferring them to squatters occupying the land informally (correspondence on file with the author).

896 De Soto (2003), *supra* note 772.

located where financiers and investors cannot see them. Because the rights to these possessions are not adequately documented, these assets cannot readily be turned into capital, cannot be traded outside of narrow local circles where people know and trust each other, cannot be used as collateral for a loan, and cannot be used as a share against an investment.

In the West, by contrast, every parcel of land, every building, every piece of equipment, or store of inventories is represented in a property document that is the visible sign of a vast hidden process that connects all these assets to the rest of the economy. Thanks to this representational process, assets can lead an invisible, parallel life alongside their material existence. They can be used as collateral for credit. The single most important source of funds for new businesses in the United States is a mortgage on the entrepreneur's house. These assets can also provide a link to the owner's credit history, an accountable address for the collection of debts and taxes, the basis for the creation of reliable and universal public utilities, and a foundation for the creation of securities (like mortgage-backed bonds) that can then be rediscounted and sold in secondary markets. By this process the West injects life into assets and makes them generate capital.[897]

De Soto's argument is subject to criticism, including a counter-argument that capital necessary to facilitate economic development could be and has been formed without FPPRs.[898] There are indeed cases of successful development absent enforceable FPPRs, as discussed in the following section, where the state played an active role in mobilizing capital for investment and industrial development without leveraging private assets. Nonetheless, the proposition that FPPRs are a prerequisite to economic growth and prosperity has been widely accepted.[899]

8.2.2 Historical challenge

By the late nineteenth century, FPPRs had become well established in the West and some other parts of the world under the colonial influence of the West. FPPRs were an integral part of the capitalist market economies. Amid the capitalist prosperity, the harsh economic conditions for laborers at the time gave rise to communism. Communism presented the most significant challenge to FPPRs, as it treated private property ownership and its protection through FPPRs as the cause of social inequality that led to social and economic decay.[900] The communist utopia is based on the idea of common ownership and equal distribution,[901]

---

897 *Ibid.,* at 6.
898 See Robert Skidelsky, "The Wealth of (Some) Nations," *The Books, New York Times on the Web* (December 24, 2000), available online at: http://movies2.nytimes.com/books/00/12/24/reviews/001224.24skidelt.html; https://perma.cc/EWG8-CZR2.
899 *Supra* note 873.
900 For the account of communism, see Karl Marx, Friedrich Engels, *et al., Capital* (Digireads.com Publishing, 2017).
901 *Ibid.*

rendering FPPRs incompatible with communist ideals. In reality, however, private property rights could not have been entirely eliminated in the communist countries; individuals had either *de jure* or *de facto* rights to some forms of property, including personal items and dwelling houses,[902] although individual ownership was not allowed for large-scale production facilities.

The communist challenge to FPPRs emerged not only from its ideological construct but also from actual economic performance. Contrary to the popular perception of economic inefficiency associated with communism, the communist economies achieved rapid economic development. For example, the Soviet Union and North Korea achieved substantial growth and underwent transformative changes in their economies—transitioning from agrarian to industrial-based systems—in a relatively short period (the Soviet Union in the 1930s and North Korea in the 1950s and 1960s), but without capitalist markets backed by FPPRs.[903] Tables 8.1 and 8.2 indicate the significant growth of national income and industrial output during these periods.

Table 8.1 Soviet industrial production and national income, 1928–1940[904]

Year	National income	Industrial output
1928	21.8	25.0
1937	95.5	96.3
1940	137.5	125.5

Note: Billion rubles at unchanged prices of 1926/1927.

Table 8.2 Average annual growth rates of North Korea, 1946–1960[905]

Year	1946		1949		1953		1956		1960
National income	100	(27.8)	209	(–7.6)	145	(30.0)	319	(20.4)	683
Gross industrial product	100	(49.9)	337	(–10.5)	216	(41.0)	605	(36.6)	2105

Note: Average annual growth percentage rate in parenthesis.

902 See, *e.g.*, Soviet Constitution 1977, art. 13.
903 Yong-Shik Lee, "Sung-Hee Jwa, A General Theory of Economic Development: Towards a Capitalist Manifesto – A Critical Review" (2017) 10(2) *Law and Development Review* 643–657, at 651.
904 Naum Jasny, *The Soviet Economy During the Plan Era* (Stanford: Stanford University, 1951), at 7. Industrial production is gross output, including double-counted intermediate products; national income is gross output, less intermediate consumption.
905 Hong Taek Jeon, "Economic Growth of North Korea: 1945–1995" (1995) 1 *Journal of Economic Development* 77–105, at 85. The North Korean economy continued to grow in the 1960s, at an average rate of 8.9 percent annually for national income during 1961–67 and 12.8 percent annually for gross industrial output. Joseph Sang-Hoon Chung, "North Korea's 'Seven Year Plan' (1961–70): Economic Performance and Reforms" (1972) 12(6) *Asian Survey* 527–545, at 518, Table 1.

The economic development in the Soviet Union continued for decades until the 1970s, and its success was also influential outside the communist bloc. For example, the economic development of the Soviet Union is known to have been an inspiration for Rostow's theory of stages of economic growth.[906] The Soviet model influenced the development of dualistic economies by Arthur Lewis[907] and also served as a development model for many other developing countries, including China and India.[908] The economic achievement of North Korea was also internationally recognized and endorsed, as demonstrated by an account of leading scholars such as Joan Robinson, a Cambridge economist.[909]

As history witnessed, however, the economic growth of the communist countries, including the Soviet Union and North Korea, was not sustained after the 1970s. Their economic growth consistently declined thereafter, as illustrated below (Figures 8.1 and 8.2).

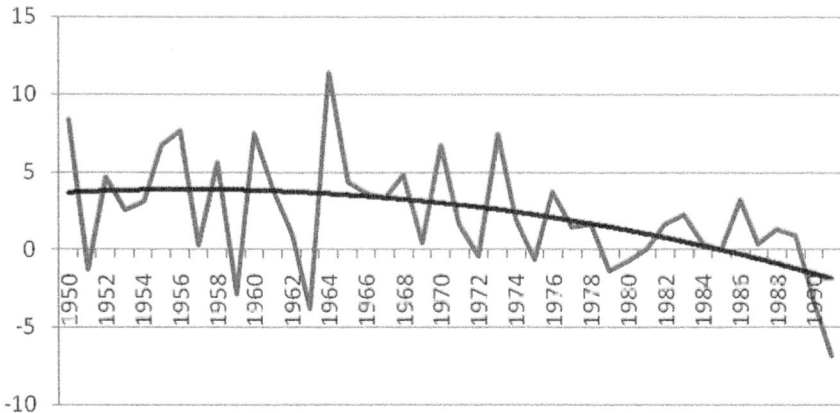

Figure 8.1 The Soviet Union GDP per capita growth rate (percentage).[910]

906 Anton Cheremukhin, Mikhail Golosov, Sergei Guriev, and Aleh Tsyvinski, "Was Stalin Necessary for Russia's Economic Development?", *NBER Working Paper*, no. 19425 (September 2013), at 1, available online at: https://economics.yale.edu/sites/default/files/files/Faculty/Tsyvinski/stalin_wp.pdf; https://perma.cc/SEX3-VVZQ.
907 Douglas Golin, "The Lewis Model: A 60-Year Retrospective" (2014) 28(3) *Journal of Economic Perspectives* 71–88.
908 *Ibid.*
909 Joan Robinson, "Korean Miracle" (1965) 16(9) *Monthly Review* 541–549.
910 A. Maddison, The World Economy, Volume 2: Historical Statistics (Paris: OECD, 2006), at 478–479.

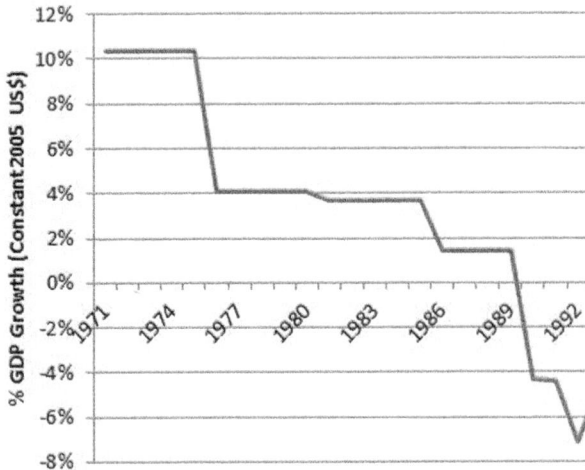

Figure 8.2 North Korea GDP growth rate.[911]

Economic problems, such as economic stagnation, provided an impetus for the fall of the communist bloc.[912] The failure to sustain and enhance productivity, as well as bureaucratic inefficiencies associated with the communist rule, and burdensome military spending, were cited as causes of this economic downfall.[913] The lack of FPPRs and the widespread state ownership may have also contributed to the outcome by causing a significant loss of economic efficiency and welfare.[914] Despite this eventual failure, the decades of successful development without strong enforcement of FPPRs,[915] exhibited by the Soviet Union, North Korea, and other countries (such as China since the 1980s), beg questioning the necessity of FPPRs as a prerequisite to successful economic development.

8.2.3 FPPRs in the development context

Concluding this section, it is necessary to identify the relevant discussion points on FPPRs in the context of economic development. First, the existence of the conflicting scenarios, which seems to suggest that FPPRs may not always be a prerequisite to economic development, necessitates an examination of both the cases for and against FPPRs as a facilitator of economic development. The first two sub-sections in Section 8.3 provide these discussions. Second, leading scholars,

---

911 United Nations, *National Accounts Main Aggregates Database*, available online at: https://unstats.un.org/unsd/snaama/countryprofile; https://perma.cc/LF7T-GBPU.
912 Archie Brown, *The Rise and Fall of Communism* (HarperCollins Publishers, 2009).
913 *Ibid.*
914 Richard Pipes, *Property and Freedom* (London: The Harvill Press, 1999).
915 See discussion *infra* Section 8.3.

such as Frank Upham, indicate that FPPRs could inhibit, rather than promote, economic development and even cause social turmoil and injustice.[916] The next section also examines the possible cause of this adverse outcome and how such a consequence could be avoided. Yet where FPPRs are found to facilitate economic development, it is also necessary to examine institutional arrangements and other socioeconomic conditions[917] that should be in place before FPPRs can function and promote economic development.

There is also an observation that development at times necessitates breach of the existing FPPRs ("creative destruction").[918] For example, successful land reform in East Asia and elsewhere redistributed land that had been lawfully owned by local masters to individual farmers, often providing the previous landowners with a small token of compensation or no compensation at all (in contravention of the existing FPPRs).[919] There are also American cases that approved certain breaches of local property rights (*e.g.*, the right to clean water) for industrialization in the 19th century.[920] The state is often the facilitator of this creative destruction (*e.g.*, in the case of land reform) or the approver of the changes that have been made in the interest of development. FPPRs are not static, and the state may decide not to protect the existing FPPRs (often justified in the name of "reform") where the change is expected to allocate the existing resources to more efficient producers or induce the development of new industries.

8.3 Are FPPRs necessary for economic development?

8.3.1 Case for FPPRs

As discussed, FPPRs have been considered an integral part of modern capitalism. Adam Smith concluded that the security of property rights against expropriation by fellow citizens or the state is an important condition for encouraging individuals to invest and accumulate capital, which, in turn, would boost economic growth.[921] Again, it is not intuitively difficult to see how FPPRs, by comparison to communal ownership, could enhance productivity. The costs and benefits from the use of property will be internalized by individual users where one has exclusive property rights (FPPRs),[922] whereas the costs and benefits will

---

916 Upham (2015), *supra* note 5, at 255–256. Professor Upham observed, "law and property rights have played a variety of roles: sometimes slowing the process of change, sometimes legitimating it, sometimes becoming the very agent of change, and sometimes playing no role at all." *Id.*, at 259. See also Xu (2013), *supra* note 32, at 119 and 136.

917 See *supra* note 233 (for a discussion of socioeconomic conditions).

918 Upham (2018), *supra* note 5, at 34–60.

919 *Ibid.* Professor Upham opined that this land reform did not achieve productivity increase but was necessary to achieve democracy. *Id.*

920 Morton Horwitz, *Transformation of American Law, 1780–1860* (Cambridge, MA: Harvard University Press, 1977).

921 Xu (2013), *supra* note 32, at 117.

922 Frank Upham argues that this is only true when Demsetz's five assumptions are met, which is never the case. Upham (2018), *supra* note 5, at 116. The five assumptions include the following: (i) all property rights must be assigned; (ii) the cost of policing property rights must be

be shared among the members of the community in the absence of FPPRs. Thus, in the former case, the property owners will have an incentive to use the property most efficiently (*i.e.,* to maximize benefits and minimize costs through optimal use, management, and investment).[923] Effective FPPRs also facilitate the transfer of property ownership to a more efficient user, improving overall economic efficiency and productivity.[924] Neo-institutional economists, such as Ronald Coase, Harold Demsetz, and Douglass North, explicitly recognize the necessity of certain institutions, such as FPPRs, for stable and secure investment and exchange.[925]

Another advantage of FPPRs is the efficient enforcement of property rights by the state and the resulting reduction in transaction costs. The public enforcement of property rights, through a state judicial system, may reduce transaction costs by providing standardized enforcement of property rights in the state's juris-diction with credible punishment for breach, and the state, with its sovereign powers, can do this on economies of scale, which individual property owners cannot replicate. By contrast, private enforcement will be costly to the individual property owners and may also result in violence not sanctioned by the state.[926] The difficulties associated with private enforcement may also limit transactions to fewer individuals with whom the owner is familiar and whom the owner trusts.[927] The enforcement of common or communal ownership could also be more com-plex and expensive, particularly for a dispute among the common users, as it involves the overlapping rights and obligations of the multiple parties the pre-cise extent of which, concerning the rights and obligations of the others, may not always be clear. The cost savings from public enforcement of FPPRs can be diverted to more economically productive and more socially peaceful uses. For example, private owners may redirect the cost of hiring private guards to improve the property, and society, as a whole, will become more peaceful, as the owners

zero; (iii) the cost of exchanging property rights must be zero; (iv) all owners of property rights must be utility maximizers; and (v) change in the distribution of wealth cannot affect demand patterns. *Id.,* at 19.

923 Demsetz (1967), *supra* note 873.

924 Xu explained how FPPRs facilitate the transfer of property ownership to more efficient users. He stated: "when property rights are clear and secure, the transaction costs involved in identifying the real owner of the property and making and enforcing a lease or sale contract are reduced to the extent that property markets can function effectively in transferring the property from less efficient uses to more efficient uses." Xu (2013), *supra* note 32, at 122. See also Richard A. Posner, *Economic Analysis of Law* (7th ed., New York: Aspen Publishers, 2002).

925 *Supra* note 873. Coasean analysis recognizes property rights as crucial to economic perfor-mance: "in all societies, primitive and modern, property rights are an important part of social technology that helps to determine economic efficiency." Martin J. Bailey, "Property Rights in Aboriginal Societies," *in* Peter Newman (ed.), *The New Palgrave Dictionary of Economics and Law* (London: Macmillan Reference LTD, 1998), at 155–157. Professor Frank Upham, how-ever, cautioned against a narrow focus on FPPRs; he observed that the early neo-institutionalists took a broad view of the types of institutions needed, including various customs, mores, mental models, and ideologies, but subsequent practitioners focused narrowly on legal rights when they turned theory into practice. See Upham (2015), *supra* note 5, at 254.

926 Xu (2013), *supra* note 32, at 120–121.

927 *Ibid.*

do not have to resort to militant groups or gang members for the protection of property, where public enforcement of FPPRs is strong.[928]

FPPRs may also facilitate investment. The certainty of title guaranteed by enforceable FPPRs can assure the value attached to the property,[929] and this assurance encourages investment.[930] According to a report, in two provinces in Thailand, farmland security (with the possession of land title) led to greater capital formation and higher levels of land improvement.[931] In northeast China, land tenure security is known to have significantly affected land investment, specifically investment in soil quality through the use of organic fertilizer.[932] In Vietnam, the 1993 Land Law, which granted households the power to exchange, transfer, lease, inherit, and mortgage their land-use rights, was found to increase the share of the total area devoted to multi-year crops and irrigation investment.[933] By contrast, the uncertainty of title associated with the absence of FPPRs lowers the asset value and creates a risk for investment return, and this risk discourages investment.[934] The certainty of title, as facilitated by FPPRs, also enables banks and other financiers to provide credit on the property as collateral. This availability of credit, in turn, promotes investment and generates capital for economic development.[935] De Soto argued this point to advocate for the protection of

---

928   For additional evidence of resource diversion, a titling program initiated by the Peruvian government resulted in the reduction of resources that untitled households devoted to maintaining tenure security through informal means and increased work hours in the labor market. In Buenos Aires, Argentina, the squatters who obtained formal land rights under the expropriation law enacted by Congress in 1984 were found to increase housing investments, reduce household sizes, and improve the education of their children. Sebastian Galiani and Ernesto Schargrodsky, "Property Rights for the Poor: Effects of Land Titling," Working Paper (Universidad Torcuato Di Tella, 2006).

929   According to a study, the prices of unit dwelling houses in the city of Davao, the Philippines, were 58 percent higher in the formal sector than in the informal sector. In another study concerning Indonesia, interviews with real estate brokers in Jakarta indicated that land prices were affected by the level of tenure security. In Thailand, 3–4 years after the issuance of title deeds under the land titling project, the land market became more active in the project area than in the non-project area. In Nicaragua, registration was found to increase land values by 30 percent. In Ecuador, holding a title led to a sizable increase in the market value of properties (on average, 23.5 percent of untitled property values). Xu (2013), *supra* note 32, at 120–121.

930   Omotunde Johnson, "Economic Analysis, the Legal Framework and Land Tenure Systems" (1972) 15 *Journal of Law and Economics* 259–276.

931   Xu (2013), *supra* note 32, at 125.

932   *Ibid.*

933   *Ibid.* In Brazil, the results of the household survey confirm that ownership plays an important role in promoting investment in land improvements. *Id.*

934   Johnson (1972), *supra* note 930.

935   A study shows that the land title secured in Thailand through FPPRs increased access to institutional credit. Galiani and Schargrodsky (2006), *supra* note 928. In Peru, land titling was found to increase loan approval rates by 9–10 percent from public sector banks for housing construction materials. *Id.* In Argentina, evidence similarly indicated the positive effect of land titling on access to mortgage credit. *Id.*

FPPRs[936] that, in his view, were absent in many developing countries and causing a lack of capital for economic development.[937]

Considering the advantages of FPPRs in the context of development, it is not surprising that the degree of FPPR protection appears to correlate with economic prosperity. As mentioned earlier, all OECD countries adopt well-defined, enforceable FPPRs: FPPRs were reinforced throughout the periods of economic development in the Western world and East Asia (Japan, South Korea, Taiwan, Hong Kong, and Singapore). There is no shortage of cases to show the enhancement of economic productivity with the adoption of FPPRs; for example, a study reported higher labor productivity in privately leased oyster grounds than in government-regulated open-access grounds in the U.S. East Coast and Gulf Coast.[938] Another study reported that the per-acre value of agricultural output on tribal-trust land and individual-trust land was 85–90 percent and 30–40 percent lower, respectively, than privately owned land.[939] A report on the use of resources related to the British Columbia halibut fishery after the privatization of property rights found that privatization led not only to efficient input usage but also to a substantial producer surplus.[940] On the strength of the case for FPPRs, the protection of FPPRs is widely justified as a precondition for economic development and the standard policy prescription of international and national development agencies today.[941]

8.3.2 FPPRs as ineffective or adverse to development and social peace

Despite the reported advantages of FPPRs, some empirical cases indicate that the introduction and the attempt to enforce FPPRs generated no significant effect on development. First, communal ownership is not always found to cause resource depletion or low productivity. For example, a communal space for cattle grazing in Töbel, Switzerland, governed by the villagers, maintained productivity in the land for centuries, and they were able to control and prevent overgrazing.[942] By contrast, in some parts of India, privatization of land has accelerated the destruction of native vegetation.[943] Second, in some areas where FPPRs have

---

936 Frank Upham argues that this titling program would create, not protect, FPPRs, and to the extent that this creation required taking title away from the previous owner, it was creative destruction. He also observes that usually it is the government who is the [dispossessed] owner, so the "destruction" is nominal (correspondence on file with the author).

937 De Soto (2003), *supra* note 772.

938 Richard J. Agnello and Lawrence P. Donnelley, "Property Rights and Efficiency in the Oyster Industry" (1975) 18 *Journal of Law and Economics* 521–533, cited in Xu (2013), *supra* note 32, at 123.

939 Terry L. Anderson and Dean Lueck, "Land Tenure and Agriculture Productivity on Indian Reservations" (1992) 35 *Journal of Law and Economics* 427–454.

940 R. Quentin Grafton, Dale Squires, and Kevin J. Fox, "Private Property and Economic Efficiency: A Study of a Common-Pool Resource" (2000) 43 *Journal of Law and Economics* 679–713.

941 See *supra* note 876.

942 N. S. Jodha, "Common Property Resources: A Missing Dimension of Development Strategies," *World Bank Discussion Paper*, no. 169 (1992).

943 *Ibid.*

been introduced, such as Africa, there are not many examples where individual property rights increased investments. For example, a study conducted on Kenya, Uganda, and Zimbabwe concluded that there was little empirical evidence to support the hypothesis that securing land tenure through land registration increased agricultural investment in these countries.[944] Cross-sectional evidence from Ghana, Kenya, and Rwanda in 1987–1988 also showed that the relationship between land rights and land improvements was unclear.[945] Findings from studies in Uganda and Madagascar further support the conclusion that land ownership has a relatively insignificant effect on investments.[946]

Third, some empirical studies have found an insignificant relationship between the possession of a title and the use of formal credit, particularly in rural Africa.[947] Fourth, securing FPPRs through land registration and titling in a significant number of cases failed to vitalize market transactions in land; in Kenya, land registration did not create a well-functioning land market.[948] A survey of 16 different areas of six African countries with titling programs (*i.e.*, Kenya, Rwanda, Burundi, Uganda, Malawi, and Zambia) showed that an average of only 16 percent of the land was acquired through market purchases: 63 percent was obtained through inheritances and various kinds of gift transfers, and 21 percent through other means, including state allocation.[949] A study also showed that in Ho Chi Minh City, Vietnam, only half the house owners had legal titles, but the real estate market continued to flourish.[950]

The attempt to protect FPPRs may also create unintended uncertainty that may hinder, rather than support, economic development, and also disrupt the established social order. First, maintaining a system that is necessary to protect FPPRs, such as a land registry, can be expensive and may raise complex problems for both landholders and the state, particularly in developing countries with limited resources. Registration can be lengthy and expensive; per the World Bank's Doing Business Report 2018, the time required for registration ranges from 1 day (Georgia) to 513 days (Kiribati), and the cost is from 0 percent of property

944 Xu (2013), *supra* note 32, at 126.
945 Shem Migot-Adholla, Peter Hazell, Benoît Blarel, and Frank Place, "Indigenous Land Rights Systems in Sub-Saharan Africa: A Constraint on Productivity" (1991) 5 *World Bank Economic Review* 155–175.
946 Hanan G. Jacoby and Bart Minten, "Is Land Titling in Sub-Saharan Africa Cost-Effective? Evidence from Madagascar" (2007) 21 *World Bank Economic Review* 461–485.
947 Frank Place and Peter Hazell, "Productivity Effects of Indigenous Land Tenure Systems in Sub-Saharan Africa" (1993) 75 *American Journal of Agricultural Economics* 10–19 and Thomas C. Pinckney and Peter K. Kimuyu, "Land Tenure Reform in East Africa: Good, Bad, or Unimportant" (1994) 3 *Journal of African Economics* 1–28.
948 Richard Barrows and Michael Roth, "Land Tenure and Investment in African Agriculture: Theory and Evidence" (1990) 28 *Journal of Modern African Studies* 265–297.
949 Jean-Philippe Platteau, *Institutions, Social Norms, and Economic Development* (Amsterdam: Harwood Academic Publishers, 2000).
950 Annette M. Kim, "A Market without the 'Right' Property Rights: Ho Chi Minh City, Vietnam's Newly-Emerged Private Real Estate Market" (2004) 12 *Economics of Transition* 275–305.

value (Georgia) to 28.0 percent (Syria).[951] The average cost and time for registration in each region are as follows (Table 8.3):

Table 8.3 Land registration by region (time and cost)[952]

Region	Time (days)	Cost (percentage of property value)
East Asia & Pacific	72.6	4.5
Europe & Central Asia	20.3	2.6
Latin America & Caribbean	63.3	5.8
Middle East & North Africa	29.7	5.7
OECD high income	20.1	4.2
South Asia	114.1	6.9
Sub-Saharan Africa	53.9	7.6

Landholders who wish to avoid the time and cost of registration will not attempt to register their property, or even if they registered initially, the time and cost might discourage them from registering subsequent land transactions and instead induce them to return to the informal system of land conveyance and land division.[953] This "deformalization" will create gaps between the land registry and actual land ownership, which results in uncertainty that inhibits economic transactions and development. Additionally, a lack of administrative capacity, which is not unusual in developing countries, would render maintaining an accurate land registry that timely records the title and its subsequent changes a challenging task. Discrepancies between the formal land registry and reality will cause new uncertainties, creating a "mixture of old and new, bottom-up and top-down, and foreign and indigenous normative structures that all too often combine the worst of all worlds."[954]

In many developing countries, the formal property law co-exists with customary land ownership, with the latter being more important—in Africa, the formal land system covers between only 2 and 10 percent of the total land area.[955] Customary land ownership is stable in many places, offering guarantees of basic

951   World Bank, *Doing Business: Registering Property*, available online at: www.doingbusiness.org/en/data/exploretopics/registering-property; https://perma.cc/8KD4-YYWR.
952   Compiled from the World Bank Doing Business Report, *ibid.*
953   Grenville Barnes and Charisse Griffith-Charles, "Assessing the Formal Land Market and Deformalization of Property in St. Lucia" (2007) 24 *Land Use Policy* 494–501.
954   Upham (2015), *supra* note 5, at 256. In Nicaragua and Bolivia, multiple government agencies delivered title to the same plot of land to separate parties when there was no clear distinction between their geographic jurisdictions or any inter-agency cooperation. Grenville Barnes, David Stanfield, and Kevin Barthel, "Land Registration Modernization in Developing Economies: A Discussion of the Main Problems in Central/Eastern Europe, Latin America, and the Caribbean" (2002) 12(4) *URISA Journal* 33–42. In Guatemala, over-centralization of registry authorities caused the registration service to be highly inaccessible for residents in remote areas. Xu (2013), *supra* note 32, at 131.
955   Klaus Deininger, *Land Policies for Growth and Poverty Reduction* (Washington, D.C.: The World Bank, 2003).

tenure security in terms of use rights and transfer rights.[956] This stability is sufficient to induce investment, and formal title does not increase security and therefore has no direct impact on investment. While the benefits from FPPRs are limited, there is substantial welfare loss associated with attempts to replace a customary land regime with FPPRs. This is demonstrated by the loss of the social safety net function served by communal land for the benefit of those vulnerable populations (*e.g.*, women, youth, seasonal users) who need the land for subsistence but who cannot claim ownership.[957] It would be very difficult to register these ancillary and overlapping interests of multiple parties to use, regulate, and manage the land;[958] thus, it may well be prudent to leave them to negotiate and settle under the dynamic and more adaptable customary land tenure system. Otherwise, imposing a formal registry may cut off the traditional rights of women, youth, and seasonal land users who may not be able to register their interests, and in this case, the imposition of FPPRs will become a source of major social conflict and injustice.

Finally, land registry, initially intended as a device to protect FPPRs, has also been misused as a means for elites to dispossess the poor and other vulnerable populations of their right to land through manipulation of titling programs. The extent of abuse is significant; according to a study, registration effectively provided a mechanism for the transfer of wealth to those with better social or economic positions, resulting in tenure insecurity for vulnerable right-holders.[959] Illegitimate land capture by elites abusing land registration and the resulting exclusion of other land users has led to disputes, with a potential of erupting into large-scale civil strife and violence.[960] In Somalia, land occupation and expropriation by the state and its governing elites has caused tragic civil conflict.[961] The widespread instances of abuse[962] indicate that the state has not yet gained

---

956 Frank Place, "Land Tenure and Agricultural Productivity in Africa: A Comparative Analysis of the Economics Literature and Recent Policy Strategies and Reforms" (2009) 37 *World Development* 1326–1336.

957 Daniel W. Bromley and Jean-Paul Chavas, "On Risk, Transactions and Economic Development in the Semiarid Tropics" (1989) 37 *Economic Development and Cultural Change* 719–736.

958 These overlapping interests are described as a "web of interests," which is a reality in many parts of Africa. Ruth Meinzen-Dick and Esther Mwangi, "Cutting the Web of Interests: Pitfalls of Formalizing Property Rights" (2008) 26 *Land Use Policy* 36–43.

959 Barrows and Roth (1990), *supra* note 948.

960 See Pauline E. Peters, "Inequality and Social Conflict over Land in Africa" (2004) 4 *Journal of Agrarian Change* 269–314 and Ben K. Fred-Mensah, "Capturing Ambiguities: Communal Conflict Management Alternative in Ghana" (1999) 27 *World Development* 951–965.

961 The Land Law of 1975 provides those privileged with access to the mechanisms of registration to obtain titles to land that local farmers had used for generations. Peters (2004), *ibid.*

962 For example, in Northwest Cameroon, land conflicts have increased because local elites sought to acquire large tracts of land under an individual title, a process facilitated by the 1974 land ordinance and by the links between local elites and national politics. In Kenya, a critical contributing factor to the growing social inequality in access to land is the capacity of the patron-client chains that link the national elite to the local level to gain control over resources that offer opportunities for wealth accumulation. In Nigeria, political and civil elites benefit disproportionately from the 1978 Land Use Decree by manipulating the authority under which property and resources are allocated. *Ibid.*

effective control over the systems necessary to protect FPPRs, such as land registration, while there is international and domestic pressure to adopt the modern land registry.[963]

8.3.3 *FPPRs and analysis under the general theory of law and development*

The preceding discussions reveal that FPPRs, despite their aspirations, do not always enhance productivity and investment in the context of economic development. FPPRs are recognized and enforced in the form of law, so to understand the conflicting outcomes, it is necessary to examine the impact on the development of laws that purport to protect FPPRs. The general theory of law and development, which assesses the impact of law on development, is relevant and can be adopted for this assessment. As discussed in Chapter 3,[964] the general theory requires an examination of regulatory design, which, in turn, involves an analysis of three sub-elements; *i.e.,* anticipated policy outcomes, the organization of LFIs (law, legal frameworks, and institutions), and the law's adaptability to the socioeconomic conditions on the ground.[965] Under the first sub-element, the examiner performs an analysis of whether the anticipated policy outcomes are consistent with the law's objectives;[966] under the second, whether the law is consistent with the relevant legal frameworks and supported by effective institutions;[967] and for the last, whether the law conforms to the identified socioeconomic conditions that are necessary for effective implementation of the law.[968]

As to the first sub-element, the analysis in the preceding sections and the theories and empirical cases discussed therein indicate whether the anticipated policy outcomes would be consistent with the objectives of laws that protect FPPRs. Such laws' objectives are the security of land tenure, enhancement of property value and investment, improvement in productivity, and generation of credit, all of which will, in turn, facilitate economic development. While these theories[969] provide support for the laws that protect FPPRs, the preceding discussion also reveals mixed outcomes,[970] with improvements of these objectives in some cases, no real impact in others, and even declines in extreme cases.[971] These varied results suggest that a presumption could not be readily made about the anticipated policy outcomes one way or the other, and the two additional sub-elements, organization of LFIs and the law's adaptation to the socioeconomic

---

963 For example, the World Bank's Doing Business Report rates each country's land registration system. *Supra* note 876.

964 Section 3.1 *supra* provides a summary of the theory. The three analytical elements of the theory are regulatory design, regulatory compliance, and the quality of implementation. *Id.*

965 See discussion *supra* Section 3.2.

966 *Ibid.*

967 *Ibid.*

968 *Ibid.*

969 See discussion *supra* Section 8.3.1.

970 See discussion *supra* Section 8.3.2.

971 *Ibid.*

conditions, could be determinative of the regulatory design and of the impact of the laws on development.

As to the organization of LFIs, laws that aim to protect FPPRs, such as property laws that set up a land registry, would not be compatible with the legal frameworks that are comprised largely of customary law such as those found in many parts in Africa. Legal pluralism, which may have been caused by supply-side constraints (*e.g.,* insufficient budget, incompetent agencies, and inadequate legitimacy, as well as enduring local legal traditions) is the reality in many African countries.[972] When the influential customary law recognizes and to some extent enforces the overlapping web of interests by multiple parties on the same parcel of land, it would be difficult for a land registry system to replace this regime altogether, even if the modern property law was adopted to replace the traditional regime. It is also unclear whether many developing countries with weak institutional apparatus have the capacity to set up and implement effective land registration systems. The institutional arrangements that implement land registries in developed countries, such as reliable bureaucracy, adequate budget, and technical know-how, are often absent or insufficient in developing countries.

The law's adaptation to socioeconomic conditions is also an issue. In many parts of Africa, land ownership is communal rather than individual. FPPRs could prevail if a socioeconomic change that necessitates private ownership was to take place, such as industrialization coupled with private corporate ownership where land use has to be exclusive and private, rather than communal. Without such change, a blanket attempt to replace the traditional land tenure with a modern regime based on FPPRs is unlikely to be successful due to its conflict with the socioeconomic conditions on the ground that support communal ownership rather than FPPRs. In this case, an attempt to impose FPPRs, which will inevitably exclude a series of incompatible but important land use rights for the community, such as subsistence rights of women and youth as well as seasonal rights, will cause injustice and social turmoil. Vulnerable land users, even if they could, in theory, register their property interests, still may not be able to afford the cost and time for registration, and this creates the opportunity for elites to capture their land illegitimately through manipulation of registration.[973]

The preceding discussion indicates that the preconditions for functional FPPRs include consistent legal and institutional frameworks, broad access to information, and competent and impartial administrative agencies. What could be done to develop necessary institutional support and meet the socioeconomic conditions? Whether it helps at all to impose FPPRs across the country should be considered. International development agencies, such as the World Bank, promote the protection of FPPRs across the board, but one size does not fit all, and caution has to be taken before promoting a particular legal device, such as land registration, that may or may not work under prevailing institutional frameworks

---

972 Daniel Fitzpatrick, "Evolution and Chaos in Property Rights Systems: The Third World Tragedy of Contested Access" (2006) 115 *Yale Law Journal* 996–1048.

973 *Supra* notes 961 and 962 (for accounts of the abuse of land registry).

and socioeconomic conditions on the ground.[974] For example, as discussed above, titling programs failed to generate additional credit in many African countries because only a small portion of people used banks and had bank accounts,[975] and dominant state banks were not able to provide competitive banking services and extend credit.[976] The introduction of FPPRs would not lead to the necessary reforms of weak banking systems in these countries, and the change of land tenure system would not be effective in generating credit unless banking reform could somehow be carried out simultaneously.

Even where there is a clear need to adopt a device, such as a land registry, to protect FPPRs, perhaps on account of an industrial development plan that requires FPPRs to secure investment and set up production facilities in certain areas, the geographical scale of its implementation should be adjusted to fit the existing institutional capacity. The implementation, even if it had initially been planned for the entire country, could be tested for a limited geographical area, and extension into other areas could be sought where initial success was secured with the institutional capacity for extension. As to the socioeconomic conditions, the government may also attempt to change the relevant conditions by, for example, providing subsistence support for the ancillary or seasonal land users and institutional support for registration should there be a clear need to consolidate land ownership through a land registry. The ability to provide subsistence support and the ability to develop adequate institutional support depend on the capacity of the state, which might also be an issue for developing countries with limited resources.

In addition to regulatory design, the two other elements under the general theory to assess the impact of law are "regulatory compliance," which refers to the conduct of the general public in complying with law,[977] and "quality of implementation," which assesses the degree to which a state meets the requirements of law and undertakes the mandates under the latter to fulfill its objectives.[978] As to regulatory compliance, the legal pluralism in many developing countries, comprised of both customary law and state law, creates difficulty for compliance with the latter. There has been an observation (in the context of Africa) that the state law failed to gain popular understanding or acceptance, and individuals continued to convey rights to

974 The World Bank supports the protection of FPPRs, but its panel report on Cambodia's Land Management and Administration Project also recognizes this problem. World Bank, "Cambodia: Land Management and Administration Project," *Investigation Report*, no. 58016-KH (November 23, 2010). Professor Frank Upham warned, "The effort to transform the superficially chaotic social norms of a poor country into a coherent, transparent, and open network often destroys pre-existing social structures invisible to best-practices expertise. What is left is not a replication of the experience of developed countries, but a mixture of old and new, bottom up and top down, and foreign and indigenous normative structures that all too often combines the worst of all worlds." Upham (2015), *supra* note 5, at 255–256.

975 Thorsten Beck, Asli Demirgüç-Kunt, and Patrick Honohan, "Access to Financial Services: Measurement, Impact, and Policies" (2009) 24 *World Bank Research Observer* 119–145.

976 James R. Barth, Gerard Caprio Jr., and Ross Levine, "Bank Regulation and Supervision: What Works Best" (2004) 13 *Journal of Financial Intermediation* 205–248.

977 See discussion *supra* Section 3.3.

978 *Ibid.*

land according to customary law, resulting in a gap between the control of rights as reflected in the land registry and as recognized by most local communities.[979]

The co-existence of these traditional and state systems causes ambiguities as to which of them has superior authority in the recognition and protection of property rights, undermining the function of FPPRs and diminishing regulatory compliance with the state law. Thus, "forum shopping," whereby parties pursue alternative channels to resolve property matters, often prevails.[980] Legal pluralism is concerning, as it weakens regulatory compliance. Xu notes:

> Legal pluralism, institutional ambiguity, and institutional shopping will further undermine social conditions that enable customary land tenure to function effectively, such as norms of reciprocity and cooperation, low-cost internal governance mechanisms, and informal sanction systems. Norm-based common property arrangements may therefore become dysfunctional, or even breakdown, especially under pressure from rising resource values. On the other hand, legal pluralism may also damage the legitimacy and credibility of formal property systems, leading to efficiency costs, in view of local people's determined resistance to drastic reshuffling of land rights. In the worst-case scenario, the norm-based resource governance system will disintegrate without the provision of effective substitutes by the state, and open access (and resource depletion) will follow.[981]

The traditional and state systems, each competing rather than complementing, weaken regulatory compliance with the state law.

As to the quality of implementation, state capacity is a central element. State capacity includes its financial, technological, and administrative capabilities, including internal controls against corruption, to implement laws and fulfill regulatory objectives.[982] According to the Fragile Country Index, compiled by the Fund for Peace, the states with properly functioning governments and due capacity to protect property rights and supply public goods seem to be the exception, rather than the rule; 112 countries out of the 178 examined countries are classified as unstable (*i.e.*, classified under "warning," "elevated warning," "high warning," "alert," "high alert," and "very high alert"), with 31 countries classified under "alert," "high alert," and "very high alert" (similar to the classification of "failing states" in the previous reports).[983] Considering the fragility of the states, it is not surprising

---

979 Barrows and Roth (1990), *supra* note 948.
980 Deininger, *supra* note 955.
981 Xu (2013), *supra* note 32, at 134.
982 See discussion *supra* Section 3.3.2(b).
983 Fund for Peace, *Fragile States Index 2020—Annual Report,* available online at: https://fragile statesindex.org/wp-content/uploads/2020/05/fsi2020-report.pdf; https://perma.cc/7YJW-JWLE.

  The Index is compiled on the examination of the following indicators:

  C1: Security Apparatus
  C2: Factionalized Elites
  C3: Group Grievance

that the governments in so many developing countries have failed to monitor and enforce FPPRs properly. These states lack due capacity, such as administrative, financial, and technical resources, required for the implementation of the laws protecting FPPRs; as a result, state institutions, such as a reliable and inexpensive land titling system, a competent and uncorrupt judiciary, and a functional police force, are non-existent. The continuing existence of legal pluralism is another sign of the lack of state capacity, as it demonstrates constraints, such as insufficient budget, incompetent agencies, and inadequate legitimacy, when most developing countries try to replace the customary land system with formal land rights protecting FPPRs.[984]

In weak states, state laws may also become a vehicle to misuse FPPRs in favor of social elites at the expense of vulnerable land users or to not enforce FPPRs for the benefit of the socially and politically powerful.[985] This misuse means that the quality of implementation is extremely low. State agents may also offer private service for the provision of typically public goods, such as the security of property rights. This type of "state capture" incurs high social costs.[986] Lastly, in many vulnerable developing countries, particularly those in Africa, problems associated with a neo-patrimonial system are found where rulers ally with local strongmen, and the latter, in return for political support, are allowed to exploit local economic opportunities, including misappropriation of property rights.[987] All of these governance issues are associated with weak state capacity, also indicating the poor quality of implementation. FPPRs cannot effectively function where the state lacks due capacity to monitor and enforce them, particularly against powerful social elites with a tendency to abuse them at the cost of the society.

E1: Economic Decline
E2: Uneven Economic Development
E3: Human Flight and Brain Drain
P1: State Legitimacy
P2: Public Services
P3: Human Rights and Rule of Law
S1: Demographic Pressures
S2: Refugees and IDPs
X1: External Intervention

Fund for Peace, *Indicators, Fragile States Index 2020*, available online at: https://fragilestatesindex.org/indicators/; https://perma.cc/K5R6-NH5V.

984 Fitzpatrick (2006), *supra* note 972.
985 Edward Glaeser, Jose Scheinkman, and Andrei Shleifer, "The Injustice of Inequality" (2003) 50(1) *Journal of Monetary Economics* 199–222; Leonid Polishchuk and Alexei Savvateev, "Spontaneous (Non)Emergence of Property Rights" (2004) 12(1) *Economics of Transition* 103–127; Konstantin Sonin, "Why the Rich May Favor Poor Protection of Property Rights" (2003) 31 *Journal of Comparative Economics* 715–731.
986 Joel S. Hellman, Geraint Jones, and Daniel Kaufmann, "Seize the State, Seize the Day: State Capture and Influence in Transition Economies" (2003) 31 *Journal of Comparative Economics* 751–773.
987 Francis Fukuyama, *State-Building: Governance and World Order in the 21st Century* (Ithaca, NY: Cornell University Press, 2004).

8.3.4 FPPRs as the subject of "creative destruction"

Frank Upham advanced an unconventional argument that FPPRs, which are considered essential for economic development, must occasionally be destroyed to allow new, more productive technology to supplant the old, where the transaction cost prevents the efficient allocation of rights and the economic and social elites tend to resist the change of the *status quo*.[988] According to this argument, the existing FPPRs are not always in the interest of economic development but may become an impediment, which, then, turn into the subject of "creative destruction."[989] Upham draws examples of creative destruction from historical instances, including the enclosure movement in England in the sixteenth century,[990] subordination of the right to clean water by American courts in the nineteenth century to the need for industrialization,[991] elimination of the economic and social status of Japanese, Korean, and Taiwanese landlords by postwar land reform,[992] and destruction of the communal right to a village's agricultural production inherent in Mao's system of people's communes with the individualization of agriculture in late-twentieth-century China.[993]

According to Upham's account, economic development proceeds with the destruction of the old FPPRs, rather than in continued compliance with them. An inquiry could follow this observation; *i.e.*, whether economic development could take place at all without extensive protection of FPPRs. The preceding discussion introduced the cases of development with communist economic systems in place, namely the Soviet Union in the 1930s and North Korea in the 1950s and 1960s, which did not recognize FPPRs in principle.[994] China presents another important case of economic development without extensive FPPR protection, as has been true for much of its development period since the 1980s. China has been trying to develop a "rule of law with Chinese characteristics," but formal legal institutions have played little role in providing security for investment that economic growth demands, as China did not fully protect private property until it adopted the Property Law of 2007.[995] While there had been administrative measures to address conflicts over property, as well as informal norms and institutions, the judiciary and formal legal institutions remained largely on the sidelines.[996] Yet, the Chinese economy grew

---

988 Upham (2015), *supra* note 5, at 256–257. See also Upham (2018), *supra* note 5, at 137–142.
989 Upham (2018), *supra* note 5, at 34–60. The term, "creative destruction," was coined by Joseph Schumpeter. Joseph A. Schumpeter, *Capitalism, Socialism and Democracy* (London: Routledge, 1994), at 82–83.
990 The villagers' rights to enter the common for turbary (the cutting of peat) and mast (the foraging of pigs) were destroyed by the sixteenth-century enclosure of English fields to allow monoculture and sheep pasturage. Upham (2015), *supra* note 5, at 257.
991 Horwitz (1977), *supra* note 920.
992 Ronald Dore, *Land Reform in Japan* (London: Oxford University Press, 1959).
993 Upham (2015), *supra* note 5, at 257.
994 See discussion *supra* Section 8.2.2.
995 Upham (2015), *supra* note 5, at 264. Frank Upham adds that the government still may not always protect property rights if the politics, usually local, dictate otherwise.
996 *Ibid.*

at close to 10 percent annually for nearly three decades since the 1980s, and this success demonstrates that the state-led development policies could replace the capital to be leveraged by FPPRs, at least in the early stages of economic development.

Another case of development without extensive FPPRs would be Cambodia; the country has achieved annual GDP growth of over 7 percent since the mid-90s.[997] Attempts to privatize land began in 1989,[998] but the land registration law of 1992 did not provide a solid platform for full tenure security or effective land management.[999] The Cambodian Land Law of 2001 attempted to formalize pre-existing *de facto* possession and prohibited subsequent informal possession. The law adopted a computerized registry system with the advent of satellite technology that would be accessible by anyone.[1000] However, despite its ambitious goals, progress was slow; from 2002 to 2010, systematic land registration projects achieved 2 million registration certificates out of an estimated set of 10 million land parcels.[1001] However, the institutional constraints, such as weak land registration, did not hinder the large inflow of public and private capital, which, in turn, vitalized the Cambodian economy and stimulated economic growth.[1002] Thus, Cambodia, like China until 2007, is a case that has shown high economic growth without FPPRs backed by land registration.

8.4 FPPRs and the public interest

This section examines the relationship between FPPRs and their restrictions, particularly those based on public interest considerations such as expropriation. Expropriation refers to the taking of privately owned property by the government under eminent domain.[1003] In all countries, including those with sophisticated

997 World Bank, *GDP Growth (annual %)—Cambodia*, available online at: https://data.worldb ank.org/indicator/NY.GDP.MKTP.KD.ZG?locations=KH; https://perma.cc/63VX-9AJL.

998 Robin Biddulph, "Cambodia's Land Management and Administration Project," *WIDER Working Paper*, no. 2014/086 (2014), at 4, available online at: www.wider.unu.edu/sites/default/files/wp2014-086.pdf; https://perma.cc/6YKD-CYFM.

999 Sar Sovann, "Land Reform in Cambodia," paper prepared for FIG Congress 2010 (2010), at 4, available online at: www.fig.net/resources/proceedings/fig_proceedings/fig2010/papers/ts07j/ts07j_sovann_4633.pdf; https://perma.cc/68Y8-5LHN.

1000 Upham (2015), *supra* note 5, at 266–267.

1001 Upham (2018), *supra* note 5, at 111. Thus, Upham has observed that Cambodia is an excellent example of how formalization was implemented unjustly (correspondence on file with the author). Land registration proceeded in Cambodia; as of 2019, Minister of Land Management, Urban Planning and Construction Chea Sophara reported that registration was around 73 percent, equal to 5.1 million plots among the nation's seven million registered plots. The government plans to complete land registration by 2021. Hin Pisei, "Government Pushes for Land Registration by 2021," *The Phnom Penh Post*, March 14, 2019, available online at: www.phnompenhpost.com/post-property/government-pushes-land-registration-2021; https://perma.cc/8LJ5-KMTC.

1002 Hal Hill and Jayant Menon, "Cambodia: Rapid Growth with Institutional Constraints," *ADB Economics Working Paper Series*, no. 331 (January 2013), available online at: www.adb.org/sites/default/files/publication/30140/economics-wp331-cambodia-rapid-growth.pdf; https://perma.cc/8JFF-6ZR4.

1003 "Expropriation," *Black's Law Dictionary* (6th ed., West Publishing, 1997), at 582.

and robust FPPR regimes, expropriation is allowed as a public policy-based limitation on FPPRs. Forms and manners in which expropriation takes place vary from one country to another; in some places, the government takes private property without much guarantee of due process, offering little or no compensation, whereas in others, the government complies with well-defined rules and procedures that are designed to protect the interests of private property holders and offer competitive compensation for a taking.[1004]

8.4.1 Expropriation for a public purpose

From ancient times, governments sought to take privately held land to be used for a public purpose, such as building roads, bridges, and other construction projects necessary for public welfare.[1005] This government need continues through modern times, and the government's right to expropriation is also recognized under international law.[1006] The general requirement for expropriation under customary international law is that a taking must be for a public purpose, as provided by law, in a non-discriminatory manner and with compensation.[1007] The adequacy of compensation has often been a subject of debate. As to its standard, a number of developed countries support the "Hull formula" that requires "prompt, adequate and effective" compensation, whereas developing countries supported the Calvo doctrine during the 1960s and 1970s, which only requires that compensation should be "appropriate."[1008] The modern trend is leaning toward the Hull formula, as often found in investment treaty provisions for compensation for a taking. Some argue that the Hull formula has achieved the status of customary international law.[1009]

1004 For a discussion of eminent domain around the world, see Iljoong Kim, Hojun Lee, and Ilya Somin (eds.), *Eminent Domain: A Comparative Perspective* (Cambridge University Press, 2017).

1005 For a historical discussion of public domain, see Susan Reynolds, *Before Eminent Domain: Toward a History of Expropriation of Land for the Common Good* (The University of North Carolina Press, 2010).

1006 See United Nations Conference on Trade and Development (UNCTAD), "Expropriation," *UNCTAD Series on Issues in International Investment Agreements II* (2012), available online at: https://unctad.org/system/files/official-document/unctaddiaeia2011d7_en.pdf; https://perma.cc/Q8PR-UGUP. The government has the power to take the title and possession of property for a public purpose. A government regulation that limits the use of private property to such a degree that it effectively deprives a property owner of economically reasonable use or value of their property could also be considered a taking, even though the regulation does not formally divest them of title to the property. *Id.* See also *Pennsylvania Coal Co. v. Mahon*, 260 U.S. 393 (1922).

1007 OECD, "'Indirect Expropriation' and the 'Right to Regulate' in International Investment Law," *OECD Working Papers on International Investment* 2004/04 (2004), at 3, available online at: www.oecd.org/daf/inv/investment-policy/WP-2004_4.pdf; https://perma.cc/9QGY-LUZ9. Hans-Bernd Schäfer argues that those affected by expropriation should be provided with incentives to fight in court against unlawful and unconstitutional takings. Hans-Bernd Schäfer and Ram Singh, "Takings of Land by Self-Interested Governments: Economic Analysis of Eminent Domain" (2018) 61(3) *Journal of Law and Economics* 427–459.

1008 OECD (2004), *supra* note 1007, at 2.

1009 *Ibid.* Frank Upham opines that the distinction is not very useful; for compensation to be "appropriate," it would have to be "prompt, adequate and effective" and *vice versa*.

In many developing countries, however, legal scrutiny of government takings is weak, particularly in places where the protection of FPPRs is insufficient; the government has large discretion to determine a public purpose and sometimes merely works as a proxy to serve the interests of the local powers and foreign investors in favorable relationships with the government. Indeed, "land grabbing," with the aid of eminent domain, and the resulting violation of the rights of the local land users has become a major international issue.[1010] In developing countries with insufficient government budgets, compensation is often inadequate; even if the purpose for a taking was to be justified, a taking with insufficient compensation could leave the displaced in economic difficulties. Expropriation may also be demanded for political reasons where a large segment of the population is in poverty; recently, South Africa's National Assembly adopted the Constitutional Review Committee's report recommending a constitutional amendment to expropriate land without compensation.[1011] The objective of this expropriation was known to be the alleviation of poverty for the landless poor and spurring economic development.[1012] In this case, the debate would be whether addressing a poverty issue by way of expropriation without adequate compensation would be justified.[1013]

8.4.2 Development as a public purpose

Economic development requires the building of necessary social and industrial infrastructure such as roads, railways, ports, airports, manufacturing factories, power stations, and large irrigation facilities, among others. All of these facilities require land for construction, and expropriation for their construction could be justified as a legitimate public purpose because it is a necessary precondition for economic development. In the early stages of economic development where facilities are insufficient, demand for building necessary infrastructure would be relatively high, particularly when the country seeks industrialization. The need for expropriation might also increase accordingly. To meet this high demand, it would be reasonable to allow governments to expropriate private land for a public purpose—which does not necessarily mean "public use," as expropriation is possible for a privately owned project such as a road or a factory—under less stringent conditions (*e.g.*, for less compensation) than those prevailing in more

---

A meaningful difference is whether compensation should be replacement value or the market value. Developing countries tend to favor the former, whereas developed ones prefer the latter (correspondence on file with the author).

1010 For a discussion of "land grabbing," see Liz Alden Wily, "The Law and Land Grabbing: Friend or Foe?" (2014) 7(2) *Law and Development Review* 207–242.

1011 Andisiwe Makinana, "Parliament Gives Go-ahead for Land Expropriation Without Compensation," *Times Live* (December 4, 2018), available online at: www.timeslive.co.za/politics/2018-12-04-parliament-gives-go-ahead-for-land-expropriation-without-compensation/; https://perma.cc/DSE5-ND7W.

1012 *Ibid.*

1013 *Ibid.*

advanced countries. The requirements of government expropriation can be tightened in the later stages of development when the need for building additional social infrastructure is reduced and more resources, including those available for compensation, are available. In the later stages of development, where much of the needed infrastructure building has been completed, the relative demand for expropriation could also be reduced.

Foreign direct investments (FDIs), which are relevant to economic development, are also subject to expropriation. A study indicated a rising trend of expropriations of FDIs since the mid-90s, although the overall level of expropriations is lower than in the 70s.[1014] From 1990 to 2006, there were 49 reported expropriation acts in 24 countries.[1015] The research also indicates that foreign firms are more vulnerable to expropriation in resource-based sectors.[1016] The expropriation of FDIs has ramifications for economic development. First, expropriation may raise a dispute over its justification and compensation, particularly when the expropriating country's domestic laws and procedures governing expropriation fall below the international standards.[1017] Second, expropriations may discourage foreign investors from engaging with the expropriating country, for fear of losing their investments, particularly when the expropriations lack adequate compensation. There is a question about the adequacy of compensation; *i.e.*, whether compensation should be assessed based on fair market value or out-of-pocket cost.[1018] Even if the parties agree on the amount of compensation, other elements, such as the currency used, could be a source of dispute when it is not stable or fully exchangeable in the international currency market. Countries negotiate investment agreements, such as bilateral investment treaties (BITs), to remove uncertainties associated with the treatment of investments, including expropriations, by providing express stipulations as to the specific grounds allowed for expropriation, the applied procedure such as notice and hearing, and details of compensation to be made in the case of expropriation.

8.4.3 Case for a balance

The preceding discussion explains the necessity of expropriation to achieve an economic development goal, but despite the need, expropriation should be balanced against other competing interests, such as potential adverse impacts on the environment, preservation of culture and residence in the affected area,

---

1014 Chris Hajzler, "Expropriation of Foreign Direct Investments: Sectoral Patterns from 1993 to 2006," *University of Otago Economics Discussion Papers*, no. 1011 (September 2010), available online at: www.otago.ac.nz/economics/research/otago077137.pdf; https://perma.cc/ 2TJW-WD32.

1015 *Ibid.*

1016 *Ibid.*

1017 See *supra* note 1007 (for a discussion of the international standards).

1018 See Andrea K. Bjorklund, A. Laird, and Sergey Ripinsky (eds.), *Investment Treaty Law: Current Issues III—Remedies in International Investment Law: Emerging Jurisprudence of International Investment Law* (British Institute of International and Comparative Law, 2009).

possible hardship on the dislocated, and insufficient compensation. Indeed, large construction projects, such as dams, could displace many people, creating a substantial social impact in the affected area and beyond.[1019] Balancing the competing interests would be particularly difficult for developing countries in the early stages of economic development when governments have a strong need for expropriation but insufficient resources to mitigate the adverse effect of expropriation. It is not clear how developing countries with limited resources can resolve this dilemma. The government should carefully set priorities in consideration of both the country's need for economic development and the key social and political interests that they must preserve at the same time. International attention and aid might be helpful to resolve this issue. For example, United Nations Educational, Scientific, and Cultural Organization (UNESCO) launched an international safeguarding campaign in the 1950s to save monuments in Nubia from being flooded by the waters of Lake Nasser due to construction of the Aswan Dam.[1020]

The question of balance is relevant not only to developing countries in the early stages of economic development but also to more developed nations. While the governments of these countries may have more resources at their disposal, which could also be used to provide greater compensation for expropriation, they also have to consider other competing interests, as listed above, in making expropriation decisions. Although the pressure for national economic development may be less for these more developed countries, the demand for the protection of other interests may be stronger, and this imposes a larger responsibility on the government, either to proceed with expropriation while minimizing the adverse effect or not to proceed at all. Stronger FPPR protections in more developed countries would also necessitate sophisticated procedures to justify expropriation and calculate adequate compensation acceptable to the property holders. For example, the proposal to amend the constitution in South Africa to allow expropriation without compensation met significant resistance and criticism,[1021] even if the objective was poverty alleviation, partly because South Africa was considered one of the most developed countries in Africa and was expected to seek higher standards for expropriation.[1022]

1019   For example, the building of Aswan Dam in Egypt in 1955 displaced as many as 60,000 local residents. See William C. Mann, "Displaced by Aswan Dam 23 Years Ago: Egypt's Nubians Dream of Home," *Los Angeles Times* (January 3, 1988), available online at: http://articles.lati mes.com/1988-01-03/news/mn-32292_1_years-ago; https://perma.cc/TC3P-GM4C.

1020   UNESCO, *Abu Simbel: The Campaign that Revolutionized the International Approach to Safeguarding Heritage*, available online at: https://en.unesco.org/70years/abu_simbel_sa feguarding_heritage; https://perma.cc/VJL9-LCY5.

1021   See *supra* note 1011 (for a discussion of the proposed expropriation in South Africa).

1022   John Campbell, "Despite Land Reform, South Africa is Not Becoming Zimbabwe or Venezuela," *Council on Foreign Relations* (August 8, 2018), available online at: www.cfr. org/blog/despite-land-reform-south-africa-not-becoming-zimbabwe-or-venezuela; https:// perma.cc/W9HF-ABBW.

8.4.4 Beyond the conventional wisdom?

This chapter has discussed the perception of FPPRs as a necessary precondition for economic development, which has become conventional wisdom and forms the mainstream view, backed by the theories of leading scholars and supported by the policies of international and national development agencies. However, a substantial number of empirical cases suggest otherwise, and the outcome of introducing FPPRs through devices like land registration has been mixed. As Frank Upham noted,[1023] FPPRs may facilitate economic development, but implementation thereof may not have much impact or could even impede economic development, the latter causing social disturbance and injustice for vulnerable populations. This chapter, adopting the general theory of law and development, attempts to analyze the institutional frameworks and socioeconomic conditions under which FPPRs may contribute to economic development. It also assesses whether the laws that purport to protect FPPRs attract regulatory compliance and also whether the laws have been effectively implemented in places where the outcome has not been encouraging.

As explained in the preceding analysis,[1024] FPPRs do not function in a vacuum but require effective institutional arrangements and supportive socio-economic conditions. For example, it would be futile to expect the introduction of FPPRs to lead to credit generation where there is no robust banking and financial industry, as seen in African cases. It would also be counterproductive to extend scarce personnel and financial resources to attempt to set up a working land registration system where an informal property system works with business transactions on the ground. The experiences of China and others have shown that FPPRs are not imperative to economic development, at least in the early stages of economic development; *i.e.,* as the economy develops and becomes more sophisticated and internationalized, there is a greater need for FPPRs, as shown by the cases of the OECD countries. The need for FPPRs in the context of economic development differs in accordance with the level of economic development and the local practices.

FPPRs are not static but dynamic over time; they are embedded in the form of law, which creates vested interests over time, and this eventually necessitates "destruction" of the existing FPPRs to move beyond the constraints of the old practice and technology to accommodate the new. Historical accounts indeed show that existing property rights have been destroyed—with courts' approval (in the name of new interpretation) and legislators' blessing (in the name of reform)—to accommodate new economic dynamism. This process is expected to continue in the future. No country protects FPPRs in absolute terms, and in all countries, the government is authorized to expropriate privately held properties under certain conditions.

1023 Upham (2015), *supra* note 5, at 259.
1024 See discussion *supra* Section 8.3.

The requirements for expropriation are not identical across the board, but international standards are applicable in disputes concerning expropriation. Expropriation has significant ramifications for economic development, and governments are also expected to consider the competing interests and seek to balance them to alleviate the adverse effect of expropriation.

9 Political governance, law, and economic development

9.1 "Good governance" and economic development

This chapter examines the role of political governance and its legal frameworks in economic development.[1025] Political governance, which may be defined as a political process by which public authority is exercised and policies are implemented,[1026] has received much attention as a key ingredient to successful development.[1027] "Good governance," which is elaborated below, has become an objective within the sustainable development goals (SDGs) promoted by the United Nations[1028] and a key mission of the World Bank. The Bank's former president Paul Wolfowitz stated:

> In the last half-century we have developed a better understanding of what helps governments function effectively and achieve economic progress. In the development community, we have a phrase for it. We call it good governance. It is essentially the combination of transparent and accountable institutions, strong skills and competence, and a fundamental willingness to do the right thing. Those are the things that enable a government to deliver

---

1025 This chapter is adapted from the author's article, "Political Governance, Law, and Economic Development" (2019) 12(3) *Law and Development Review* 723–759.

1026 The World Bank's governance project report defined governance as "the traditions and institutions by which authority in a country is exercised," which "includes (i) the process by which governments are selected, monitored, and replaced, (ii) the capacity of the government to effectively formulate and implement sound policies, and (iii) the respect of citizens and the state for the institutions that govern economic and social interactions amongst them." Kaufmann *et al.* (1999), *supra* note 37, at 1.

1027 See, *e.g.*, Kaufmann *et al.* (1999), *ibid.*; Dani Rodrik, "Thinking about Governance," *in* World Bank, *Governance, Growth, and Development Decision-Making* (Washington, D.C., World Bank, 2008) and World Bank, *World Development Report 2017: Governance and the Law* (Washington, D.C., World Bank, 2017).

1028 Goal 16 of the SDGs includes targets such as the development of "effective, accountable and transparent institutions at all levels" (Target 16.6), assurance of "responsive, inclusive, participatory and representative decision-making at all levels" (Target 16.7), and insurance of "public access to information and protect[ion of] fundamental freedoms, in accordance with national legislation and international agreements" (Target 16.10). United Nations, *Sustainable Development Goals, supra* note 9.

DOI: 10.4324/9781003090175-12

services to its people efficiently (…) An independent judiciary, a free press, and a vibrant civil society are important components of good governance. They balance the power of governments, and they hold them accountable for delivering better services, creating jobs, and improving living standards.[1029]

Paul Wolfowitz's statement reflects the importance of "good governance" and highlights core elements of Western-style democratic governance based on "transparent and accountable institutions," "an independent judiciary," "a free press," and "a vibrant civil society," all of which "balance the power of government and hold them accountable for delivering better services, creating jobs, and improving living standards,"[1030] as Wolfowitz described. The vast majority of developed countries today, such as OECD member countries, have democratic governance systems that meet the good governance criteria as described earlier.[1031]

However, history has also revealed cases of unprecedented economic development, such as in several East Asian countries (South Korea, Taiwan, Singapore, and China),[1032] where governance was largely authoritarian and demonstrated significant democratic deficits (*i.e.,* lack of institutional transparency and democratic accountability, questionable judicial independence, restricted freedom of the press, and a weak civil society).[1033] Not only the East Asian countries just mentioned, but other successful developing countries of the twentieth century, such as Spain under General Franco and Chile under General Pinochet, achieved substantial economic development despite atrocities committed under their respective regimes—in other words, without "good governance" under the Wolfowitz definition.[1034] In addition, there is an argument that today's exemplary democracies with developed economies, such as the United States, United Kingdom, and Germany, did not have "good governance" as per the modern definition when they underwent rapid economic development in the nineteenth century.[1035] This leads to a pressing question: how could these countries—East

---

1029　Paul Wolfowitz, "Good Governance and Development—A Time for Action," remarks at Jakarta, Indonesia (April 2006), cited in Jean-Marie Baland, Karl Ove Moene, and James A. Robinson, "Governance and Development," *in* J. Baland, Dani Rodrik, and M. R. Rosenzweig (eds.), *Handbook of Development Economics,* vol. 5 (North Holland, 2009), at 4598.

1030　*Ibid.*

1031　*Ibid.*

1032　These countries achieved remarkable economic development, escaping from widespread poverty for most of their populations and attaining the status of high-income countries within a single generation. See *supra* note 28 (for a discussion of the rapid development of these countries).

1033　See Songok Han Thornton and William H. Thornton (2008), *supra* note 56.

1034　See *supra* note 29 (for a discussion of the development of Spain and Chile).

1035　Chang (2002), *supra* note 203, at 71–76. In the West, political governance was controlled by a privileged minority (*i.e.,* an elite white male class) during the period of their rapid development (the nineteenth century), which does not fit the notion of "good governance" today. *Id.*

Asian countries, including China, in the twentieth century and Western countries in the preceding periods—achieve successful economic development despite lack of "good governance"?

The preceding historical observation suggests that governance which is effective for economic development is not synonymous with "good governance" in its current guise. "Good governance" represents a holistic approach to development, as demonstrated by the SDGs;[1036] non-economic values, such as peace, justice, gender equality, and environmental protection, are now included in the notion of "development."[1037] Regardless of its impact on economic development, "good governance" that promotes "peace, justice, and strong institutions" and ensures "responsive, inclusive, participatory and representative decision-making at all levels" as well as "public access to information and protect[ion of] fundamental freedoms"[1038] has become the objective of development *per se*.[1039] Thus, the two notions, "good governance" under the holistic notion of development and "effective governance" for economic development, cannot be treated as synonymous; on the contrary, they need to be distinguished. This distinction is central to the analysis presented in this chapter.

The scope of the relationship between good governance and economic development is currently uncertain, but there is a strong correlation between economic development and political stability, which itself is understood as presuming effective government without necessarily exhibiting the democratic characteristics that are today associated with good governance. Section 9.2 discusses political stability in the context of economic development. The system of political governance that creates political stability may differ from one place to another, depending upon political needs, cultural priorities, historical contexts, and popular aspirations (including economic requirements). It will be explained that political stability is a notion that is separate from democracy: while civil liberty has been considered a key ingredient for prosperity,[1040] historical evidence suggests that the promotion of democracy, its normative importance and attraction notwithstanding, does not necessarily lead to economic development. Section 9.3 addresses the question of democracy in the context of "good governance" based on the holistic notion of development. Section 9.4 returns to the issue of political stability and considers legal frameworks that will be conducive to creating political stability. While political stability cannot be created by laws alone, an effective legal framework for political governance, such as a constitution, can facilitate political stability.

1036   For a description of the SDGs, see United Nations, *Sustainable Development, supra* note 9.

1037   *Ibid*. For a discussion of the holistic approach to development, see *supra* Section 1.3.

1038   *Supra* note 1028 (for the inclusion of these objectives in Goal 16 of the SDGs).

1039   *Ibid*.

1040   Hayek (1960), *supra* note 201.

9.2 Political stability and economic development

9.2.1 *Historical references*

A study of successful developing countries in the last two centuries, including those in East Asia—South Korea, Taiwan, Singapore, and China (in the twentieth century)—and the Western countries in Europe and North America (in the nineteenth century), reveals substantial diversity in the form of governance, but also a common political characteristic. As to the form of governance, the East Asian countries were under authoritarian rule, through military government or martial law (South Korea and Taiwan), through a civilian dominant-party regime (Singapore), or a communist single-party regime (China).[1041] Another group of economically successful developing countries in twentieth-century Europe and South America, Spain and Chile, were also under militaristic authoritarian rule by Franco and Pinochet, respectively. As to Western Europe and North America, governance took the form of limited democracy with political control by a privileged minority such as an elite white male class, accompanied by restrictions in voting rights throughout the nineteenth century.[1042] Historically, none of these successful developing countries exercised "good governance" under the modern definition[1043] when they were undergoing rapid economic development.[1044]

Despite these democratic limitations and differences in the nature of each nation's political regime, these successful developing countries shared a common political element, namely a substantial degree of political stability. For example, from the 1960s to the mid-1990s, the period of rapid economic development for South Korea, Taiwan, and Singapore, these countries maintained stable political regimes without government collapses. China, after the crisis of the Cultural Revolution in the 1970s, was similarly characterized by political stability and achieved successful economic development under Deng Xiaoping's reform policies.[1045] In Spain and Chile, the regimes of Franco and Pinochet, respectively, ensured political stability, despite human rights atrocities, leading to successful economic development.[1046] In the West, the United Kingdom maintained a stable constitutional monarchy under the leadership of its Parliament throughout the eighteenth and nineteenth centuries when its industrial progress and economic development enabled the country to achieve global dominance in trade and

---

1041 For studies of political foundations of East Asian growth, see Mark R. Thompson, *Authoritarian Modernism in East Asia* (New York: Palgrave Pivot, 2018); Louis D. Hayes, *Political Systems of East Asia* (Abington: Routledge, 2015).
1042 Chang (2002), *supra* note 203, at 71–76.
1043 Wolfowitz (2006), *supra* note 1029.
1044 Chang (2002), *supra* note 203, at 71–76.
1045 See Yong-Shik Lee and Xiaojie Lu, "China's Trade and Development Policy under the WTO: An Evaluation of Law and Economics Aspect" (2016) 2(2) *China and WTO Review* 339–360, at 341–342 and Lee (2016), *supra* note 102, at 318.
1046 See *supra* note 29 (for a discussion of the development of Spain and Chile).

manufacturing.[1047] Germany and the United States, which industrialized after Britain, also achieved political stability after the Civil War for the United States and after unification for Germany. By the early twentieth century, both countries overtook Britain economically and became the two largest manufacturing countries in the world. It should be clear, then, that sustained political stability has been instrumental for successful development for all these countries. An empirical study, based on a survey of 113 countries from 1950 to 1983, corroborates this conclusion, demonstrating that economic growth is negatively correlated with political instability.[1048]

Political stability is thus essential for economic development but not synonymous with democratic governance and the guarantee of individual freedoms (*i.e.,* good governance in its contemporary understanding). For example, the East Asian countries, which maintained political stability throughout the period of successful economic development (the 1960s to 1980s), restricted civil liberties and imposed severe penal sanctions on political dissidents.[1049] The Western countries, which also maintained political stability throughout their respective periods of industrialization and economic development, restricted the right to vote to a white male class, and as a result, women and racial minorities were excluded from full participation in political governance.[1050] Ha-Joon Chang has observed that democracy tends to be an outcome, rather than a cause, of economic development.[1051] Thus, political stability refers to a state of relatively stable continuation of a political process by which public authority is exercised and policies are implemented without substantial government collapses; it does not, however, necessarily entail an absence of authoritarian oppression, political resistance, or social and political injustice and unfairness. Throughout the periods of economic development in various successful countries, political dissidents continued to struggle, and when they formed a critical mass, major political shifts occurred, as witnessed by the democratic transitions of these countries.[1052]

9.2.2 Socioeconomic conditions for political stability

The preceding discussion has established that political stability is essential for economic development. Any inquiry into the conditions conducive to economic development must accordingly include an examination of the conditions that help to

---

1047 For an account of political and economic developments in Britain, see P. J. Marshall (ed.), *The Oxford History of the British Empire*, vol. II (Oxford: Oxford University Press, 1998) and Andrew Porter (ed.), *The Oxford History of the British Empire*, vol. III (Oxford: Oxford University Press, 2001).

1048 Alesina *et al.* (1992), *supra* note 445.

1049 Lee (2018), *supra* note 339.

1050 Chang (2002), *supra* note 203, chapter 3, at 69–124.

1051 *Ibid.*

1052 See, *e.g.,* Lee (2018), *supra* note 339, at 442–443. Section 9.3 *infra* provides a further discussion.

generate political stability. In this regard, attention must be given to those who are governed as well as a system of governance. Baland *et al.* observed:

> Most of the governance literature considers how society is governed in isolation from how it is organized. To apply an old-fashioned distinction, most attention is devoted to the superstructure of society, very little to the base of the economy. Governance, however, is not only about those who govern, but also about those who are governed.[1053]

As mentioned earlier, the system of political governance that sustains political stability may vary from one place to another, depending upon relevant factors such as political needs, cultural priorities, historical contexts, and popular aspirations. The following discussion examines these elements as the conditions relevant to creating and sustaining political stability. Political leadership must also be factored into the equation, which is addressed in the subsequent section.

(a) Political needs

Political stability requires governance to be perceived by the governed as responding to the political needs of a society, which include, for example, the allocation of resources (often among competing groups), the inclusion of the priorities of the majority, or their participation in the decision-making process, protection of rights and privileges, and preservation of social orders (that the majority in a society can accept). Where political governance fails to meet these needs, political stability is jeopardized. For example, when the South African government that had adopted the policy of Apartheid could not meet the political needs of the black majority in terms of equal rights without discrimination, political participation, and equitable access to economic opportunities, violent struggles ensued, and political stability was disrupted to the point that the white minority then controlling political governance in South Africa had to abandon the Apartheid policy and accept a government elected by the oppressed majority.[1054]

It is unlikely for any system of political governance to be able to reach an optimal arrangement that meets all the competing and often conflicting political needs of the various constituent groups in society. Thus, elements of potential political instability exist in all systems of political governance. Effective political governance identifies the most potent sources of potential instability and attempts to fulfill the related unmet political needs to the extent possible. For example, in the United States, the Johnson administration (1963–1969) undertook political and legal reforms to meet the needs of the black minority and protect their civil rights,[1055] while its South African counterpart continued with

---

1053   Baland *et al.* (2009), *supra* note 1029, at 4600.
1054   See *supra* Section 5.1.
1055   For example, the Civil Rights Act of 1964 is a key civil rights statute in the United States that prohibits discrimination based on race, color, religion, sex, or national origin. Civil Rights Act of 1964, 42 U.S.C. § 2000d *et seq.*

the oppressive Apartheid policy against South Africa's black majority during this same period. That choice tore South African society apart, disrupting political stability and potentially affecting economic performance. In contrast, after the civil rights reform under the Johnson administration, the gross national income (GNI) per capita growth rates of the United States were 2.1 percent (1971), 4.2 percent (1972), and 4.9 percent (1973), which were substantially higher than South Africa's growth rates of 1.8 percent (1971), minus 1.3 percent (1972), and 1.6 percent (1973).[1056]

Meeting the needs of the governed also requires access to and investment of substantial administrative and technical capabilities. For example, to allocate limited resources to groups in need of financial assistance, the government must have the administrative capabilities to identify and assess the needs of the different groups and transfer the needed resources to the right recipients. To preserve public order, the government must have the financial, technical, and human resources to administer law and order.[1057] Resource constraints are a critical challenge for many developing countries, to the point that some commentators argue that poor countries cannot afford good governance.[1058] There is merit in this view: all "failing states" (*e.g.*, 31 countries classified under "alert," "high alert," or "very high alert" by the Fragile Country Index)[1059] are developing countries with severe resource constraints. Despite the difficulty associated with such resource constraints, the countries identified earlier as having been successful in achieving economic development were able to meet the most pressing societal needs—relief from poverty—by prioritizing economic development and securing popular support for this endeavor.[1060] During their respective periods of economic development, each country's government was able to suppress some of the political needs, such as enhancement of labor rights and social welfare, while still managing to save resources and maintain political stability, although the suppressed needs surfaced more strongly once economic development had been achieved and rendered the policy transition inevitable.

1056   World Bank, *GNI per capita Growth (annual %)—United States, South Africa*, available online at: https://data.worldbank.org/indicator/NY.GNP.PCAP.KD.ZG?locations=US-ZA; https://perma.cc/6VKT-JXJX.

1057   A study highlighted the importance of state capacity in administering law and order; the study reported that the suppression of sexual and gender-based violence has not been very effective in Liberia where the government had enacted laws that substantially increased penalties for these crimes, but the state lacked the capacity to implement these laws effectively, due to the absence of resources necessary to supply a sufficient police force and prosecutorial services, and for courts to monitor, prosecute, convict, and punish offenders. Zwier (2017), *supra* note 291.

1058   Jeffrey D. Sachs *et al.*, "Ending Africa's Poverty Trap," *Brookings Papers on Economic Activity*, 2004(1) (2004), at 117–240.

1059   Fund for Peace, *Fragile States Index 2020—Annual Report*, *supra* note 983.

1060   See Lee (2018), *supra* note 339, at 442–444. See also Lee (2017), *supra* note 4, at 463–464 and 467–468.

(b) Cultural priorities

Political stability also requires compliance with the cultural priorities of a society. Political governance was effective in the East Asian countries which emphasized the role of the state in economic development because it met the cultural requirements of the Confucian tradition of society, emphasizing the duty that individuals owed to larger communities (*e.g.*, loyalty to the state) and that which the state owed to its citizens (*e.g.*, the welfare of its citizens). Such an approach may not have been particularly effective in cultures where individual autonomy is emphasized and the state is expected to protect individual rights rather than to take up a more active role in ensuring the economic welfare of individuals.[1061] Likewise, in places where the majority of society abide by some religious norms and where there is no clear separation between church and state, effective political governance will embrace the dominant or prevailing religious norms and codes, and policies will comply with them.[1062]

Government policies prioritizing economic development can influence the culture; for example, as the process of economic development continued and the living standard of people improved in the East Asian countries, their cultures came to value industrialization and modernization.[1063] Public education that promotes government policies and national interests can also facilitate the change of cultural priorities.[1064] For instance, a decades-long public campaign in South Korea that promoted the use of domestically produced goods from the 1960s through the 1980s instilled in Korean society a cultural tendency against using imported consumer products, such as cigarettes, and this cultural tendency remained for years after the campaign stopped and the government allowed imports (and to an extent encouraged them under foreign pressure). It has been observed that the cultural traits and requirements of the East Asian countries have been "westernized" as a result of successful economic development; by the 1990s, these countries underwent political transitions from authoritarian rule to more democratic governance with an emphasis on the rule of law and individual freedoms, following the Western liberal constitutional model.[1065] Government policies also changed to support the market as a whole rather than directly supporting particular industries.[1066] Maintaining political stability necessitates adjustment of political governance to meet the changing cultural priorities and requirements, which is often a complex task that requires political expediency.

1061 See discussion *supra* Section 6.3.1(c).
1062 Thus, a number of Muslim-majority countries formally adopted Shari'a law in compliance with the code of Islamic religion. Arif Hyder Ali and Ali Ehassi, "Shari'a Law Approaches to Arbitration," *in* Paul E. Mason and Horacio A. Grigera Naón (eds.), *International Commercial Arbitration Practice: 21st Century Perspectives* (LexisNexis, 2018). Religion can also be co-opted as an instrument of "control" and used as an instrument of governance.
1063 Lee (2017), *supra* note 4, at 467–468.
1064 *Ibid.*, at 460.
1065 *Ibid.*
1066 Pistor and Wellons (1999), *supra* note 265, at 110–111.

(c) Historical contexts

Political governance relies, to a substantial degree, on the collective memory of a society, which forms the historical canvas against which the government operates and its performance is evaluated. Political governance that does not take into account historical contexts is unlikely to sustain political stability. For example, the U.S. military government in post-war Japan could not remove the Japanese Imperial Court in whose name war-time crimes had been committed, because of the historical context in Japan, where a majority of Japanese people had accepted the Emperor as the sacred head of state.[1067] Considering the historical context, it would have been difficult to maintain political stability in Japan if the Emperor had been forcefully removed or prosecuted as a war criminal.[1068] In a related vein, the majority of Koreans did not accept a proposal that the country be ruled under the trusteeship of the United Nations for five years after the Second World War because of Korea's history of oppressive colonial rule by Japan, and most Koreans were not willing to accept yet another period of foreign rule.[1069]

The preceding examples illustrate how historical contexts limit political choices for the government. However, historical contexts sometimes provide opportunities for new initiatives and facilitate effective political governance. For example, the South Korean government in the 1960s used a historical lens to justify and seek political support for its economic development policies; the government reminded Koreans of the generations of poverty and suffering under brutal Japanese colonial rule and the destructive Korean War and argued, successfully, that its economic development policies were an opportunity for the Korean people to lift themselves from crushing poverty to prosperity that would set a new mark for them and their nation in history.[1070] This historical context assisted the Korean government in pushing through its economic development policies, which required that individual Koreans make a number of short-term sacrifices (*e.g.*, no house mortgages due to the government policy mobilizing all available financial resources for industrial production) without disrupting political stability.

(d) Popular aspirations

Politics are never divorced from popular aspirations. In a democracy, governments that do not meet the aspirations of the voters will be voted out. Even under authoritarian rule, political stability is unlikely to last should governance remain continually divorced from the aspirations of the population. For example, the continued economic failures of the former Soviet Union and its government's

---

1067   For a study of the Emperor of Japan, see Donald Keene, *Emperor of Japan: Meiji and His World, 1852–1912* (New York: Columbia University Press, 2005) and Peter Martin, *The Chrysanthemum Throne: A History of the Emperors of Japan* (Honolulu: Latitude 20, 1997).
1068   *Ibid.*
1069   For a history of Korea, see Hwang (2016), *supra* note 342; Seth (2010), *supra* note 342; Eckert and Lee (1991), *supra* note 342.
1070   Lee (2017), *supra* note 4, at 463–464. See also Section 4.2.2. *supra*.

inability to remedy these failures were an important cause of the downfall of the Soviet bloc.[1071] The economic disaster caused by the Great Depression in the 1930s and the failure of the then German government to address this issue caused the rise of Hitler that ended the Weimar Republic.[1072] In contrast, the formerly authoritarian East Asian countries were able to maintain political stability and pursue economic prosperity because their governments were able to adjust their policies and approaches to meet the changing aspirations of their populations—from overcoming poverty to securing political freedom, including more equitable and democratic political participation based on the rule of law.[1073]

Leadership is another essential factor for political stability, particularly under challenging economic and social environments. Aligning changing popular aspirations with national interests and maintaining political stability require pragmatic political leadership. For example, in a developing country where jobs are scarce and other economic opportunities are limited, it will be important to increase the savings rate so that capital can be accumulated and made available for industrial investments that will create jobs and other economic opportunities. However, it is difficult to increase the savings rate in many developing countries, where incomes are insufficient to make ends meet. In such circumstances, it will take effective political leadership to persuade constituencies to understand the need for short-term sacrifices to realize longer term growth and prosperity and to create sufficient trust so that citizens are willing to comply with government policy and suppress their demands for immediate consumption. The history of East Asian economic development has shown such political leadership.[1074] The next sub-section discusses the interrelationship between leadership and political stability.

9.2.3 Leadership and political stability

The successful developing countries had effective leaders during their respective periods of rapid economic development and political stability. Legendary examples include Park Jung Hee of South Korea (1917–1979), Chang Kai-Shek of Taiwan (1885–1975), Lee Kuan Yew of Singapore (1923–2015), and Deng Xiaoping of China (1904–1997). In the West, prominent parliamentary leaders (prime ministers) such as Robert Walpole, William Pitt, Robert Pill, Lord Palmerston (Henry John Temple), Benjamin Disraeli, and William Gladstone led the United Kingdom into unprecedented economic prosperity and industrial development. In Germany, Otto von Bismarck (1815–1898) unified the German nation and provided the necessary political stability that facilitated Germany's rapid industrial and economic

---

1071   For a discussion of the economic problems in the Soviet Union, see Philip Hanson, *The Rise and Fall of the Soviet Economy: An Economic History of the USSR from 1945* (Abington: Routledge, 2014), at 70–97, 128–176, 218–255.

1072   See Detlev J. K. Peukert, *The Weimar Republic: The Crisis of Classical Modernity* (New York: Hill and Wang, 1993), 249–267.

1073   See discussion *supra* Section 1.3.1.

1074   See discussion *supra* Section 3.3.2(c).

development. In the United States, Abraham Lincoln preserved the integrity of the Union by preventing the separation of the Southern States through a costly civil war and paved the way for the United States to become the world's major industrial and economic power.

A recent study has examined the role of leadership in the context of law and development.[1075] The study discusses the long impasse on the contest between structure and agent as a cause of social change and inquires whether a more integrative approach is possible.[1076] This inquiry is relevant to the discourse of this chapter; as observed, effective leadership was in place in the successful developing countries during their respective periods of political stability and economic development. This observation leads to the question of whether the emergence of such leadership is an entirely exogenous factor or whether it could be facilitated by certain socioeconomic conditions. A possible hypothesis is that effective leaders contribute to the political stability that is necessary for economic development and that sustained political stability, in turn, is conducive to producing effective leadership. This hypothesis suggests a synergetic relationship between political stability and leadership.

The political developments in the United Kingdom during the eighteenth and nineteenth centuries may provide support for this hypothesis. An unintended historical incident, as follows, settled the long-standing strife between the Crown and the Parliament: a new king (George I), who had been a foreigner and had not been acquainted with Britain, needed a trusted agent (prime minister), who was to be appointed by the leaders of the parliamentary factions, to form the government on his behalf. Prime ministers who had lost the confidence of the Parliament were replaced, and new leaders were appointed without government collapses or civil wars. In other words, political stability was maintained.[1077] As a result, several leaders emerged as prime ministers, including those from outside the traditional ruling class, such as Benjamin Disraeli and William Gladstone, without violent struggles and civil wars which often accompanied the change of regimes in other European countries.[1078]

Factors that were relevant to creating political stability in the United Kingdom of the eighteenth and nineteenth centuries, such as the acceptance of the political needs of the growing middle-class, cultural priorities valuing individual merits over hereditary entitlements, the historical contexts in which the British society promoted a more inclusive system of governance to adjust to the rapidly changing social and economic environment, and popular aspirations of the British society seeking effective leadership that would harness and promote the development of commerce and trade, were also conducive to producing a new breed of leadership (*i.e.,* non-ruling class leadership). This new leadership, in turn, contributed to sustaining political stability necessary for economic development. Under this

1075   Jamie Baxter, "Leadership, Law and Development" (2019) 12(1) *Law and Development Review* 119–158.
1076   *Ibid.,* at 119.
1077   See Marshall (ed.) (1998), *supra* note 1047 and Porter (ed.) (2001), *supra* note 1047.
1078   *Ibid.*

analysis, institutions and agents are no longer separated but form an inseparable amalgam that creates indivisible synergies between them.

Finally, on the question of leadership, the majority of successful developing countries with "benevolent" or "good" authoritarian leaders in the twentieth century have been located in East Asia, where the prevailing Confucian tradition emphasized the duty of the elite to their state and people.[1079] It has been observed that this cultural tradition may have been a reason for the production of a higher ratio of leaders devoted to economic development in East Asia, compared to that of other regions in the world without such tradition.[1080] On another view, the governments in countries with rich natural resource endowments are more vulnerable to capture by individuals and groups interested in predation rather than development, as they can easily appropriate large economic rents.[1081] None of the successful East Asian developing countries were resource-rich. Also, the East Asian countries mentioned earlier are relatively homogeneous in ethnicity and culture (*i.e.,* over three-quarters of the populations are a single race with common cultural traits) and did not suffer from the degree of contentious ethnic, religious, and cultural divisions experienced by many developing countries in other regions.[1082] Those divisions create a hurdle for producing united leadership toward development.

9.3 The question of democracy

9.3.1 Democracy as a development target

As discussed previously, the promotion of "good governance" is included in the Sustainable Development Goals: Goal 16 refers to targets such as the development of effective, accountable, and transparent institutions at all levels (Target 16.6),[1083] assurance of responsive, inclusive, participatory and representative decision-making at all levels (Target 16.7),[1084] and assurance of public access to information and protection of fundamental freedoms, in accordance with national legislation and international agreements (Target 16.10).[1085] With these inclusions, good governance has arguably become an objective of development, regardless of its impact on economic development.[1086] The requirements for "good governance," including "institutional transparency and accountability," "an independent judiciary," "a free press," and "a viable civil society,"[1087] as well as those described in the cited SDG targets—"responsive, inclusive, participatory

---

1079   *Supra* note 332 (for a discussion of pro-development political leadership in East Asia).
1080   For a discussion of the Confucian tradition in East Asia, see Tu (1996), *supra* note 315.
1081   See Auty (1997), *supra* note 332, at 651.
1082   See *e.g.,* discussion *supra* Section 5.2.4(b) in the context of South Africa.
1083   United Nations, *Sustainable Development Goals, supra* note 1028.
1084   *Ibid.*
1085   *Ibid.*
1086   Wolfowitz (2006), *supra* note 1029.
1087   *Ibid.*

and representative decision-making at all levels" and "public access to information and protect[ion of] fundamental freedoms"—are the traits of a working democracy,[1088] although the term democracy is not explicitly mentioned in the SDGs. As such, "good governance" under the preceding definition is synonymous with an administratively competent, working democracy, and democracy has become an objective of development under the SDGs.

Recognizing democracy as a development objective may be justified for the following reasons. First, democracy, as a form of constitutional government, has overwhelming support in the international community.[1089] The majority of countries have achieved working democracies or at least attempted to do so: according to the "Democracy Index 2020" compiled by the Economist Intelligence Unit,[1090] nearly two-thirds of the world's 167 investigated countries, including all of the economically advanced OECD countries, are either fully fledged (liberal) democracies or regimes with the elements of democracy ("hybrid regimes").[1091] Second, a democratic form of government can be defended as a constituent element of development under the holistic approach. Leading scholars such as Amartya Sen view "development" as a notion that comprises political freedom, as well as economic choice and protection from abject poverty,[1092] and thus advocate for a democratic form of government.

In reality, however, it is not always straightforward to determine whether a particular regime can be considered a "democracy." Democracy is broadly understood as "a political regime that protects the freedom of individuals and expresses the will of the majority through free and fair elections, protection of minority rights and respect for basic human rights."[1093] However, democracy takes varied forms; for instance, parliamentary rule with heads of the state in different types

1088 See also, Michael J. Trebilcock and Mariana Monta Prado, *What Makes Poor Countries Poor? Institutional Determinants of Development* (Cheltenham: Edward Elgar, 2011), at 120. For an explanation of the varied approaches to democracy, including "thin" and "thick" definitions of democracy (*i.e.*, a competitive struggle for people's vote v. several constituent elements—basic rights, elections, an independent judiciary, legal equality, due process, institutional checks and balances, presence of civil society, civil control over military), see *id.*, at 121–122.

1089 A report indicates that an EU polls in 2007 found that about 80 percent of respondents around the world, regardless of country, continent, age, gender, or religion, believed democracy was the best way to run a society. Ian Morris, "Democracy: The Least Bad Form of Government," *Stratfor Worldview* (October 7, 2015), available online at: https://worldview.stratfor.com/article/democracy-least-bad-form-government; https://perma.cc/UZ7J-5LMW.

1090 The Economist, *Democracy Index 2020*, available online at: www.eiu.com/n/campaigns/democracy-index-2020/; https://perma.cc/Q97S-3L8C. It rates 167 countries on 60 indicators across five categories: electoral process and pluralism, the functioning of government, political participation, political culture, and civil liberties. *Id.*

1091 *Ibid.* According to another report, some 116 countries claimed to be democracies in 2010, compared to only 39 in 1974. Freedom House, *Freedom in the World 2010: Global Erosion of Freedom* (Washington, D.C.: Freedom House, 2010), available online at: https://freedomhouse.org/sites/default/files/2020-03/FIW_2010_Complete_Book_Scan.pdf; https://perma.cc/76YG-U8B7.

1092 Sen (1999), *supra* note 49.

1093 Trebilcock and Prado (2011), *supra* note 1088, at 120.

and roles (such as a traditional but "constitutional" monarch who plays only ceremonial roles, while more extensive power is vested in an elected president) or presidential rule with limited or more extensive parliamentary or congressional checks. There is no universal standard to determine whether or not a particular regime is a "democracy." The simple dichotomy between democracy and non-democracy has accordingly been criticized.[1094] Reflecting this complexity, the recent Democracy Index subdivides democracy into "full democracy" and "flawed democracy" and introduces yet another category of "hybrid regime."[1095] Under this categorization, Turkey, an OECD member country, is classified as a "hybrid regime," and the United States, a country that has been considered the champion of democracy, as a "flawed democracy."[1096] According to this Index, only 8.4 percent of the world population is living under a full democracy.[1097] These categorizations may not be met with universal approval, but they underscore that the determination of democracy is far from straightforward and may entail a degree of subjectivity.

9.3.2 *Democracy in the context of economic development*

Paul Wolfowitz has observed that good governance also promotes economic development.[1098] However, as discussed earlier, "good governance" *qua* democracy under the current definition may not always be effective in cultivating economic development. The two notions need to be distinguished from each other.[1099] This sub-section discusses the arguments for and against democracy with respect to economic development, which is necessary to assess the causal link between democracy and economic development, and examines further whether the suggested distinction between "good governance" and "effective governance" for economic development is warranted.

Trebilcock and Prado succinctly identify the four advantages of democracy in the context of economic development.[1100]

> First, democracy provides greater protection of property rights than non-democratic or authoritarian regimes. Second, democracy exhibits an enhanced capacity for mediating intergroup and distributional conflicts. Third, democracy generates better information and more reliable feedback on the effects of present or proposed policies when dissent or criticism is an avenue of recourse available to ordinary citizens and is not dependent on extraordinary, self-sacrificial heroes. Finally, democratic regimes are more

1094   Peter Lindert, "Voice and Growth: Was Churchill Right?" (2003) 63(2) *Journal of Economic History* 315–350.
1095   The Economist, *Democracy Index 2020, supra* note 1090.
1096   *Ibid.*
1097   *Ibid.*
1098   See discussion *supra* Section 9.1.
1099   *Ibid.*
1100   Trebilcock and Prado (2011), *supra* note 1088, at 123.

likely than totalitarian or authoritarian regimes to act in the general interest, or at least to reduce predatory tendencies that will often be exhibited by autocratic rulers.[1101]

The preceding discussion in Chapter 3 has explained that there are also drawbacks to being a democracy in the context of economic development, mainly due to its deliberative and elective nature:[1102] democratic governance may present considerable challenges when making long-term development decisions that may require voters to make immediate sacrifices, particularly in the early stages of economic development[1103] when resources are limited and difficult choices must be confronted.[1104] For example, the South Korean government did not authorize the provision of home mortgages to individuals in the 1960s and the 1970s in an effort to mobilize all available capital for industrial investments, by which the government hoped to create jobs and incomes for the people and promote national economic development.[1105] Such a policy might be justified for the nation's long-term economic development interests, but it would have been an extremely unpopular policy to voters who then had to save much of their limited income to buy their homes without the assistance of mortgages. In a full democracy, it would be difficult for the government to implement policies that might be conducive to long-term development but which are nevertheless unpopular in the short term. By way of example, a study found that democratic regimes will also have difficulty in undertaking fundamental institutional restructuring involving privatizing state enterprises, reforming the tax system, and creating new financial and regulatory institutions because this restructuring would incur a loss of jobs, income, status, and other perquisites and rents for the populations.[1106]

In addition, a change of administration, which is an inevitable outcome in elective democracies, may lead to changes in development policy and development objectives. The parties running for office cannot ignore the popular demands, even if unpopular policies might be necessary for the country's long-term interests. While extraordinary leadership may be able to align popular

---

1101   *Ibid.* Trebilcock and Prado introduce additional benefits of democracy: democracy provides a better incentive for the enhancement of future welfare of citizens (compared to roving or stationary "bandits"); the participatory political system is better for acquiring local knowledge to develop institutions necessary for development; and populations are more public-spirited and willing to compromise from deliberative processes associated with democracy. *Ibid.*, at 124–125.

1102   See discussion *supra* Section 3.3.2(c). See also Lee (2017), *supra* note 4, at 455.

1103   See *supra* note 262 (for a discussion of the stages of economic development).

1104   Thus, it took several decades before democratic India was able to embark on sustained economic growth, whereas the other successful developing countries under authoritarian rules achieved more rapid economic development.

1105   See discussion *supra* Section 3.3.2(c).

1106   Leszek Balcerowicz, "Understanding Post-Communist Transitions" (1994) 5(4) *Journal of Democracy* 75–89.

aspirations with long-term national interests,[1107] there is no guarantee that such leadership will be available at the time of need.

Despite the aforementioned advantages of democracy, history has shown that the most successful countries in achieving economic development (*e.g.*, South Korea, Taiwan, Singapore, Spain, Chile, and China in the twentieth century and the Western countries in the nineteenth century) were under authoritarian regimes or limited democracies. These countries protected individual property rights under the established private/civil law systems (in the case of China, through the new civil code and the Property Law implemented in 1987 and adopted in 2007, respectively), developed administrative bureaucracies, and set up judicial courts to resolve disputes efficiently (although the latter were not always fully independent from the administration on political matters). They promoted well-trained and capable administrators that planned, developed, implemented, and monitored policies for economic development and had dedicated national leaders who offered a clear vision, rationale, and plans for economic development in the national interest and followed up by implementing effective policies that led to successful economic development.[1108]

As discussed in Chapter 3, the inherent difficulty with elective democracy and the record of success under authoritarian rule does not, however, lead to the conclusion that dictatorships or authoritarian regimes are the answer.[1109] These regimes do not automatically generate the political commitment and institutional frameworks conducive to development, as evidenced by a number of authoritarian regimes in Africa and elsewhere, which have failed to make notable progress in development. Authoritarian leadership in several successful developing countries has produced decades of successful economic development, but a system of

---

1107   See discussion *supra* Section 9.2.3.

1108   See Lee (2018), *supra* note 339. See also *supra* note 336 (for a list of literature discussing successful development cases).

1109   See discussion *supra* Section 3.3.2(c). Empirical studies are not conclusive as to which form of government is more conducive to economic development. In a 1993 summary by Przeworski and Limongi of 18 studies including 21 observations about the relationship between democracy and growth, eight observations favored democracy, eight favored authoritarianism, and five found no difference. Adam Przeworski and Fernando Limongi, "Political Regimes and Economic Growth" (1993) 7(3) *Journal of Economic Perspectives* 51–69, cited in Trebilcock and Prado (2011), *supra* note 1088, at 123. Helliwell's study of 100 countries from 1965 to 1980 also revealed the minimal effect of introducing democracy on subsequent economic development. John F. Helliwell, "Empirical Linkages between Democracy and Economic Growth" (1994) 24(2) *British Journal of Political Science* 225–248. A 2000 study by Przeworski *et al.* investigating 137 countries between 1950 and 1990 concluded that the net effect of democracy or autocracy on economic growth is zero. Przeworski *et al.*, *supra* note 328, at 142–179. By contrast, a study by Halperin, Siegle, and Weinstein of a large sample of countries for the period between 1960 and 2001 finds that democracies (at least full liberal democracies) generally outperform autocracies in terms of economic growth by a significant margin, as well as exhibit less economic volatility and far fewer "economic disasters." Morton Halperin, Joseph Siegle, and Michael Weinstein, *The Democracy Advantage: How Democracies Promote Prosperity and Peace* (New York: Routledge, 2010). Lindert pointed out the weakness of these studies: the simple dichotomy between democracy and non-democracy is problematic, and liberal democracy is a relatively recent development. Lindert (2003), *supra* note 1094, at 315–350.

dictatorship or authoritarian governance does not necessarily promote economic development. The dilemma is that no political system automatically generates the kind of political leadership and institutional framework under which the government is able to consistently adopt, pursue, and adjust coherent and well-conceived economic development policies, resisting popular demand for short-term economic gain in order to meet long-term development objectives.[1110]

9.3.3 Economic development: a pathway to democracy

The preceding discussion suggests that a certain base level of economic development may realistically be necessary before a democratic system of governance can operate efficiently and promote development. A working democracy requires economic and social resources, such as public education, access to information, and the rule of law, which may not be achievable without economic development in place.[1111] In this respect, Chang is correct in claiming that democracy is a result of economic development, rather than one of its causes.[1112] This observation is consistent with the historical developments chronicled in Section 9.2: the successful developing countries, which were authoritarian or only partially democratic, underwent political transitions by the 1990s, in response to popular demands for political participation and protection of fundamental rights, and achieved democracy based on the rule of law.[1113]

The following hypothesis offers an intuitive account of the feasibility of democracy in the context of economic development. Suppose that a developing country decides to build a dam in an area where several towns are located, to supply electricity to adjacent manufacturing plants being built in the region, and to control flooding that has been repeated on a regular basis. The manufacturing plants are expected to generate employment and produce income for the employees and tax revenues for the government. The production from the manufacturing plants is consistent with the country's economic development initiatives, and the control of flooding will protect crops and prevent property damage and even loss of life. However, the construction of the dam will also create a reservoir, and several towns in the area will be submerged under the water. As a result, the residents will have to abandon their homes and move to safe locations.

This dam project may well find its economic justification in the country's national interest, but it will also cause severe grievances for the displaced residents. The government will presumably have the legal authority (*i.e.*, the power of

---

1110   The cited systemic issues with elective democracies and the uncertainty characterizing authoritarian regimes are likely reasons that only a small number of countries achieved development successfully since the Second World War and became developed ones. See *supra* note 333 (for a discussion of additional development cases other than the countries cited above).

1111   See Chang (2002), *supra* note 203, at 69–124. See also Paul Collier, *Wars, Guns, and Votes: Democracy in Dangerous Places* (New York: HarperCollins, 2009), at 45.

1112   Chang, *ibid.*

1113   See discussion *supra* Section 1.3.1.

eminent domain) to expropriate the residents' properties for the construction project,[1114] but the principles of democracy require certain due processes; *e.g.*, hearings and other processes to assess the grievance of the residents, to determine or re-determine the necessity of the project, and to examine the environmental impact. All this could take years. In the midst of the process, unsatisfied residents could file a lawsuit against the government, and courts could issue an interim injunction to halt work on the dam project until the case is decided, which may also take several years or longer. Even if the government and the residents agree on the necessity of the dam's construction, negotiations to determine the amount of compensation could also take a considerable amount of time to resolve.

Democracies will have to endure these types of delays and processes for non-emergency matters—it is the deliberative nature of the system. The advanced, developed economies of the world, vested with abundant resources, may well be able to afford to tolerate these types of delays and even the discontinuation of a particular project if it should be an outcome of the process. The impact of each individual project on the national economy is likely limited, and alternative opportunities will be available. It is unlikely that the success or failure of an individual project will have immediate ramifications for the livelihood of populations in developed countries. However, for developing countries, the magnitude of a single key infrastructure project is much larger for the entire economy and often essential for the relief of poverty. A series of well-intended democratic processes then become an impediment to economic development where the availability of alternative economic opportunities is limited, and there is a more immediate impact on the livelihood of populations. Thus, in developing countries, particularly those in the early stages of economic development, there is a call for a more expedient regime, such as those adopted by administrations of successful developing countries in the past that had been labeled as "authoritarian" or "limited democracies" (even if such a regime may not necessarily "guarantee" the success of economic development as discussed earlier).

Successful economic development provides a pathway to democracy. The history of economic development has shown a pattern whereby once a degree of economic development has been achieved, the people who are freed of day-to-day subsistence concerns and endowed with resources as a result of successful economic development, demand increased political participation and legal protection of fundamental rights.[1115] Indeed, the successful developing countries cited, including South Korea, Taiwan, Spain, and Chile, have transitioned into democracies based on the rule of law. In the West, the limited democracies of the eighteenth and nineteenth centuries matured into full democracies with universal suffrage during the twentieth century.[1116] Trebilcock and Prado aptly summarize

---

1114 The government has the power to take the title and possession of property for a public purpose. For a discussion of eminent domain around the world, see Iljoong Kim, Hojun Lee, and Ilya Somin (eds.) (2017), *supra* note 1004.

1115 Lee (2018), *supra* note 339, at 461.

1116 Chang (2002), *supra* note 203, at 73.

the relationship between democracy and economic development: "Democracy may not be conducive to the emergence of capitalism and its early growth, but [...] it is the regime most likely to develop and be sustainable once societies reach a certain level of economic development."[1117]

On a final note, in many of the successful developing countries, the transition to democracy came about not only as a result of economic development but also because of civil challenge and strife.[1118] The authoritarian regimes in these countries led their countries into economic prosperity, but at the same time, they maintained a tight grip on governmental power and did not allow civil challenges.[1119] Not all economic development has shown transition into democracy; since the 1980s, China has achieved rapid economic development, but the country still maintains an authoritarian rule under its single-party system (although China has not yet reached the status of a developed country unlike the other successful developing countries). There is also a debate as to whether Singapore is a full democracy.[1120] As such, there is no absolute guarantee that economic development will always lead to democracy, and even if it eventually happens, the timing of such a transition is difficult to predict. Despite this uncertainty, economic development provides socioeconomic conditions (*e.g.*, economic resources, education, access to information) under which democracy can develop and prosper.

9.4 Establishing legal frameworks for political stability

9.4.1 Law and political stability

Having established that political stability is essential for economic development,[1121] this section turns to examine the role of law in creating political stability and the necessary frameworks to sustain the latter. As repeatedly mentioned, the successful developing countries were authoritarian regimes or limited democracies with a high degree of political stability. This sub-section focuses on the importance of law to create and maintain political stability where the authoritarian ruler can adopt any and all measures deemed necessary for developmental purposes. At the outset, it should be acknowledged that laws are necessary, even in the authoritarian context, to maintain political stability, as legal rules instill consistency and regularity in policy implementation.[1122] All of the successful

---

1117   Trebilcock and Prado (2011), *supra* note 1088, at 123.
1118   Lee (2018), *supra* note 339, at 432–434. See also Hart-Landsberg (1993), *supra* note 418 and Alan M. Wachman, *Taiwan: National Identity and Democratization* (Abington: Routledge, 2016).
1119   *Ibid.*
1120   Freedom House, "Singapore," *Freedom in the World 2019*, available online at: https://freedomhouse.org/country/singapore/freedom-world/2019; https://perma.cc/RY64-H36E.
1121   See discussion *supra* Section 9.2.
1122   Thus, the "thin" conception of the rule of law requires that government officials and citizens are bound by and must act consistently with the law, whatever the law might require. Brian Tamanaha, "A Concise Guide to the Rule of Law," *Legal Studies Research Paper Series, St.*

developing countries cited in this chapter, with the exception of China until the 1980s, had well-developed public law systems that defined the powers of the state and the rights of people. Although courts were often unable to check authoritarian rulers in relation to politically sensitive matters, the governments in these countries nevertheless used the laws to enable themselves to adopt measures that they considered necessary to maintain political stability.

Sustaining political stability requires the government to restrain itself from engaging in activities that could make economic sense but are risky from a stability perspective, such as using the legal power to expropriate private property without justification, which is likely to trigger civilian resistance. At the same time, prudent governments will engage in activities that are conducive to reinforcing political stability, such as subsidizing services that are viewed as meeting the public interest (*e.g.*, subsidizing public healthcare). Doing so requires the exercise of lawmaking or regulatory power to formulate a legal rule that is accessible and understandable—one that also identifies the conditions under which subsidies will be made available. As discussed above, the socioeconomic conditions to sustain political stability vary from one place to another, and the activities in which the government is required to engage or disengage to maintain political stability would also vary according to the conditions on the ground.[1123] For example, the conditions of prevalent poverty and starvation, which would be fertile ground for political dissidents, will require the government to focus on the eradication of poverty. Law can assist in maintaining political stability by functioning as both an inhibitor on the state and an enabler, as further discussed below.

9.4.2 Law as an inhibitor on the state

Legal rules, perhaps most notably those contained in a country's constitution, may inhibit the state from engaging in activities not conducive to political stability. Constitutions typically identify the "rights" and "freedoms" of individuals with which the state must not interfere. Property rights, freedom of contract, freedom of religion, the right to travel, and the right to a fair trial are examples of such rights and freedoms protected against unjustified government interference.[1124] The doctrine of constitutional supremacy means that these rights and freedoms stipulated in the constitution are binding on all levels of government and that all other laws must comply with its prescriptions to be valid.[1125] The legal protection of these rights and freedoms, including constitutional protection,

John's University School of Law, #07–0082 (September 2007), at 17, available online at: http://content.csbs.utah.edu/~dlevin/conlaw/tamanaha-rule-of-law.pdf; https://perma.cc/UZ2W-FLXU.

1123   See discussion *supra* Section 3.2.

1124   For example, the Bill of Rights of the U.S. Constitution (Amendments 1–10) lists fundamental rights, binding on all levels of the government. American courts also started to protect the right to contract (freedom of contract) under the due process of the Fourteenth Amendment by the late nineteenth century. Bernstein (2008), *supra* note 312.

1125   *Ibid.*

represents more than the mere embodiment of human aspirations; it represents an acknowledgment of the necessity of maintaining political stability by deterring state interference. For example, unwarranted state interference with religion could instigate intense opposition and disrupt political stability. As another example, unjustified interferences with property rights and freedom of contract will also disturb the established economic order and adversely impact political stability.

Under an authoritarian regime, the government often restricts the exercise of political rights, such as freedom of (political) speech and freedom of the press, to prevent the circulation of statements that leaders deem objectionable from the standpoint of the authoritarian government. Such government restrictions often lead to resistance, including public demonstrations and other forms of organized opposition by the public, which, in turn, instigates oppressive measures from the government, including arrests and prosecutions.[1126] This contentious cycle continues until the country completes its transformation into a fully fledged constitutional democracy in later stages of economic development.[1127] In non-political areas, the successful developing countries protected individual rights and freedoms (*e.g.*, property rights and freedom of contract), except in cases where government development strategies required restrictions, such as cases of government-led "economic restructuring" to sort out overlapping investments by competing enterprises.[1128] The government protected these rights to preserve and promote private incentives for economic transactions, which was essential to promote market-based economic development.[1129]

9.4.3 Law as an enabler of the state

Law also "enables" the state to promote certain activities that would bolster political stability. There are two ways in which law may function as an enabler of the state; first, by recognizing socioeconomic rights to be enjoyed by the people, such as the right to employment, the right to education, the right to healthcare, and the right to a clean environment.[1130] These socioeconomic rights can be distinguished from the civil and political rights and freedoms cited above in that

---

1126 Lee (2018), *supra* note 339, at 432–434. See also Hart-Landsberg (1993), *supra* note 418 and Wachman (2016), *supra* note 1118.

1127 *Ibid.*

1128 See, *e.g.*, Sang Chul Lee, "A Study on the Industrial Restructuring Policy in Korea during the 1980s," *NRF Research Project*, no. 2012S1A5A2A01020629 (2012) (in Korean).

1129 Professor Maartje de Visser has suggested another dimension alongside rights protection: the constitution (and related legislation) will also prescribe how policies are to be made; *e.g.*, the need for parliamentary legislation to determine the basic details of a policy, voting rules, the need to consult advisory bodies or the people through a referendum, or involvement of the lower echelons in the case of a federation. These, too, limit the government's ability to maneuver in prescribing the format of policies (*e.g.*, via statute as opposed to regulation) and the speed with which policies can be introduced or amended (correspondence on file with the author).

1130 For a discussion of socioeconomic rights, see David Bilchitz, *Poverty and Fundamental Rights: The Justification and Enforcement of Socio-Economic Rights* (Oxford: Oxford

the state has the positive duty to facilitate these rights: mere non-interference does not suffice. For example, to facilitate the right to education, the state has to build schools and recruit teachers. Where the state has the resources to do so, the law "enables" the state to use its resources to facilitate such rights for the people. Socioeconomic rights are directly relevant to the state's effort to facilitate economic development; for instance, the right to employment and the right to development[1131] authorize the state to spend resources for the economic wellbeing of its citizens and thereby secure the effective realization of these legal guarantees.[1132]

Second, the law enables the state to adopt specific measures to promote industrial and economic development. Developmental states[1133] often adopt specific statutes designed to facilitate the development of particular industries. For example, successful developing countries, such as South Korea, enacted several statutes mandating direct state support for specific manufacturing industries.[1134] These statutes authorized the government to provide tax incentives, loans whose terms, such as interest rates, were more favorable than the prevailing commercial terms (*i.e.,* "policy loans"), subsidy grants, tariff rebates and import control, and overseas loan guarantees for the designated industries.[1135] Countries also pass laws that enable their respective governments to raise tariff rates to protect domestic industries against competition with imports, lower taxes for businesses to expand their domestic operations, promote research and development that will benefit industries, and adjust regulatory restrictions to promote industries.

9.4.4 Problems with rights-based approaches

(a) Controversy over justiciability

A recent study illustrates problems associated with rights-based approaches.[1136] The study concluded that the environmental protection clause (Section 20) of

University Press, 2007) and Sandra Liebenberg, *Socio-Economic Rights: Adjudication Under a Transformative Constitution* (Juta Academic, 2010).

1131 For a discussion of the RTD, see Lee (2019), *supra* note 594.

1132 *Ibid.*

1133 A "developmental state" is a sovereign state that assumes the key role for economic development and which "creates [economic development] plans, relocate[s] surplus, combat[s] resistance, invest[s] and manage[s] key sectors, and control[s] foreign capital." *Supra* note 166.

1134 For example, the Korean government enacted several statutes for this purpose, including the Act on Temporary Measures for Textile Industrial Facilities (1967); the Acts facilitating the development of specific industries, such as Mechanical Industries (1967), Shipbuilding Industries (1967), Electronic Industries (1969), Petrochemical Industries (1970), and Steel Industries (1970); the Act on Refining Service of Non-Ferrous Metals (1971); and the Act on Promotion of the Modernization of Textile Industries (1979). See Section 4.2.3 *supra*.

1135 See *supra* Section 4.2.3. These statutes were replaced with the Manufacturing Industry Development Act in 1986, which granted more selective assistance to industries based on a need to improve their efficiency by restructuring or reorganization. By the 1980s, industry-specific support was no longer required thanks to the progress of industrial development in Korea. *Id.*

1136 Peter Oniemola and Oyinkan Tasie, "Engendering Constitutional Realization of Sustainable Development in Nigeria" (2020) 13(1) *Law and Development Review* 159–191.

the Nigerian constitution supports sustainable development requirements but found that another constitutional provision precludes courts from adjudicating claims arising from this constitutional provision.[1137] Section 6 of the Nigerian constitution provides in relevant part:

> The judicial powers vested in accordance with the foregoing provisions of this section
>
> [...]
>
> shall not except as otherwise provided by this Constitution, extend to any issue or question as to whether any act of omission by any authority or person or as to whether any law or any judicial decision is in conformity with the Fundamental Objectives and Directive Principles of State Policy set out in Chapter II of this Constitution [where the environmental protection clause is located] (explanation added).[1138]

The authors of the study claim that the non-justiciability of the constitutional provision has weakened sustainable development requirements and accordingly argue that a constitutional amendment is necessary to provide remedies for the claims arising under this provision.[1139]

Ensuring environmental protection requires affirmative action on the part of the state, which accounts for its status as a socioeconomic right in the growing number of countries that offer constitutional recognition for such protection. Socioeconomic rights "enable" the state to adopt measures to maintain political stability, but the more challenging question is whether the state must be "required" to take action to fulfill every socioeconomic right listed in its constitution. In developing countries where resources are limited, such as Nigeria, the state must prioritize the areas to which it will dedicate its limited resources and thereby facilitate the relevant rights. In theory, courts may also take the country's limited resources into consideration and determine whether the state is justified in declining to facilitate a particular right or trying to fulfill it in a manner which the claimant may find objectionable. However, it is doubtful that, as judicial institutions, courts are in the best position to make that determination, given that they are unlikely to be experts in budgetary and resource-allocation matters. By this logic, the non-justiciability of socioeconomic rights, as in the Nigerian example, seems prudent. Perhaps a more feasible approach is for the parliament to enact detailed statutes that obligate the government to spend resources to fulfill the rights specified therein to the extent possible under the available budget.[1140]

1137 *Ibid.*
1138 Constitution of Nigeria, Section 6(6)(c).
1139 Oniemola and Tasie (2020), *supra* note 1136, at 185.
1140 Oniemola and Tasie recognize that legislation is another option to realize the right. *Ibid.*

(b) Socioeconomic constraints

Rights-based approaches to development tend to overlook the socioeconomic constraints faced by the government. The SDGs include a number of development objectives, fulfillment of which requires a massive amount of resources that most developing countries lack. For example, according to a report, Nigeria would need US$ 337 billion to implement the SDGs from 2019 to 2022.[1141] The required amount, US$ 337 billion, is more than 11 times the annual government budget of Nigeria. Given the massive financial demands, it would be simply impossible for Nigeria and most other developing countries to implement all the SDG targets simultaneously with equal strength; sequencing and prioritization are inevitable. The cost of implementing SDGs globally has been estimated at US$ 2.5 trillion per year,[1142] which exceeds the financial capabilities of developing countries. International aid might be available but is likely insufficient to cover this high cost and will not remove the need for sequencing and prioritization.

Thus, rights-based approaches to development are essentially incompatible with the fiscal reality of developing countries. The challenging fiscal conditions and severe resource constraints facing most developing countries cannot be ignored, and the realization of socioeconomic rights is not a matter of assigning rights and making rights-based demands, as the approaches suggest, but of capabilities and resources. Another study emphasizes the need for the United States to approve the right to development and recognize socioeconomic rights under its federal constitution.[1143] Its context, however, is completely different from that of developing countries; the United States has the largest and most advanced economy in the world, and the U.S. government commands the largest budget among all countries. Yet, social welfare provisions in the United States are weaker than those offered by many other developed countries,[1144] mostly on political grounds, and the economic circumstances of the United States justify new approaches—the recognition of the RTD and socioeconomic rights—which will enable the U.S. government, and to some extent obligate it, to provide for its citizens.[1145] The socioeconomic conditions that justify this approach either do not exist or are very different in most developing countries.

9.4.5 *Designing legal frameworks to facilitate political stability*

The preceding discussion has examined the role of law in creating political stability and promoting economic development. Against that backdrop, the remainder of this section explores how effective legal frameworks can be designed to facilitate the political stability that is essential for successful economic development.

1141 *Ibid.*, at 187.
1142 AIDDATA, *Realizing Agenda 2030*, available online at: www.aiddata.org/sdg; https://perma.cc/D8TG-VYU9.
1143 Lee (2019), *supra* note 594.
1144 *Ibid.*
1145 *Ibid.*

(a) Constitution as a blueprint

A national constitution, as the supreme law of the land, is the primary architecture of the country's governing structures and of the fundamental rights and obligations owed by the state to its people. These structures, rights, and obligations together form the basic legal apparatus that creates the regulatory conditions for political stability. For example, where a majority of the population suffers from economic deprivations, a long list of detailed socioeconomic rights stipulated in the constitution could create a presumption on the part of people that the fulfillment of these rights is a matter of making the government hear and accept their rights-based demands,[1146] particularly when the constitution does not clarify the conditions under which the government is required to fulfill these rights, such as the availability of financial and technical resources. The existence of such a presumption may render political stability under constant threat by those who are dissatisfied with the government for its real or perceived failure to realize their "rights."[1147] Some national constitutions, such as the South African Constitution and the Indian Constitution, include extensive lists of socioeconomic rights, fulfillment of which may not always be feasible due to fiscal and other resource constraints. The provisions of the constitution must be realistic to promote stability. This suggests that, for example, a long list of socioeconomic rights stipulated in the constitution of a developing country with resource constraints should be augmented by a clause that specifies the conditions under which the state must fulfill those rights.

The "realism" to be embodied in the constitution must reflect the reality facing the country. For the countries facing prevalent poverty and an acute need for economic development, the constitution should set forth provisions that emphasize the importance of economic development, establish dedicated state agencies, and assign these agencies clear duties to develop and implement the necessary measures to promote economic development. The details for the implementation of these duties can be set out in specific statutes and government regulations, but the constitution should present the foundational "blueprint" for this endeavor. By contrast, in countries that have achieved a sufficiently high degree of economic development but face other socioeconomic issues as a result of development, such as inequitable income distributions and labor issues, the constitution could helpfully include provisions that promote more equitable income distributions and protect labor rights. South Korea's 1987 constitutional amendment added provisions that clarify the state's duty to ensure proper

---

1146   Thus, T. K. Pooe criticized rights-based approaches in the context of the South African constitution. See T. K. Pooe, "Developmental State No Birth Right: South Africa's Post-1994 Economic Development Story" (2017) 10(2) *Law and Development Review* 361–387.

1147   *Ibid*. The demands may go beyond the bounds of the constitution. South Africa's National Assembly, for example, adopted the constitutional review committee's report recommending a constitutional amendment to expropriate land without compensation. Makinana (2018), *supra* note 1011.

distribution of income.[1148] Constitutional amendments signify changes in the regulatory blueprint in response to the changing socioeconomic conditions.[1149]

(b) Law as both inhibitor and enabler

The constitutional "blueprint" will need to be augmented and reinforced by more detailed statutes and government regulations. In this context, the dual function of law as an inhibitor and enabler must be coordinated to facilitate political stability. Drafters of the statutes and regulations must identify the activities and measures that the state shall adopt and should refrain from pursuing, taking relevant factors into consideration, such as the political needs of the constituents, cultural priorities, historical contexts, and popular aspirations.[1150] The government will face difficult decisions when drafting legislation, confronted as it will be with competing and conflicting demands from stakeholders. For example, those who stand to benefit from liberalizing trade with a foreign country may demand that the government legislate for free trade, whereas those who expect to be harmed by those same measures will resist such legislation and may even demand the adjustment of the current tariff laws to increase trade barriers. One way or the other, political stability will be affected by those unsatisfied with government action or inaction.

An expedient government will devise action plans to maximize the national interest while minimizing harm to the losing stakeholders and any adverse impact on political stability. For example, the government may authorize free trade with another country if it determines that this course of action will increase the overall economic interest for the nation. At the same time, the government may also enact a statute to provide subsidies to the losing industries or constituencies (*e.g.*, employment and training assistance).[1151] This is an example of the government using the law as an enabler to promote political stability. The government may also use the law as an inhibitor to sustain political stability. Government attempts to impose restrictions on cryptocurrency markets have been a controversial issue in many countries.[1152] Growing discontent by those who oppose such

---

1148   Article 119(2) of the 1987 Constitution provides, "The State may regulate and coordinate economic affairs in order to maintain the balanced growth and stability of the national economy, *to ensure proper distribution of income, to prevent the domination of the market and the abuse of economic power and to democratize the economy through harmony among the economic agents*" (emphasis added).

1149   Thus, failure to engage in timely amendments could also, in the longer term, result in political instability as the constitution is perceived to be incompatible with socioeconomic realities on the ground.

1150   See discussion *supra* Section 9.2.2.

1151   The Trade Adjustment Assistance Program, established in the United States under the Trade Act of 1974, would be an example of such an effort. Trade Act of 1974, 19 U.S.C. § 2271 *et seq.*

1152   According to a Library of Congress report, nine countries ban cryptocurrency markets outright and sixteen imposed "implicit ban[s]" on the markets. Library of Congress, *Legal Status of Cryptocurrencies*, available online at: www.loc.gov/law/help/cryptocurrency/map1.pdf; https://perma.cc/FP62-49NG.

government restrictions may adversely affect political stability, particularly if the general public has already made substantial investments in the market by the time government restrictions take effect. If there is a social consensus that the government must refrain from imposing these types of restrictive measures, the government may adopt a law that clarifies the rights of the market users, such as the rights to sell and buy cryptocurrencies, not to be breached by the state. Such a law will contribute to political stability by inhibiting specific state action. Statutory enactments and amendments should reflect regulatory adjustments in response to changes in socioeconomic conditions.

(c) Securing compliance and implementation

For the legal rules just canvassed to have the desired effect on political stability, compliance and implementation are required. As readers will recall, the general theory of law and development explains that three analytical factors—"regulatory design," "regulatory compliance," and "quality of implementation"—determine the impact of law on economic development.[1153] Compliance refers to the conduct of the general public in complying with the law.[1154] There is active compliance when compliance exceeds fulfilling the minimum requirements under the law and when the public seeks to assist the state in meeting the law's regulatory objective by actively participating in the process mandated by law, often with encouragement to others to do the same.[1155] Active compliance will maximize the impact of law, and people are likely to show active compliance when they believe that the law meets their own interests and agendas, whether they are political needs, cultural priorities, historical contexts, or popular aspirations.

The quality of implementation is measured by the extent to which a state meets the requirements set forth by the terms of law and fulfills the mandates under these terms, including its enforcement and monitoring terms.[1156] The two factors, "state capacity," which refers to the financial, technological, and administrative capabilities of a state, and "political will," which means the commitment and devotion of a country's political leadership to the implementation of a particular law, influence the quality of implementation.[1157] The latter is particularly important when the implementation of a law with developmental aspirations is subject to political challenge.[1158] For example, political will was important when the South Korean government promoted the (unpopular) policy restricting home mortgages to mobilize and commit all available capital to industrial production for the interest of long-term economic development.[1159]

1153 See discussion *supra* Section 3.1.
1154 See discussion *supra* Section 3.3.1.
1155 *Ibid.*
1156 See discussion *supra* Section 3.3.2.
1157 *Ibid.*
1158 *Ibid.*
1159 See discussion *supra* Section 9.2.2(c).

9.4.6 *Political governance, law, and economic development: interrelationships*

This chapter has discussed the interrelationships among political governance, law, and economic development. Political governance has been identified as a key determinant of successful economic development. Major intergovernmental organizations, such as the World Bank, actively promote "good governance," which includes the constitutive elements of a working democracy, such as "transparent and accountable institutions," "an independent judiciary," "a free press," "responsive, inclusive, participatory and representative decision-making at all levels," and "public access to information and protect[ion of] fundamental freedoms."[1160] As the Bank's former president Paul Wolfowitz explained, the assumption is that "good governance" helps governments function effectively and achieve economic progress.[1161] According to this explanation, "good governance" is thus conducive to economic development and needs to be promoted.

However, history has shown that the countries that achieved the most successful economic development, such as South Korea, Taiwan, Singapore, Spain, Chile, and even many countries in the West during the Industrial Revolution and thereafter, were under authoritarian rules or limited democracy (*e.g.*, with the right to vote reserved to a certain class); to be sure, they were not exemplars of countries practicing "good governance" under the modern definition. What these successful developing countries had in common was *not* the presence of "good governance" or democracy but sustained political stability and effective leadership. This chapter has identified various factors, such as political needs, cultural priorities, historical contexts, and popular aspirations (including economic requirements), as bearing particular influence on political stability, with effective leaders playing a crucial role in creating the conditions for political stability and for economic development to proceed apace. A working democracy requires considerable resources, such as economic resources, education, and access to information. As such, it is difficult, if not entirely impossible, for countries with severe resource constraints to practice working democracy and achieve economic development at the same time. Democracy is a result of economic development rather than its cause. This conclusion is consistent with the historical developments: the successful developing countries which had been under authoritarian rule or limited democracy transitioned to become democracies only *after* a degree of economic development was achieved.[1162]

Laws and legal frameworks influence political governance and political stability. Even in authoritarian regimes, law helps to create consistency and predictability in policy implementations, which cannot be achieved by *ad hoc* instructions from the rulers. Indeed, all of the successful developing countries used the law

---

1160   See discussion *supra* Section 9.1.
1161   *Ibid.*
1162   See discussion *supra* Section 9.3.3.

to adopt measures necessary to promote economic development. In this regard, law functions as an inhibitor on the state, preventing the latter from engaging in activities that may threaten political stability, and also as an enabler of the state, authorizing it to promote activities that are conducive to political stability and economic development. Effective governance ensures that the state adopts well-designed laws in a coordinated combination of effective inhibitors and enablers for the purpose of promoting political stability and economic development. Rights-based approaches to development, notably including the recognition of justiciable socioeconomic rights, may not be compatible with the realities of developing countries facing severe fiscal constraints. Resource constraints render sequencing and prioritization inevitable in pursuing development objectives. Laws and legal frameworks, including constitutions, must adapt to the changing socioeconomic conditions on the ground to remain effective.

10 Legal frameworks for business transactions and economic development

10.1 Contract law and economic development

10.1.1 Introduction

This chapter examines the legal frameworks for business transactions in the context of economic development, with an emphasis on contract law.[1163] Economic development is synonymous with the proliferation of business transactions, and the legal frameworks relevant to business transactions must be carefully studied, as they set forth legal parameters of business. The legal frameworks include a wide range of private and public laws, such as contract law and laws governing property rights, government regulations on business transactions, and secured transactions. Among these laws, this chapter focuses on contract law, which regulates the formation of a contract and defines the rights and obligations of the parties to a contract. A contract may be defined as a legally binding commitment,[1164] and contracts are also categorized into different types, such as private contracts and public contracts.[1165] Contracts are an essential constituent element for business transactions, as they create a "price" (*e.g.*, damages to be paid) for failing to perform the promised transaction and clarify the terms of the transaction. Contracts are formed with or without documentary execution and often arise from day-to-day transactions. For example, someone who hails a taxi in a city and mutters only

---

1163 This chapter is developed from the author's recent article, "The Legal Framework for Business Transactions and Economic Development" (2020) 44(2) *Southern Illinois University Law Journal* 273–297.

1164 Restatement Second of Contracts (Restatement Second) defines a contract as "a promise or a set of promises for the breach of which the law gives a remedy, or the performance of which the law in some way recognizes as a duty." American Law Institute (ALI), *Restatement of the Law Second Contracts* (Washington, D.C.: ALI, 1979), Section 1.

1165 Private contracts refer to contracts arising between private parties who may not necessarily share a social nexus. Breach of private contracts entails legal sanctions that are civil in nature, such as monetary damages. Public contracts involve the work or improvement desired by a public authority for the benefit of the public at large, often with standardized terms, and entail regulatory sanctions. See Thomas W. Merrill, "Public Contracts, Private Contracts, and the Transformation of the Constitutional Order" (1987) *Case Western Reserve Law Review* 597–630.

DOI: 10.4324/9781003090175-13

one word about his or her destination to the driver forms a binding contractual relationship with the taxi driver.[1166] These terms include payment of the fare by the passenger and transportation of the passenger to the destination by the driver, even if they are not explicitly spelled out.

Some other contracts are more explicit and sophisticated, and the details of their terms are set out in a document or multiple documents. Regardless of transactional complexity, protection and enforcement of contractual rights and obligations are important for business transactions and economic growth, because this protection and enforcement improves the predictability of transaction outcomes and thereby reduces transaction costs.[1167] The terms of contract law stipulate such protection and facilitate enforcement; thus, contract law is relevant to economic development and needs to be examined in this context, although law may not be the only device for the protection and enforcement of contractual rights and obligations.[1168] Formal contract enforcement, referring to a form of contract enforcement performed by the state under the terms of law, is also relevant to economic development. A conventional view emphasizes the role of formal contract enforcement for economic development.[1169] However, a contrasting view, citing empirical works, holds that contract law and formal enforcement are not important for business transactions, because the majority of issues and difficulties arising from business transactions are resolved informally, without reference to contractual terms.[1170]

In the presence of opposing views, the governments promoting economic development will have to consider an appropriate regulatory approach; *e.g.*, to what extent the state must use its limited resources to develop formal contract law and enforce contracts to facilitate economic development. This decision will be particularly important for developing countries facing resource constraints. Freedom of contract[1171] also needs to be balanced with the public interest, including economic development: the government may find it necessary to intervene in private contractual relations to meet the needs of economic development, such as expropriation for infrastructure projects. A point of optimal balance between freedom of contract and public interest limiting such freedom may change over

1166 Such contracts are referred to as "implied contracts" or "contracts implied-in-fact." Farnsworth (2004), *supra* note 753.

1167 Ronald H. Coase developed a theory of transaction cost. Coase (1937), *supra* note 205, and Coase (1960), *supra* note 205.

1168 For example, social risks, such as reputational risks and the risk of exclusion, may deter breach and enable private enforcement of contract. North (1990), *supra* note 34, at 19.

1169 Supporting this view, Douglass North stated that "the inability of societies to develop effective, low-cost enforcement of contracts is the most important source of both historical stagnation and contemporary underdevelopment in the Third World." *Ibid.,* at 54.

1170 Avner Greif, "Contracting, Enforcement, and Efficiency: Economics beyond the Law," *in* Michael Bruno and Boris Pleskovic (eds.), *Annual World Bank Conference on Development Economics 1996* (Washington, D.C.: World Bank, 1997), at 239.

1171 Freedom of contract refers to the freedom of individuals and legal persons (legally recognized entities), including corporations, to form contracts and determine contractual terms. Freedom of contract is essential to the free market economy. Bernstein (2008), *supra* note 312.

the course of economic development. Finally, national and international development agencies emphasize the importance of promoting secured transactions for economic development and proposed law reforms.[1172] Since the facilitation of laws and institutions to encourage secured transactions requires a considerable amount of resources and administrative capacity, it is also necessary to examine whether secured transactions are imperative to economic development.

This chapter is organized as follows. Section 10.2 briefly discusses contract validity and formation issues in the context of economic development, examines the views that support or detract from the role of formal contract enforcement in economic development, and assesses the importance of formal contract enforcement for economic development. This section also examines the conditions required for the regulatory frameworks in contract law that are conducive to economic development, as well as a strategic regulatory approach for developing countries. Section 10.3 considers limitations on freedom of contract supported by public interest considerations, such as economic development. Section 10.4 turns to secured transactions, which have been promoted by national and international development agencies as a vehicle for economic development, and evaluates the claim that law reforms promoting secured transactions are important for economic development.

10.2 Contract enforcement and economic development

Today, most jurisdictions in both civil law and common law traditions have a set of laws that recognize, protect, and enforce contractual rights.[1173] Such laws are collectively referred to as contract law, and they include provisions pertaining to the formation of contracts, the validity of contracts, the rights and obligations of parties, the forms which contracts may take, and defenses against alleged contracts or breaches thereof.[1174] Private property rights form the essential basis for valid contractual transactions among private individuals;[1175] for example, a private contract to purchase a house would be an invalid contract under a communist regime that does not allow private ownership of a house. Thus, private property rights and freedom of contract are the two key elements for a market

---

1172   For example, the United Nations (including the United Nations Commission on International Trade Law (UNCITRAL) and the General Assembly), the Organization of American States (OAS), Organization for the Harmonization of Business Law in Africa (OHADA), the European Union, the World Bank, the United States Agency for International Development, and other similar agencies have identified secured transactions reform as a critical component in economic development in developing countries. American Bar Association, *Report Adopted by the House of Delegates* (August 8–9, 2011), at 2.

1173   For example, in German law, contract law is found in Bürgerliches Gesetzbuch (BGB) (civil code of Germany). In common law jurisdictions, such as the United States, contract law is developed by judicial precedents originated in English courts. See Farnsworth (2004), *supra* note 753, at 9–41.

1174   *Ibid.*

1175   De Soto (2003), *supra* note 772.

economy. The facilitation of various market transactions therein would not be possible without the recognition and protection of valid contracts. Also important is contract enforcement, which is influenced by institutional effectiveness and state capacity.[1176]

10.2.1 Contract validity and contract formation

The validity of a particular contract raises a question concerning the subject matter of the contract; *i.e.*, as to what private parties may agree upon in a legally enforceable contract. There are two regulatory approaches: liberal and restrictive. The liberal approach permits parties to contract freely (*i.e.*, freedom of contract) without restrictions, except where specific transactions are prohibited by law (*e.g.*, transactions on illegal drugs). Most market economies adopt liberal approaches and endeavor to secure freedom of contract. In contrast, the restrictive approach limits and controls what can be contracted among private parties. For example, communist regimes restricted freedom of contract and did not allow private transactions over means of production, such as manufacturing facilities and agricultural farms.[1177] Even in market economies, the government may restrict private property rights in the context of industrial strategy, and this may lead to the diminution of freedom of contract; for example, the restriction of private ownership of strategic minerals would render a private contract for the sale of these minerals invalid.

In the development context, the government may use licensing schemes to control the contractual capacity of private parties. For example, the government may control exports and imports by requiring traders to obtain a license prior to transactions. The government may set the terms for issuance and renewal of such licenses so that international trade contributes to development goals; *e.g.*, the government may set policies to grant a lucrative import license to firms with a certain level of export performance as a means to promote export-led development policies.[1178] The government can also operate a licensing scheme to secure revenue sources, such as tariffs imposed on imports. In addition to trade, the government may also affect domestic business transactions and promote specific policy objectives by setting up laws that require prior authorizations. For example, the government may require authorization for land or real property transactions in areas where strong demands drive up land prices rapidly and create social problems associated with radical price increases. Contracts formed without

---

1176 Formal contract enforcement requires that courts render a timely decision and implement the decision effectively. The quality of implementation is also influenced by state capacity. See Lee (2017), *supra* note 4, at 451–454. See also John R. Commons, *Legal Foundations of Capitalism* (New York: The Macmillan Company, 1924).

1177 See, *e.g.*, Wenceslas J. Wagner, "The Law of Contracts in Communist Countries (Russia, Bulgaria, Czechoslovakia and Hungary)" (1963) 7(4) *Saint Louis University Law Journal* 292–310.

1178 Lee (2018), *supra* note 339, at 445.

such authorization will be invalid and hence unenforceable. Thus, the government can control the scope of legal business transactions by using licensing and authorization schemes. Such licensing and authorization schemes are further discussed in Section 10.3.

Contract law also addresses the technical issues of contract formation. In most jurisdictions, contract formation requires an act that expresses intent to create a legally binding commitment, accompanied by clear and definite terms (*e.g.*, the quantity of products), and an unequivocal act of accepting such intent, commonly referred to as "offer" and "acceptance," respectively.[1179] In common law, contracts also require "consideration," which refers to a bargained-for benefit or detriment that each party agrees to assume in return for the promise made by the other party.[1180] For example, in a contract to buy a computer for $1,000, the consideration for the seller is $1,000, and for the buyer, it is the computer. Consideration is not normally an issue in commercial transactions, in which a service or a good is exchanged for an economic benefit (*e.g.*, money). The difficulty in contract formation arises where the terms of an offer and acceptance vary (*e.g.*, an offer to sell a car for $1,000 in cash and an acceptance of the price with a suggestion to pay by a check). Common law requires that acceptance mirror the terms of an offer without any variation,[1181] but in real life, such discrepancies are commonplace and need to be accommodated; *i.e.*, it is necessary to recognize a contract even if there are discrepancies in the terms between the offer and acceptance.[1182]

Regulatory treatment is not identical across the board in this case, but clarity and simplicity will be important in the context of economic development. The Uniform Commercial Code (UCC)[1183] distinguishes between merchants and non-merchants and applies different rules in each scenario.[1184] The UCC rules are notoriously complex when parties exchange forms with varying terms in contract formation stages ("battle of the forms").[1185] Some civil codes governing contracts are simpler (hence more appealing in the interest of economic development) and treat an acceptance that varies the term of the original offer as a rejection and a new offer subject to acceptance by the other party.[1186] In international trade,

---

1179   See Farnsworth (2004), *supra* note 753, at 129–152.
1180   *Ibid.*, at 47–53. Consideration is not required in most civil law jurisdictions.
1181   *Ibid.*, at 140–145.
1182   Otherwise, numerous transactions will lose contractual protection for technical reasons where parties intend to have transactions but merely fail to match the terms of their offers and acceptances.
1183   The Uniform Commercial Code, first published in 1952, is an outcome of a joint project of the National Conference of Commissioners on Uniform State Laws (NCCUSL) and the American Law Institute (ALI) that aimed to harmonize the laws of sales and other commercial transactions throughout the United States. All states and Washington, D.C. have adopted the UCC through legislation.
1184   See, *e.g.*, UCC § 2–207.
1185   *Ibid.*
1186   See, *e.g.*, Civil Code of Korea § 534.

the dissimilar rules of contract laws among trading nations become a significant impediment to cross-border transactions. The United Nations Convention on Contracts for the International Sale of Goods (CISG, 1980) was drafted to address the differences in the regulatory treatment of contracts among nations. The CISG governs contract formation and rights and obligations of the parties for the sale of goods in 96 participating countries.[1187]

10.2.2 Private v. formal contract enforcement

A contract will not be very effective if its terms are not enforced in the case of a breach, thereby leaving the non-breaching party without remedy. A party may attempt to enforce a contract privately without involving a state agency such as the court.[1188] The party may resort to any number of means at its disposal, including, for example, use of a third-party collector, social pressure such as a warning to exclude the breaching party from further transactions, a bad review on the internet, or even self-help (*e.g.*, taking possession of the breaching party's property) that may or may not be legitimate under the law.[1189] There is an argument that private enforcement is an effective alternative to formal contract enforcement,[1190] but private contract enforcement can be costly, the outcome might be unpredictable, and the adopted measure carries with it some risk (particularly when the method used to enforce the contract is not strictly legal), thereby increasing transaction costs and deterring investments.[1191] The elements of uncertainty, cost, and risk associated with private enforcement have led to an argument supporting formal enforcement of contracts by the state following the outcome of court proceedings.

The mainstream position, advocated by numerous academics, including Douglass North, and by international development agencies, such as the World Bank, supports the development of formal enforcement mechanisms. North argued that the rules and norms governing economic interactions (including both formal law and informal norms) are the most significant drivers of an economy's success or failure.[1192] According to North, private enforcement may work in

---

1187 United Nations, *Treaty Collection*, available online at: https://treaties.un.org/pages/View Details.aspx?src=TREATY&mtdsg_no=X-10&chapter=10&clang=_en; https://perma.cc/ HW7M-WVZE.

1188 See Bruce L. Benson, *The Enterprise of Law: Justice without the State* (The Independent Institute, 2011).

1189 For further discussion of private contract enforcement, see Hamish R. Gow, Deborah H. Streeter, and Johan F. M. Swinnen, "How Private Contract Enforcement Mechanisms Can Succeed Where Public Institutions Fail: The Case of Juhocukor a.s." (2000) 23(3) *Agricultural Economics* 253–265.

1190 *Ibid.*

1191 Thus, the World Bank report emphasized the importance of courts (formal enforcement) for reducing the risks firms face to increase their willingness to invest more. World Bank, *World Development Report 2005: A Better Investment Climate for Everyone* (2004), at 86, available online at: https://openknowledge.worldbank.org/handle/10986/5987; https://perma.cc/ 5TNP-DQJC.

1192 North (1990), *supra* note 34, at 3.

the initial stages of economic development, in which transacting parties have more extensive personal knowledge about one another,[1193] and repeat dealings are pervasive; however, as the economies become more fully integrated into the broader global economy, formal contract enforcement mechanisms become more important.[1194] The World Bank, in support of developing formal enforcement mechanisms, also stated that "better courts reduce the risks firms face, and so increase the firms' willingness to invest more."[1195] In fact, all of the OECD countries have developed formal contract enforcement mechanisms, *albeit* with varying degrees of expediency, as illustrated by the table below (Table 10.1).

Table 10.1 Time in days to enforce a contract by means of a suit[1196]

Group 1		Group 2		Group 3	
Country	Days	Country	Days	Country	Days
Singapore	164	Chile	480	Algeria	630
New Zealand	216	Sweden	483	Ireland	650
Belarus	275	Denmark	485	Botswana	660
Korea	290	Finland	485	Czech Rep	678
Russia	337	China	496	Poland	685
Mexico	341	Germany	499	Venezuela	720
Japan	360	Belgium	505	Uruguay	725
Ukraine	378	Iran	505	Brazil	731
Hong Kong	385	Morocco	510	Portugal	755
France	395	Spain	510	Canada	910
Austria	397	Romania	512	Philippines	962
Vietnam	400	Netherlands	514	Israel	975
Australia	402	Ethiopia	530	Argentina	995
Indonesia	403	Rep. Congo	560	Egypt	1,010
USA	420	Bulgaria	564	Pakistan	1,071
Malaysia	425	Bolivia	591	Italy	1,120
Peru	426	Switzerland	598	Colombia	1,288
UK	437	South Africa	600	Bangladesh	1,442
Nigeria	454	Hungary	605	India	1,445
Kenya	465	Turkey	609	Greece	1,580

The above table shows a substantial discrepancy in the amount of time required for contract enforcement, even among "developed countries" where a formal system is in place, indicating that a formal system does not necessarily guarantee a speedy resolution of contract disputes. Additionally, formal enforcement requires considerable institutional capability: the state must have access to considerable financial, technical, and personnel resources to set up and maintain a judicial

1193   *Ibid.*, at 55.
1194   *Ibid.*, at 59.
1195   World Bank (2004), *supra* note 1191.
1196   World Bank, *Doing Business* (Washington, D.C., 2018).

system that effectively adjudicates contract disputes, identifies appropriate remedies, and enforces them against the unwilling breaching party.[1197] Developing countries that are facing serious resource constraints may not have access to these resources—that is, not to the extent necessary to set up and maintain a functioning system for formal enforcement. As a result, judicial reform intended to improve effectiveness has often failed to take root once external aid is discontinued.[1198] A well-functioning court system and effective formal enforcement may be an outcome of economic development, which enables the government to afford the resources needed for the court system. The push for judicial reform to improve formal enforcement, without due consideration of the state's resources and capacity, may prove to be ineffective and fail to result in effective formal enforcement.

The importance of contract law and formal enforcement may have been overemphasized, particularly as it relates to the early stages of economic development.[1199] Both in developed and developing economies, the vast majority of business disputes are resolved without ever resorting to contract law or formal enforcement. It is also not conclusive that the absence of effective formal enforcement necessarily lowers investments and impedes economic development. The cost of enforcement and the risk of contract breach is only a part of the cost assessment for investors, even in the absence of effective formal enforcement. In other words, entrepreneurs and investors may well consider such a risk an acceptable cost and may not necessarily refrain from making investments and engaging in transactions if the other benefits, such as market viability and growth potential, outweigh the cost. This explains the rapid growth of investment and economic development in China since the 1980s[1200] when there was no developed contract law or robust formal contract enforcement.[1201]

1197 On the importance of institutions, the OECD states "Having a contract law on the books is not sufficient. What matters equally are the role and practices of the legal institutions that support the effective implementation of contract law. The legal institutions relate to the organization of courts, an independent and competent judiciary, the legal profession, the enforcement services and the process of law making itself." OECD, "Contract Enforcement and Dispute Resolution," *Policy Framework for Investment*, available online at: www.oecd.org/investment/toolkit/policyareas/investmentpolicy/contractenforcementanddisputeresolution.htm; https://perma.cc/L2NX-EA7M.

1198 For a discussion of the issues arising from externally driven judicial reform, see Roberto Laver, "The World Bank and Judicial Reform: Overcoming 'Blind Spots' in the Approach to Judicial Independence" (2012) 22 *Duke Journal of International and Comparative Law* 183–238.

1199 See *supra* note 262 (for a discussion of the stages of economic development).

1200 China initiated an economic reform process in the late 1970s, accommodating market mechanisms in the economy gradually throughout the 1980s. Jiangyu Wang, "The Evolution of China's International Trade Policy: Development through Protection and Liberalization," *in* Yong-Shik Lee (ed.), *Economic Development through World Trade: A Developing Country Perspective* (Alphen aan den Rijn: Kluwer Law International, 2008), at 192–196.

1201 Opportunistic behavior was nevertheless controlled by informal sanctions, such as exclusion from future transactions.

Leading scholars have observed that a lack of formal enforcement is not necessarily a barrier to economic development in the early stages of economic development.[1202] According to this view, formal enforcement becomes more relevant only in the later stages when informal business arrangements and private enforcement based on community networks and personal ties become less effective due to the increasing complexity of transactions and the involvement of parties from outside the community networks who may not necessarily share common business practices or traditions.[1203] As discussed above, institutional capacity is an issue for the establishment and operation of effective courts and formal enforcement systems.[1204] As economic development progresses, the economy will secure, as a result of economic development, the resources necessary to set up and operate formal enforcement mechanisms, and the government will be in a better position to facilitate them as necessary. However, there is no cut-off point or a universal guideline as to when formal enforcement systems become imperative and how much should be invested into formal enforcement. Even a developed economy, such as Japan, may still prefer out-of-court adjudication over formal court proceedings and enforcement—although globalization requires a degree of formalization, the actual use of formal enforcement will vary among the developed economies.

10.2.3 Strategy for developing countries

Effective contract enforcement is conducive to fostering business transactions, but it is not conclusive whether formal enforcement is imperative to economic development, particularly in the early stages of economic development where a majority of transactions are based on community networks and informal arrangements.[1205] The successful development cases of the East Asian countries, where formal contract law and formal enforcement were not emphasized, indicate that formal law and formal enforcement are not key requirements for economic development in the early stages of development.[1206] Nonetheless, the expansion of economic transactions and globalization necessitates formal mechanisms (*i.e.*, contract law and formal enforcement). As discussed above, the development and successful operation of these formal mechanisms require substantial institutional capability and resources; thus, there is a case for gradual adoption of formal mechanisms, in pace with the available resources, as a working strategy for developing countries.

1202   Trebilcock and Leng (2006), *supra* note 134.

1203   *Ibid.*

1204   Local residents in developing countries may prefer to use informal, traditional venues to resolve disputes. A study emphasized the necessity to engage customary dispute resolution processes in developing countries. See Zwier (2017), *supra* note 291.

1205   See discussion *supra* Section 10.2.2.

1206   Jayasuriya (1999), *supra* note 443, at 7; Ginsburg (2000), *supra* note 443; Perry (2002), *supra* note 443.

Developing countries may adopt a flexible regulatory approach which allows both informal and formal enforcement mechanisms, to the extent that these two mechanisms do not conflict; the government, for example, could disallow self-help approaches taken by creditors who attempt to forcefully take possession of the debtor's property outside a legal process. An attempt to overhaul the existing contract law and enforcement mechanisms through blanket legal transplant, without due consideration of the institutional capacity and available resources, would be costly and ineffective. The general theory of law and development sets forth regulatory compliance as one of its key elements.[1207] Thus, even if the government were able to set up laws and formal enforcement mechanisms, they would not be effective without due compliance, which is, in turn, affected by socioeconomic conditions on the ground.[1208] For example, efforts to improve court efficiency would not be very useful in adjudicating contract disputes and facilitating contract enforcement where a majority of the population does not resort to courts for dispute resolution but prefers an alternative, informal means of dispute settlement.[1209]

For developing countries facing resource constraints, another workable strategy would be to focus on recurring problems in business transactions that may have the effect of suppressing economic growth. For example, if fraud involving loan agreements is a recurring issue (*e.g.*, a borrower entering into a loan agreement without an intention to repay the principal and/or the interest), the government may adopt a criminal penalty for this type of contract breach. The adoption of criminal sanctions may deter recurring fraud in loan transactions, although it is often difficult for the non-breaching party to secure evidence of such fraudulent intention on the part of the borrower. Lowering the standard of proof for ease of punishment may undermine the rights of the accused. Alternatively, the government may facilitate the development of a credit reporting system in collaboration with business communities. The credit reporting system would be particularly important with the development of formal lending businesses (*e.g.*, bank loans).[1210] The government may also facilitate the use of arbitration and mediation for contract disputes in lieu of or in conjunction with the formal court system.

Lastly, international investment agreements (IIAs) are relevant for developing countries in attracting foreign investments for economic development. IIAs set forth enforceable contractual terms between the government of the host country and foreign investors of the signatory country. The terms of IIAs mandate adherence to the most-favored-nation (MFN) principle (foreign investors

---

1207 Lee (2017), note 4, at 446–450. See also discussion *supra* Section 3.3.1.
1208 *Ibid.*
1209 This lack of use may stem from limited access to the court due to the cost of litigation, an absence of the knowledge required to use the court, the physical remoteness of the court, or cultural reasons. See Zwier (2017), *supra* note 291.
1210 World Bank, *Credit Reporting* (October 5, 2015), available online at: www.worldbank.org/en/topic/financialsector/brief/credit-reporting; https://perma.cc/AAX7-FZD3.

from the signatory country will receive no less favorable treatment than investors from any other country), the national treatment principle (foreign investors will receive no less favorable treatment than domestic investors, subject to stipulated exceptions), and protection of foreign investments from undue government interference (such as a demand to transfer technology) and expropriation (without due process and fair compensation).[1211] IIA terms that encapsulate these principles may induce foreign investments, as they accord legal protection, but at the same time, they also restrict the policy space for the host developing country.[1212] For example, the government will not be able to offer subsidies exclusively to domestic investors to facilitate domestic industries if the terms of an IIA prohibit such differential treatment to domestic investors. Thus, developing countries must carefully weigh the benefit and cost in concluding an IIA and set the terms to ensure that the IIA does not preclude its key development policies related to investment.[1213]

10.3 Limitations on contracts

Freedom of contract is a cornerstone of the market economy and a key element for economic development. The preceding discussion has advanced the proposition that freedom of contract, regardless of whether it is protected by formal contract law and facilitated by formal enforcement or *de facto* secured by an informal arrangement, enables market transactions that will lead to economic growth and development. Nonetheless, governments regularly impose limitations on freedom of contract[1214] under particular circumstances to promote strategic economic considerations or to meet broader policy objectives. This section discusses limitations on contracts that are imposed to serve these needs and examines the socioeconomic considerations that call for such limitations. The section also inquires where an optimal balance between freedom of contract and its limitations should be found and whether it is desirable at all to implement general restrictions on freedom of contract in any stage of economic development.

1211 See Chrispas Nyombi and Tom Mortimer, *Rebalancing International Investment Agreements in Favour of Host States* (Wildy, Simmons, and Hill Publishing, 2018).

1212 *Ibid.*

1213 *Ibid.*

1214 Limitations on freedom of contract or limitations on contracts refer to specific limitations imposed by the government on the scope of a valid contract. The government imposes such limitations by setting qualifications for entering into a certain type of contract (*e.g.,* a license requirement for export and import transactions), imposing restrictions on the subject matter of a valid contract (*e.g.,* a contract for an international sale of a product subject to an export quota when the quantity covered by the contract is over the quota limit), or requiring government authorization for a specific type of contract (*e.g.,* a contract for a land transaction in an area that requires government authorization).

10.3.1 *Contract limitations for strategic development needs*

The government may impose limitations on contracts in various forms when it serves the country's strategic development needs. For example, a country may impose limitations on international contracts for the sale of strategic natural resources, such as rare earth materials. These limitations are called "export restrictions." In 2009, China imposed export restrictions in multiple forms, including export duties and export quotas, on rare earth minerals such as bauxite and fluorspar, used for a range of modern industries such as chemical industries and ceramics.[1215] Export duties are the charges imposed on exporters for exportation of the covered commodity, the effect of which is to increase the export prices and reduce the export quantities. Export quotas are quantitative restrictions that set the maximum amount of the covered products that can be exported. A contract that provides for the sale of a covered product in a quantity that exceeds the quota would not be enforceable. Thus, export restrictions, along with the licensing schemes as discussed above, impose limitations on freedom of contract associated with international trade.

The government imposes these contract limitations for strategic economic concerns. In the case of China's export restrictions, the government intends to secure a sufficient quantity of rare earth minerals for the use of domestic producers by restraining exports,[1216] and this policy facilitates domestic industries using these minerals. The government may also run general licensing schemes for export and import businesses, and under such schemes, only the licensed exporters and importers would be authorized to engage in international trade. Such licensing schemes were prevalent before trade liberalization under the General Agreement on Tariffs and Trade (GATT) and the World Trade Organization (WTO) and still exist today.[1217] As discussed earlier,[1218] the government may affect trade and the economy with licensing schemes by, for instance, setting the license renewal terms to provide incentives for preferred economic activities such as exports (favoring firms with export performance in the license renewal process for lucrative imports).[1219]

Licensing schemes have a more general effect on freedom of contract beyond international trade. Licensing schemes set limits on those who can engage in certain types of contracts, and such schemes have a general impact on freedom of contract and the economy. For example, a licensing scheme that stipulates credentials for certain professionals, such as doctors, lawyers, and accountants,

---

1215   For a further account, see Ruth Jebe, Don Mayer, and Y.S. Lee, "China's Export Restrictions on Raw Materials and Rare Earths: A New Balance between Free Trade and Environmental Protection" (2012) 44 *George Washington International Law Review* 579–642.
1216   *Ibid.*
1217   For further discussion of the international trading system under the GATT and the WTO regimes, see Lee (2016), *supra* note 102.
1218   See discussion *supra* Section 10.2.1.
1219   *Ibid.*

limits those who may engage in professional contracts under these professions to the individuals who meet the defined credentials stipulated under the law. Such licensing requirements relate to public concern for safety and to professional reliability (*e.g.*, it will be in the society's interest to allow only qualified doctors to perform surgery), which may outweigh the negative impact on freedom of contract, and such licensing is in an increasing trend. Lastly, as discussed earlier, the government may also require "authorization" for specific categories of contracts (*e.g.*, authorization required for contracts on land transactions to prevent speculative transactions that drive up the land price).[1220]

Licensing schemes and government authorization may be adopted in conjunction with economic development policies, particularly in the early stages of economic development where the private sectors are relatively weak, and the government can support and facilitate economic transactions conducive to economic development. The aforementioned example of licensing schemes for international trade illustrates this point well.[1221] Such government interventions, however, limit freedom of contract, and their economic effect has been debated for centuries.[1222] Cases of government misuse and abuse of these schemes abound, although several successful developing countries, such as the East Asian countries—South Korea, Taiwan, Singapore, and, more recently, China—have been remarkably successful with the government-led development policies.[1223] In these countries, government control over certain contracts (*e.g.*, licensing and authorization) was stronger in the early stages of economic development, and the governments relaxed them in later stages as the private sector grew and became robust.[1224]

10.3.2 Control for public policy considerations

The government may also impose limitations on contracts for broader public policy considerations such as the need to address unequal bargaining power between parties, the need to protect consumers against better organized producers and suppliers, and the need to prioritize public interest over private interest by reserving in government the power of eminent domain ("expropriation").[1225] Growing concern for social welfare in the twentieth century led to calls for government interventions in many areas of market transactions which had initially been left to the market, and the government responded by beginning to regulate contractual relations on public policy grounds.[1226] These grounds are

1220   *Ibid.*
1221   *Ibid.*
1222   See Lee (2016), *supra* note 102, at 14–32.
1223   See *supra* note 28 (for an account of the remarkable economic development in the East Asian countries).
1224   See discussion *supra* Section 3.2.1.
1225   Professor Holcombe warns that government limitations on freedom of contract, including expropriation, are subject to abuse, as demonstrated by the frequent abuse by local governments in the United States (correspondence with the author).
1226   For further discussion of the public policy concerns relevant to contracts, see Farnsworth (2004), *supra* note 753, at 308–311.

broader than economic development interests, but the limitations on contracts based on broader public policy grounds need to be addressed because they may still affect economic development.

The development of banking and financing industries has also led to a unique circumstance in which consumers are not in an equal position *vis-à-vis* banks and other financiers ("suppliers") in mass financial transactions, such as consumer finance and insurance contracts. In such financial transactions, individual consumers are not on equal footing with the suppliers in terms of knowledge, access to information, experience, and bargaining power, which renders consumers unable to effectively negotiate the terms of a contract. The terms of such contracts are also standardized to maximize the benefit and minimize the risks for the suppliers.[1227] Freedom of contract presumes that parties are free to negotiate the terms, but under these circumstances, such a presumption is not a reality. The government, thus, has justification for intervening and regulating the terms of such contracts to "level the playing field" and protect consumer interests.[1228]

To be sure, the lack of inter-party parity in contracts exists beyond the banking and financing industries. The majority of consumer contracts are standardized throughout industries, and consumers are presented with contracts containing standardized or preset terms prepared by the suppliers with little or no chance for terms negotiations. This standardization is supported by economic rationale. For example, the cost of a flight ticket would be much higher if airliners were to engage each passenger in the negotiation of the terms of each flight. Increasing government regulations and interventions may fill in the gaps by preserving the standardized contracts and their economic utility but protecting the rights and interests of consumers who cannot negotiate with the suppliers. In the early stages of economic development, lack of competition among producers and the existence of dominant producers will cause unequal bargaining power between suppliers and consumers, and in such circumstances, the government would be justified in regulating contracts on behalf of the weaker customers.[1229]

Lastly, the state's power to expropriate private property for public interest (eminent domain) imposes a substantial limit on freedom of contract. The government may take possession of a private property through expropriation for public interest, regardless of a prior contract concerning such property. Contract law normally treats unexpected government action, including expropriation, as legitimate grounds to rescind the contract without incurring any legal liability for breach on the part of the parties.[1230] Nonetheless, to the extent that the parties are unable to perform under the contract, expropriation creates a substantial limitation on freedom of contract, and it becomes a significant impediment to the

---

1227   *Ibid.*, at 285–294.
1228   *Ibid.*, at 308–311.
1229   Thus, consumer protection agencies have addressed these issues in some of the successful developing countries, such as South Korea.
1230   Farnsworth (2004), *supra* note 753, at 619–647.

development of a market economy when the government exercises this power without due care and prudence.[1231] This means that the countries that pursue economic development must treat expropriation with caution, even where it is justified for economic development, and prudent governments will only use expropriation after considering its ramification for private ownership and private contracts.

10.3.3 General restrictions on freedom of contract?

As discussed above, freedom of contract has never been completely removed in any economic system at any time in history;[1232] conversely, it has never received unfettered protection anywhere. There have always been some limitations on contracts, based on strategic or broader public policy grounds. Market transactions have sustained economic development; whether the development strategy is one of government-led industrial policy, export promotion, or the neoliberal prescriptions minimizing government interventions, market transactions have formed the foundation for continued economic development, and freedom of contract is at their core. Thus, any attempt to completely remove the freedom to contract or place general restrictions on contracts would simply be unfeasible and unproductive in any stage of market-based economic development. The proliferation of "marketplaces" in today's most isolated and restrictive country, North Korea, and its subsequent economic growth due to increased levels of market transactions (before the imposition of strong international economic sanctions in response to its nuclear ambitions) bear testament to the importance of freedom of contract for economic development.[1233]

The real question is not whether freedom of contract is conducive to economic development or whether general restrictions on freedom contract have any positive effect on economic development, but where the government should try to strike a balance between protection of freedom of contract and promotion of public interest, including economic development. There is likely no universal answer to this question, but the cases of successful development in the past offer some guidance for determining the appropriate balance. The East Asian countries, which have achieved the most successful economic development in history,[1234] all maintained market economies but introduced strong government measures to promote exports and facilitate domestic industries, the effect of which

---

1231   See George Leef, "It's Bad Policy to Use Eminent Domain for Economic Development, Even if It Sometimes 'Works'," *Forbes* (August 28, 2015), available online at: www.forbes.com/sites/georgeleef/2015/08/28/its-bad-policy-to-use-eminent-domain-for-economic-development-even-if-it-sometimes-works/#4c884d0a7f80; https://perma.cc/DD5F-E962.

1232   See, *e.g.*, Jasny (1951), *supra* note 904.

1233   For a discussion of economic development in North Korea, see Yong-Shik Lee, "A Note on Economic Development in North Korea: Call for a Comprehensive Approach" (2019) 12(1) *Law and Development Review* 247–259 and Yong-Shik Lee, Young-Ok Kim, and Hye Seong Mun, "Economic Development of North Korea: International Trade Based Development Policy and Legal Reform" (2010) 3(1) *Law and Development Review* 136–156.

1234   See *supra* note 28.

inevitably imposed limitations on private contracts.[1235] This suggests that strategic government interventions, which are carefully contemplated, designed, and selected, could be effective, despite the consequential limitations on contracts, where freedom of contract is protected in principle. The courts in those countries protected contractual rights and enforced contracts.

10.4 Secured transactions: a vehicle for economic development?

This final section offers a brief account of secured transactions and discusses their effect on economic development. Secured transactions refer to a loan or a credit transaction in which the lender acquires a security interest in collateral owned by the debtor. The availability of secured transactions is expected to enhance access to credit by creating a security interest in collateral in the form of a preferential right to possession or control in the case of default. The collateral can include both real property and personal property, but law reform initiatives have focused on personal property for individuals and small businesses that do not own real property. Former U.S. Secretary of State Hillary Rodham Clinton described the importance of secured transactions reform:

> We're also working on reforms with the OAS [the Organization of American States] to update what is called the 'secured transactions law.' Now put simply, that is to allow small businesses and entrepreneurs to use assets like refrigerators or sewing machines as collateral for loans. Many of these businesses could grow and employ more people, but they don't own the property that they work in or the home that they live in. But they have a refrigerator or a sewing machine, and we want to change the laws so that that can serve as collateral.[1236]

10.4.1 Advantages for economic development

Secured transactions create advantages for borrowers. For example, a single property can be used to support a series of loans, and debtors do not have to surrender the title to the property; thus, multiple loan arrangements could be made on single collateral, *albeit* with different priorities among the creditors. There is also substantial flexibility with the types of collateral that can be used for secured transactions: a security interest can be created in any property susceptible to monetary valuation, whether it is property presently owned by the debtor or property to be owned in the future, either tangible or intangible. This is an inherent strength embedded in secured transactions, and a secured transaction is a device that empowers borrowers to leverage a substantial amount of financing from lenders.

1235 For example, firms without export performance could not secure the license for lucrative imports for the government's strong export promotion policy, which should have restrained the opportunities for import contracts. See discussion *supra* Section 10.2.1.
1236 American Bar Association (2011), *supra* note 1172, at 3.

A security interest is created by contract, the terms of which specify the credit arrangement between the parties, including the duration of the loan, payment of interest, repayment of the principal, and disposition of collateral in case of default. However, these contracts do not protect the interests of third parties, such as subsequent creditors who may seek a security interest in the same collateral; thus, a core function of secured transaction law is the protection of third-party interest. To promote confidence in a secured transaction system, third parties must have access to information on the status of the collateral in which the party wishes to create a security interest. A public notice would provide such information.[1237] The possession or control of collateral by a creditor may give such notice, but it is necessary to devise another system that will give public notice if the debtor should be allowed to use the collateral (*e.g.*, machinery) for business purposes.

The method that systematically provides public notice, such as a registration system, will, therefore, be particularly important: registration of a security interest facilitates secured transactions by providing access to information on any security interest created in the collateral, while the debtor does not have to surrender the possession or control of the collateral. Priority will also be an issue where multiple security interests are created in a single item of collateral. There are potentially multiple ways to determine priority, but the time of filing tends to be preferred, subject to variations in the legal provision governing this issue.[1238] As seen in the context of property rights in Chapter 8, setting up a working registry is not always straightforward, particularly in developing countries with resource and personnel constraints.[1239]

Despite this perceived difficulty, many national and international development agencies and non-governmental organizations (NGOs), such as the UNCITRAL, the Organization of American States (OAS), the Organization for the Harmonization of Business Law in Africa (OHADA), the European Union, the World Bank, the USAID, and other development agencies, have identified secured transactions reform as a critical component in economic development in developing countries and have thus supported relevant law reform.[1240] The OAS reported the progress of law reform in secured transactions: according to the OAS, several countries in Latin America, including Guatemala, Honduras, Peru, and Colombia, enacted modern secured transactions laws (Ley de Garantías Mobiliarias) to address rapidly changing commercial and financing needs.[1241]

1237   For further discussion of public notice, see Jens Hausmann, "The Value of Public-Notice Filing under Uniform Commercial Code Article 9: A Comparison with the German Legal System of Securities in Personal Property" (1996) 25(3) *Georgia Journal of International and Comparative Law* 427–478.

1238   *Ibid.*

1239   See discussion *supra* Section 8.3.2. Also, the registry may not work well for certain types of assets which change quickly over time, like a herd of cows.

1240   *Supra* note 1172.

1241   OAS, *Secured Transactions Reform in the Americas* (August 2013), available online at: www. oas.org/en/sla/dil/docs/secured_transactions_newsletter_aug_2013.pdf; https://perma.cc/V6UH-6TFT.

According to an OAS report, Mexico put into operation its moveable assets registry (Registro Único de Garantías Mobiliarias) in 2010, creating access to financing for small- and medium-sized businesses.[1242] Costa Rica and El Salvador also enacted their respective secured transactions laws with registries of security interests on personal property in place.[1243]

10.4.2 *Limitations*

The availability of secured transactions, facilitated by laws that support them, may indeed assist small businesses and individuals without substantial real property to access cheaper credit. However, it is not clear whether the promotion of secured transactions can lead to economic development for the following reasons. First, the proliferation of secured transactions depends on the efficacy of public notice and the accessibility and reliability of the registration system. As noted above, building a reliable system takes considerable administrative resources and expertise, which many developing countries facing resource constraints lack. The promotion of secured transactions may also create conflicts with communal rights in property, which may not be registered. The legal facilitation of secured transactions must be promoted in a manner that will avoid or minimize such conflicts, and careful consideration must be given to informal property rights and local lending practices. However, such regulatory calibration is complex and might not be easily achievable. The development and operation of an effective registration system in developing countries have proven to be a challenging task; for example, in Peru, there were 17 registries for different kinds of assets, each with its own regulations and requirements, and the system was considered to be "a recipe for confusion and uncertainty."[1244]

Also, it is not clear whether, even if the system operates as intended, the small-scale consumer loans to be raised by secured transactions will replace the need for larger loans and investments to promote economic development on a national scale. Secured transactions could be a device to raise small-scale loans, but it is not certain whether it can be an effective vehicle for economic development; for instance, financial investments for the successful economic development of East Asia came from sources such as international loans, foreign direct investments, and public savings rather than small-scale loans raised by secured transactions.[1245] It remains to be seen whether small-scale credit that can be raised

---

1242   *Ibid.*
1243   Secured Transactions Law Reform Project, *El Salvador*, available online at: https://securedt ransactionslawreformproject.org/reform-in-other-jurisdictions/central-america/el-salvador/; https://perma.cc/XWL4-9TBH; Secured Transactions Law Reform Project, *Costa Rica*, available online at: https://securedtransactionslawreformproject.org/reform-in-other-jurisd ictions/central-america/costa-rica/; https://perma.cc/YGP8-JY6X.
1244   World Bank, *Doing Business: Case Study of Peru* (March 2020), available online at: www. doingbusiness.org/content/dam/doingBusiness/media/Reforms/Case-Studies/2008/ DB08-CS-Peru.pdf; https://perma.cc/933R-QFZN.
1245   See discussion *infra* Section 11.3 (for a discussion of the development path of the East Asian countries).

by secured transactions on movable collateral could work as an engine for economic development.

There is also a risk that easier access to credit created by secured transactions may exacerbate, rather than alleviate, poverty by inducing individuals, who will be unable to repay debts, to collateralize whatever they own, obtain credit, and lose the property upon failure to repay the debt, deepening poverty. The magnitude of the positive impact of small collateral on the terms of a loan is not certain, and borrowers may still have to take loans at relatively high-interest rates in addition to offering what they own. An observer has pointed out possible misuse of secured transactions, which will result in enriching the creditor and impoverishing the grantor upon failure to repay the debt.[1246] In the worst case scenario, small collaterals can be used to encourage predatory lending practices, and the system may deepen impoverishment rather than facilitate economic development. The government can enact laws to prevent such practices (*e.g.*, setting limits on interest rates and heightening requirements for taking or selling secured collateral), but this may also have the effect of restraining secured transactions.

10.4.3 Concluding remarks

This chapter examines the legal frameworks for business transactions that may contribute to economic development by clarifying and protecting the rights and obligations of the parties to transactions and thereby reducing transaction costs. Advocates of contract law and formal enforcement have argued that the lack thereof is a reason for economic stagnation in developing countries.[1247] In contrast, dissidents have pointed out the cases of successful development in which the absence of formal mechanisms did not necessarily impede economic development.[1248] Informal arrangements, based on a social nexus and reputational elements, can be practical in protecting and enforcing contractual rights and can indeed support market transactions, particularly in the early stages of economic development. The development of contract law that is congruent with the socioeconomic conditions on the ground[1249] and the facilitation of effective enforcement require resources and expertise that many developing countries lack.

This explains why many judicial reforms have had limited success,[1250] which only lasted for the duration of external aid. The lesson is that efforts to develop contract law and facilitate formal enforcement should be paced with the availability of resources and expertise so that the reform can be sustained after the

---

1246   Nicolas Rouiller, *International Business Law: An Introduction to the Legal Instruments and to the Legal Environment of Business from an International Perspective* (Zürich: Schulthess, 2015), at 471.

1247   See discussion *supra* Section 10.2.

1248   *Ibid.*

1249   The contents of contract law tend to have common elements across the board, but the terms also need to recognize prevalent local practice to increase applicability and effectiveness.

1250   See *supra* Section 10.2.2.

expiration of external aid. As shown by the cases of East Asian development, the progress of economic development broadens the ambit of business transactions well beyond those sharing a common business and cultural heritage, and informal mechanisms based on the latter become insufficient to afford the protection and enforcement of contractual rights. The increased resources and expertise, as a result of economic development, would enable courts to secure the capacity required for effective enforcement. Well-developed contract law and effective formal enforcement are as much a result of economic development as a potential cause. A need-based, gradual adoption of the formal mechanisms, rather than a prescriptive transplant, stands a better chance for success.

Governments have imposed limitations on contracts to achieve strategic development objectives or to meet broader policy considerations. These objectives and needs have necessitated that the government impose various forms of limitations on contracts, such as regulating the terms of the contract and requiring licensing schemes and authorization on particular transactions. Scholars disagree as to the economic utility of these schemes, but the successful developing countries in the past used them to promote industrial development and economic growth. Expropriation also imposes limitations on private ownership and private transactional interests in the property. The economic effect of expropriation is controversial,[1251] but regardless of the debate, even if the call for economic development should broadly justify expropriation, abuse of eminent domain without due process and compensation will disrupt and reduce the reliability of the market-based economic system, and this will not be conducive to economic development.

Secured transactions have been widely promoted as an essential element for economic development, and there has been a focus of international assistance on secured transactions law reform.[1252] Secured transactions may indeed facilitate small-scale credit access by enabling small businesses and individuals to leverage their personal property to obtain credit, but it is not certain whether the facilitation of small-scale loans would be an adequate substitute for the large-scale investments necessary for successful economic development on a national scale. The development of a reliable and accessible registry of security interests could be a challenging task for developing countries lacking resources and administrative capacity, and it may also impede communal property interests that are not registered, which can become a cause of social unrest. In the worst case, predatory loan practices in secured transactions can result in impoverishment rather than economic development. Careful consideration should be given to the potential benefit drawn from secured transactions reform against the economic and social costs in implementation.

1251 Leef (2015), *supra* note 1231.
1252 See discussion *supra* Section 10.4.1.

11 State industrial promotion

11.1 State industrial policy

This chapter examines state industrial policy in the context of law and development and discusses the role of the state in promoting industries.[1253] The term state industrial policy refers to any economic, financial, and/or other policy adopted by a state to promote industries. This term has not been popularly used since the emergence of neoliberalism in the 1980s, which discouraged government interventions in the economy and found support from mainstream economists.[1254] Neoliberalism may have lost much of its appeal since the 2007 financial crisis, but the caution against government interventions in the economy remains.[1255] In reality, however, nearly all states today adopt policies to promote industries, even if they may not necessarily call such policies "state industrial policies" or "industrial policies": governments have adopted a wide range of policy tools, such as financial grants, loan guarantees, tax rebates, R&D support, facilitation of social infrastructures, and trade measures (*e.g.*, tariffs on imports), to support industrial development.

The government adopts these policies due to practical concerns about unemployment and the resultant economic, social, and political issues rather than economic ideologies. The government is under constant pressure to resolve these issues. The private sector creates the majority of job opportunities, and growth in industries tends to increase employment opportunities; thus, the government has an incentive to adopt a range of policies to promote the growth of industries. The government will have a stronger need to adopt these policies when the economy is weak and poverty is prevalent. Thus, industrial policies in developing countries are also called "development policies" (although the term development is broader

---

1253 This chapter is developed from the author's article, "State Industrial Promotion and Law" (2019) 13(3) *Review of Institution and Economics* 11–49.

1254 Milton Friedman, *Capitalism and Freedom* (Chicago: University of Chicago Press, 1962) and Friedrich Hayek, *Individualism and Economic Order* (Chicago: University of Chicago Press, 1948).

1255 Terry Miller, "Government Intervention: A Threat to Economic Recovery," *The Heritage Foundation* (2009), available online at: www.heritage.org/testimony/government-intervention-threat-economic-recovery; https://perma.cc/879K-2L9J.

DOI: 10.4324/9781003090175-14

than just economic development).[1256] A study accounts that both developed and developing countries have used industrial policies.[1257] In particular, the successful developing countries in East Asia, such as South Korea, Taiwan, Singapore, and, more recently, China, have adopted effective industrial policies and achieved successful economic development.[1258]

Among the varied industrial policies, government subsidies and trade measures (such as increases in tariffs) are two major policy tools of state industrial promotion.[1259] As discussed in later sections, however, there is a substantial regulatory impediment to the adoption of these policies. Scholars have criticized industrial policy as causing an inefficient allocation of resources, but Dani Rodrik has argued that industrial policy is concerned with the provisions of public goods for the productive sector, such as public labs and public research and development (R&D), health and infrastructure facilities, sanitary and phytosanitary standards, infrastructure, and vocational and technical training, and concluded that "industrial policy is just good economic policy of the type that traditional, orthodox approaches prescribe."[1260] Industrial policy may be even broader than what Rodrik described; it may also include measures that have a more direct effect on industries than the measures cited by Rodrik, such as industry-specific subsidies and measures that affect international trade. As a result, controversies continue as to the economic efficiency of these measures.

There is a large body of literature examining the economic effect of state industrial promotion,[1261] but fewer studies are addressing the relationship between state industrial promotion and law. Economic policies are implemented through law, and several factors, such as those adopted by the general theory of law and development (*i.e.*, regulatory design, regulatory compliance, and quality of implementation), affect the impact of law on state industrial promotion.[1262] The regulatory frameworks and specific legal provisions may alter the outcome of an otherwise identical development policy. This chapter introduces a case study of successful developing countries in the past, such as the East Asian countries, as well as the United States, to illustrate how the law has facilitated state industrial promotion.

Section 11.2 discusses the economic efficacy of state-led development policies and further reviews the centuries-old debate on the proper role of the state in the economy and provides a background for further analysis. The section also introduces the New General Theory of Economic Development and examines how the theory explains the role of the state in economic development. Section 11.3 examines the successful cases of state industrial promotion

1256 See discussion *supra* Sections 1.3.1 and 1.3.2.
1257 Chang (2002), *supra* note 203.
1258 See *supra* note 28.
1259 Lee (2016), *supra* note 102, at 19–32.
1260 Rodrik (2004), *supra* note 264, at 38–39.
1261 Amsden (1992), *supra* note 336; Westphal (1990), *supra* note 336; Kim and Park (1985), *supra* note 336; Brohman (1996), *supra* note 336; Krueger (1984), *supra* note 336; Srinivasan (2001), *supra* note 336; Helleiner (1992), *supra* note 336; World Bank (1993), *supra* note 336.
1262 Lee (2017), *supra* note 4.

in East Asia and analyzes key industrial policies as well as legal and institutional frameworks. Section 11.4 explains the industrial policies and relevant legal and institutional frameworks in the United States as a case study of industrial policy in a developed country.

11.2 Debate on the efficacy of state-led development policies

11.2.1 The "invisible hand"—proliferation of the pro-market approach

Since Adam Smith argued that the "invisible hand" of the market optimizes supply and demand, leading to economic efficiency, market forces have been considered the core element of prosperous economies creating wealth for a nation and its people, except in the limited cases of market failures, such as monopoly, monopsony, externalities, public goods, and asymmetric information.[1263] According to this classical market theory, individuals make the best economic choice for themselves, given that they have access to information and the freedom to make an economic choice, and state involvement in the economy leads only to economic inefficiency. Adam Smith stated:

> What is the species of domestic industry which his capital can employ, and of which the produce is likely to be of the greatest value, every individual, it is evident, can, in his local situation, judge much better than any statesman or lawgiver can do for him.[1264]

According to the classical economic theory, economic growth comes from a division of labor, not from state protection of domestic industries; thus, the measures of industrial protection, such as government subsidies and tariffs against competing imports, would be inconsistent with the classical economic approach. This liberal, pro-market theory laid the foundation for mainstream economics and culminated in the "Washington Consensus," which refers to a set of policies representing the lowest common denominator of policy advice advanced by Washington-based institutions, such as fiscal discipline, a redirection of public expenditure priorities toward areas offering both high economic returns and the potential to improve income distribution (such as primary healthcare, primary education, and infrastructure), tax reform to lower marginal rates and broadening the tax base, interest rate liberalization, a competitive exchange rate, trade liberalization, liberalization of inflows of foreign direct investment, privatization, deregulation (to abolish barriers to entry and exit), and protection of property rights.[1265]

The policy preferences reflected in the Washington Consensus have dominated the policies of international financial institutions, such as the International

---

1263   Adam Smith, *An Inquiry into the Nature and Causes of the Wealth of Nations* (1776).
1264   *Ibid.*
1265   Williamson (1990), *supra* note 8.

Monetary Fund and the World Bank, and formed the regulatory makeup of the World Trade Organization.[1266] The mainstream pro-market approach has broad appeal beyond the realm of a simple economic policy choice; it implicates the essential importance of civil liberty and democracy: to facilitate market transactions, individuals must have access to information and freedom to make commercial transactions. Also, individuals must have the right to retain property that has been obtained through market transactions. These requirements necessitate a free and democratic society with the rule of law that protects fundamental rights, such as the right to property; *i.e.*, the requirements of the market economy correspond to the call for liberal democracy based on the rule of law, one of the most important sociopolitical movements since the eighteenth century. The pro-market economic system supports this important sociopolitical agenda, which is palatable to the sociopolitical priorities of the West.

11.2.2 *The reality at odds*

The classical market theory and the subsequent neoclassical theories presume that information is available and an individual makes a rational choice based on the available information. However, in reality, information is not always readily available, and in such circumstances, government intervention becomes useful to address information-related problems. These problems include information externalities (*i.e.*, the risk of no-compensation or under-compensation for those who first engage in new ventures) and coordination issues (*i.e.*, lack of other support services and infrastructure necessary for the new production activities that incur high fixed costs).[1267] The "rational person" presumption does not always hold, either, as has been seen by the 2007 financial crisis when the decisions of the sophisticated experts and the public were as much influenced by irrational greed, panic, and fear, as by rational discourse.[1268]

The cases of successful economic development in the past also exhibit clear inconsistencies with the pro-market prescriptions. The detailed account of economic development in the United States and the United Kingdom, two among the most successful countries in history, reveals strong government interventions in their economies at a crucial juncture of their economic development. Britain, which has long been known as a champion of the free market economy, had adopted intensive government interventions, including export bans on wool to protect its rising wool industries, until it started to dominate the world trade and manufacturing in the nineteenth century.[1269] The United States, another

---

1266 Lee (2016), *supra* note 102, at 22.
1267 Rodrik (2004), *supra* note 264.
1268 Rachelle Yonglai, Doug Palmer, and Teresa Carson, "Financial Crisis Caused by 'Greed and Stupidity': Geithner," *Reuters* (April 25, 2012), available online at: www.reuters.com/article/us-usa-economy-geithner/financial-crises-caused-by-stupidity-and-greed-geithner-idUSBRE83P01P20120426, accessed October 12, 2020.
1269 Chang (2002), *supra* note 203, at 19–24.

strong advocate of free trade and the free market economy, had adopted the highest tariffs in the world until the Second World War. Adam Smith warned the Americans:

> Were the Americans, either by combination or by any other sort of violence, to stop the importation of European manufactures, and, by thus giving a monopoly to such of their own countrymen as could manufacture the like goods, divert any considerable part of their capital into this employment, they would retard instead of accelerating the further increase in the value of their annual produce, and would obstruct instead of promoting the progress of their country towards real wealth and greatness.[1270]

Despite this warning, Alexander Hamilton argued that to start new industries in the United States that could soon become internationally competitive, the initial losses of those industries should be guaranteed by government aid, which could take the form of import duties or prohibition of imports altogether.[1271] Henry Clay, who was Abraham Lincoln's early mentor, advocated the "American System" of trade protection in opposition to what he called the "British System" of free trade, which, he subsequently argued, was part of the British imperialist system that consigned the United States to a role of primary product exporter.[1272] Ha-Joon Chang discussed cases of so-called infant industry protection, not only in the United States and the United Kingdom as cited above, but also in Germany, France, Sweden, Belgium, the Netherlands, Switzerland, Japan, and other newly industrialized countries (NICs) in East Asia, showing that the governments of successful developing countries in the past adopted policies of government intervention at odds with the classical and neoclassical market approaches.[1273]

The infant industry promotion policy, which holds that initial government support is necessary to assist domestic industries until they achieve economies of scale and international competitiveness, was promoted by a German economist, Friedrich List, who had also been influenced by Alexander Hamilton and Daniel Raymond. By the 1970s, most developing countries adopted a form of this policy, including government subsidies and trade measures, but success was relatively rare, and most of them did not achieve sustained economic development. Mainstream economists criticize the infant industry promotion policy and point out difficulties associated with the policy, such as the inherent difficulty in identifying the industries that will be successful with support, the difficulty of removing government support, and misuse of public funds due to corruption and poor judgment.[1274] A few successful developing countries, such as the aforementioned

---

1270   Smith (1776), *supra* note 1263.
1271   J. Dorfman and R. Tugwell, *Early American Policy—Six Columbia Contributors* (New York: Columbia University Press, 1960), at 31–32.
1272   Conkin (1980), *supra* note 318.
1273   Chang (2002), *supra* note 203, at 19–51.
1274   Dominick Salvatore, *International Economics* (8th ed., Hoboken, NJ: John Wiley & Sons, 2003), at 287–288.

NICs, were able to combine government support effectively with export opportunities and achieved industrial and economic development, as further discussed in Section 11.3. Nonetheless, this type of government support policy began to recede in the 1970s, and the neoliberal policies that discourage government interventions in the economy have prevailed since the 1980s.

11.2.3 Settling the debate

The mainstream academic and policy discourse supports the liberal, pro-market approach as discussed above. However, studies have also revealed that in practice, the governments of successful developing countries in East Asia and the West adopted various industrial policies that do not fit under mainstream prescriptions but nevertheless achieved a degree of success in economic development. Realizing this, contemporary trends, such as New Development Economics (NDE), tend to seek a synthesis between the two camps, as described by Michael Trebilcock:

> By the late 1990s, the consensus in development economics had shifted dramatically. The Washington Consensus was agreed to have often been a failure and two principal paths forward have emerged... A more promising approach is represented by the New Development Economics (NDE) which eschews truisms such as 'getting institutions right' and represents a break with big-picture paradigms that advance one-size-fits-all solutions. Drawing on the neoclassical paradigm, it recognizes that markets are not nearly as inefficient as the early structuralists believed; rather the fundamental principle of rational responses to incentives continues to organize economic behavior. Further, with the rise of the New Institutional Economics, the distinction between government and markets has become blurred – each operating via similar fundamental mechanisms. As such, NDE advocates a complementary role for governments and markets, finding both to be susceptible to failures in coordination, imperfect information, and agency problems.[1275]

The state and the market are not mutually exclusive, and policies that complement the strength of each can be devised and implemented; *e.g.*, a state may adopt an industrial policy to protect the domestic industry while focusing on exports to facilitate the industry's international competitiveness. The orthodox theory maintains that where investment is unrelated to schools or infrastructure, success depends on private information, which bureaucrats lack but some business people possess. However, as Dani Rodrik has opined, the private sector also has imperfect information,[1276] and this problem tends to pose more of a burden in the early stages of economic development, where a country's resource constraints, including means to acquire information, are greater. This means

---

1275   Michael J. Trebilcock, "Between Theories of Trade and Development: The Future of the World Trading System" (2015) 16(1) *Journal of World Investment & Trade* 122–140.
1276   Rodrik (2004), *supra* note 264.

that governments that are strongly motivated to support economic development and staffed with officials able to coordinate private investments to serve national economic development objectives, such as the South Korean government in the 1960s through the 1980s, can work with private entrepreneurs by providing resources and information that they may lack.[1277]

The New General Theory of Economic Development also explains the role of the state in economic development. This theory, according to which economic growth, distribution, and innovation are the constitutive elements of economic development, explains that state industrial promotion led to economic development in the early stages thereof, even in non-market economies, such as the Soviet Union in the 1920s and 1930s and North Korea in the 1950s and 60s, as well as in market economies, such as South Korea.[1278] The Soviet Union achieved a rapid industrialization and increased domestic production in the 1930s through centralized government planning that mobilized resources into industrial sectors.[1279] Government investment and reallocation of surplus labor from agriculture, rather than the activities of corporations and market transactions, drove the economic achievement of the Soviet Union in the 1930s; the Soviet system did not allow the private ownership of corporations or other free market activities.[1280] Communist North Korea also showed a similar pattern of economic development: in the late 1940s and the 1950s, North Korea adopted the development strategy of the Soviet Union in the 1930s and initiated economic development through government planning and mobilization of resources into industrial sectors, leading to industrialization and economic growth.[1281]

The communist rule in North Korea and the Soviet Union banned private ownership of corporations and market activities, and both countries developed their economies and industries through government planning and mobilization of resources into industrial sectors.[1282] In both countries, the elements of economic development—growth, distribution (through a state distribution system), and innovation (as evidenced by the shift of industrial structure and the expansion of the manufacturing sector)—were evident in the economic transitions,[1283] although the new theory also accounts that their economic development was not sustained, and the economies in both countries started to decline due to the inefficiencies associated with government planning and resulting bureaucracies without any other mechanisms to correct them.[1284] In contrast, South Korea,

---

1277   The government devised economic development plans with specific growth targets and industrial development goals, and private enterprises made specific investment decisions, often in coordination with and support from the government. For the process of economic development in South Korea, see Chapter 4 *supra*.

1278   Yong-Shik Lee, "New General Theory of Economic Development: Innovative Growth and Distribution" (2020) 24(2) *Review of Economic Development* 402–423, at 413–414.

1279   See Table 8.1, Section 8.2.2 *supra*.

1280   Lee (2020), *supra* note 1278, at 413.

1281   See Table 8.2, Section 8.2.2 *supra*.

1282   Lee (2020), *supra* note 1278, at 413.

1283   *Ibid.*

1284   *Ibid.*, at 415.

which had a robust market economy coupled with extensive state industrial policies, sustained rapid economic development for over three decades.[1285]

If government support is instrumental to fostering economic development, particularly in the early stages of economic development, there is a question as to whether the government may provide sector-specific support or if its support should instead focus on "new activities," such as developing new technology, providing training, and supporting new goods and services. Rodrik indicated that blanket support for specific sectors is likely to be less productive,[1286] but different sectors have different support needs, and it might not be possible to respond to all those needs with limited public resources. This limitation may necessitate sector-specific support to maximize the impact of government support on the economy and development. Another important finding is that a "good" economic policy is not sufficient to bring about economic development; there are numerous cases in which an identical economic policy, such as deregulation and privatization, has resulted in starkly divergent outcomes in different places (*e.g.*, the successful economic reform in the U.K. in the 1980s versus the dismal economic outcome in post-Soviet Russia). Relevant factors, such as a stable and efficient government, a working institutional arrangement between the public and private sectors, consistent economic policy, social peace, an educated population, access to capital, and a cultural environment that fosters working ethics, affect the outcome as much as a specific economic policy does.[1287]

The importance of sectoral support is also evidenced by the successful development process of South Korea: the South Korean government enacted legislation targeting the development of specific industries, including new industries in which there was no proven market player.[1288] The government legislated statutes that mandated direct support for specific manufacturing industries, including textile, mechanical, shipbuilding, electronic, petrochemical, and steel industries.[1289] These statutes authorized the government to adopt support measures for the designated industries, including tax incentives; "policy loans" whose terms, such as interest rates, were more favorable than the prevailing commercial terms; subsidy grants; tariff rebates and import control; and overseas loan guarantees.[1290] The government also instructed certain corporations to enter into such new industries (*e.g.*, Hyundai into the shipbuilding industry in the 1970s) and provided support (*e.g.*, government loan repayment guarantees) without a proven market performance record in place.[1291] This focused sectoral support led to the rapid economic development of South Korea in the early stages of economic development.[1292]

1285   See discussion *supra* Chapter 4.
1286   Rodrik (2004), *supra* note 264.
1287   Lee (2016), *supra* note 102, at 30.
1288   Lee (2020), *supra* note 1278, at 414.
1289   See Kim (ed.) (2011), vol. 1, *supra* note 176, at 216–227.
1290   See *supra* discussion Section 4.2.3(a).
1291   *Ibid.*
1292   South Korea recorded the real GDP growth rates of 8.0 percent and 9.7 percent in the periods of 1962–1966 and 1967–1971, respectively. See *supra* Table 4.1.

Lastly, the current international legal disciplines for international trade under the auspices of the World Trade Organization ("WTO law") impose substantial restrictions on the ability of WTO Member States ("Members") to adopt certain industrial policies, particularly trade-related subsidies and trade measures, as further discussed in Chapter 12. WTO law is binding on its 164 Members, which include all of the world's major economies and traders and both developed and developing countries. The subsidy rules of WTO law (Agreement on Subsidies and Countervailing Measures or "SCM Agreement," Article 3) prohibit export subsidies (subsidies contingent upon exports) and import-substitution subsidies (subsidies contingent upon the use of domestic products). WTO law (General Agreement on Trade and Tariffs or "GATT," Article II) also regulates tariffs applicable by individual Members under their schedules of concessions agreed upon with the rest of the WTO membership.[1293] Under these WTO rules, Members may not adopt certain trade-related subsidies, including export subsidies and import-substitution subsidies, or raise tariffs beyond the maximum binding rates upon which they have agreed with the other Members.[1294] WTO law (GATT, Article XI) also generally prohibits quantitative restrictions, and Members may not adopt a quota against imports unless specifically authorized under WTO rules (*e.g.*, a safeguard measure under the Agreement on Safeguards).[1295] As Rodrik lamented, the current trade rules have made "a significant dent in the abilities of developing countries to employ intelligently-designed industrial policies."[1296]

11.3 A case of success: the East Asian experience

11.3.1 From poverty to prosperity

The Newly Industrializing Countries (NICs) in East Asia, including Korea, Taiwan, Hong Kong, and Singapore, have achieved the most successful economic development in history. These NICs recorded unprecedented economic growth, sustained for over three decades; between 1961 and 1996, South Korea increased its GDP (gross domestic product) by an average of 8.75 percent per annum, Hong Kong by 7.61 percent, Taiwan by 8.64 percent, and Singapore by 8.61 percent (calculated with real GDP figures at constant 2005 national prices). Meanwhile, the world's average annual GDP increase and the annual GDP increase of the low- and middle-income countries for the corresponding period were 3.85 and 4.39 percent, respectively.[1297] This unprecedented, sustained growth was accompanied by economic transformation from primary industries of low productivity (*e.g.*, agriculture, fishery) to sophisticated manufacturing-based industries with technological advances. The NICs were among the poorest countries in the

---

1293   See discussion *infra* Chapter 12.
1294   *Ibid.*
1295   *Ibid.*
1296   Rodrik (2004), *supra* note 264, at 34–35.
1297   Feenstra, Inklaar, and Timmer (2015), *supra* note 28.

world, endowed with modest financial resources, scarce natural resources, low levels of technology, and weak manufacturing capacity. Within three decades, however, these countries were transformed from underdeveloped economies with prevalent poverty to advanced economies with high per-capita income and world-class industries.[1298]

This phenomenal economic transformation had been facilitated by state industrial promotion. The specific industrial policies of each country were not identical, although all of them focused on exports; for example, Singapore and Hong Kong adopted free trade policies and focused on attracting foreign investments, while South Korea and Taiwan protected domestic industries and focused on industrial development.[1299] Despite these specific differences, the NICs were successful "developmental states," *i.e.,* sovereign states that assume the key role for economic development and "create [economic development] plans, relocate surplus, combat resistance, invest and manage key sectors, and control foreign capital," exhibiting the apparent traits of state industrial promotion.[1300] The governments of the NICs planned for economic development and implemented strong industrial policies by influencing what would be produced and by whom through policy instruments such as subsidies and tax rebates. They chose the recipients of their support in accordance with their market performance, letting weak performers go, and this market-based selection was a key reason for success.[1301]

The success of the NICs became a model for many developing countries, such as China. Although China has never explicitly admitted that they are following the paths of these countries and instead argued that they are adopting their own, namely the "socialist market economy,"[1302] China has adopted strong industrial policies, extensively using government subsidies and trade measures, while also adopting various market mechanisms and supporting the growth of the private sectors.[1303] China's accession into the WTO accelerated its export drive, which parallels the export promotion by the NICs; within a decade after its accession, China became the largest exporter in the world. By 2010, China had become a solidly middle-income country, lifting hundreds of millions of its populations from absolute poverty.[1304] China's economic rise was met with substantial caution from the West, culminating in its recent trade conflicts with the United States.[1305] It remains to be seen whether the country's path will lead to the same level of economic prosperity for the majority of its populations as enjoyed by the NICs.

1298   Lee (2016), *supra* note 102, at 16.
1299   Pangestu (2002), *supra* note 30, at 153.
1300   Trubek and Santos (2006), *supra* note 81, at 5.
1301   See discussion *supra* Section 4.2.3(a).
1302   Lee and Lu (2016), *supra* note 1045.
1303   *Ibid.*
1304   *Ibid.*
1305   See Yong-Shik Lee, "International Trade Law Post Neoliberalism" (2020) 68(2) *Buffalo Law Review* 413–478, at 454–457.

11.3.2 *The marriage between state and market*

The economic development policies of most developing countries in the 1950s and 1960s were import substitution industrialization (ISI) policies, which aimed to substitute imports with domestically produced goods. ISI was as much a politically motivated initiative as an economic policy, in the sense that ISI was an effort to prevent the recurrence of the past practice that created an economic dependency on imports from the then-powerful industrial countries in the West to meet domestic economic demands.[1306] This economic dependency was believed to have led to political dependency and military domination, which resulted in colonial rule, a mistake that the newly independent developing countries vowed not to repeat.[1307] However, ISI policies failed in most places because of lack of sustainability; the government may, for instance, build a factory using tax revenue or an international loan, only to discover there is not enough demand in the domestic market to sustain the factory's production, due to the insufficient purchasing power of domestic consumers. The government would have to continue providing subsidies to support the factory, while it may never become competitive enough to sustain itself.[1308]

The NICs also adopted ISI policies in the 1950s and early 1960s, but they subsequently shifted policies toward export promotion.[1309] Export promotion policies aim to break the "cycle of poverty," which refers to the conditions that perpetuate poverty: existing poverty causes low purchasing power, which leads to low market demand, and this low market demand results in low income because production, which generates income, remains at a low level due to the low market demand. Exports break this circle by finding demands for domestic products in overseas export markets.[1310] Export promotion also accords domestic industries several advantages, such as the economies of scale, lowering production costs and increasing profit levels; improved productivity and product quality because of increased competition in the export markets; improved managerial efficiency; and accelerated technological progress thanks to the greater contacts with foreign institutions and ideas through exports.[1311]

Commentators contrast the failed ISI policies with the "successful" outward export promotion policies of the NICs, but such a dichotomy does not reflect the truth. As mentioned earlier, Singapore and Hong Kong adopted free trade policies and opened their borders for imports and foreign investments, but South Korea and Taiwan maintained protective tariff structures for decades to safeguard

---

1306 See Vincent Ferraro, "Dependency Theory: An Introduction," *in* Giorgio Secondi (ed.), *The Development Economics Reader* (London: Routledge, 2008), 58–64.
1307 *Ibid.*
1308 See, *e.g.*, Leland J. Johnson, "Problems of Import Substitution: The Chilean Automobile Industry" (1967) 15(2) *Economic Development and Cultural Change* 202–216.
1309 Pangestu (2002), *supra* note 30, at 153.
1310 Lee (2016), *supra* note 102, at 16–17.
1311 *Ibid.*

and promote domestic industries while they initiated the export drive.[1312] In other words, the successful developing countries, such as Korea and Taiwan, adopted both ISI and export promotion policies at the same time, and these two types of policies were complementary and not mutually exclusive. Another dichotomy between a free-market economy and government interventions also does not hold. While the success of the NICs has been praised as an outcome of market-based policies,[1313] the governments of these countries were closely involved in managing their economies through economic planning, extensive public campaigns, and more direct interventions with banks and corporations.[1314]

The policies of the NICs can be described as a "marriage between state and market."[1315] All of the NICs were market economies that offered the legal protection of property rights and freedom of contract, but their governments also intervened in the economy—*albeit* to different degrees at different times—by making key economic decisions for the nation and adopting measures of state industrial promotion, such as subsidies and trade measures, which would substantially alter the allocation of resources. In all of the NICs, the government had plans to develop industries and expand exports,[1316] with the economic targets (*e.g.*, growth rate) to be met within the established time frames. In the process, civil liberties and individual autonomy were curtailed; some of the NICs, such as Singapore, remain authoritarian, while South Korea and Taiwan democratized by the 1990s. Despite the democratic deficit, the NICs sustained economic development and political stability, as the populations were satisfied with the economic success of the marriage between state and market. This marriage was bonded by law, legal frameworks, and institutions. The next sub-section examines how the governments of the NICs used laws and institutions to promote the development of industries.

11.3.3 State industrial promotion, law, and institutions

(a) Law

The NICs used laws to empower the government to adopt industrial policies such as subsidies and trade measures. For example, South Korea enacted specific statutes intended to promote exports and specific industries, such as the Act on Temporary Measures for the Grant of Export Subsidies (1961), the Export Promotion Act (1962) (subsequently repealed and replaced by the Trade Transactions Act of 1967), and the Regulation of Tax Reduction and Exemption Act (1965).[1317] As discussed in Chapter 4, these statutes authorized the government to grant tax rebates for the profits generated by exports, ensure timely payment of subsidies contingent upon exports, make priority allocation of scarce foreign reserves

1312 *Ibid.*
1313 World Bank (1993), *supra* note 336.
1314 Lee (2016), *supra* note 102, at 330–332.
1315 *Ibid.*, at 331.
1316 Pangestu (2002), *supra* note 30, at 153.
1317 See discussion *supra* 4.2.3(a).

for the purchase of raw material to produce export products, and permit only those traders with qualified export performance to engage in the lucrative import business.[1318] The Korean government also enacted several statutes mandating direct support for specific manufacturing industries, as discussed above.[1319] These statutes authorized the government to adopt measures of support for the designated industries, including grants, tax rebates, policy loans, subsidy grants, tariff rebates and import control, and loan guarantees. Support was provided to businesses on a conditional basis: in return for support, businesses were required to show market performance, particularly in export markets.

The other NICs also used laws to promote industries. For example, Taiwan legislated the Statute for Encouragement of Investment (SEI) in 1960.[1320] The SEI authorized the government to provide numerous tax benefits to qualified domestic and foreign businesses making investments in specific key areas, such as manufacturing, mining, agriculture, transportation, warehousing, or technical services.[1321] In addition, the SEI enabled the government to grant special tax benefits for exports[1322] and R&D investments; it facilitated industrial infrastructure, promoted energy conservation, and reduced pollution.[1323] The SEI also established a government fund to assist with R&D investments.[1324] The SEI provisions supported cooperation between the public and private sectors, such as in the process of privatizing state enterprises, where the government was able to direct proceeds from privatization to a development fund that the government used to invest in high-tech industries.[1325] In 1990, the government legislated the Statute for Upgrading Industries (SUI) to replace the SEI.[1326] The SUI authorized the government to expand tax benefits for investing in areas of the country which were less economically developed.[1327] The SUI provided for the establishment of a development fund similar to the one from the SEI but with an added focus on newer, high-technology industries.[1328] The SUI also facilitated the establishment of industrial parks, granting the government authority to expropriate land for the parks and regulate their operation.[1329]

For Singapore, laws also provided for industrial promotion and export expansion. The Pioneer Industries Ordinance, enacted in 1959, allowed the government to provide two to five-year tax holidays to firms producing certain products

---

1318   *Ibid.*

1319   *Ibid.*

1320   Neil L. Meyers, "Statutory Encouragement of Investment and Economic Development in the Republic of China on Taiwan," *Occasional Papers/Reprints Series in Contemporary Asian Studies* (1994), at 14.

1321   SEI, art. 3.

1322   *Ibid.*, arts. 31–32.

1323   *Ibid.*, arts. 34–37, 44–48.

1324   *Ibid.*, art. 35.

1325   Meyers (1994), *supra* note 1320, at 39–42.

1326   *Ibid.*, at 42.

1327   SUI, art. 7.

1328   *Ibid.*, art. 21.

1329   *Ibid.*, arts. 25–26, 37–40.

prioritized for economic development.[1330] The qualifying firms under the Ordinance were also allowed to carry forward losses from the pioneer period and write off depreciation allowances against their profits after the pioneer period.[1331] The Industrial Expansion Ordinance, also enacted in 1959, gave special tax relief to expanding enterprises, and the period of tax relief would vary based on new capital expenditure.[1332] The Control of Manufacture Ordinance, enacted in the same year, allowed the Minister of Finance to set limits on the total number of firms producing specific goods to prevent over-competition.[1333] The Control of Manufacture Ordinance also established protective tariffs and import quotas.[1334] The Economic Expansion Incentives Act, passed in 1967, reduced corporate tax rates on the profits of approved exporters from 40 percent to 4 percent.[1335] The Act also provided tax relief for income resulting from capital expansion, a 90 percent remission on profits for up to 15 years, and tax exemptions for interest on foreign loans, royalties, and technical assistance fees.[1336] In 1970, this law was amended to raise the threshold for businesses to qualify for pioneer status and changed the benefit structure of this status. Pioneer firms would enjoy tax exemption for up to ten years, while non-pioneer firms could be exempt from taxation on up to 90 percent of their export profits for five years.[1337]

In the case of Hong Kong, the colonial government was known to have adopted a laissez-faire economic policy with minimal government involvement ("positive non-intervention"), under which the government only intervened to maintain general economic stability.[1338] However, Catherine Schenk suggested that this perception was a myth and argued that the government subsidized industry indirectly through public housing, which restrained the rise in the cost of living that would have threatened Hong Kong's labor-cost advantage in manufacturing.[1339] Regardless, government spending remained low across the board compared to the other NICs, and the government focused on building and maintaining physical infrastructure, ensuring the functioning of the legal system, and developing institutions to facilitate markets.[1340] In the late 1980s,

1330 Rachel van Elkan, "Singapore's Development Strategy," *in* K. Bercusson (eds.), *Singapore: A Case Study in Rapid Development* (Washington, D.C.: International Monetary Fund, 1995), at 12, note 2.

1331 Augustine Tan, "Official Efforts to Attract FDI: Case of Singapore's EDB," *in* 1999 EWC/KDI Conference on Industrial Globalization in the 21st Century: *Impact and Consequences for East Asia and Korea* (1999), at 5.

1332 *Ibid.*

1333 *Ibid.*, at 12.

1334 *Ibid.*, at 5.

1335 Van Elkan (1995), *supra* note 1330, at 13, note 5.

1336 Teck-Wong Soon and C. Suan Tan, *Singapore: Public Policy and Economic Development* (Washington, D.C.: World Bank, 1993), at 10.

1337 Tan (1999), *supra* note 1331, at 6–7.

1338 Lai Si Tsui-Auch, "Has the Hong Kong Model Worked? Industrial Policy in Retrospect and Prospect" (1998) 29 *Development and Change* 55–79, at 68.

1339 Schenk (2008), *supra* note 260.

1340 Tsui-Auch (1998), *supra* note 1338, at 68.

however, the government started to support high-technology industry, first by providing subsidized land in the Industrial Estates of Tai Po, Yuen Long, and Tseung Kwan O,[1341] and in tandem with the 1997 political transition, by taking a more proactive role in promoting innovation and technological development.[1342] In 1999, the Legislative Council passed the Innovation Technology Fund (ITF) Resolution, indicating that the government would assume a more active role in industrial development.[1343] Under the ITF resolution, the Financial Secretary was authorized to apply money from the fund to projects that "contribute to innovation" and the upgrading and technological development of the manufacturing and service industries.[1344]

(b) Institutional framework

Crucial to the success of the NICs' laws facilitating economic development was their implementation of effective institutional frameworks. For example, South Korea set up several development-supporting institutions, both inside and outside the government.[1345] As discussed in Chapter 4, South Korea established the Economic Planning Board (EPB) within the central government in 1961, which worked as the control center for the development and implementation of development policies.[1346] The EPB coordinated with other government departments on policy measures concerning economic development for over three decades; the EPB had authority over personnel appointment and budget allocation in other government departments and agencies, which empowered the EPB to instruct and lead the entire government on the development and implementation of economic development policy.[1347] In addition to the EPB, the government also set up other financial institutions to support economic development, including the Korea Development Bank and the Korea Export-Import Bank, which provided loans for select industries and export credit, respectively.[1348] Korea also launched and operated trade-support organizations, such as the Korea Trade Promotion Corporation (KOTRA), which supported exporters with access to overseas market information and business networks, and the Korea International Trade Association (KITA), which promoted the interests of Korean traders and provided trade information to its members.[1349]

1341 *Ibid.*, at 69.
1342 Legislative Council of Hong Kong, Panel on Commerce and Industry, *Updated Background Brief on the Funding Schemes under the Innovation and Technology Fund*, LC Paper No. CB(1)535/19–20(04) (2020), at 1.
1343 Hong Kong E-Legislation, *Cap. 2Q Innovation and Technology Fund*, available online at: www.elegislation.gov.hk/hk/cap2Q@2017-02-15T00:00:00?xpid=ID_1438402956369_003; https://perma.cc/9HPY-ANUK.
1344 *Ibid.*
1345 See discussion *supra* Section 4.2.3(b).
1346 *Ibid.*
1347 *Ibid.*
1348 *Ibid.*
1349 *Ibid.*

In Taiwan, the Industrial Development Bureau (IDB) played a similar role as South Korea's EPB in the development of industrial policy, but unlike the EPB, it was under the control of another ministry, the Ministry of Economic Affairs,[1350] and it had a different institutional status and mandate. The Executive Yuan, essentially the Cabinet of the Taiwanese government, was responsible for much of the top-level administration and industrial policy coordination.[1351] The Executive Yuan carried out two major functions in this context: first, the Executive Yuan consulted with the ministries and agencies that govern certain sectors to promulgate industry-specific regulation,[1352] and second, it administered and oversaw the development funds that were allocated and administered under various pieces of industrial legislation.[1353] The Ministry of Economic Affairs, a department of the Executive Yuan in charge of administering economic development policy, oversaw administrative agencies such as the IDB and the Bureau of Foreign Trade, as well as state-owned enterprises.[1354]

Singapore established the Economic Development Board (EDB) in 1961.[1355] The EDB was in charge of promoting industry, encouraging investment, and facilitating economic development.[1356] Additionally, the EDB was empowered to take on any other function "conferred upon the Board under any written law."[1357] Thus, the EDB was tasked with managing the overall process of economic development[1358] and pursued a variety of development-related policy objectives, including investment promotion, consultancy services, and industrial training.[1359] Toward the end of the 1960s, however, some of the EDB's functions were transferred to other agencies: for example, the financing functions of the EDB were transferred to the Development Bank of Singapore (DBS), which became an independent body.[1360] The Jurong Town Corporation, a separate statutory board, was established to handle much of the industrial promotion functions.[1361] Despite these transfers of power, the EDB remained responsible for administering key industrial promotion policies, including administering tax

1350 Robert H. Wade, "The Economic Bureaucracy," *in* Robert Wade (ed.), *Governing the Market: Economic Theory and the Role of Government in East Asian Industrialization* (Princeton, NJ: Princeton University Press, 1990), at 20.

1351 Meyers (1994), *supra* note 1320.

1352 *Ibid.*, at 22.

1353 *Ibid.*, at 41, 53.

1354 See also Ministry of Economic Affairs, *History*, available online at: www.moea.gov.tw/MNS/english/EconomicHistory/EconomicHistory.aspx?menu_id=32897; https://perma.cc/GH3Z-NB7X.

1355 The EDB was created by Economic Development Board Act of 1961. See Singapore Government Agency, *Economic Development Board Act*, available online at: https://sso.agc.gov.sg/Act/EDBA1961; https://perma.cc/MD7Q-YJEN.

1356 *Ibid.*

1357 *Ibid.*

1358 Soon and Tan (1993), *supra* note 1336, at 25.

1359 *Ibid.*, at 26.

1360 *Ibid.*, at 26.

1361 *Ibid.*

incentives, coordinating with ministries for industry-specific development, and optimizing the regulatory framework for private enterprises in Singapore.[1362]

For much of its colonial period, Hong Kong, known to have adopted a laissez-faire policy for industrialization, did not set up strong institutional frameworks for industrial promotion like the other NICs. The government of Hong Kong set up an Industrial Development Board in 1977 to plan and monitor local industries, but it was placed under the Office of the Financial Secretary (whose responsibility was to oversee government expenditure), thus implying a relatively weaker government commitment than the other NICs.[1363] Since the early 1990s, however, the government began to increase its efforts to promote the technical capacity of Hong Kong's manufacturing industry. For example, the government set up the Industry and Technology Development Council in 1992, replacing the Industrial Development Board, to ensure Hong Kong's speedy response to the fast-changing technological environment and to enhance the connection between industry and technology that was considered vital for industrial development in Hong Kong.[1364] In addition, the Hong Kong Trade Development Council, which was set up in 1966, promoted trade and the service sector, exploring new export markets, providing information to local manufacturers about overseas buyers, and cooperating with local producers to improve the quality and design of their products.[1365]

(c) Evaluation

The NICs adopted statutory devices to empower their respective governments to promote industrial development through subsidization and export promotion. The law in the NICs guided the path over which local industrial development was sustained through continued export expansion and technological innovation, which, in turn, led to unprecedented economic development.[1366] The extent of direct industrial promotion by the state varied among the NICs, as discussed above, but all of them monitored the development of industries and promoted exports through effective institutions, *albeit* in different forms and statuses. The NICs also made adjustments to their laws and institutional frameworks as their industrial and economic development progressed: the statutes enacted to promote specific industries were repealed or revised as those industries attained international competitiveness and no longer required direct governmental support, and the institutions that once controlled the national development and industrial policies, such as the EPB of South Korea, were also repealed and adjusted to the

---

1362   Tan (1999), *supra* note 1331, at 5–14.

1363   See Tsui-Auch (1998), *supra* note 1338, at 68. See also Mee-Kau Nyaw and Chan-leong Chan, "Structure and Development Strategies of the Manufacturing Industries in Singapore and Hong Kong: A Comparative Study" (1982) 22(5) *Asian Survey* 449–469, at 463.

1364   Edward Chen and Raymond Ng, "Economic Restructuring of Hong Kong on the Basis of Innovation and Technology," *in* Seiichi Masuyama, Donna Vandenbrink, and Chia Siow Yue (eds.), *Industrial Restructuring in East Asia* (ISEAS Publishing, 2019), at 9.

1365   *Ibid.*

1366   See *supra* note 28 (for an account of the NICs' rapid economic development).

new economic environment.[1367] The NICs had both consistency in the implementation of laws and institutions and flexibility to make adjustments when the latter were required—a rare combination of important qualities that led to historic success.

Two other important legal and institutional features of the NICs were the reliability of the judicial system and the protection of property rights and economic freedom. Even though for most of their rapid economic development from the 1960s through 1990s, the administrations of the NICs were either largely authoritarian (South Korea, Taiwan, and Singapore) or colonial (Hong Kong), their laws were well-developed from the European civil law system (South Korea and Taiwan) or common law system (Singapore and Hong Kong), and they solidly protected property rights and freedom of contract. The legal system thus worked as an important economic incentive for private enterprises. Their judiciaries, which were able to recruit elites from their societies, were largely effective, reliable, and relatively independent from interventions from the executive branch over non-political matters.[1368] The authoritarian and colonial regimes of the NICs, which were not receptive to political challenges,[1369] nevertheless, respected the rule of law at least in the economic and business sphere and sought to implement development policies through law in relevant institutional frameworks.

The success of the NICs was publicized around the world, and many other developing countries emulated development-facilitating laws and development-supporting institutions adopted by the NICs, but it did not lead to success for most of them.[1370] As the general theory of law and development has explained earlier,[1371] the adaptation of laws and institutions is not sufficient to guarantee success; other elements, such as regulatory design, regulatory compliance, and the quality of implementation, are also important. In many cases, the regulatory design failed to conform to socioeconomic conditions on the ground and was weak due to the lack of institutional support. Additionally, regulatory compliance was absent among the people, and the quality of implementation was low on account of lack of state capacity and political will.[1372] The NICs, unlike many other developing countries, retained political leadership—despite it having been authoritarian or colonial—that had strong interests in economic development, and implemented, over a period of time, consistent development

---

1367   See discussion *supra* Section 4.2.
1368   For a relevant discussion of the development of the judiciary in East Asia, see Tom Ginsburg, "Judicial Independence in East Asia: Implications for China," *Public Law and Legal Theory Working Papers* (2010), available online at: https://chicagounbound.uchicago.edu/cgi/viewcontent.cgi?article=1172&context=public_law_and_legal_theory; https://perma.cc/SRT8-P9MM.
1369   See, *e.g.*, Hart-Landsberg (1993), *supra* note 418 and Wachman (2016), *supra* note 1118.
1370   See, *e.g.*, discussion *supra* Chapter 5 (for a discussion of limited economic success in South Africa).
1371   See discussion *supra* Chapter 3.
1372   See, *e.g.*, discussion *supra* Section 5.2.

policies and laws that may not have been immediately popular with general populations due to short-term sacrifices associated with long-term investments (*e.g.*, promotion of savings for economic development over short-term disbursement of capital).[1373] Such effective political leadership, active compliance by the public, and well-designed and flexible laws and institutions were key for the NICs' success.

11.4 Industrial policy of developed countries: the U.S. Case

11.4.1 Introduction

This section examines industrial policy adopted by a developed country, the United States. As the concept of development and law and development approaches are found relevant in addressing chronic economic problems in both developing and developed countries,[1374] state industrial promotion by developed countries, such as the United States, is also relevant to the discourse of this chapter. As discussed at the beginning of this chapter, virtually all states apply industrial policy, whether or not the country in question announces it as such.[1375] The United States is not an exception; as further discussed in this section, the United States has adopted various state industrial promotion measures, including subsidies and trade measures. The U.S. government has adopted these measures through legal means, and a number of institutions have been created to administer the laws fostering industrial development. The recent trade measures by the United States to protect and promote relevant domestic industries, such as its steel and aluminum tariffs,[1376] have created a significant impact for international trade and a precedent that will be adversarial to the multilateral trade order under the auspices of the WTO that the United States worked to establish in 1995.[1377]

There is a deep historical root for the U.S. industrial policy: in 1791, shortly after the United States achieved independence from Britain, Alexander Hamilton advocated for the use of subsidies and tariffs at Congress to support the nation's emerging industries.[1378] For several decades thereafter, the United States remained largely an agrarian country, but in the late nineteenth century, industrialization rapidly progressed in the United States, and along with it, the implementation of trade measures and subsidies: Abraham Lincoln adopted protectionist trade policies and implemented massive government investments in

---

1373   See discussion *supra* Section 3.3.2(c).

1374   See discussion *supra* Section 6.1.

1375   See discussion *supra* Section 11.1.

1376   Proclamation 9705 of March 8, 2018, *Adjusting Imports of Steel into the United States* and Proclamation 9704 of March 8, 2018, *Adjusting Imports of Aluminum into the United States*, reported in *Federal Register*, vol. 83, no. 51 (March 15, 2018), docs. 2018–11625 and 2018–11619, respectively.

1377   See Lee (2019), *supra* note 598.

1378   Alexander Hamilton, *Report on the Subject of Manufactures* (December 5, 1791), available online at: https://founders.archives.gov/documents/Hamilton/01-10-02-0001-0007; https://perma.cc/55T8-8YYU.

infrastructure, such as the transcontinental railroad.[1379] U.S. tariff rates gradually increased throughout the 19th century, and by the 1930s, amidst the Great Depression, the Smoot-Hawley Tariff Act pushed the country's tariffs to among the highest in the world.[1380] The policies of the New Deal also increased government subsidies and investments to an unprecedented level.[1381] After the Second World War, when the United States had recovered from the Great Depression and attained a dominant economic position in the world, it began to advocate free trade and the market economy without government interventions, as reflected by the Washington Consensus.[1382] Despite this advocacy, the United States has maintained, for decades, state industrial promotion policy as will be further discussed in the remainder of this section.

11.4.2 Subsidies

Since the massive railroad subsidies in the nineteenth century,[1383] the United States has granted large amounts of subsidies to specific industries, such as steel, oil, and agricultural industries.[1384] Despite subsidy grants to specific industries, however, the overall policy structure is different from the one adopted by the NICs, which focused on centralized planning and high-profile government direction; instead, American industrial policy has adopted a "developmental network state,"[1385] which is oriented toward identifying technological needs in the economy and coordinating the actions of different bodies conducting research, through R&D subsidization, to improve the quality of research and accelerate the process of turning research breakthroughs into commercial applications and ultimately new technological products.[1386] For example, in 1983, the U.S. government established the Strategic Computing Initiative (SCI).[1387] The SCI was a ten-year program in which the government provided funding for research of key technological hurdles in the development of advanced computing technologies; the government provided initial research grants to a series of competing

---

1379   Robert D. Hormats, "Abraham Lincoln and the Global Economy" (2003) *Harvard Business Review*, available online at: https://hbr.org/2003/08/abraham-lincoln-and-the-global-economy#:~:text=And%20the%20success%20he%20and,opportunity%20to%20settle%20Western%20lands; https://perma.cc/3JQS-ESU3.

1380   Tariff Act of 1930, 19 U.S.C. §§ 1201–1641.

1381   Robert H. Wade, "The Paradox of US Industrial Policy: The Developmental State in Disguise," in José Manuel Salazar-Xirinachs, Irmgard Nübler, and Richard Kozul-Wright (eds.), *Transforming Economies: Making Industrial Policy Work for Growth, Jobs and Development* (Geneva: ILO, 2014), at 386–387.

1382   See *supra* note 8 (for a discussion of the Washington Consensus).

1383   Hormats (2003), *supra* note 1379.

1384   For a general discussion, see Felicia J. Deyrup, "Government Support of Industry in American History" (1950) 17(3) *Social Research* 346–364.

1385   Fred Block, "Swimming Against the Current: The Rise of a Hidden Developmental State in the United States" (2008) 36(2) *Politics and Society* 169–206, at 171.

1386   *Ibid.*, at 172–174.

1387   *Ibid.*, at 181.

research groups and provided an additional subsidy to research groups which demonstrated success or promising results to commercialize those results.[1388] As another example, in 1987, the government created Sematech, a consortium of public research organizations and private technology firms which would support the development and improvement of semiconductor technology in the United States.[1389]

The United States has systematically granted subsidies through legal devices. For example, Congress legislated the Stevenson-Wydler Technology Innovation Act in 1980, which provided for supportive measures, including subsidy grants, to promote technological innovation.[1390] Under the Act, the Director of Office of Industrial Technology, appointed by the Secretary of Commerce, was tasked with identifying technological needs in American industry, finding areas that needed assistance in developing technology, supporting the development of new technologies through subsidy grants, and improving coordination between industry and the Department of Commerce to advance technology.[1391] Research and development support has also been extended to small businesses. In 1982, Congress passed the Small Business Innovation Development Act.[1392] The Act required every federal agency with an R&D budget of over $100 million per year to set up their own Small Business Innovation Research (SBIR) Program.[1393] Each agency's SBIR Program is then required to determine what kind of projects it will fund, issue solicitations for funding applications, select awardees for funding grants, and make payments to the recipients of funding.[1394]

11.4.3 Trade measures

Since Hamilton proposed to use tariffs as a means to protect domestic industries in the United States, U.S. tariff rates gradually increased throughout the nineteenth century and had become among the highest in the world with the enactment of the Smoot-Hawley Tariff Act in 1930, increasing tariffs already at high levels (some 40 percent) by an average of 40–50 percent.[1395] The government reduced the tariff rates after the Second World War but has actively used "administered protection" authorized under WTO law, such as countervailing duties (CVDs) and anti-dumping (AD) measures, which are additional duties applicable against subsidized imports and against imports priced under "normal

---

1388   *Ibid.*
1389   *Ibid.*
1390   Stevenson-Wydler Technology Innovation Act of 1980, 15 U.S.C. §§ 3710–3753.
1391   *Ibid.* The Act also provides for the Centers for Industrial Technology to be set up in conjunction with a host university or a non-profit organization and supported by both the Office of Industrial Technology and the National Science Foundation. *Id.*
1392   Small Business Innovation Development Act of 1982, 15 U.S.C. § 638.
1393   *Ibid.*
1394   *Ibid.*
1395   Brady P. Priest, "Steel Tariffs: A Shining Example of the Tension between Politics and Economics in the United States" (2002) 28(3) *Brooklyn Journal of International Law* 1025–1057, at 1035, note 53.

value," respectively.[1396] The United States imposed more AD measures and CVDs than any other country, applying a total of 514 AD measures out of 4012 measures invoked around the world from 1995 to 2020,[1397] and half of the CVD measures (168 measures out of 337) applied during the same period.[1398] The United States justified the imposition of these measures in the name of restoring a "level-playing field,"[1399] but these measures were industrial policy measures, as they have been invoked to protect and promote the interests of domestic industries.

The recent controversial tariffs ("the steel and aluminum tariffs") imposed by the Trump administration illustrate the nature of U.S. trade measures as industrial policy. In March 2018, the Trump administration adopted trade measures that increased tariffs on steel and aluminum products by 25 percent and 10 percent, respectively, in addition to any duties already in place, including AD measures and CVDs.[1400] The U.S. government justified the tariffs on national security grounds,[1401] which is permitted to protect essential security interests under GATT Article XXI[1402] and section 232 of the Trade Expansion Act.[1403] However, several countries have criticized the U.S. steel and aluminum tariffs as lacking justification under GATT Article XXI for national security concerns and argued further that those tariffs were adopted as a trade protection measure.[1404] The government applied steel and aluminum tariffs to all items of imported products of iron or steel as well as all entries of aluminum products, rendering the scope of products subject to the tariffs too wide to justify any "essential security interest."[1405] These are the product areas in which the U.S. government had applied numerous AD measures and CVDs, but without any clear evidence justifying these extensive tariffs for an essential security interest. The steel and aluminum tariffs were likely applied for the protection and promotion of domestic industries for a commercial purpose.[1406]

1396 For further discussion of CVDs and anti-dumping measures, see discussion *infra* Sections 12.2.2 and 12.2.3, respectively.

1397 WTO, *Anti-dumping Measures: Reporting Member vs Exporter 01/01/1995—30/06/2020*, available online at: www.wto.org/english/tratop_e/adp_e/AD_MeasuresRepMemVsExp.pdf; https://perma.cc/3UFS-H25C.

1398 WTO, *Countervailing Measures: by Reporting Member 01/01/1995—30/06/2020*, available online at: www.wto.org/english/tratop_e/scm_e/CV_MeasuresByRepMem.pdf; https://perma.cc/S4KX-ZA3G.

1399 Lee (2016), *supra* note 102, at 61–62.

1400 Proclamations 9704 and 9705 of March 8, 2018, *supra* note 1376.

1401 *Ibid.*

1402 GATT, 1867 U.N.T.S. 194 (October 30, 1947), art. XXI.

1403 As amended 19 U.S.C. § 1862.

1404 WTO, *Disputes by Member*, available online at: www.wto.org/english/tratop_e/dispu_e/dispu_by_country_e.htm; https://perma.cc/J6H8-FFPJ; *United States—Certain Measures on U.S. Steel and Aluminum Products* (*United States—Steel and Aluminum Products*), DS550, DS563, DS548, DS547, DS551, DS552, DS554, DS556, DS564, cited in Lee (2019), *supra* note 598, at 488, note 38.

1405 Lee (2019), *ibid.*, at 482, notes 7 and 8.

1406 Perhaps recognizing the weakness of its case, the United States argued that its claim under Article XXI is a self-judging matter, unreviewable by the WTO, but there is no support in WTO jurisprudence for this claim. For a further discussion, see *Ibid.*, at 490–491.

11.4.4 Evaluation

Developed countries, as well as developing countries, have adopted industry policy measures and promoted industrial development. The United States has adopted subsidies and extensive trade measures to promote the interests of its domestic industries. Compared to the policies adopted by NICs during the early stages of their economic development, which focused on sectoral development, the U.S. industrial policy after the Second World has been characterized as a "developmental network state," more oriented toward subsidizing R&D, facilitating coordination, and supporting the commercialization of new technologies.[1407] Sectoral support, however, remained prevalent in some areas, such as agriculture and oil industries.[1408] The NICs have also transitioned toward these types of more indirect support since the 1990s as their economies progressed into advanced economies based on the high level of technologies. The United States has also maintained extensive trade measures, which have been invoked to protect domestic industries, despite international controversies about their justifications.[1409] Trade measures remain an important means of industrial policy today. The increasing economic disparity and structural economic issues in the United States, discussed in Chapter 6, call for a new legal and institutional approach, reinforcing the role of the government in support and coordination.[1410] It remains to be seen whether the United States will embark on the new path.

11.4.5 Concluding remarks–state industrial promotion, law, and economic development

Scholars disagree on the efficacy of state industrial promotion and the role that a state must play in the economy. The recent theories, including the New General Theory of Economic Development, suggest that state industrial promotion and the market economy are not necessarily mutually exclusive and can lead to economic development. History has shown that the most successful developing countries, such as the NICs, adopted extensive state industrial promotion policies and lifted their economies from poverty to prosperity while maintaining the market economy. The success has not been replicated in most other developing countries, and this chapter has discussed the key factors that have affected the success of the NICs and the failure of others. There have been relatively fewer studies examining the interrelationship between state promotion of policy and law. This chapter has examined the laws and institutions that the NICs have

---

1407   See discussion *supra* Section 11.4.2.
1408   *Ibid.*
1409   See discussion *supra* Section 11.4.3.
1410   See discussion *supra* Section 6.3.

adopted to promote industries. The outcome of this examination confirms that a policy alone does not lead to an anticipated outcome in economic development and industrial promotion. The causal elements presented by the general theory of law and development, such as regulatory design, regulatory compliance, and quality of implementation, are determinative in the impact of law on state industrial promotion.

This chapter has also examined the industrial policy of a developed country, the United States. The United States, under the Trump administration, invoked traditional trade measures in the form of extensive tariffs on imports from particular countries, such as China, and in specific product categories, such as steel and aluminum.[1411] The United States defends these tariff measures on the grounds of national security protection (in the case of steel and aluminum tariffs) and of its right to curtail unfair trade practices (in the case of China), but they are trade measures adopted for commercial reasons and for the protection and promotion of U.S. domestic industries.[1412] To the extent that the tariff measures benefit the domestic industries, the measures qualify as state industrial promotion. The concern is that the recent U.S. trade protectionism has triggered retaliatory measures from other exporting countries, a practice that has the potential to destabilize the international trading system.[1413]

1411 Lee (2019), *supra* note 598.
1412 *Ibid.*
1413 *Ibid.*

12 International legal frameworks

Trade and development

12.1 Trade and development

This chapter, which concludes Part III, examines development issues in international legal frameworks, focusing on international trade law ("trade and development issues"), and assesses the impact of international trade law on economic development.[1414] The facilitation of development has become a key objective for the multilateral trading system under the auspices of the World Trade Organization (WTO),[1415] of which three-quarters of the membership is currently comprised of developing countries.[1416] Yet, the legal disciplines of the WTO, including the legal disciplines of its predecessor, the General Agreement on Tariffs and Trade (GATT),[1417] are marked with a significant development deficit, as further discussed in this chapter. The Doha Round, which was initiated to advance development interests under the Doha Development Agenda (DDA),[1418] failed to deliver on the promises of development after 14 years of negotiations. Despite numerical superiority, developing countries have not substantially improved their positions in the

---

1414   This chapter has been developed from the author's previous works, including "The Long and Winding Road – Path Towards Facilitation of Development in the WTO: Reflections on the Doha Round and Beyond" (2016) 9(2) *Law and Development Review* 437–465 and Lee (2016), *supra* note 102, at 175–196.

1415   The Preamble of the WTO Agreement provides in relevant part, "There is a need for positive efforts designed to ensure that developing countries, and especially the least developed among them, secure a share in the growth of international trade commensurate with the needs of their economic development… ." WTO Agreement, *supra* note 305, preamble. See also WTO, *Singapore Ministerial Declaration*, WT/MIN(96)/DEC (December 18, 1996), para. 13.

1416   WTO membership currently includes all major trading nations in the world, 164 countries as of November 2020, making the WTO the "United Nations" of international trade. WTO, *Members and Observers*, available online at: www.wto.org/english/thewto_e/whatis_e/tif_e/org6_e.htm; https://perma.cc/QJR3-JMVN.

1417   GATT, 1867 U.N.T.S. 194 (October 30, 1947), art. XVIII.

1418   The Doha Round was signified by its development agenda (DDA), which aimed to advance the interests of developing countries in the major negotiation areas, including agriculture, non-agricultural market access, services, intellectual property, trade and development, trade and environment, trade facilitation, WTO rules, and Dispute Settlement Understanding. WTO, *The Doha Round*, available online at: www.wto.org/english/tratop_e/dda_e/dda_e.htm#development; https://perma.cc/MS28-LK2F.

DOI: 10.4324/9781003090175-15

world trading system, as demonstrated by the failure to advance their development interests at the Doha Round. This chapter discusses the impact that international trade and international trade law have on economic development, analyzes the difficulties in promoting development interests in the WTO system, identifies the development deficit in the current rules of international trade law, and examines the effects that the proliferation of regional trade agreements (RTAs) have on development.

International trade and the expansion of export have been essential to economic development. Their importance to economic development has been demonstrated by successful developing countries. As discussed in the preceding chapter, the NICs adopted the "outward development strategy,"[1419] pursuing aggressive export promotion policies to overcome the "cycle of poverty."[1420] In this outward development model, export becomes the engine for development by creating demands for domestically produced products otherwise not consumed in their small domestic markets.[1421] Export revenues can be reinvested to expand export industries further, and therefore, the output of the domestic economy improves over time with the expansion of the share of manufacturing sectors in the economy.[1422] This is the common element observed in the development process of the NICs. In those East Asian countries, a series of economic factors preferable for industrial expansion, such as lower labor costs and a high rate of savings, helped export industries, but governments also played an important role by promoting those industries with various subsidies and tariff protection.[1423]

The success of this development strategy would, thus, depend on the government's ability to promote exports.[1424] The current regulatory framework for international trade, however, places certain limitations on the ability of developing countries to adopt some trade-related development policies, such as export subsidies, without which the successful economic development of the East Asian countries would have been difficult. Recognizing these regulatory restraints in place, Dani Rodrik commented that the current trade rules have made "a significant dent in the abilities of developing countries to employ intelligently designed industrial policies."[1425] The legal framework for international trade controls which development policies can be implemented with respect to international trade and how they are implemented.[1426] Therefore, the legal disciplines of international

---

1419 See discussion *supra* Section 11.3. For an evolution of the NICs' industrial policies, see Pangestu (2002), *supra* note 30, at 153, Table 17.1.
1420 The cycle of poverty is a continuation of causal elements perpetuating poverty: the low purchasing power of consumers induced by low levels of income affords only low levels of production which, in turn, leads to low levels of income and low levels of consumption.
1421 Lee (2016), *supra* note 102, at 16.
1422 *Ibid.*
1423 See discussion *supra* Section 11.3.
1424 Lee (2016), *supra* note 102, at 18.
1425 Rodrik (2004), *supra* note 264.
1426 Lee (2016), *supra* note 102, at 18–19.

trade are closely relevant to poverty and development, and international trade law affects the ability of developing countries to adopt effective development policies.

The emphasis on development has evolved since the GATT era (1947–1994).[1427] Initially, little progress was made in meeting development objectives, but attention to the importance of development grew over time as the participation of developing countries increased.[1428] With the number of developing countries reaching over three-quarters of WTO membership today, development has become a key issue in the WTO. The WTO Agreement (*i.e.*, the Marrakesh Agreement Establishing the WTO) includes the facilitation of development among its major objectives. As shown in the preamble to the WTO Agreement,[1429] the WTO recognizes the role of international trade in development and the need to ensure that developing countries share in the growth of international trade. The first WTO Ministerial Conference also addressed the importance of integrating developing countries in the multilateral trading system for their economic development,[1430] recalling that "the WTO Agreement embodies provisions conferring differential and more favorable treatment for developing countries, including special attention to the particular situation of least developed countries."[1431]

Despite this emphasis on development, WTO law displays considerable deficiencies in promoting development interests. For instance, a substantial number of exceptions exist in the regulations on trade in agriculture, such as domestic subsidies that would otherwise be actionable under WTO law,[1432] adversely affecting the interests of many developing countries relying on exports of agricultural products.[1433] While market access was demanded of developing countries,

---

1427　The late Professor Robert Hudec's insightful work, *Developing Countries in the GATT Legal System*, provides an account of how the GATT as an institution came to accommodate the increasing involvement of developing countries in the world trading system. R. E. Hudec, *Developing Countries in the GATT Legal System*, Thames Essay no. 50 (Aldershot: Gower, for the Trade Policy Research Centre, London, 1987).

1428　A GATT ministerial decision in November 1957 cited "the failure of the trade of less developed countries to develop as rapidly as that of industrialized countries" as a major problem. GATT, Decision of November 29, 1957, B.I.S.D. 6S/18 (1958). This decision led to the publication of the "Haberler Report," which supported the perception that the export earnings of developing countries were not satisfactory. G. Haberler *et al.*, *Trends in International Trade* (October 1958), available online at: www.wto.org/english/res_e/booksp_e/gatt_trends_in_international_trade.pdf, accessed November 9, 2020.

1429　WTO Agreement, *supra* note 305, preamble.

1430　WTO, WT/MIN(96)/DEC, *supra* note 1415.

1431　*Ibid.* The WTO also recognizes and grants certain regulatory preferences to least developed countries (LDCs). LDCs are identified by the United Nations (U.N.) based on multiple criteria such as a low-income criterion, a human resource weakness criterion, and an economic vulnerability criterion. 47 LDCs are on the U.N. list as of November 2020. For further details of LDCs, see United Nations, *Least Developed Countries (LDCs)*, available online at: www.un.org/development/desa/dpad/least-developed-country-category.html; https://perma.cc/6A6X-MK7S; 36 LDCs have become WTO Members to date. See WTO, *Least-developed Countries*, available online at: www.wto.org/english/thewto_e/whatis_e/tif_e/org7_e.htm; https://perma.cc/49RV-5EVS.

1432　SCM Agreement, *infra* note 1455.

1433　See also Lee (2016), *supra* note 102, at 141–148.

and trade-related subsidies were banned or made actionable despite their use as an effective tool for economic development,[1434] development-facilitation provisions in the GATT, such as Article XVIII, have never been expanded into more enforceable agreements, creating a regulatory imbalance in the system. Trade facilitation is an important part of development strategy[1435] and needs to be supported by the WTO. The successful development of East Asian economies—such as those of South Korea, Taiwan, Singapore, Hong Kong, and, more recently, China—was fostered by rapid increases in their exports, which, in turn, transformed their industrial structure and enhanced economic growth.[1436]

12.2 Development "deficit" in the current rules and reform proposal

The rules of international law, as currently constructed, exhibit significant development deficits, thus justifying extensive regulatory reform beyond the scope of reform attempted by the Doha Round.[1437] Some WTO provisions attempt to support the interests of developing countries by granting special and differential treatment ("S&D treatment"), applied for the benefit of developing countries. S&D provisions aim to increase the trade opportunities of developing countries, require Members to safeguard the interests of developing countries, allow some flexibility to developing countries for commitments and use of policy instruments, provide additional transitional time periods to implement commitments, and offer technical assistance.[1438] According to a 2018 WTO report, 155 S&D provisions were scattered throughout WTO agreements, and additional Ministerial, General Council, and other Decisions allowed for special treatment to developing and least developed country (LDC) Members.[1439] As discussed below, the current S&D provisions are insufficient to support development interests, and more extensive regulatory reform is required in each of the following areas.

12.2.1 Tariff bindings

GATT Article II requires WTO Members to "bind" maximum tariff rates through their Schedule of Concessions. Paragraph I of Article II provides:

a Each contracting party shall accord to the commerce of the other contracting parties treatment no less favourable than that provided for in the appropriate Part of the appropriate Schedule annexed to this Agreement.

1434 *Ibid.*, at 14–32.
1435 *Ibid.*
1436 *Ibid.* See also discussion *supra* Chapter 4.
1437 WTO, *supra* note 1418.
1438 WTO, *Special and Differential Treatment Provisions in WTO Agreements and Decisions – Note by the Secretariat*, WT/COMTD/W/239 (October 12, 2018).
1439 *Ibid.*

b The products described in Part I of the Schedule relating to any contracting party, which are the products of territories of other contracting parties, shall, on their importation into the territory to which the Schedule relates, and subject to the terms, conditions or qualifications set forth in that Schedule, be exempt from ordinary customs duties in excess of those set forth and provided therein. Such products shall also be exempt from all other duties or charges of any kind imposed on or in connection with the importation in excess of those imposed on the date of this Agreement or those directly and mandatorily required to be imposed thereafter by legislation in force in the importing territory on that date...[1440]

While this requirement of maximum tariff binding provides essential stability for the international trading system, it also restrains the ability of developing countries to adopt tariff measures above the maximum bindings to promote domestic industries for development purposes.[1441]

GATT Article XVIII, entitled "Government Assistance to Economic Development,"[1442] offers S&D treatment to developing country Members with respect to the tariff bindings. Specifically, Article XVIII enables developing country Members, whose economies can only support low standards of living and are in the early stages of development,[1443] "to maintain flexibility in their tariff structure to be able to grant the tariff protection *required for the establishment of a particular industry* and to apply quantitative restrictions for balance of payment purposes in a manner which takes full account of the continued high level of demand for imports likely to be generated by their programmes of economic development" (emphasis added).[1444] The purpose of Article XVIII is to assist developing country Members in implementing programs and policies of economic development designed to raise their general standard of living, and it does so by authorizing those Members to take protective or promotional measures affecting imports (*e.g.*, raising tariffs beyond their bound concessions).[1445]

Article XVIII addresses the need of developing countries to establish and promote industries for economic development by authorizing import restrictions. However, the provisions of this Article also require developing countries to conduct negotiations with other interested Members and to offer reciprocal concessions.[1446] This requirement of consultations and negotiations may cause considerable delays in implementing necessary trade measures for development

---

1440 GATT, art. II, paras. 1(a) and 1(b).
1441 While there has been controversy as to the effectiveness of tariff protection as a means of facilitating domestic industries and fostering economic development, the GATT approves measures for this purpose, as in GATT Article XVIII.
1442 GATT, art. XVIII.
1443 *Ibid.*, para. 4(a).
1444 *Ibid.*, para. 2.
1445 See also Lee (2016), *supra* note 102, at 72–77.
1446 GATT, art. XVIII, para. 7.

purposes, and the reciprocal concessions may also burden their economies and prove counter-effective to their development interests. Although it is desirable to allow developing countries additional facilities to have a more flexible tariff structure, as Article XVIII attempts to do, this type of multilateral scrutiny diminishes their effectiveness in assisting with development.[1447] As a result, this article has never been invoked, except to address the balance of payment issues, since the beginning of the WTO regime in 1995, demonstrating its limited utility.[1448]

The "Development-Facilitation Tariff" or "DFT" has been proposed to address this issue.[1449] The DFT scheme enables developing countries to set the maximum additional tariff rate above the tariff binding under Article II to assist the development of their infant industries.[1450] It assigns a different maximum DFT rate to an individual developing country on a sliding scale, to be determined by its level of economic development, measured by relevant economic indicators such as per-capita gross national income (GNI) figures.[1451] For instance, suppose that the maximum DFT rate is set at 100 percent over the tariff binding and the economic threshold for an eligible developing country to benefit from a DFT is 8,000 USD per capita GNI. In such a case, any country that has a higher per-capita income than 8,000 USD will not be eligible for a DFT. Country A with the per capita GNI of 2,000 USD, which is 25 percent of the threshold income, will be allowed to apply a DFT of 75 percent (100% x (1–0.25) = 75%). Country B with the per capita GNI of 6,000 USD, which is 75 percent of the threshold income, will be allowed to apply a DFT of 25 percent (100% x (1–0.75) = 25%). Although the imposition of negotiation and compensation requirements on developing countries is not proposed in the DFT, a series of procedural requirements—such as a report setting forth rationales for the proposed increase in tariffs, a public hearing, notice, and gradual liberalization and elimination of the DFT after a set period of time—should reduce the possibility of abuse.[1452]

1447 This may explain the relatively few numbers of Article XVIII measures. From 1947 to 1994, Section A of Article XVIII was invoked only nine times (by Benelux on behalf of Suriname (1958), Greece (1956, 1965), Indonesia (1983), Korea (1958), and Sri Lanka, twice in 1955 and once each in 1956 and 1957), and has not been invoked since the establishment of the WTO. *Special and Differential Treatment Provisions in WTO Agreements and Decisions, supra* note 1438. BOP measures have been invoked more often, over 20 times before the WTO Agreement entered into force. *Id.* Since the establishment of the WTO, 14 developing countries have used BOP measures. *Id.*

1448 *Ibid.*

1449 Yong-Shik Lee, "Facilitating Development in the World Trading System: A Proposal for Development Facilitation Tariff (DFT) and Development Facilitation Subsidy (DFS)" (2004) 38(2) *Journal of World Trade* 935–954. See also Yong-Shik Lee, "WTO Disciplines and Economic Development: Reform Proposal" (2014) 1(2) *Journal of International and Comparative Law* 300–301.

1450 *Ibid.*

1451 *Ibid.*

1452 The Agreement on Safeguards also includes those procedural requirements. Agreement on Safeguards ("SA"), WTO Agreement, Annex 1A, 1869 U.N.T.S. 154 (April 15, 1994), arts. 3, 7, and 12.

12.2.2 Subsidies

A similar type of reform needs to be considered for subsidies.[1453] As discussed in Chapter 11, government subsidies are an important development tool for developing countries,[1454] and their importance has been recognized by the WTO.[1455] Yet, some of the key trade-related subsidies, such as export subsidies and import-substitution subsidies, are prohibited by the current WTO rules.[1456] Other kinds of subsidies that adversely affect the trade of other Members are also "actionable": *i.e.*, subject to trade sanctions, including countervailing measures.[1457] As Dani Rodrik aptly described, the current subsidy rules have made "a significant dent in the ability of developing countries to employ intelligently designed industrial policies."[1458]

Historically, subsidies have played an important role in the economic development of today's developed countries.[1459] It thus stands to reason that developing countries should also be able to adopt trade-related subsidies without fear of retaliatory measures by developed countries or prohibition by the WTO.[1460] The concept of the sliding income scale, proposed in the DFT, can be applied to subsidies otherwise prohibited or actionable under the current WTO rule.[1461] The "Development-Facilitation Subsidy" (DFS) can be considered in favor of developing countries under certain per-capita income thresholds. Under this scheme, developing countries are allowed to adopt otherwise prohibited or actionable subsidies in accordance with their per-capita income status.[1462] Since the objective of the DFS is to promote economic development through export facilitation, it cannot be used to support exports from developing countries whose share in the export market is above certain thresholds, making them already competitive. The procedural requirements, comparable to those for the DFT, would also be important for the DFS scheme to prevent abuse.

1453   Lee (2004), *supra* note 1449. See also Lee (2014), *supra* note 1449, at 300–301.
1454   See discussion *supra* Section 11.1.
1455   Agreement on Subsidies and Countervailing Measures (SCM Agreement), WTO Agreement, Annex 1A, 1869 U.N.T.S. 14 (April 15, 1994), art. 27, para. 1.
1456   *Ibid.* art. 3.
1457   *Ibid.* arts. 5–7.
1458   Rodrik (2004), *supra* note 264.
1459   See Chang (2002), *supra* note 203, at 19–21. For instance, the United Kingdom provided extensive export subsidies to textile products in the eighteenth century, *id.*, at 21–22; the United States offered subsidies to railway companies in the nineteenth century and invested heavily in research and development of new technologies, *id.*, at 30–31; Germany also subsidized several industries, including textiles and metals, *id.*, at 33–34. Other developed countries today, including France, the Netherlands, Sweden, Japan, and the East Asian countries (NICs) all provided subsidies to promote their industries, *id.*, at 35–51.
1460   Lee (2004), *supra* note 1449. See also Lee (2014), *supra* note 1449, at 301–302.
1461   *Ibid.*
1462   *Ibid.*

12.2.3 Anti-dumping measures

Anti-dumping (AD) is another area in which substantial trade interests of developing countries are adversely affected. WTO rules allow Members to adopt AD measures in the form of added tariffs where they determine that imports are "dumped"; *i.e.*, sold at prices below normal value.[1463] The "normal value" is determined by comparison to the home price or, where a proper comparison cannot be made due to the market situation or a low sales volume in the domestic market, to an export price in a third country.[1464] The normal value can also be "constructed" based on costs and reasonable profits.[1465] This regulatory flexibility allows national authorities a degree of latitude in anti-dumping investigations, making AD measures the most prevalently adopted trade measures of all.[1466] There is little economic rationale for imposing anti-dumping measures; for example, "predatory dumping"—a practice whereby a producer sells below cost to drive competitors out of the market and then raises prices to cover the interim loss—is unlikely to succeed in today's global market where a number of producers may enter into the market at any time. Further, other kinds of dumping, such as one to clear out temporary surplus products, are considered by most economists to be beneficial, rather than harmful, to consumers.[1467] In particular, cheaper imports from developing countries have been a major target for AD measures, undermining the trade and development interests of developing countries.[1468]

The determination of "normal value" is inherently arbitrary and imprecise. For example, there may not be a single home market price to compare, in which case a complex adjusted average may have to be calculated to come up with a reference home price.[1469] Where a comparison should be made to an export price in a third country, there may not be a single export price but potentially many substantially different prices. Where a normal value needs to be constructed, depending on a specific methodology adopted to calculate costs and average prices, the result can be vastly different, not to mention that the measure of "reasonable profit" can also vary.[1470] National authorities have a virtually free hand to determine the existence of dumping and the dumping margin. Limited reform of the WTO Anti-Dumping Agreement has been proposed,[1471] but it is unlikely to remove the

---

1463 Agreement on Implementation of Article VI of the GATT 1994 ("Anti-Dumping Practice Agreement" or "ADP Agreement"), WTO Agreement, Annex 1A, 1868 U.N.T.S. 201 (April 15, 1994), art. 1.
1464 *Ibid.*, arts. 1–2.
1465 *Ibid.*, art. 2.
1466 At the end of June 2020, there were as many as 1,926 AD measures in force. WTO, *Report (2020) of the Committee on Anti-Dumping Practices*, G/L/1366, G/ADP/27 (October 20, 2020).
1467 Lee (2016), *supra* note 102, at 119.
1468 Between July 2019 and June 2020, over three-quarters of the 303 AD investigations targeted imports from developing countries. WTO (2020), *supra* note 1466.
1469 Lee (2016), *supra* note 102, at 121–122.
1470 *Ibid.*, at 122.
1471 See WTO, *supra* note 1418.

inherent arbitrariness from the AD regime. As Yale economist T.N. Srinivasan characterized, AD is indeed tantamount to a "nuclear weapon in the armoury of trade policy,"[1472] and regulatory reform is necessary to restrain AD measures against imports from developing countries altogether.

12.2.4 Trade-related investment measures

Certain trade-related investment measures (TRIMs) are also regulated by WTO rules. TRIMs are important government development policy tools, so the rules regulating TRIMs need to be examined. Provisions of the WTO Agreement on Trade-Related Investment Measures[1473] ("TRIMs Agreement") prohibit a range of investment measures that affect international trade.[1474] Those prohibited TRIMs include local content requirements (mandating the use of a certain amount of local inputs in production); import controls (requiring imports used in local production to be equivalent to a certain proportion of exports); foreign exchange balancing requirements (requiring the foreign exchange made available for imports to be a certain proportion of the value of foreign exchange brought in by the foreign investment from exports and other sources); and export controls (obligating exports to be equivalent to a certain proportion of local production).[1475]

Investment can contribute significantly to economic development by bringing needed capital, technology, and management expertise to the host nation, and some of the TRIMs are designed to maximize investment's contribution to the host country's development agenda.[1476] While the economic utility of TRIMs has been debated and the distorting trade effect of TRIMs has been underscored,[1477] the decision to adopt TRIMs must rest with developing countries. According to a study, all of today's developed countries have, in the course of their development, adopted investment measures to meet their development objectives.[1478] To address this concern, 12 developing countries proposed a change to the text of the TRIMs Agreement to make commitments thereunder optional rather than mandatory.[1479] It would indeed be fair for today's developing countries to be accorded the same opportunity to use TRIMs to promote economic development.

1472 International Institute for Sustainable Development, *Report on the WTO's High-Level Symposium on Trade and Development* (Geneva, March 17–18, 1999), available online at: www. wto.org/english/tratop_e/devel_e/summhl_e.pdf; https://perma.cc/6FF9-J57T.

1473 Agreement on Trade-Related Investment Measures ("TRIMs Agreement"), WTO Agreement, Annex 1A, 1868 U.N.T.S. 168 (April 15, 1994).

1474 The TRIMs Agreement prohibits investment measures that are inconsistent with Articles III and XI of the GATT, which require national treatment and the general elimination of quantitative restrictions, respectively. *Ibid.*, art. 2, and GATT, arts. III, XI.

1475 TRIMs Agreement, paras. 1(a)–2(c).

1476 Lee (2016), *supra* note 102, at 148–149, 151–152.

1477 *Ibid.*, at 150–151.

1478 Ha-Joon Chang and D. Green, *The Northern WTO Agenda on Investment: Do as We Say, Not as We Did* (Geneva: South Centre, 2003), at 33.

1479 WTO, *Preparations for the 1999 Ministerial Conference*, WT/GC/W/354 (October 11, 1999), paras. 20–21.

A study has reported that several African countries had already legislated for the adoption of certain TRIMs, such as local content requirements prohibited under the TRIMs Agreement.[1480] This practice would be a deviation from the requirements under the TRIMs Agreement, but as of November 2020, no complaint against these measures had been filed at the WTO Dispute Settlement Body (DSB).[1481] Such a complaint against developing countries in Africa would have been politically challenging, even if the cited practice is a rule violation under the TRIMs Agreement. Regardless of the existence of a formal complaint, this creates an inconsistency between the rule and the practice that needs to be resolved. To resolve this conflict, it is necessary to lift the application of the TRIMs Agreement in favor of developing countries through a regulatory reform.

12.2.5 Trade-related intellectual property rights

The current WTO rules on intellectual property rights ("TRIPS Agreement"[1482]) should also be reconsidered in the context of development. Acquiring advanced technology and knowledge is important for developing countries to improve their industries and promote economic development.[1483] However, the effort to acquire advanced technology and knowledge tends to create tension between developing countries, whose priority is to acquire them expediently, and developed countries, whose interest is to control access to their intellectual property. The latter countries protect their intellectual property by assigning proprietary rights to technology and knowledge domestically through local law and internationally through international convention.[1484] The TRIPS Agreement—the most extensive of all WTO provisions[1485]—sets out mandatory standards for the protection of several intellectual property rights (IPRs), including patents, trademarks, copyrights, designs, and geographical indications. The Agreement also requires the protection of foreign IPR holders by incorporating other major IPR conventions and provides for enforcement against IPR violations.[1486]

1480 C. Nwapi, "Defining the 'Local' in Local Content Requirements in the Oil and Gas and Mining Sectors in Developing Countries" (2015) 8(1) *Law and Development Review* 187–216.

1481 WTO, *Dispute Settlement: The Disputes – Disputes by Agreement*, available online at: www.wto.org/english/tratop_e/dispu_e/dispu_agreements_index_e.htm; https://perma.cc/44R4-2M2P.

1482 Agreement on Trade-Related Intellectual Property Rights ("TRIPS Agreement"), WTO Agreement, Annex 1C, 1869 U.N.T.S. 299 (April 15, 1994).

1483 Lee (2016), *supra* note 1414, at 455; Lee (2016), *supra* note 102, at 158–159.

1484 For instance, the Paris Convention offers protection for foreign patent holders. Paris Convention for the Protection of Industrial Property, 21 U.S.T. 1583, 828 U.N.T.S. 11851 (March 20, 1883), art. 2, para. 1. The Berne Convention does so for foreign copyright holders. The Berne Convention for the Protection of Literary and Artistic Works, 28 U.S.T. 7645, 1161 U.N.T.S. 30 (September 9, 1886), arts. 1–2, para. 1.

1485 TRIPS Agreement is composed of 73 Articles in seven parts. See TRIPS Agreement, *supra* note 1482.

1486 *Ibid.*, arts. 9–12.

The TRIPS Agreement is unique among WTO rules in that it goes beyond what seems directly relevant to trade issues. It attempts to establish IPR regimes in all WTO Members, including those whose economic and social developments may not be ready to embrace the concept of IPRs yet.[1487] There is a question as to whether the prescription of an economic and legal system such as an IPR regime, implemented to promote a set of values and interests pertaining mostly to developed countries, should be the role of the trade disciplines. In general, WTO rules address the behavior of nations that directly affects international trade and attempt to control such behavior by imposing certain obligations and authorizing trade sanctions.[1488] Members are required to bring their laws and regulations in conformity with the WTO disciplines.[1489] Yet, they are not required to establish a specific legal regime as they are by the requirements of the TRIPS Agreement.

While IPR protection is a legitimate interest, those extensive requirements are counterproductive to the development effort of developing countries whose legal and financial resources may not be sufficient for extensive IPR protection.[1490] Regulatory reform should exempt developing countries from the application of the provisions in the TRIPS Agreement which impose legislative requirements on them. A better alternative is to develop a new set of rules to elaborate on the relevant provision of GATT Article XX, which allows Members to take measures to protect their IPR interests.[1491] Such a set of rules would specify applicable measures together with the procedural and substantive requirements for the application of the measures, as does the WTO Agreement on Safeguards, which, in turn, was developed based on GATT Article XIX.[1492]

1487   A historical study shows that IPRs began to be recognized and protected when considerable economic and social developments had taken place. Chang (2002), *supra* note 203, at 83–85.

1488   Dani Rodrik opined that the purpose of international rules should be not to impose common rules on countries with different regulatory systems, but to accept these differences and regulate the interface between them to reduce adverse spillovers. Dani Rodrik, *The Global Governance of Trade as If Development Really Mattered* (New York: UNDP, 2001).

1489   WTO Agreement, art XVI.4.

1490   According to a study, implementing the TRIPS obligations would require "the least developed countries to invest in buildings, equipment, training, and so forth that would cost each of them $150 million—for many of the least developed countries this represents a full year's development budget." Finger (2000), *supra* note 307, at 435.

1491   GATT Article XX provides in relevant part:

   Subject to the requirement that such measures are not applied in a manner which would constitute a means of arbitrary or unjustifiable discrimination between countries where the same conditions prevail, or a disguised restriction on international trade, nothing in this Agreement shall be construed to prevent the adoption or enforcement by any contracting party of measures: . . . (*d*) necessary to secure compliance with laws or regulations which are not inconsistent with the provisions of this Agreement, including those relating to . . . the protection of patents, trade marks and copyrights, and the prevention of deceptive practices . . . .

   GATT, art. XX.

1492   The Agreement on Safeguards elaborates on GATT Article XIX and provides a detailed set of substantive and procedural requirements for the application of a safeguard measure. See Yong-Shik Lee, *Safeguard Measures in World Trade: The Legal Analysis* (3rd ed., Cheltenham: Edward Elgar Publishing, 2014), for a detailed study of safeguard measures.

12.2.6 *Preference for least developed countries*

As of November 2020, there are 47 least developed countries on the U.N. list, and 36 of the LDCs had become WTO Members.[1493] Several developed countries and some developing countries offer preferential treatment to LDCs. For instance, the European Union provides the "Everything But Arms" (EBA) initiative, offering duty-free, quota-free (DFQF) treatment to products currently exported by LDCs.[1494] Other countries, such as the United States and Canada, offer similar preferential treatment to LDCs, although less comprehensive and more limited in scope than the EBA initiative.[1495] Considering the dire economic need of LDCs, an EBA-type of DFQF treatment needs to be implemented by developed countries and participating developing countries in the WTO. A transitional period can be established for the complete removal of trade barriers to sensitive products.[1496] The WTO issued a Ministerial Decision on DFQF Market Access for LDCs, but it did not create a legally binding obligation.[1497]

Members would also have to ensure that non-tariff measures do not undermine the trade benefit of these preferences for LDCs. These non-tariff measures include rules of origin, which determine the country origin of a product and, transitively, the applicability of trade preference to it. Each WTO Member has separate rules of origin, and these rules have not yet been harmonized.[1498] It has been observed that stringent rules of origin limit exports from LDCs significantly.[1499]

1493 See *supra* note 306.

1494 Regulation (EU) No 978/2012 of the European Parliament and of the Council of 25 October 2012 (applying a scheme of generalized tariff preferences and repealing Council Regulation (EC) No 732/2008). OJ L 303 (October 31, 2012), at 1–82. For an initial evaluation of the EBA initiative, see Paul Brenton, "Integrating the Least Developed Countries into the World Trading System: The Current Impact of European Union Preferences Under 'Everything but Arms'" (2003) 37(3) *Journal of World Trade* 623–646.

1495 For instance, the United States has implemented the *Africa Growth and Opportunity Act*, which offers improved access to certain African, but not Asian, LDCs. African Growth and Opportunity Act of 2000, Public Law 106–200, 114 Stat. 251, U.S.C. ch. 23 § 3701 *et seq.* See also Brenton (2003), *ibid.*, at 644–645.

1496 At the adoption of the EBA initiative, trade liberalization had been complete except for three products: fresh bananas, rice, and sugar, where tariffs were to be gradually reduced to zero (in 2006 for bananas and 2009 for rice and sugar). Duty-free tariff quotas for rice and sugar were to be increased annually. *Ibid.*, at 625.

1497 The Decision states "Developed-country Members that do not yet provide duty-free and quota-free market access for at least 97% of products originating from LDCs, defined at the tariff line level, shall *seek to improve* their existing duty-free and quota-free coverage for such products, so as to provide increasingly greater market access to LDCs" (emphasis added). WTO, *Duty-Free and Quota Free (DFQF) Market Access for Least-Developed Countries, Ministerial Decision of 7 December 2013*, WT/MIN(13)/44, WT/L/919 (December 11, 2013).

1498 The WTO Agreement on Rules of Origin aims to harmonize rules of origin, but there is disagreement as to whether the harmonization is necessary. WTO, "Members Divided on Way Forward for Rules of Origin," *2013 News Items* (September 26, 2013), available online at: www.wto.org/english/news_e/news13_e/roi_26sep13_e.htm; https://perma.cc/3ZLX-9ZL8.

1499 Stefano Inama, "Market Access for LDCs: Issues to Be Addressed" (2002) 36(1) *Journal of World Trade* 85–116, at 115.

The 2013 Bali Decision and the 2015 Nairobi Decision attempt to relax rules of origin for the benefit of LDCs and offer recommended guidelines rather than enforceable obligations on Members.[1500] Applications of administered protection, such as AD measures, countervailing duties, and safeguards, can also diminish the beneficial effect of preference for LDCs. Divergent rules of origin and rampant applications of trade remedy measures substantially interfere with exports from developing countries, including LDCs, against their development interests. Thus, the WTO has been developing guidelines for the application of rules of origin for exports from developing countries, but the key recommendations, such as the use of non-originating materials up to 75 percent of the final value of the product,[1501] must be turned into enforceable obligations to benefit LDCs.

12.3 Dispute settlement, new agreement, and institutional reform

12.3.1 Dispute settlement mechanism

Consideration should also be given to the operation of the dispute settlement mechanism in the WTO and how it may facilitate development. WTO disciplines prohibit the adoption of a unilateral trade sanction and require that a trade dispute be adjudicated multilaterally by the Dispute Settlement Body (DSB), comprised of WTO membership. The Understanding on Rules and Procedures Governing the Settlement of Disputes ("Dispute Settlement Understanding" or "DSU") provides for procedures to deal with a trade dispute.[1502] A Member may refer a trade dispute arising from a violation of WTO disciplines to the DSB, which may lead to the establishment of a dispute settlement panel.[1503] Decisions by a panel may be appealed to the standing Appellate Body, which renders final decisions.[1504] The Appellate Body decisions are adopted by the DSB, and failure to comply with the decision may lead to the authorization of a retaliatory measure against the non-complying party.[1505]

Developing countries may breach WTO disciplines where it is inevitable to meet their key development interest. An example would be the use of trade-related government subsidies for development purposes, as discussed earlier,

---

1500   WTO, *Preferential Rules of Origin for Least-Developed Countries, Ministerial Decision of 7 December 2013*, WT/MIN(13)/42, WT/L/917 (December 11, 2013), available online at: www.wto.org/english/thewto_e/minist_e/mc9_e/desci42_e.htm; https://perma.cc/6YP4-VNLY; WTO, *Preferential Rules of Origin for Least-Developed Countries, Ministerial Decision of 19 December 2015*, WT/MIN(15)/47, WT/L/917 (December 21, 2015), www.wto.org/english/thewto_e/minist_e/mc10_e/l917_e.htm; https://perma.cc/4Q85-S44D.

1501   *Ibid.*

1502   WTO, Understanding on Rules and Procedures Governing the Settlement of Disputes ("DSU"), WTO Agreement, Annex 2, 1869 U.N.T.S. 401, 33 I.L.M. 1226 (1994), available online at: www.wto.org/english/docs_e/legal_e/legal_e.htm#dispute; https://perma.cc/G8RU-VEX8.

1503   DSU, art. 6.

1504   *Ibid.*, art. 17.

1505   *Ibid.*, art. 22.

which may be either prohibited or actionable under the current WTO disciplines. Another example would be the widespread adoption of local content requirements prohibited under the TRIMs Agreement.[1506] This chapter proposes regulatory reforms throughout, but particular consideration should be given to a broader "development exemption" concerning the application of the DSU.[1507] The proposal is to allow those measures deemed necessary for development purposes that may otherwise be in breach of WTO disciplines, even if they were referred to the DSB for adjudication, and not to require their withdrawal or authorize any sanction. This would be a broad exemption, and a question may be raised as to whether this type of broad exemption would dismantle WTO disciplines altogether. Adjustment to the DSU, which would allow the WTO DSB to consider development interests, particularly in the consultation process,[1508] would be necessary to resolve this issue. At the time of writing, the United States has blocked several appointments of Appellate Body members, resulting in paralysis of the WTO dispute settlement process. Reform should also include an adjustment to the current appointment practice that requires consensus and thereby enables a dominant WTO Member, such as the United States, to disrupt the functioning of the WTO.

12.3.2 Agreement on development facilitation

The feasibility and desirability of a separate set of rules facilitating development also need to be considered. As discussed earlier, WTO provisions offering S&D treatment to developing countries, although insufficient, are scattered throughout various provisions of WTO disciplines[1509] without any coherent regulatory structure. Some of the S&D provisions, such as the subsidy rules for developing countries,[1510] were granted temporarily and expired, and they need to be restored and converted into permanent rules. The inclusion of these scattered provisions in a separate and enforceable agreement may also provide a coherent and permanent regulatory structure to S&D treatment that is currently lacking. For instance, such inclusion could provide clear and objective standards for determining developing country status; under the current system, developing country status is self-declaratory, and the absence of a definition for developing country Members seems to create regulatory ambiguity.[1511]

A separate agreement, which may be entitled "the Agreement on Development Facilitation" or "the ADF," will function as a set of rules prevailing over the

---

1506   Nwapi (2015), *supra* note 1480.
1507   This proposal has merit particularly when considering the potential difficulty associated with the proposed changes in substantive WTO disciplines.
1508   DSU, art. 4, para. 1.
1509   WTO, WT/COMTD/W/196, *supra* note 1438.
1510   See also Lee (2016), *supra* note 102, at 297.
1511   See also F. Cui, "Who are the Developing Countries in the WTO?" (2008) 1(1) *Law and Development Review* 124–153.

other WTO rules. The ADF may include a clarification of the thresholds for developing countries entitled to S&D treatment, as mentioned above, and the reform proposals discussed in the preceding sub-sections, including adjustments to tariff bindings (DFT), subsidy rules (DFS), AD measures, TRIMs, TRIPS, and the DSU. By concluding a separate agreement, the WTO will be able to advance development interests without undertaking potentially complex revisions to the existing agreements. The ADF might require a special status in the WTO Agreement, as it would affect the operation of the other WTO rules such as the TRIPS Agreement, as well as the Uruguay Round agreements on trade in goods. The establishment of the ADF would affirm that development issues are elevated to the status of focal regulatory importance. Where TRIPS, which have been promoted primarily by the fewer developed countries, have been granted separate regulatory treatment, the same treatment for development issues, which concern the majority of WTO membership, would be justifiable and appropriate. A renewed interest in new initiatives enhancing development interests in the WTO would be even more important and necessary given the unsuccessful conclusion of the Doha Round.

12.3.3 Institutional reform: proposal for the WTO Council on Trade and Development

There is a question as to the sufficiency of the current organizational apparatus—which consists of the Committee on Trade and Development and the Sub-Committee on LDCs, aided by the Institute for Training and Technical Cooperation under the WTO Secretariat—to address complex and long-term development issues. First, this question can be addressed by way of comparison with the treatment of TRIPS; a full council, not a committee, is organized to cover complex and long-term TRIPS issues.[1512] As discussed in the context of the ADF, if the magnitude of development issues should be considered to be no less important than that of developed country issues such as TRIPS, consideration should also be given to elevating the level of the institutional body on trade and development to the full council level. This elevation will not only make a statement recognizing the essential importance of development issues but also meet practical needs as follows.

Some of the development issues addressed in WTO working groups, such as trade, debt, finance, and technology transfer, have fundamental implications for development. Should these issues become monitored and addressed by the WTO on a permanent rather than temporary basis, then the importance of these issues and the long-term requirement for personnel and other resources to address these issues necessitates elevating the current working groups and establishing separate committees to replace the working groups. A separate Council for Trade and Development can oversee the operations of these committees. There should

---

1512   The Council for Trade-Related Aspects of Intellectual Property Rights is organized under Article IV of the WTO Agreement. See also Lee (2016), *supra* note 102, at 294, note 1493.

be at least one full committee devoted to the problems of LDCs and another separate committee to assist developing countries with capacity building, which will facilitate fuller participation of developing countries in the trading system to secure its benefits.[1513]

Greater assistance should also be provided to developing country Members involved in costly and time-consuming trade disputes. Consideration should be given to assigning the function of the existing Advisory Centre on WTO Law (ACWL),[1514] which provides support to developing countries with a panel or Appellate Body proceedings, to a committee under the proposed Council for Trade and Development to better serve the needs of developing country Members. The current ACWL, if it is to be preserved, needs to be expanded so that it can offer assistance to every developing country Member in need of support, not only LDCs.

In addition, the reform may include a mandatory reporting requirement for all developed country Members and participating developing country Members, requiring participants to file a "Trade-Related Development Assistance Report," or "TDAR," periodically. This report would identify and examine trade practices and activities of each Member that comply with the trade and development agenda set by the Council, as well as those that are inconsistent with it. The Council should examine TDARs regularly and consult with relevant Members to discuss their development assistance activities. The Council could agree on specific commitments to be fulfilled by the developed country Members and participating developing country Members to promote the trade and development agenda, and the Council could further examine, within a certain time period, whether these commitments are being met.

12.4 Regional trade agreements[1515]

While multilateralism in international trade is the key principle forming the legal disciplines of the WTO, another parallel and equally important trend is increasing regionalism in international trade, as represented by "regional trade agreements" or "RTAs," referring to reciprocal trade agreements between two or more countries. RTAs are a salient feature of the international trading system today. RTAs have been rapidly proliferated since 1990, from 22 RTAs in force in 1990 to 305 as of September 2020.[1516] RTAs are critically important in the

---

1513   The Aid for Trade initiative launched by the WTO has been helpful for developing countries in this regard. See WTO, *Aid for Trade*, available online at: www.wto.org/english/tratop_e/devel_e/a4t_e/aid4trade_e.htm; https://perma.cc/J4K8-KAFG.

1514   For legal assistance, 32 WTO governments set up "the Advisory Centre on WTO Law (ACWL)" in 2001. Its members consist of countries contributing to the funding and those receiving legal advice. LDCs are automatically eligible for advice, and other developing countries and transition economies have to be fee-paying members to receive advice.

1515   This section has been developed from the author's previous work, Lee (2016), *supra* note 102, at 175–196.

1516   WTO, *Regional Trade Agreements*, available online at: www.wto.org/english/tratop_e/region_e/region_e.htm; https://perma.cc/4Q2K-5ZZG. On the proliferation of RTAs,

current international trading system because the terms of RTAs govern not only the trade relations among the participating countries as they are designed to do, but also create additional sets of trade disciplines that exist parallel to multilateral WTO disciplines such as the establishment of a separate dispute settlement mechanism, separate rules of origin, rules for IPRs and international investment, and adjustment of trade remedies.[1517] Since every Member is now a signatory of one or more RTAs, and the majority portion of world trade[1518] is governed by the terms of RTAs and by WTO disciplines, Members have to deal with both WTO disciplines and those of RTAs at the same time.

12.4.1 RTAs and economic development

Hundreds of RTAs today involve developing countries.[1519] Of these, the majority are formed under GATT Article XXIV and GATS (General Agreement on Trade in Services) Article V, requiring the liberalization of "substantially all trade," while a minority of the RTAs are formed under the Enabling Clause, which does not have this "substantially all trade" requirement.[1520] Developing countries are participating in the recent RTA drive to increase their access to export markets while the progress of the Doha Round is stagnant. However, it is not clear whether RTAs, as they stand now, would necessarily benefit developing countries and meet their development goals despite conventional wisdom under the classical trade theories, as discussed below.

Some trade measures, such as the adoption of an infant industry promotion policy, will inevitably cause welfare loss.[1521] The implementation of RTAs, which liberalizes trade, will prevent this because RTAs eliminate trade barriers that cause such loss; thus, regional trade liberalization by these RTAs is considered to promote development for the participating developing countries.[1522] According to the classical trade theories, the elimination of trade barriers would enable specialization in the production of goods in which a country has a relative

see Rafael Leal-Arcas, "Proliferation of Regional Trade Agreements: Complementing or Supplanting Multilateralism?" (2011) 11(2) *Chicago Journal of International Law* 597–629. See also Gonzalo Villalta Puig and Omiunu Ohiocheoya, "Regional Trade Agreements and the Neo-Colonialism of the United States of America and the European Union: A Review of the Principle of Competitive Imperialism" (2011) 32(3) *The Liverpool Law Review* 225–235.

1517 For a further discussion on these issues, see Lee (2016), *supra* note 102, at 175–196.

1518 According to the OECD, RTAs cover more than half of international trade and operate alongside multilateral agreements under the WTO. OECD, *Regional Trade Agreements*, available online at: www.oecd.org/tad/benefitlib/regionaltradeagreements.htm.

1519 WTO, *Regional Trade Agreements*, *supra* note 1516.

1520 *Ibid.*

1521 See Lee (2016), *supra* note 102, at 82 for discussion of trade measures. For a discussion of welfare loss, see Dominick Salvatore, *International Economics* (11th ed., Hoboken, NJ: John Wiley & Sons, 2013), at 221–228, 257–260.

1522 Mitsuo Matsushita, "Legal Aspects of Free Trade Agreements in the Context of Article XXIV of the GATT 1994," paper presented at the seminar, The Way Forward to Successful Doha Development Agenda Negotiation, United Nations University, Tokyo, Japan (May 24–25, 2004).

advantage, and this specialization would improve economic efficiency.[1523] This rationale underlies the premise that promoting free trade will foster economic development. Nonetheless, a conclusion has been drawn from the historical study that *this specialization alone* did not bring about economic development, and virtually all developed countries today had applied industrial promotion policies to establish some manufacturing basis with the extensive use of subsidies and trade protections.[1524] A study also concluded that developing economies tend to diversify, rather than concentrate, production patterns in a large cross-section, suggesting that the driving force of economic development cannot be the forces of comparative advantage.[1525]

Free trade between developing and developed countries may hamper the growth of manufacturing industries in developing countries since eliminating trade barriers according to applicable terms of the RTA would remove the ability of developing countries to offer trade protection for their infant industries. As a result, RTAs may lock the current industrial structure of developing countries in place. Suppose that South Korea and Chile have entered into an RTA which eliminates trade barriers on all export products, including automobiles, in which South Korea has an advantage over Chile, and grapes, in which Chile has the advantage. By eliminating trade barriers, including tariffs, Chile may have secured a larger market for its grapes, but developing an automobile industry, which is potentially more beneficial for their overall economic development, would become much more difficult due to the increased number of automobile imports from South Korea. Note that South Korea had previously protected its domestic automobile market against imports until it achieved a level of competitiveness in its automobile industry. While the effectiveness of the theory of infant industry has been debated for decades,[1526] history reveals that all of the developed countries today protected their industries during their periods of economic development,[1527] and WTO disciplines also authorize the promotion of infant industries for economic development purposes.[1528]

12.4.2 Developing countries under RTA drives

Developing countries are often under significant pressure to join RTAs driven by developed countries for fear of losing their export markets in the developed countries to competing countries. Their negotiation position against developed countries will thus be substantially weaker than that which they would find in the multilateral negotiation rounds, where a greater number of developing countries can work in collaboration and form alliances to promote their common interests.

1523   Lee (2016), *supra* note 102, at 192.
1524   *Ibid.*, at 193.
1525   Jean Imbs and Romain Wacziarg, "Stages of Diversification" (2003) 93(1) *American Economic Review* 63–86.
1526   See Lee (2016), *supra* note 102, at 72–77 for further discussion.
1527   See Chang (2002), *supra* note 203.
1528   GATT, art. XVIII. For further discussion, see Lee (2016), *supra* note 102, at 72–77.

Developed countries may find it easier to negotiate with developing countries outside the multilateral framework, concluding RTAs with a smaller group of developing countries on their terms.[1529] This type of RTA drive is not a positive development for developing countries, whose development interests have become a key agenda for the multilateral trading system.[1530]

Problems are compounded as a new breed of RTAs, promoted by certain developed countries like the United States, not only seek to eliminate tariff barriers but also attempt to instill certain regulatory elements in developing countries. These elements include IPR enforcements, requirements for environmental and labor standards, and uninhibited cross-border capital transfers.[1531] This new type of RTA will have greater ramifications on the development of developing countries than the traditional RTAs (which focused primarily on the elimination of tariff barriers) by restricting policy space for developing countries even more than WTO agreements have; the additional requirements in the new RTAs affect wider aspects of the economic and regulatory systems of developing countries, under which development policies are adopted and implemented.

These new requirements go beyond the facilitation of international trade, just as the introduction of the TRIPS Agreement did in the context of WTO legal disciplines. Developed countries that promote the additional requirements may have their own economic and political agendas and interests to include in trade disciplines. Nonetheless, it creates certain risks for the trading system. The danger of imposing a set of values and regulatory frameworks not essential to the facilitation of international trade has been discussed in the context of the TRIPS Agreement.[1532] The same concerns and conclusions can also be applied here: those new requirements in RTAs would burden the economies of participating developing countries and would be counterproductive to their development interests.

12.4.3 Preserving development in RTAs

One way to restore the ability of developing countries to adopt trade-related development policy measures would be to allow developing countries to withdraw from their RTA commitments, notwithstanding the RTA provisions, when it is deemed necessary for them to use trade measures to promote economic development. GATT Article XVIII also authorizes developing countries to deviate from their WTO commitments under certain conditions to promote domestic industries for economic development. An RTA could include such a provision, but WTO disciplines may also stipulate it as a right of developing-country Members that cannot be varied by the terms of an RTA. An example

---

1529   WTO, *Regional Trade Agreements, supra* note 1516.
1530   See, *e.g., supra* note 1418.
1531   Alvin Hilaire and Yongzheng Yang, "The United States and the New Regionalism/Bilateralism" (2004) 38 *Journal of World Trade* 609. See also Rodrik (2004), *supra* note 264, at 33.
1532   See discussion *supra* Section 12.2.5.

of this type of regulation is Article 11 of the SA,[1533] which invalidates gray-area measures, regardless of an agreement otherwise by Members.

The gains from RTAs for developing countries, such as securing export markets on more favorable terms, should be preserved, while the barriers to economic development, such as undermining long-term development potential by locking in the current industrial structure for developing countries, should be removed. A comprehensive investigation should also be conducted to examine the extent to which RTAs have affected the economic development of developing countries, with references to any change in their abilities to adopt trade-related development policies, terms of trade, access to export markets, and technology and capital transfers. If RTAs have caused negative impacts on them or brought some positive outcomes but at substantial social and political costs—such as a substantial loss of employment in the vulnerable domestic industry adversely affected by the RTA—then efforts should be made to reduce the problems. The extent of gains and losses from RTAs could vary among developing countries. For example, smaller developing countries tend to have weaker leverage *vis-à-vis* developed countries than larger developing countries in RTA relationships, so attention should be given to small and vulnerable developing countries whose economic and trade interests can be easily affected by external influence, such as RTA arrangements.

12.4.4 Concluding international legal frameworks: trade and development

This chapter has examined the development issues associated with international trade law. The inability of Members to conclude the Doha Round successfully after 14 years of negotiations is a testament to the degree of difficulty in facilitating development in the WTO system. The Doha Round negotiations slowed down due to disagreements over key issues[1534] and were marginalized by major trading nations to promote other interests, such as RTAs. RTAs have proliferated since the establishment of the WTO, encroaching on the MFN principle of the multilateral trading system[1535] and creating trade disciplines parallel to those of the multilateral trading system. This encroachment further compromises the position of developing countries and development interests where RTAs are promoted by developed countries with substantial market leverage *vis-à-vis* developing countries.

1533 Article 11 regulates "gray area measures" that include any voluntary export restraints and orderly marketing arrangements which are sought to control the amount of imports. See SA, art. 11, para. 2. For further discussion, see Lee (2016), *supra* note 102, at 131.

1534 These key issues included agricultural domestic support, agricultural market access, and non-agricultural market access (NAMA), called "the triangle of issues." Lee (2016), *supra* note 1414, at 443.

1535 The MFN principle, stipulated in GATT Article I, prohibits arbitrary discrimination in trade among WTO Members. GATT, 1867 U.N.T.S. 194 (October 30, 1947), art. I.

Three-quarters of WTO membership is comprised of developing countries, but the multilateral trading system will not be sustainable unless the promises of development facilitation, as reflected in the DDA, are fulfilled. In this respect, the failure of the Doha Round negotiations is a major setback for the efforts to facilitate development interests. The WTO may not be a development institution *per se*, but given the key impact that international trade has on economic development, it will be critically important for WTO law to facilitate development through trade, rather than inhibiting it. As discussed, extensive regulatory and institutional reform—more extensive than that promoted by the DDA—needs to be considered and promoted to fill the development gap in the WTO system and restore the balance of trade interests between developed and developing countries.

At the end of the day, the successful development of developing countries would serve not only their own interests, but also those of all countries. In this relatively open trading system, successful economic development would create affluent consumer markets for today's developed countries, as proven by the development cases of East Asian economies. As Trebilcock notes, the current regulatory and institutional apparatus of the WTO places considerable limitations on the policy space that is required for the adoption of effective development policies for developing countries.[1536] It is not clear whether the limited regulatory reform undertaken during the Doha Round, including an amendment to the Agreement on Government Procurement ("GPA")[1537] and promulgation of the new Agreement on Trade Facilitation ("Trade Facilitation Agreement" or "TFA"),[1538] effectively promotes the development interests of developing countries to an extent sufficient to justify its considerable regulatory burden thereupon. The more effective and desirable way to fill the development gap would be to redress the current imbalance by extensive regulatory reform and not to require developing countries to offer reciprocal concessions for the reforms necessary to fill this gap.

1536 See Michael J. Trebilcock, "Between Universalism and Relativism: Reflections on the Evolution of Law and Development Studies" (2016) 66 *University of Toronto Law Journal* 351–352.

1537 For an explanation of the GPA amendment, see WTO, *Revised Agreement on Government Procurement*, available online at: www.wto.org/english/tratop_e/gproc_e/gp_revised_gpa_e.htm; https://perma.cc/GZF5-UAFN.

1538 For an introduction of the TFA, see WTO, *Trade Facilitation*, available online at: www.wto.org/english/tratop_e/tradfa_e/tradfa_e.htm; https://perma.cc/A9QK-FEL4.

13 Conclusion

13.1 Law and development at the crossroads

Over four decades ago, law and development scholars were described as "self-estranged" due to their failures to associate studies in the field with realities on the ground.[1539] Law and development studies since then have drifted, and the field has been stagnant, particularly with respect to the development of coherent theories and methodologies that explain the important interrelationships between law and development. Law and development projects based on the neoliberal policy stance have flourished, but they have not been successful in bringing about development throughout the world.[1540] Those development projects and initiatives, thus, have been criticized as a means of serving the political and economic agendas of the developed world rather than meeting the economic development needs of the developing world.[1541]

How, then, may law and development be revitalized as a field with a real prospect of contributing to development? It should begin with formulating solid analytical frameworks to explain the interrelationships between law and development and clarify the parameters of the key constituent concepts, "law" and "development." I have taught courses in law and development for years now, and the suggested focus corresponds to the most frequently asked questions that I receive from students: (i) how exactly law affects development, and (ii) what the substance and conceptual boundaries of "law" and "development" under analysis are. I have developed the general theory of law and development to respond to these key inquiries. Some may find my effort to be a bold attempt because the mechanisms by which law impacts development are extremely complex, depending on a number of socioeconomic conditions on the ground, and there is not yet a consensus as to the conceptual elements of development, or even of law, that should be included in this endeavor.[1542]

1539 Trubek and Galanter (1974), *supra* note 33, cited in Lee (2015), *supra* note 16, at 59. Some passages in these concluding remarks are drawn from Lee (2015), *ibid.*, section 5, at 59–61.
1540 See discussion *supra* Section 2.1.
1541 The critics include Arturo Escobar, Sundhya Pahuja, and Balakrishnan Rajagopal. See *supra* note 44.
1542 See discussion *supra* Sections 1.2 and 1.3.

DOI: 10.4324/9781003090175-16

Nevertheless, there must be a start; the failure to build robust law and development scholarship lies in the lack of clear theoretical frameworks by which one can assess the interrelationships between law and development and that may also bind varied and somewhat fragmented interests currently pursued in the ambit of law and development with a coherent disciplinary framework.[1543] This is by no means a straightforward task, but one has to begin somewhere to stop the continuing drift and to break out of intellectual stagnation. My general theory is a modest effort toward building law and development as a solid field of study. As with general theories in other fields, my theory may be unable to answer all questions concerning the important relationship between law and development and might also be subject to criticism due to its imperfections. Nevertheless, nothing will bring me more pleasure if scholars would use my theory to develop even fuller theories to explain the interrelationships between law and development and clarify the operating concepts of its constituent elements.

In the new addition (Chapters 8 through 12), I have also explored the interrelationship between law and development in specific legal areas, such as property rights (Chapter 8), political governance (Chapter 9), business transactions (Chapter 10), state industrial promotion (Chapter 11), and international trade (Chapter 12). In those chapters, I have shown that, *inter alia*, the conventional wisdom—such as the protection of FPPRs, the guarantee of freedom of contract, and the regulatory frameworks to promote free trade—does not always promote economic development, and its contribution to economic development may vary by relevant stages of economic development and other socioeconomic conditions under which they apply. The one-size-fits-all type of approach, based on a certain ideological stance, has not proven to promote economic development successfully; the law and development analysis in Part II has shown that an analytical and pragmatic approach responsive to varied socioeconomic conditions on the ground is likely to be more effective.

Efforts are being made to revitalize law and development studies through enhancing dialogue among scholars, publishing academic journals devoted to law and development, and analyzing international development projects. For example, the Law and Development Institute (LDI), an international network of scholars and experts in law and development launched in 2009, has convened law and development conferences annually since 2010, published a rare, peer-reviewed academic journal in the area of law and development ("Law and Development Review") since 2008,[1544] and offered training and academic programs in law and development.[1545] Several universities, primarily European, have also recently set up the "Law and Development Research Network (LDRN)" to foster communications and research collaborations among law and

---

1543   See discussion *supra* Section 3.1.
1544   Law and Development Review (LDR) has been in continuous operation since 2008, publishing 27 issues in fourteen annual volumes as of March 2021.
1545   The details of LDI activities are available online at: www.lawanddevelopment.net; https://perma.cc/JGD9-VTVM.

development scholars.[1546] With the introduction and development of solid theoretical frameworks in law and development, one may expect a growing academic interest in law and development, particularly from students and young scholars. The renewed interest and new initiatives will enhance the future of law and development.

13.2 Law and industrial development

It has been decades since the international community extended the boundaries of development goals beyond economic growth and included non-economic values, such as the environment, democratic and transparent governance, gender equality, and the rule of law.[1547] Such extension was a move in the right direction; after all, few societies would argue that economic progress is all that is needed, and there are certainly non-economic values to be realized. Nonetheless, due consideration should also be given to sequencing and prioritization, particularly for developing countries with resource constraints.[1548] A senior scholar at Emory Law School has vividly shown through his field study how difficult it is to achieve non-economic values without a proper economic foundation:[1549] ensuring the safety of women from violation may not be an economic development objective, but a critical social agenda, and he has observed a severe problem in controlling serious crimes against women in a developing country that could support only one police station with a two-man staff covering a 50-mile radius, coupled with a critical shortage of prosecutors, courts, and prisons, despite the considerable government efforts and political determination to change the laws and stop this tragedy.[1550]

External aid alone cannot meet the financial needs of developing countries to fulfill non-economic development objectives, and successful economic development is imperative to building the necessary economic foundations to support non-economic development objectives. It is difficult to find a country that has achieved non-economic development objectives fully when it failed in economic development. We only find the reverse cases; for example, the East Asian countries focused on economic development under authoritarian rule until the 1980s.[1551] By the 1990s, they achieved important non-economic development objectives, such as elective democracy, the rule of law, improved gender equality, and a cleaner and safer environment for human beings and natural habitats. The economic constraints do not mean that all non-economic development objectives should be ignored in the process of development, but the resource constraints faced by developing countries create practical difficulties in pursuing all development

---

1546   LDRN, *Law and Development Research Network*, available online at: https://lawdev.org/; https://perma.cc/EU94-GPC9.
1547   See discussion *supra* Section 1.3.
1548   *Ibid.*
1549   Zwier (2017), *supra* note 291.
1550   *Ibid.*
1551   See discussion *supra* Sections 1.3.1 and 11.3.

objectives simultaneously with equal strengths. As such, developing countries should be allowed to prioritize among varied development objectives and undertake them in sequence for their effective realization.[1552]

From this perspective, law and development studies should give more attention to the relationship between law and industrial development, as economic development would not be feasible without the latter. It is also necessary to rethink the role of government in economic development.[1553] Chapter 11 has discussed the efficacy of state industrial promotion and cases of success. The neoliberal approach emphasizing privatization and deregulation has not been very successful in bringing development to most developing countries,[1554] but the alternative approach, adopted by the successful developing countries in the past,[1555] has not been actively adopted or recommended by international financial institutions and development agencies. In successful development cases such as Korea, Taiwan, Singapore, Spain, and Chile, the government departed from the traditional free-market prescriptions by actively supporting and facilitating industries and coordinating with the private sector. More recently, countries like China, Rwanda, and Ethiopia followed suit and achieved considerable success in economic development.[1556] Government planning and economic control by the government may not be a recipe for success, *per se*, as seen in many other failed countries, but the conditions for the success in this alternative approach and the role of law and institutions, which this book has addressed, need to be studied further.

In this vein, Chapters 4 and 5 of this book have examined the very different development trajectories shown in the cases of Korea and South Africa. By the early 1960s, South Africa, which was the most advanced country in Africa at that time, was far ahead of Korea in the progress of development, as measured by its GNI per capita, which was then three times higher than that of Korea. In less than two generations, however, the economic positions of the two countries have completely reversed; Korea, devoid of natural resources and under constant security threats from its northern neighbor (North Korea), currently generates five times more economic output and income than South Africa, measured by aggregate terms and per capita. Despite several development initiatives, South Africa has continued to suffer from stagnant economic growth, severe unemployment, and critical economic disparity for decades, while Korea has become one of the most advanced economies and vibrant democracies in the world after continuous success in development during the same period. One of the notable differences between these two countries is that the Korean government focused on industrialization consistently for over three decades, with the aid of effective LFIs, and such continued focus and leadership was absent in South Africa.[1557]

1552   *Ibid.*

1553   See *infra* note 1568 (for a discussion of the need for a broader study on the role of the state in economic development).

1554   See discussion *supra* Section 2.1.

1555   See discussion *supra* Section 11.3.

1556   For an account of the development of these countries, see *supra* note 500.

1557   Culture might be relevant to explain this difference. In correspondence with the author, Simon Deakin raised a question as to how far the success of the East Asian countries can

13.3 A new horizon for law and development

There are lessons from both successful and unsuccessful experiences in development; there is no monolithic path for economic development and no universal legal or institutional arrangement that works for economic development.[1558] While the economic efficiency of the market economy and rule of law have been advocated as necessities for economic development,[1559] the history of successful economic development shows that their adaptation has not been universal; for example, China has developed rapidly since the 1980s without adopting the level of rule of law promoted by the West, and with the government retaining control over much of the economy, contrasting the conventional market approaches.[1560] As discussed earlier, the economic development of Korea and other successful developing countries in the preceding periods showed the same pattern (*i.e.,* authoritarian rule and extensive government engagement with the economy). They shifted policies and relaxed government control over the economy as they achieved economic development, and the previous discussion explains how this shift worked for continuing successful development in these countries.[1561]

be ascribed to Confucian culture. He pointed out the difficulty associated with drawing clear conclusions about cultural factors and warned against the danger of post-hoc rationalizations. He discussed the case of Japan that presented specific conditions that allowed for its post-1945 recovery which have little to do, in his view, with culture, but more to do with specific factors in the way the economy was organized (limiting the role of market-based finance in corporate governance, for example). In his assessment, China has also been following a path of confining the role of finance or subordinating it to industrial policy. Therefore, he would, overall, favor emphasizing specific policies that seemed to have worked, over Confucian or other cultural factors. His view raises a question as to why, then, in many other developing countries which adopted the policies implemented in successful developing countries, such as state industrial promotion, the outcome of those policies was not as successful. For example, President Zuma in South Africa attempted to adopt state "developmental policies" for eight years without much success. An important difference is the consistency and strength of policy implementation, and culture is relevant as it generates a difference in political will, as discussed in Chapter 3. Many successful developing countries share Confucian cultural traditions, but there are also others, such as Chile and Spain, which share some of the characteristics of the Confucian leadership during the periods of their successful development after the Second World War. Policies are important, but culture, which may change over time, is also relevant, and political leadership, which is also affected by culture, has an essential role.

1558   See, *e.g.,* Rodrik (2005), *supra* note 207.
1559   Davis and Trebilcock (2008), *supra* note 87. Another study also suggests that the economic growth of Europe owes much to the rise of learned law and its teaching in Universities. Hans-Bernd Schäfer and Alexander Wulf, "Jurists, Clerics and Merchants: The Rise of Learned Law in Medieval Europe and Its Impact on Economic Growth" (2014) 11(2) *Journal of Empirical Legal Studies* 266–300.
1560   Government involvement/control in the economy in China is justified under the notion of the "socialist market economy," which is a form of state capitalism. See Suliman (ed.) (1998), *supra* note 380.
1561   See discussion *supra* Section 3.2.1.

Chapter 10, which examines the interrelationship among political governance, law, and economic development, and Chapter 11, which discusses state industrial promotion, have explained that there is no universal system of political and economic governance ensuring successful development.

In addition to the analytical issues for law and development studies, there is also a concern that industrialized countries in Europe, North America, and Asia may not enthusiastically support industrialization efforts in developing countries due to the need to safeguard their own economic (and political) interests. This apprehension stems from the traditional world powers' collective learning experience that successful economic development in East Asia, including China, has created strong industrial rivals and also affected the international political hegemony once held by North America and Europe. According to this line of thinking, a developed and industrialized Africa, Asia, or South America might undermine the economic and political hegemony enjoyed by the West even further; thus, it is not a type of development that could be welcomed by the developed world.

This sort of protective stance does not, however, appreciate the full possibility to be created by successful development in the developing world. The recent economic progress in China may have heightened rivalries from some economic and international political perspectives, but China's successful economic development has also offered tremendous economic opportunities for many developed countries, as evidenced by some of their largest corporations setting up branches and operating in major Chinese cities such as Beijing and Shanghai.[1562] Politically, there is also a substantial benefit as well as a potential rivalry—the world will also be more secure with China as a responsible member of the international community, as shown by its cooperation regarding the enforcement of the United Nations' economic sanctions against North Korea for its nuclear tests and ballistic missile test launches.[1563] The same can also be expected of successful development elsewhere; *i.e.,* successful economic development in Africa, Asia, and South America will also offer invaluable economic opportunities for developed countries and provide foundations for future partnerships to develop and pursue shared political interests.

The development of the ADM is both necessary and feasible, although the scale of the project may require many years for its completion. The ADM will present working legislative guidance for countries that seek to develop LFIs that will support economic development under their own political, social, and economic conditions. As the general theory indicates, law and development projects will likely produce a positive outcome when they are designed to fit the socioeconomic conditions on the ground and when they meet the local development needs, rather than serving the political and economic agendas and priorities of

---

1562   As of 2018, China is the second-largest import market in the world, next only to the United States.

1563   "China to Enforce UN Sanctions Against North Korea," *The Guardian,* September 23, 2017, available online at: www.theguardian.com/world/2017/sep/23/china-to-enforce-un-sanctions-against-north-korea; https://perma.cc/R2B3-SCRR.

the developed world. The proposed ADM will offer developing countries a leg-islative guide for the development-facilitating LFIs in each of the key areas,[1564] which will work in the stage of their economic development and under their own socioeconomic conditions. It is a markedly different approach from the one-size-fits-all mentality, which has not proven particularly successful. By understanding and responding to the real needs of the developing world, aided by the proposed ADM, rather than insisting on the ideal aspirations and preferences of the devel-oped world, scholars in law and development will finally find themselves out of "self-estrangement"[1565] and in tune with the realities on the ground.

A note should also be made that law and development is relevant and useful not only to developing countries but to developed ones as well, as discussed in Chapter 6. The financial crisis in the last decade, which caused a worldwide economic downturn, demonstrated potential flaws in the current regulatory system of developed countries, which may have contributed to the outbreak of this crisis.[1566] The regional economic gaps within developed countries, stag-nant economic growth, and widening income gaps among populations in developed countries[1567] also require regulatory reform under new legal and institutional approaches. The proposed law and development approaches can also be adopted to address the economic problems of developed countries, and this will substantially increase the scope of study and practice for law and development.[1568]

Finally, the law and development analysis undertaken for specific areas in Chapters 8 through 12 could be further expanded into additional areas rele-vant to development, such as banking and financing, taxation, competition, labor rights, and intellectual property rights. As shown by those new chapters, one needs to re-evaluate the conventional wisdom that has been believed to pro-mote development in those areas, such as protection of the autonomy of banking and financial industries, assurance of flexibility in the labor market, enhancement of competition, and reinforcement of IPRs, against alternative approaches (such as government control over banking and financing, labor protection, allowance of economic concentration: monopolies and oligopolies, and less-stringent IPR protection). Successful developing countries in the past, such as the NICs, adopted many of these alternative practices. The former and the latter catego-ries of practices may not necessarily be mutually exclusive; *e.g.*, allowing the for-mation of a few mega-firms controlling an industry but enhancing competition

---

1564   See *supra* Section 7.3.
1565   Trubek and Galanter (1974), *supra* note 33.
1566   See *supra* note 798 (for references on the causes of the financial crisis).
1567   See discussion *supra* Section 6.1.
1568   This might require a broader academic approach; Simon Deakin has opined that more research is necessary to understand the role of law in development or industrialization in the West and that a theory of the state and of the legal system is currently insufficient. This suggests that the work done by preeminent predecessors, such as Max Weber and Friedrich Hayek, on the role of law for the economic prosperity of the West may not have been sufficient to understand the causes of the economic development and industrialization in the West.

among them, as successfully practiced in the NICs to facilitate rapid economic development. Relevant stages of economic development and dissimilar socioeconomic conditions may determine the effectiveness of a chosen legal and regulatory approach, whether it is one under the conventional wisdom, an alternative approach, or a combination thereof.

Bibliography

Academic references and reports

Acemoglu, Daron, Simon Johnson, and James A. Robinson, "The Colonial Origins of Comparative Development: An Empirical Investigation" (2001) 91(5) *American Economic Review* 1369–1401.

Acemoglu, Daron, Stephen Gelb, and James A. Robinson, *Black Economic Empowerment and Economic Performance in South Africa* (August 2007), available online at: www.treasury.gov.za/publications/other/growth/06-Procurement%20and%20BEE/02-BLACK%20ECONOMIC%20EMPOWERMENT%20AND%20ECONOMIC%20PERFORMANCE%20IN%20SO.pdf; https://perma.cc/UM53-L4J2.

Agnello, Richard J. and Lawrence P. Donnelley, "Property Rights and Efficiency in the Oyster Industry" (1975) 18 *Journal of Law and Economics* 521–533.

Ahmad, E. and N. Stern, "Taxation for Developing Countries," *in* Hollis Chenery and T. N. Srinivasan (eds.), *Handbook of Development Economics*, vol. 2 (New York: North-Holland, 1989).

AIDDATA, *Realizing Agenda 2030*, available online at: www.aiddata.org/sdg; https://perma.cc/D8TG-VYU9.

Alesina, Alberto *et al.*, "Political Instability and Economic Growth," *National Bureau of Economic Research Working Paper*, no. 4173 (September 1992).

Alichi, Ali, Kory Kantenga, and Juan Solé, "Income Polarization in the United States," *IMF Working Paper*, WP/16/121 (June 2016).

Alm, James and Asmaa El-Ganainy, "Value-Added Taxation and Consumption" (2013) 20(1) *International Tax and Public Finance* 105–128.

American Bar Association, *Report Adopted by the House of Delegates* (August 8–9, 2011).

American Law Institute (ALI), *Restatement of the Law Second Contracts* (Washington, D.C.: ALI, 1979).

Amsden, Alice H., *Asia's Next Giant: Korea and Late Industrialization* (New York: Oxford University Press, 1992).

Anderson, Terry L. and Dean Lueck, "Land Tenure and Agriculture Productivity on Indian Reservations" (1992) 35 *Journal of Law and Economics* 427–454.

AnEconomicSense.org, "How Fast Can GDP Grow? Not as Fast as Trump Says," *An Economic Sense* (August 1, 2017), available online at: https://aneconomicsense.org/2017/08/01/how-fast-can-gdp-grow-not-as-fast-as-trump-says/; https://perma.cc/D8UN-74VU.

Aoki, Masohiko, *Information, Corporate Governance, and Institutional Diversity* (New York: Oxford University Press, 2000).

Aoki, Masohiko, *Toward a Comparative Institutional Analysis* (Cambridge, MA: MIT Press, 2001).

Asian Development Bank, *The Saemaul Undong Movement in the Republic of Korea* (2012), available online at: www.adb.org/sites/default/files/publication/29881/saemaul-undong-movement-korea.pdf; https://perma.cc/9WJD-P7LM.

Auty, Richard M., "Natural Resource Endowment, the State, and Development Policy" (1997) 9(4) *Journal of International Development* 435–673.

Bailey, Martin J., "Property Rights in Aboriginal Societies," *in* Peter Newman (ed.), *The New Palgrave Dictionary of Economics and Law* (London: Macmillan Reference LTD, 1998).

Baland, Jean-Marie, Karl Ove Moene, and James A. Robinson, "Governance and Development," *in* Dani Rodrik and M. R. Rosenzweig (eds.), *Handbook of Development Economics*, vol. 5 (New York: North-Holland, 2009).

Balcerowicz, Leszek, "Understanding Post-Communist Transitions" (1994) 5(4) *Journal of Democracy* 75–89.

Bank of Korea, *Economic Statistics System*, available online at: http://ecos.bok.or.kr/, accessed October 12, 2020.

Barden, Garrett and Tim Murphy, *Law and Justice in Community* (New York: Oxford University Press, 2010).

Bardhan, Pranab, "Economics of Development and the Development of Economics" (1993) 7(2) *The Journal of Economic Perspectives* 129–142.

Barnes, Grenville and Charisse Griffith-Charles, "Assessing the Formal Land Market and Deformalization of Property in St. Lucia" (2007) 24 *Land Use Policy* 494–501.

Barnes, Grenville, David Stanfield, and Kevin Barthel, "Land Registration Modernization in Developing Economies: A Discussion of the Main Problems in Central/Eastern Europe, Latin America, and the Caribbean" (2002) 12(4) *URISA Journal* 33–42.

Barrows, Richard and Daniel Bromley, "Employment Impacts of the Economic Development Administration's Public Works Program" (1975) 57(1) *American Journal of Agricultural Economics* 46–54.

Barrows, Richard and Michael Roth, "Land Tenure and Investment in African Agriculture: Theory and Evidence" (1990) 28 *Journal of Modern African Studies* 265–297.

Barth, James R., Gerard Caprio Jr., and Ross Levine, "Bank Regulation and Supervision: What Works Best" (2004) 13 *Journal of Financial Intermediation* 205–248.

Baxter, Jamie "Leadership, Law and Development" (2019) 12(1) *Law and Development Review* 119–158.

Bayley, David H., "Law Enforcement and the Rule of Law: Is There a Tradeoff?" (2002) 2(1) *Criminology and Public Policy* 133–154.

Beck, Thorsten, Asli Demirgüç-Kunt, and Patrick Honohan, "Access to Financial Services: Measurement, Impact, and Policies" (2009) 24 *World Bank Research Observer* 119–145.

Belton, Rachel Kleinfeld, "Competing Definitions of the Rule of Law: Implications for Practitioners," *Carnegie Papers, Rule of Law Series* (2005), available online at: http://carnegieendowment.org/files/CP55.Belton.FINAL.pdf; https://perma.cc/2PRN-PQLX.

Benson, Bruce L., *The Enterprise of Law: Justice without the State* (Oakland: The Independent Institute, 2011).

Berblinger, Anne, "Federal Aid for Rural Economic Development" (1993) 529(1) *The Annals of the American Academy of Political and Social Science* 155–163.

Berg, Elliot M., "Law and Development: A Review of the Literature and a Critique of 'Scholar in Self-Estrangement'" (1977) 25(2) *American Journal of Comparative Law* 492–530.

Berger, Adolf, *Encyclopedic Dictionary of Roman Law* (Philadelphia: The American Philosophical Society, 1953).

Berger, Peter L. and Hsin-Huang Michael Hsiao, *In Search of an East Asian Development Model* (Piscataway: Transaction Publishers, 1988).

Bergstein, Jonas, "Foreign Investment in Uruguay: A Law and Development Perspective" (1989) 20(2) *University of Miami Inter-American Law Review* 359–392.

Bernstein, David, "Freedom of Contract," *in* David S. Tanenhaus (ed.), *Encyclopedia of the Supreme Court of the United States*, vol. 2 (Palgrave Macmillan Reference, 2008).

Bernstein, Lisa, "Opting Out of the Legal System: Extralegal Contractual Relations in the Diamond Industry" (1992) 21(1) *Journal of Legal Studies* 115–157.

Beseley, T. and M. Gothak, "Property Rights and Economic Development," *in* Dani Rodrik and M. R. Rosenzweig (eds.), *Handbook of Development Economics*, vol. 5 (New York: North-Holland, 2009).

Biddulph, Robin, "Cambodia's Land Management and Administration Project," *WIDER Working Paper*, no. 2014/086 (2014), available online at: www.wider.unu.edu/sites/default/files/wp2014-086.pdf; https://perma.cc/6YKD-CYFM.

Bilchitz, David, *Poverty and Fundamental Rights: The Justification and Enforcement of Socio-Economic Rights* (Oxford: Oxford University Press, 2007).

Bjorklund, Andrea K., A. Laird, and Sergey Ripinsky (eds.), *Investment Treaty Law: Current Issues III—Remedies in International Investment Law: Emerging Jurisprudence of International Investment Law* (British Institute of International and Comparative Law, 2009).

Black, Henry Campbell, *Black's Law Dictionary* (6th ed., St. Paul: West Publishing Co., 1990).

Block, Fred, "Swimming Against the Current: The Rise of a Hidden Developmental State in the United States" (2008) 36(2) *Politics and Society* 169–206.

Boettke, Peter J. and Peter T. Leeson, *The Economic Role of the State* (Aldershot: Edward Elgar, 2015).

Bogopane, L. P., "Evaluation of Black Economic Empowerment (BEE) Policy Implementation in the Ngaka Modiri Molema District, North West Province, South Africa" (2013) 34(3) *Journal of Social Sciences* 277–288.

Brauner, Yariv and Miranda Stewart (eds.), *Taxation, Law and Development* (Cheltenham: Edward Elgar, 2013).

Brenton, Paul, "Integrating the Least Developed Countries into the World Trading System: The Current Impact of European Union Preferences under 'Everything but Arms'" (2003) 37(3) *Journal of World Trade* 623–646.

Brohman, John, "Postwar Development in the Asian NICs: Does the Neoliberal Model Fit Reality?" (1996) 72(2) *Economic Geography* 107–130.

Bromley, Daniel W. and Jean-Paul Chavas, "On Risk, Transactions and Economic Development in the Semiarid Tropics" (1989) 37 *Economic Development and Cultural Change* 719–736.

Brown, Archie, *The Rise and Fall of Communism* (New York: HarperCollins Publishers, 2009).

Campbell, John, "Despite Land Reform, South Africa Is Not Becoming Zimbabwe or Venezuela," *Council on Foreign Relations* (August 8, 2018), available online at: www.cfr.org/blog/despite-land-reform-south-africa-not-becoming-zimbabwe-or-venezuela; https://perma.cc/W9HF-ABBW.

Carothers, Thomas, "The Rule of Law Revival," *Foreign Affairs* (March/April 1998), available online at: www.foreignaffairs.com/articles/53809/thomas-carothers/the-rule-of-law-revival; https://perma.cc/G4DN-GVWN.

Carothers, Thomas, "The Problem of Knowledge," *in* Thomas Carothers (ed.), *Promoting the Rule of Law Abroad: In Search of Knowledge* (Washington, D.C.: Carnegie Endowment for International Peace, 2006).

Carroll, Archie B., "A Three-Dimensional Conceptual Model of Corporate Social Performance" (1979) 4 *Academy of Management Review* 497–505.

"Challenging Moments in Korean History (2): Five-Year Economic Development Plans," *Korean Economy Daily*, August 2008.

Chang, Ha-Joon, *Kicking Away the Ladder: Development Strategy in Historical Perspective* (London: Anthem Press, 2002).

Chang, Ha-Joon and D. Green, *The Northern WTO Agenda on Investment: Do as We Say, Not as We Did* (Geneva: South Centre, 2003).

Chen, Edward and Raymond Ng, "Economic Restructuring of Hong Kong on the Basis of Innovation and Technology," *in* Seiichi Masuyama, Donna Vandenbrink, and Chia Siow Yue (eds.), *Industrial Restructuring in East Asia* (Singapore: ISEAS Publishing, 2019).

Cheremukhin, Anton, Mikhail Golosov, Sergei Guriev, and Aleh Tsyvinski, "Was Stalin Necessary for Russia's Economic Development?" *NBER Working Paper*, no. 19425 (September 2013), available online at: https://economics.yale.edu/sites/default/files/files/Faculty/Tsyvinski/stalin_wp.pdf; https://perma.cc/SEX3-VVZQ.

Chesterman, Simon, "An International Rule of Law?" (2008) 56(2) *American Journal of Comparative Law* 331–361.

Chibundu, Maxwell, "Law in Development: On Tapping, Gourding and Serving Palm-Wine" (1997) 29(2) *Case Western Reserve Journal of International Law* 167–261.

Chimni, Bhupinder, "The Sen Conception of Development and Contemporary International Law Discourse: Some Parallels" (2008) 1(1) *Law and Development Review* 1–22.

"China to Enforce UN Sanctions Against North Korea," *The Guardian*, September 23, 2017, available online at: www.theguardian.com/world/2017/sep/23/china-to-enforce-un-sanctions-against-north-korea; https://perma.cc/R2B3-SCRR.

Chinkin, C. M., "The Challenge of Soft Law: Development and Change in International Law" (1989) 38(4) *International and Comparative Law Quarterly* 850–866.

Chua, Amy, "Markets, Democracy, and Ethnicity: Toward A New Paradigm for Law and Development" (1998) 108(1) *Yale Law Journal* 1–107.

Chung, Joseph Sang-Hoon, "North Korea's 'Seven Year Plan' (1961–70): Economic Performance and Reforms" (1972) 12(6) *Asian Survey* 527–545.

Claessens, Stijn and Fabian Valencia (eds.), *Financial Crises: Causes, Consequences, and Policy Responses* (Washington, D.C.: International Monetary Fund, 2014).

Claessens, Stijn and Leora Klapper, "Bankruptcy Around the World: Explanations of Its Relative Use" (2005) 7(1) *American Law and Economics Review* 253–283.

Clarke, Julie, "The Increasing Criminalization of Economic Law—A Competition Law Perspective" (2012) 19(1) *Journal of Financial Crime* 76–98.

Coase, Ronald H., "The Nature of the Firm" (1937) 4(16) *Economica* 386–405.

Coase, Ronald H., "The Problem of Social Cost" (1960) 3 *Journal of Law and Economics* 1–44.

Cody, Edward, "Tensions Flare in France over Veil Ban," *Washington Post*, August 9, 2012, available online at: www.washingtonpost.com/world/tensions-flare-in-france-over-veil-ban/2012/08/08/67b56fc2-e150-11e1-98e7-89d659f9c106_story.html?utm_term=.2a15a15b3dea; https://perma.cc/3R4E-5U9Q.

Collier, Paul, *Wars, Guns, and Votes: Democracy in Dangerous Places* (New York: HarperCollins, 2009).

Commons, John R., *Legal Foundations of Capitalism* (New York: The Macmillan Company, 1924).

Commons, John R., *Institutional Economics* (New York: Palgrave Macmillan, 1934).

Congressional Budget Office, *Letter to Honorable Nancy Pelosi* (June 9, 2020), available online at: www.cbo.gov/system/files/2020-06/56395-CBO-Pelosi-Letter.pdf; https://perma.cc/E8FL-JB7H.

Conkin, P., *Prophets of Prosperity: America's First Political Economists* (Bloomington: Indiana University Press, 1980).

Cooter, Robert and Hans-Bernd Schäfer, *Solomon's Knot: How Law Can End the Poverty of Nations* (Princeton: Princeton University Press, 2012).

Corsetti, Giancarlo, Paolo Pesenti, and Nouriel Roubini, "What Caused the Asian Currency and Financial Crisis? Part I: A Macroeconomic Overview," *National Bureau of Economic Research Working Paper*, no. 6833 (1998), available online at: www.nber.org/papers/w6833; https://perma.cc/J2P6-N4VS.

Cronje, Jan, "World Bank Predicts Just 1.1% GDP Growth for SA in 2018," *fin 24*, January 10, 2018, available online at: www.fin24.com/Economy/world-bank-predicts-just-11-gdp-growth-for-sa-in-2018-20180109; https://perma.cc/R2ZD-J58Z.

Cross, Frank, "Law and Economic Growth" (2001) 80(7) *Texas Law Review* 1737–1775.

Cross, Frank, "Identifying the Virtues of the Common Law" (2007) 15(1) *Supreme Court Economic Review* 21–59.

Cuéllar, Mariano-Florentino, "The Mismatch between State Power and State Capacity in Transnational Law Enforcement" (2004) 22(1) *Berkeley Journal of International Law* 15–58.

Cui, F., "Who Are the Developing Countries in the WTO?" (2008) 1(1) *Law and Development Review* 124–153.

Cypher, James M., "Is Chile a Neoliberal Success?" *Dollars & Sense: Real World Economics* (September–October 2004), available online at: http://dollarsandsense.org/archives/2004/0904cypher.html; https://perma.cc/R65K-HDDY.

Dadayan, Lucy and Donald J. Boyd, *By the Numbers: 2016: Another Lackluster Year for State Tax Revenue* (Rockefeller Institute of Government) (May 2017), available online at: http://rockinst.org/wp-content/uploads/2018/02/2017-05-08-By-numbers-brief-no9-1.pdf; https://perma.cc/DQ5A-ESBZ.

Dam, Kenneth, *The Law-Growth Nexus: The Rule of Law and Economic Development* (Washington, D.C.: Brookings, 2006).

Dann, Philipp, *The Law of Development Cooperation* (Cambridge: Cambridge University Press, 2013).

Davis, Kevin, "What Can the Rule of Law Variable Tell Us about Rule of Law Reforms?" (2004) 26 *Michigan Journal of International Law* 141–161.

Davis, Kevin and Michael Trebilcock, "Legal Reforms and Development" (2001) 22(1) Third World Quarterly 21–36.

Davis, Kevin and Michael Trebilcock, "The Relationship between Law and Development: Optimists Versus Skeptics" (2008) 56(4) *American Journal of Comparative Law* 895–946.

Deakin, Simon, "Legal Origin, Juridical Form and Industrialisation in Historical Perspective: The Case of the Employment Contract and the Joint-Stock Company" (2008) 4(7) *Comparative Research in Law and Political Economy* 1–39.

Deaton, A., "Data and Econometric Tools for Development Analysis," *in* J. Behrman and T. N. Srinivasan (eds.), *Handbook of Development Economics*, vol. 3 (New York: North-Holland, 1995).

Deininger, Klaus, *Land Policies for Growth and Poverty Reduction* (Washington, D.C.: The World Bank, 2003).

De la Escosura, Leandro Prados, Joan Rosés, and Isabel Sanz Villarroya, "Stabilisation and Growth under Dictatorships: Lessons from Franco's Spain," *VOX: CEPR's Policy Portal* (March 22, 2010), available online at: http://voxeu.org/article/stabilisation-and-gro wth-under-dictatorships-new-lessons-franco-s-spain; https://perma.cc/Y2EU-VS78.

Demsetz, Harold, "Toward a Theory of Property Rights" (1967) 57 *American Economic Review* 347–359.

De Soto, Hernando, *The Mystery of Capital: Why Capitalism Triumphs in the West and Fails Everywhere Else* (New York: Basic Books, 2003).

Deyrup, Felicia J., "Government Support of Industry in American History" (1950) 17(3) *Social Research* 346–364.

Dlamini, C. R. M., "The Role of Customary Law in Meeting Social Needs" (1991) *Acta Juridica* 71–85.

Dolasia, Meera, "PyeongChang 2018 Winter Olympics Open with Intel's Spectacular Shooting Star Drones," *Dogonews*, February 12, 2018, available online at: www. dogonews.com/2018/2/12/pyeongchang-2018-winter-olympics-open-with-intels-spectacular-shooting-star-drones; https://perma.cc/79P4-VYYK.

Domingo, Rafael, "The Law of Property in Ancient Roman Law" (June 2017), available online at: https://papers.ssrn.com/sol3/papers.cfm?abstract_id=2984869, accessed October 12, 2020.

Dore, Ronald, *Land Reform in Japan* (London: Oxford University Press, 1959).

Dorfman, J. and R. Tugwell, *Early American Policy—Six Columbia Contributors* (New York: Columbia University Press, 1960).

Dubow, Saul, *Apartheid, 1948–1994* (Oxford: Oxford University Press, 2014).

Eckert, Carter J. and Ki-Baik Lee, *Korea Old and New: A History* (Seoul: Ilchokak Publishers, 1991).

Economic Development Administration, *EDA Fiscal Year 2017 Budget Request at-a-Glance: Supporting 21st Century Economic Development*, available online at: www. eda.gov/pdf/EDA-FY-2017-Budget-Fact-Sheet_FINAL.pdf; https://perma.cc/ 2V7L-PEQQ.

Economic Development Administration, *2018 Annual Report* (2019), available online at: www.eda.gov/files/annual-reports/fy2018/EDA-FY2018-Annual-Report-full.pdf; https://perma.cc/T9WS-R3FE.

Economic Development Administration, *Fiscal Year 2021 Congressional Budget Request* (February 10, 2020), available online at: www.commerce.gov/sites/default/files/ 2020-02/fy2021_eda_congressional_budget_justification.pdf; https://perma.cc/ 6SST-XU8G.

Economic Planning Board, *Government Budget Allocation in 1962*, BA0084326 [National Archives of Korea document call number] (1962) (in Korean).

Economist, *Democracy Index 2020*, available online at: www.eiu.com/n/campaigns/ democracy-index-2020/; https://perma.cc/Q97S-3L8C.

"Egyptian Law," *Encyclopaedia Britannica*, available online at: www.britannica.com/ topic/Egyptian-law; https://perma.cc/5TK9-8D48.

El-Erian, Mohamed A., "Why Advanced Economies Need to Learn from Developing Nations," *Bloomberg View*, July 11, 2016.

Ellickson, Robert, *Order Without Law: How Neighbors Settle Disputes* (Cambridge: Harvard University Press, 1997).

Encyclopedia of the Nations, *Korea, South*, available online at: www.nationsencyclopedia. com/economies/Asia-and-the-Pacific/Korea-South.html; https://perma.cc/B8GC-5ZFW.

Escobar, Arturo, *Encountering Development: The Making and Unmaking of the Third World* (Princeton: Princeton University Press, 2011).

Étienne, Julien, "La Conformation Des Gouvernes. Une revue de la littérature théorique" (2010) 60(3) *Revue Française de Science Politique* 493–517.

European Institute for Gender Equality, *Economic Benefits of Gender Equality in the European Union: Report on the Empirical Application of the Model* (2017), available online at: http://eige.europa.eu/sites/default/files/documents/mh0217174enn_ web.pdf; https://perma.cc/S3MV-EEJ8.

"Expropriation," *Black's Law Dictionary* (6th ed., St. Paul: West Publishing, 1997).

Farnsworth, E. Allen, *Contracts* (4th ed., New York: Aspen Publishers, 2004).

Farrar, Salim and Ghena Krayem, *Accommodating Muslims under Common Law: A Comparative Analysis* (Abington: Routledge, 2016).

Federal Reserve Economic Data, *Employment-Population Ratio—25–54 Yrs.*, available online at: https://fred.stlouisfed.org/series/LNS12300060, accessed January 3, 2021.

Federal Reserve Economic Data, *Employment Rate: Aged 25–54: Males for the United States*, available online at: https://fred.stlouisfed.org/series/LREM25MAUSM156S, accessed January 3, 2021.

Federal Reserve Economic Data, *Real GDP at Constant National Prices for Republic of Korea*, available online at: https://fred.stlouisfed.org/series/RGDPNAKRA666N RUG, accessed January 3, 2021.

Feenstra, Robert C., Robert Inklaar, and Marcel P. Timmer, *Penn World Table Version 8.1* (April 13, 2015), available online at: www.rug.nl/ggdc/productivity/pwt/pwt-releases/pwt8.1; https://perma.cc/AUP9-FPZC.

Ferraro, Vincent, "Dependency Theory: An Introduction," *in* Giorgio Secondi (ed.), *The Development Economics Reader* (London: Routledge, 2008).

Finger, J. Michael, "The WTO's Special Burden on Less Developed Countries" (2000) 19(3) *Cato Journal* 425–437.

Fitzpatrick, Daniel, "Evolution and Chaos in Property Rights Systems: The Third World Tragedy of Contested Access" (2006) 115 *Yale Law Journal* 996–1048.

"Four Tables and Graphs You Should See Ahead of South Africa's Matric Results," *Business Tech*, January 5, 2020, available online at: https://businesstech.co.za/news/governm ent/363480/4-tables-and-graphs-you-should-see-ahead-of-south-africas-matric-resu lts/, accessed December 9, 2020.

Fraile, Lydia, "Lessons from Latin America's Neo-Liberal Experiment: An Overview of Labour and Social Policies since the 1980s" (2009) 148(3) *International Labour Review* 215–233.

Francis, Norton, "What Do State Economic Development Agencies Do?" *Economic Development Strategies Information Brief* 6 (Urban Institute) (July 2016), available online at: www.urban.org/sites/default/files/publication/83141/2000880-What-Do-State-Economic-Development-Agencies-Do.pdf; https://perma.cc/4MJB-JPED.

Fred-Mensah, Ben K., "Capturing Ambiguities: Communal Conflict Management Alternative in Ghana" (1999) 27 *World Development* 951–965.

Freedman, David A., *Statistical Models: Theory and Practice* (New York: Cambridge University Press, 2005).

Freedom House, *Freedom in the World 2010: Global Erosion of Freedom* (Washington, D.C.: Freedom House, 2010), available online at: https://freedomhouse.org/sites/default/files/2020-03/FIW_2010_Complete_Book_Scan.pdf; https://perma.cc/76YG-U8B7.

Freedom House, "Singapore," *Freedom in the World 2019*, available online at: https://freedomhouse.org/country/singapore/freedom-world/2019; https://perma.cc/RY64-H36E.

Freeman, R. B., "Labor Regulations, Unions, and Social Protection in Developing Countries: Market Distortions or Efficient Institutions?" *in* Dani Rodrik and M. R. Rosenzweig (eds.), *Handbook of Development Economics*, vol. 5 (New York: North-Holland, 2009).

Friedman, Jeffrey (ed.), *What Caused the Financial Crisis* (Philadelphia: University of Pennsylvania Press, 2010).

Friedman, Milton, *Capitalism and Freedom* (Chicago: University of Chicago Press, 1962).

Fukuyama, Francis, *State-Building: Governance and World Order in the 21st Century* (Ithaca: Cornell University Press, 2004).

Fund for Peace, *Fragile States Index 2020—Annual Report*, available online at: https://fragilestatesindex.org/wp-content/uploads/2020/05/fsi2020-report.pdf; https://perma.cc/7YJW-JWLE.

Fund for Peace, *Indicators, Fragile States Index 2020*, available online at: https://fragilestatesindex.org/indicators/; https://perma.cc/K5R6-NH5V.

Gabriel, Trip, "How Erie Went Red: The Economy Sank, and Trump Rose," *The New York Times*, November 12, 2016, available online at: www.nytimes.com/2016/11/13/us/politics/pennsylvania-trump-votes.html; https://perma.cc/AB25-Z4ZB.

Galiani, Sebastian and Ernesto Schargrodsky, "Property Rights for the Poor: Effects of Land Titling," Working Paper (Universidad Torcuato Di Tella, 2006).

GAN Business Anti-Corruption Portal, *South Africa Corruption Report* (December 2015), available online at: www.business-anti-corruption.com/country-profiles/south-africa; https://perma.cc/3DRU-BD6X.

Gardner, James, *Legal Imperialism: American Lawyers and Foreign Aid in Latin America* (Madison: University of Wisconsin Press, 1980).

Ghai, Yash, "Whose Human Right to Development?" *Human Rights Unit Occasional Papers* (Commonwealth Secretariat) (November 1989).

Gilson, Ronald J., Charles Sable, and Robert Scott, "Braiding: The Interaction of Formal and Informal Contracting in Theory, Practice and Doctrine" (2010) 110(6) *Columbia Law Review* 1377–1447.

Gilson, Ronald J. and Curtis J. Milhaupt, "Economically Benevolent Dictators: Lessons for Developing Democracies" (2011) 59(1) *American Journal of Comparative Law* 227–288.

Ginsburg, Tom, "Does Law Matter for Economic Development? Evidence from East Asia" (2000) 34(3) *Law and Society Review* 829–856.

Ginsburg, Tom, "Judicial Independence in East Asia: Implications for China," *Public Law and Legal Theory Working Papers* (2010), available online at: https://chicagounbound.uchicago.edu/cgi/viewcontent.cgi?article=1172&context=public_law_and_legal_theory; https://perma.cc/SRT8-P9MM.

Glaeser, Edward, "Secular Joblessness," *in* Coen Teulings and Richard Baldwin (eds.), *Secular Stagnation: Facts, Causes and Cures* (CEPR Press, 2014), available online at: https://scholar.harvard.edu/files/farhi/files/book_chapter_secular_stagnation_nov_2014_0.pdf; https://perma.cc/6ZC7-TRML.

Glaeser, Edward, Jose Scheinkman, and Andrei Shleifer, "The Injustice of Inequality" (2003) 50(1) *Journal of Monetary Economics* 199–222.

Godoy, Sergio and Joseph Stiglitz, "Growth, Initial Conditions, Law and Speed of Privatization in Transition Countries: 11 Years Later," *National Bureau of Economic Research Working Paper*, no. 11992 (2006).

Golin, Douglas, "The Lewis Model: A 60-Year Retrospective" (2014) 28(3) *Journal of Economic Perspectives* 71–88.

Goodman, Peter S., "End of Apartheid in South Africa? Not in Economic Terms," *The New York Times*, October 24, 2017, available online at: www.nytimes.com/2017/10/24/business/south-africa-economy-apartheid.html; https://perma.cc/2EKB-MWCA.

Gordon, Robert J., "The Turtle's Progress: Secular Stagnation Meets the Headwinds," *in Secular Stagnation: Facts, Causes and Cures* (CEPR Press, 2014), available online at: https://scholar.harvard.edu/files/farhi/files/book_chapter_secular_stagnation_nov_2014_0.pdf; https://perma.cc/6ZC7-TRML.

Gordon, Robert J., *The Rise and Fall of American Growth: The U.S. Standard of Living since the Civil War* (Princeton: Princeton University Press, 2016).

Gordon, Ruth E. and Jon H. Sylvester, "Deconstructing Development" (2004) 22(1) *Wisconsin International Law Journal* 1–98.

Gow, Hamish R., Deborah H. Streeter, and Johan F. M. Swinnen, "How Private Contract Enforcement Mechanisms Can Succeed Where Public Institutions Fail: The Case of Juhocukor a.s." (2000) 23(3) *Agricultural Economics* 253–265.

Grafton, R. Quentin, Dale Squires, and Kevin J. Fox, "Private Property and Economic Efficiency: A Study of a Common-Pool Resource" (2000) 43 *Journal of Law and Economics* 679–713.

Greif, Avner, "Contracting, Enforcement, and Efficiency: Economics beyond the Law," *in* Michael Bruno and Boris Pleskovic (eds.), *Annual World Bank Conference on Development Economics 1996* (Washington, D.C.: World Bank, 1997).

Griffiths, John, "Do Laws Have Symbolic Effects?" *in* Nicolle Zeegers, Willem Witteveen, and Bart van Klink (eds.), *Social and Symbolic Effects of Legislation under the Rule of Law* (Lewiston: The Edwin Mellen Press, 2005).

Gupta, Sanjeev, Hamid Davoodi, and Rosa Alonso-Terme, "Does Corruption Affect Income Inequality and Poverty?" (2001) 3(1) *Economics of Governance* 23–45.

Haberler, G., *et al.*, *Trends in International Trade* (October 1958), available online at: www.wto.org/english/res_e/booksp_e/gatt_trends_in_international_trade.pdf, accessed November 9, 2020.

Haggard, Stephan and Lydia Tiede, "The Rule of Law and Economic Growth: Where Are We?" (2011) 39(5) *World Development* 673–685.

Hagler, Yoav, "Introduction: Identifying Underperforming Regions," *in* Petra Todorovich and Yoav Hagler (eds.), *America 2050: New Strategies for Regional Economic Development* (2009), available online at: https://s3.us-east-1.amazonaws.com/rpa-org/pdfs/2050-New-Strategies-for-Regional-Economic-Development.pdf; https://perma.cc/85SV-WGAJ.

Hahn, Robert W., Jason K. Burnett, Yee-Ho I. Chan, Elizabeth A. Mader, and Petrea R. Moyle, "Assessing Regulatory Impact Analyses: The Failure of Agencies to Comply with Executive Order 12,866" (2000) 23(3) *Harvard Journal of Law and Public Policy* 859–877.

Hajzler, Chris, "Expropriation of Foreign Direct Investments: Sectoral Patterns from 1993 to 2006," *University of Otago Economics Discussion Papers*, no. 1011 (September

2010), available online at: www.otago.ac.nz/economics/research/otago077137.pdf; https://perma.cc/2TJW-WD32.

Halperin, Morton, Joseph Siegle, and Michael Weinstein, *The Democracy Advantage: How Democracies Promote Prosperity and Peace* (New York: Routledge, 2010).

Hamilton, Alexander, *Report on the Subject of Manufactures* (December 5, 1791), available online at: https://founders.archives.gov/documents/Hamilton/01-10-02-0001-0007; https://perma.cc/55T8-8YYU.

Hanson, Philip, *The Rise and Fall of the Soviet Economy: An Economic History of the USSR from 1945* (Abington: Routledge, 2014).

Harkness, Peter, "Detroit and New Orleans Have More in Common Than Most Think," *Governing* (January 2016), available online at: www.governing.com/archive/gov-detroit-new-orleans-resilience.html; https://perma.cc/ZV3P-33AD.

Harris, John, "If You Have Got Money, You Vote in … If You Haven't, You Vote Out," *The Guardian*, June 24, 2016.

Harrison, A., "Trade, Foreign Investment, and Industrial Policy for Developing Countries," *in* Dani Rodrik and M. R. Rosenzweig (eds.), *Handbook of Development Economics*, vol. 5 (New York: North-Holland, 2009).

Hart, H. L. A., *The Concept of Law* (2nd ed., New York: Oxford University Press, 1994).

Hart-Landsberg, Martin, *The Rush to Development: Economic Change and Political Struggle in Korea* (Monthly Review Press, 1993).

Harwood, John, "Trump's Tax Cut Isn't Giving the US Economy the Boost It Needs," *CNBC*, August 16, 2019, available online at: www.cnbc.com/2019/08/16/trumps-tax-cut-isnt-giving-the-us-economy-the-boost-it-needs.html; https://perma.cc/UYV4-D2S5.

Hausmann, Jens, "The Value of Public-Notice Filing under Uniform Commercial Code Article 9: A Comparison with the German Legal System of Securities in Personal Property" (1996) 25(3) *Georgia Journal of International and Comparative Law* 427–478.

Hayek, Friedrich, *The Road to Serfdom* (London: Routledge, 1944).

Hayek, Friedrich, *Individualism and Economic Order* (Chicago: University of Chicago Press, 1948).

Hayek, Friedrich, *The Constitution of Liberty* (Chicago: University of Chicago Press, 1960).

Hayek, Friedrich, *Law, Legislation, and Liberty*, vols. 1–3 (Chicago: University of Chicago Press, 1979).

Hayes, Louis D., *Political Systems of East Asia* (Abington: Routledge, 2015).

Hazlett, Thomas W., "Is Federal Preemption Efficient in Cellular Phone Regulation?" (2003) 56(1) *Federal Communications Law Journal* 155–238.

Helleiner, G. K. (ed.), *Trade Policy, Industrialization, and Development* (Oxford: Oxford University Press, 1992).

Helliwell, John F., "Empirical Linkages between Democracy and Economic Growth" (1994) 24(2) *British Journal of Political Science* 225–248.

Hellman, Joel S., Geraint Jones, and Daniel Kaufmann, "Seize the State, Seize the Day: State Capture and Influence in Transition Economies" (2003) 31 *Journal of Comparative Economics* 751–773.

Hilaire, Alvin, and Yongzheng Yang, "The United States and the New Regionalism/ Bilateralism" (2004) 38 *Journal of World Trade* 609.

Hill, Hal and Jayant Menon, "Cambodia: Rapid Growth with Institutional Constraints," *ADB Economics Working Paper Series*, no. 331 (January 2013), available online at:

www.adb.org/sites/default/files/publication/30140/economics-wp331-cambodia-rapid-growth.pdf; https://perma.cc/8JFF-6ZR4.

Himonga, Chuma and Thandabantu Nhlapo (eds.), *African Customary Law: In South Africa: Post-Apartheid and Living Law Perspectives: Private Law* (Oxford: Oxford University Press, 2015).

Hofheinz, Roy Jr. and Kent E. Calder, *The East Asia Edge: Why an Entire Region Is Overtaking the West in Technology, Exports and Management* (New York: Basic Books, 1982).

Hogan, William W., "Economic Reforms in the Sovereign States of the Former Soviet Union," *Brookings Papers on Economic Activity*, no. 2 (1991), available online at: www.brookings.edu/wp-content/uploads/1991/06/1991b_bpea_hogan.pdf; https://perma.cc/NZF9-JM8K.

Holmes, Frank, "FATCA: Good Intentions, Poor Design," *U.S. Global Investors* (June 25, 2014), available online at: www.usfunds.com/investor-library/frank-talk/fatca-good-intentions-bad-execution/#.V-28rIKQL3g; https://perma.cc/N5W3-S6D3.

Hong Kong E-Legislation, *Cap. 2Q Innovation and Technology Fund*, available online at: www.elegislation.gov.hk/hk/cap2Q@2017-02-15T00:00:00?xpid=ID_1438402956369_003; https://perma.cc/9HPY-ANUK.

Hormats, Robert D., "Abraham Lincoln and the Global Economy" (2003) *Harvard Business Review*, available online at: https://hbr.org/2003/08/abraham-lincoln-and-the-global-economy#:~:text=And%20the%20success%20he%20and,opportunity%20to%20settle%20Western%20lands; https://perma.cc/3JQS-ESU3.

Horwitz, Morton, *Transformation of American Law, 1780–1860* (Cambridge: Harvard University Press, 1977).

Hubbard, William H. J., "Yong-Shik Lee, 'Call for a New Analytical Model for Law and Development': A Comment" (2015) 8(2) *Law and Development Review* 271–276.

Hudec, R. E., *Developing Countries in the GATT Legal System*, Thames Essay no. 50 (Aldershot: Gower, for the Trade Policy Research Centre, London, 1987).

Hwang, Kyung Moon, *A History of Korea* (New York: Palgrave Macmillan, 2016).

Ilg, Michael, "Profit, Persuasion, and Fidelity: Why People Follow the Rule of Law" (2017) 10(2) *Law and Development Review* 275–303.

Im, Gang Taek and Sung Chul Kim, "Unofficial Undertaking of Property Rights in North Korea (in Korean)," Research Report 03-19, Korea Unification Research Institute (2003), available online at: http://repo.kinu.or.kr/bitstream/2015.oak/712/1/0000598245.pdf; https://perma.cc/EB9Q-2NA4.

Imbs, Jean, and Romain Wacziarg, "Stages of Diversification" (2003) 93(1) *American Economic Review* 63–86.

Inama, Stefano, "Market Access for LDCs: Issues to Be Addressed" (2002) 36(1) *Journal of World Trade* 85–116.

International Institute for Sustainable Development, *Report on the World Trade Organization's High-Level Symposium on Trade and Development* (Geneva, March 17–18, 1999), available online at: www.wto.org/english/tratop_e/devel_e/summhl_e.pdf; https://perma.cc/6FF9-J57T.

Jacoby, Hanan G. and Bart Minten, "Is Land Titling in Sub-Saharan Africa Cost-Effective? Evidence from Madagascar" (2007) 21 *World Bank Economic Review* 461–485.

Jain, Arvind K., "Corruption: A Review" (2001) 15(1) *Journal of Economic Surveys* 71–121.

Jasny, Naum, *The Soviet Economy During the Plan Era* (Stanford: Stanford University, 1951).

Jayasuriya, Kanishka, "Introduction: A Framework for the Analysis of Legal Institutions in East Asia," *in* Kanishka Jayasuriya (ed.), *Law, Capitalism, and Power in Asia* (London: Routledge, 1999).

Jebe, Ruth, Don Mayer, and Y.S. Lee, "China's Export Restrictions on Raw Materials and Rare Earths: A New Balance between Free Trade and Environmental Protection" (2012) 44 *George Washington International Law Review* 579–642.

Jeon, Hong Taek, "Economic Growth of North Korea: 1945–1995" (1995) 1 *Journal of Economic Development* 77–105.

"Jindal Rejects La.'s Stimulus Share," *The Washington Times*, February 21, 2009, available online at: www.washingtontimes.com/news/2009/feb/21/lousiana-gov-rejects-states-stimulus-share; https://perma.cc/FER7-ZUNP.

Jodha, N. S., "Common Property Resources: A Missing Dimension of Development Strategies," *World Bank Discussion Paper*, no. 169 (1992).

Johnson, Chalmers, "The Development State: Odyssey of a Concept," *in* Meredith Woo-Cumings (ed.), *The Developmental State* (Ithaca, NY: Cornell University Press, 1999).

Johnson, Leland J., "Problems of Import Substitution: The Chilean Automobile Industry" (1967) 15(2) *Economic Development and Cultural Change* 202–216.

Johnson, Omotunde, "Economic Analysis, the Legal Framework and Land Tenure Systems" (1972) 15 *Journal of Law and Economics* 259–276.

Jolowicz, H. F., *Historical Introduction to the Study of Roman Law* (3rd ed., Holmes Beach, FL: Gaunt, 1996).

Jung, Woosik and K. Lee, "The Effectiveness of Export Promotion Policies: The Case of Korea" (1986) 122 *Weltwirtschaftliches Archiv* 340–357.

Jung, Y. H., "How Did Law Matter for Korean Economic Development? Evidence from 1970s," paper prepared for the Korean Economic Association Conference (June 2012).

Jwa, Sung-Hee, *A General Theory of Economic Development Towards a Capitalist Manifesto* (Cheltenham: Edward Elgar, 2017).

Kadish, Sanford H., "Some Observations on the Use of Criminal Sanctions in Enforcing Economic Regulations" (1963) 30(3) *The University of Chicago Law Review* 423–449.

Kaiser Family Foundation, *Status of State Medicaid Expansion Decisions: Interactive Map* (November 2, 2020), available online at: www.kff.org/medicaid/issue-brief/status-of-state-medicaid-expansion-decisions-interactive-map/; https://perma.cc/S2KW-8S5B.

Kaldor, Nicholas, "Taxation for Economic Development" (1963) 9(1) *The Journal of Modern African Studies* 7–23.

Kanda, Hideki and Curtis J. Milhaupt, "Re-Examining Legal Transplants: The Director's Fiduciary Duty in Japanese Corporate Law" (2003) 51(4) *American Journal of Comparative Law* 887–901.

Katz, Larissa, "Governing through Owners: How and Why Formal Private Property Rights Enhance State Power" (2012) 160 *University of Pennsylvania Law Review* 2029–2059.

Kaufmann, Daniel, "Rule of Law Matters: Unorthodoxy in Brief," *Brookings Report* (January 21, 2010), available online at: www.brookings.edu/research/reports/2010/01/21-governance-kaufmann; https://perma.cc/324Y-928D.

Kaufmann, Daniel *et al.*, "Governance Matters," *World Bank Policy Research Working Papers*, no. 2196 (1999).

Keefer, Philip and Stephen Knack, "Why Don't Poor Countries Catch Up? A Cross-National Test of an Institutional Explanation" (1997) 35(3) *Economic Inquiry* 590–602.

Keene, Donald, *Emperor of Japan: Meiji and His World, 1852–1912* (New York: Columbia University Press, 2005).

Kennedy, David, "The 'Rule of Law,' Political Choices, and Development Common Sense," *in* David M. Trubek and Alvaro Santos (eds.), *The New Law and Economic Development* (New York: Cambridge University Press, 2006).

Khan, Hider A., *Global Markets and Financial Crises in Asia* (New York: Palgrave Macmillan, 2004).

Kim, Annette M., "A Market without the 'Right' Property Rights: Ho Chi Minh City, Vietnam's Newly-Emerged Private Real Estate Market" (2004) 12 *Economics of Transition* 275–305.

Kim, Cynthia, "S. Korea Crackdown on Underground Economy Stokes Angst," *Bloomberg*, February 2, 2014, available online at: www.bloomberg.com/news/articles/2014-02-02/south-korea-s-crackdown-on-underground-economy-stokes-angst; https://perma.cc/H55Q-K2R4.

Kim, Duol (ed.), *History of Economic Laws in Korea: From Liberation to Present*, vols. 1–4 (Seoul: Haenam Publishing Co., 2011).

Kim, Iljoong, Hojun Lee, and Ilya Somin (eds.), *Eminent Domain: A Comparative Perspective* (Cambridge University Press, 2017).

Kim, Kwang-Suk and Joon-kyung Park, *Sources of Economic Growth in Korea: 1963–1981* (Seoul: Korea Development Institute, 1985).

Kim, Marie Seong-Hak, "In the Name of Custom, Culture, and the Constitution: Korean Customary Law in Flux" (2013) 48(3) *Texas International Law Journal* 357–391.

Koh, Ran and Jai Sheen Mah, "The Effect of Export Composition on Economic Growth: The Case of Korea" (2013) 47(1) *Journal of Developing Areas* 171–179.

Korea National Statistical Office, *Statistical Assessment of Changes in Korea's Economy and Society for the Past 60 Years* (August 2008) (in Korean), available online at: https://web.archive.org/web/20140219065908/http://kostat.go.kr/portal/korea/kor_nw/2/1/index.board?bmode=download&bSeq=&aSeq=60300&ord=1, accessed January 13, 2021.

Korea National Statistical Office, E-National Statistical Index, *The Number of Administrative Lawsuits* (in Korean), available online at: www.index.go.kr/potal/main/EachDtlPageDetail.do?idx_cd=1724; https://perma.cc/X44R-CS7P.

Kose, M. A., "Financial Globalization and Economic Policies," *in* Dani Rodrik and M. R. Rosenzweig (eds.), *Handbook of Development Economics*, vol. 5 (New York: North-Holland, 2009).

Kossick, Robert, "The Rule of Law and Development in Mexico" (2004) 21 *Arizona Journal of International and Comparative Law* 715–834.

Krier, James E., "Evolutionary Theory and the Origin of Property Rights" (2009) 95 *Cornell Law Review* 139–159.

Krueger, A. O., "Trade Policies in Developing Countries," *in* R. W. Jones and P. B. Kenen (eds.), *Handbook of International Economics*, vol. 1 (New York: North-Holland, 1984).

Krugman, Paul, *The Rise and Fall of Development Economics*, available online at: http://web.mit.edu/krugman/www/dishpan.html; https://perma.cc/H6KW-VJEZ.

Kuran, Timur, "The Scale of Entrepreneurship in Middle Eastern History: Inhibitive Roles of Islamic Institutions," *in* William J. Baumol, David S. Landes, and Joel Mokyr (eds.), *Entrepreneurs and Entrepreneurship in Economic History* (Princeton: Princeton University Press, 2010).

Kutubi, Shawgat S., "Combating Money-Laundering by the Financial Institutions: An Analysis of Challenges and Efforts in Bangladesh" (2011) 1(2) *World Journal of Social Sciences* 36–51.

Kwon, Youngjoon and Yong-Shik Lee, "Legal Analysis of Traditional Leasehold in Korea (Chonsegwon) from Comparative Legal Perspective" (2012) 29(2) *Arizona Journal of International and Comparative Law* 263–286.

La Porta, Raphael, Florencio Lopez-de-Silanes, Andrei Shleifer, and Robert Vishny, "Law and Finance" (1998) 106(6) *Journal of Political Economy* 1113–1155.

La Porta, Raphael, Florencio Lopez-de-Silanes, Andrei Shleifer, and Robert Vishny, "Investor Protection and Corporate Governance" (2000) 58 *Journal of Financial Economics* 3–27.

La Porta, Raphael, Florencio Lopez-de-Silanes, Andrei Shleifer, and Robert Vishny, "Investor Protection and Corporate Valuation" (2002) 5(3) *Journal of Finance* 1147–1170.

La Porta, Raphael, Florencio Lopez-de-Silanes, Andrei Shleifer, and Robert Vishny, "The Economic Consequences of Legal Origins" (2008) 46(2) *Journal of Economic Literature* 285–332.

Lauterpacht, Hersch, "Recognition of States in International Law" (1944) 53(3) *Yale Law Journal* 385–458.

Laver, Roberto, "The World Bank and Judicial Reform: Overcoming 'Blind Spots' in the Approach to Judicial Independence" (2012) 22 *Duke Journal of International and Comparative Law* 183–238.

Law, David S. and Mila Versteeg, "The Declining Influence of the United States Constitution" (2012) 87(3) *The New York University Law Review* 762–858.

Law and Development Research Network, available online at: https://lawdev.org/; https://perma.cc/EU94-GPC9.

Leal-Arcas, Rafael, "Proliferation of Regional Trade Agreements: Complementing or Supplanting Multilateralism?" (2011) 11(2) *Chicago Journal of International Law* 597–629.

Lee, Jong Suk, "The Launching of Economic Development Plan (The Half Century of Korean Economy)," *E Daily*, May 5, 2005 (in Korean).

Lee, Sang Chul, "A Study on the Industrial Restructuring Policy in Korea during the 1980s," *NRF Research Project*, no. 2012S1A5A2A01020629 (2012) (in Korean).

Lee, Tae Hee, "Issues and Solutions at the Time of the IMF," *The Hankyoreh*, December 17, 1997 (in Korean).

Lee, Yong-Shik, "Facilitating Development in the World Trading System: A Proposal for Development Facilitation Tariff (DFT) and Development Facilitation Subsidy (DFS)" (2004) 38(2) *Journal of World Trade* 935–954.

Lee, Yong-Shik, *Safeguard Measures in World Trade: The Legal Analysis* (3rd ed., Cheltenham: Edward Elgar Publishing, 2014).

Lee, Yong-Shik, "WTO Disciplines and Economic Development: Reform Proposal" (2014) 1(2) *Journal of International and Comparative Law* 300–301.

Lee, Yong-Shik, "Call for a New Analytical Model for Law and Development" (2015) 8(1) *Law and Development Review* 1–67.

Lee, Yong-Shik, *Reclaiming Development in the World Trading System* (2nd ed., Cambridge: Cambridge University Press, 2016).

Lee, Yong-Shik, "The Long and Winding Road—Path Towards Facilitation of Development in the WTO: Reflections on the Doha Round and Beyond" (2016) 9(2) *Law and Development Review* 437–465.

Lee, Yong-Shik, "A General Theory of Law and Development" (2017) 50(3) *Cornell International Law Journal* 415–472.

Lee, Yong-Shik, "Sung-Hee Jwa, A General Theory of Economic Development: Towards a Capitalist Manifesto—A Critical Review" (2017) 10(2) *Law and Development Review* 643–657.

Lee, Yong-Shik, "Trans-Pacific Partnership Agreement: A Commentary on Developing/Developed Country Divide and Social Considerations" (2017) 9(2) *Trade, Law and Development* 21–53.

Lee, Yong-Shik, "Law and Development: Lessons from South Korea" (2018) 11(2) *Law and Development Review* 433–465.

Lee, Yong-Shik, "A Note on Economic Development in North Korea: Call for a Comprehensive Approach" (2019) 12(1) *Law and Development Review* 247–259.

Lee, Yong-Shik, "Law and Economic Development in the United States: Toward a New Paradigm" (2019) 68(2) *Catholic University Law Review* 229–290.

Lee, Yong-Shik, "Political Governance, Law, and Economic Development" (2019) 12(3) *Law and Development Review* 723–759.

Lee, Yong-Shik, "Reflections on Sustainable Development: A Note on Current Development" (2019) 9 *KLRI Journal of Law and Legislation* 193–204.

Lee, Yong-Shik, "South Korean Economy at the Crossroads: Structure Issues under External Pressure—An Essay from a Law and Development Perspective" (2019) 12(3) *Law and Development Review* 865–885.

Lee, Yong-Shik, "State Industrial Promotion and Law" (2019) 13(3) *Review of Institution and Economics* 11–49.

Lee, Yong-Shik, "Three Wrongs Do Not Make a Right: The Conundrum of the U.S. Steel and Aluminum Tariffs" (2019) 18(3) *World Trade Review* 481–501.

Lee, Yong-Shik, "International Trade Law Post Neoliberalism" (2020) 68(2) *Buffalo Law Review* 413–478.

Lee, Yong-Shik, "New General Theory of Economic Development: Innovative Growth and Distribution" (2020) 24(2) *Review of Economic Development* 402–423.

Lee, Yong-Shik, *Managing COVID-19: Legal and Institutional Issues* (November 6, 2020), available online at: https://papers.ssrn.com/sol3/papers.cfm?abstract_id=3724655, accessed December 10, 2020.

Lee, Yong-Shik, "Property Rights and Economic Development" (2020) 14(1) *Review of Institution and Economics* 25–64.

Lee, Yong-Shik, "The Legal Framework for Business Transactions and Economic Development" (2020) 44(2) *Southern Illinois University Law Journal* 273–297.

Lee, Yong-Shik, "State Capitalism and the Law," *in* Geoffrey Wood (ed.), *Oxford Handbook of State Capitalism and The Firm* (Oxford: Oxford University Press, forthcoming 2022), available online at: https://papers.ssrn.com/sol3/papers.cfm?abstract_id=3368065; https://perma.cc/G5L4-M3DM.

Lee, Yong-Shik *et al.* (eds.), *Law and Development Perspective on International Trade Law* (Cambridge: Cambridge University Press, 2011).

Lee, Yong-Shik and Xiaojie Lu, "China's Trade and Development Policy under the WTO: An Evaluation of Law and Economics Aspect" (2016) 2(2) *China and WTO Review* 339–360.

Lee, Yong-Shik, Young-Ok Kim, and Hye Seong Mun, "Economic Development of North Korea: International Trade Based Development Policy and Legal Reform" (2010) 3(1) *Law and Development Review* 136–156.

Leef, George, "It's Bad Policy to Use Eminent Domain for Economic Development, Even if It Sometimes 'Works,'" *Forbes* (August 28, 2015), available online at: www.forbes.com/sites/georgeleef/2015/08/28/its-bad-policy-to-use-eminent-domain-for-economic-development-even-if-it-sometimes-works/#4c884d0a7f80; https://perma.cc/DD5F-E962.

Legislative Council of Hong Kong, Panel on Commerce and Industry, *Updated Background Brief on the Funding Schemes under the Innovation and Technology Fund*, LC Paper No. CB(1)535/19-20(04) (2020).

Library of Congress, *Legal Status of Cryptocurrencies*, available online at: www.loc.gov/law/help/cryptocurrency/map1.pdf; https://perma.cc/FP62-49NG.

Liebenberg, Sandra, *Socio-Economic Rights: Adjudication under a Transformative Constitution* (Cape Town: Juta Academic, 2010).

Lindert, Peter, "Voice and Growth: Was Churchill Right?" (2003) 63(2) *Journal of Economic History* 315–350.

Lindsey, Tim, *Law Reform in Developing and Transitional States* (New York: Routledge, 2006).

Liptak, Adam, "'We the People' Loses Appeal with People around the World," *The New York Times*, February 6, 2012, available online at: www.nytimes.com/2012/02/07/us/we-the-people-loses-appeal-with-people-around-the-world.html; https://perma.cc/JLK5-77V7.

Lodge, Tom (ed.), *Politics in South Africa: From Mandela to Mbeki* (Cape Town: David Philip, 2003).

Long, Heather, "Trump Vows 25 Million Jobs, Most of any President," *CNN Money*, January 20, 2017, available online at: https://money.cnn.com/2017/01/20/news/economy/donald-trump-jobs-wages/index.html; https://perma.cc/K5V9-QJWY.

Macaulay, Stewart, "Non-Contractual Relations in Business: A Preliminary Study" (1963) 28 *American Sociological Review* 55–67.

Maddison, A., *The World Economy, Volume 2: Historical Statistics* (Paris: OECD, 2006).

Maggio, Giuseppe, Alessandro Romano, and Angela Troisi, "The Legal Origin of Income Inequality" (2014) 7(1) *Law and Development Review* 1–22.

Mah, Jai S., "Export Promotion Policies, Export Composition and Economic Development of Korea" (2011) 4(2) *Law and Development Review* 3–27.

Mahoney, Paul, "The Common Law and Economic Growth: Hayek Might Be Right" (2001) 30(2) *Journal of Legal Studies* 503–525.

Maine, Henry Sumner, *Ancient Law: Its Connection with the Early History of Society, and Its Relation to Modern Ideas* (New York: Henry Holt and Company, 1861).

Makinana, Andisiwe, "Parliament Gives Go-ahead for Land Expropriation Without Compensation," *Times Live* (December 4, 2018), available online at: www.timeslive.co.za/politics/2018-12-04-parliament-gives-go-ahead-for-land-expropriation-without-compensation/; https://perma.cc/DSE5-ND7W.

Mann, William C., "Displaced by Aswan Dam 23 Years Ago: Egypt's Nubians Dream of Home," *Los Angeles Times* (January 3, 1988), available online at: http://articles.latimes.com/1988-01-03/news/mn-32292_1_years-ago; https://perma.cc/TC3P-GM4C.

Marks, Stephen, "The Human Right to Development: Between Rhetoric and Reality" (2004) 17 *Harvard Human Rights Journal* 137–168.

Marshall, P. J. (ed.), *The Oxford History of the British Empire*, vol. II (Oxford: Oxford University Press, 1998).

Martin, Peter, *The Chrysanthemum Throne: A History of the Emperors of Japan* (Honolulu: Latitude 20, 1997).

Martin, Randolph and Robert Graham, "The Impact of Economic Development Administration Programs: Some Empirical Evidence" (1980) 62(1) *The Review of Economics and Statistics* 52–62.

Marx, Karl, Friedrich Engels, *et al.*, *Capital* (Digireads.com Publishing, 2017).

Mason, Paul E. and Horacio A. Grigera Naón (eds.), *International Commercial Arbitration Practice: 21st Century Perspectives* (LexisNexis, 2018).

Matsushita, Mitsuo, "Legal Aspects of Free Trade Agreements in the Context of Article XXIV of the GATT 1994," paper presented at the seminar, The Way Forward to Successful Doha Development Agenda Negotiation, United Nations University, Tokyo, Japan (May 24–25, 2004).

Matthews, Chris, "America's Investment Crisis Is Getting Worse," *Fortune Finance* (December 5, 2015), available online at: http://fortune.com/2015/12/02/corpor ate-investment-crisis/; https://perma.cc/MGF7-X637.

McGarity, Thomas O., "Regulatory Analysis and Regulatory Reform" (1987) 65(7) *Texas Law Review* 1243–1333.

McInerney, Thomas, "Law and Development as Democratic Practice" (2007) 37 *Vanderbilt Journal of Transnational Law* 935–969.

Meinzen-Dick, Ruth and Esther Mwangi, "Cutting the Web of Interests: Pitfalls of Formalizing Property Rights" (2008) 26 *Land Use Policy* 36–43.

Merrill, Thomas W., "Public Contracts, Private Contracts, and the Transformation of the Constitutional Order" (1987) *Case Western Reserve Law Review* 597–630.

Merrill, Thomas W., "Melms v. Pabst Brewing Co. and the Doctrine of Waste in American Property Law" (2011) 94(4) *Marquette Law Review* 1055–1094.

Merryman, Jon Henry, "Comparative Law and Social Change: On the Origins, Style, Decline & Revival of the Law and Development Movement" (1977) 25 *American Journal of Comparative Law* 457–483.

Meyers, Neil L., "Statutory Encouragement of Investment and Economic Development in the Republic of China on Taiwan," *Occasional Papers/Reprints Series in Contemporary Asian Studies* (1994).

Michaely, M., "Exports and Growth" (1977) 4(1) *Journal of Development Economics* 49–53.

Migot-Adholla, Shem, Peter Hazell , Benoît Blarel, and Frank Place, "Indigenous Land Rights Systems in Sub-Saharan Africa: A Constraint on Productivity" (1991) 5 *World Bank Economic Review* 155–175.

Miller, Terry, "Government Intervention: A Threat to Economic Recovery," *The Heritage Foundation* (2009), available online at: www.heritage.org/testimony/government-intervention-threat-economic-recovery; https://perma.cc/879K-2L9J.

Ministry of Economic Affairs, *History*, available online at: www.moea.gov.tw/MNS/english/EconomicHistory/EconomicHistory.aspx?menu_id=32897; https://perma.cc/GH3Z-NB7X.

Morris, Ian, "Democracy: The Least Bad Form of Government," *Stratfor Worldview* (October 7, 2015), available online at: https://worldview.stratfor.com/article/democr acy-least-bad-form-government; https://perma.cc/UZ7J-5LMW.

Mthanti, Thanti, "Systemic Racism behind South Africa's Failure to Transform Its Economy," *The Conversation* (January 31, 2018), available online at: https://theconve rsation.com/systemic-racism-behind-south-africas-failure-to-transform-its-economy-71499; https://perma.cc/4R5J-N4NN.

Murphy, Tim, "Living Law, Normative Pluralism, and Analytic Jurisprudence" (2012) 3(1) *Jurisprudence* 177–210.

Mwabu, G., "Health Economics for Low-Income Countries" *in* T. Paul Schultz and John Strauss (eds.), *Handbook of Development Economics*, vol. 4 (New York: North-Holland, 2008).

Nam, Ae Ri, *The Regulation on Family Rite*, National Archives of Korea (in Korean), available online at: http://theme.archives.go.kr/next/koreaOfRecord/homeRule.do; https://perma.cc/U4BV-PGLD.

National Archives of Korea, *The Path that Hangul (Korean Alphabet) Walked On* (in Korean), available online at: http://theme.archives.go.kr/next/hangeulPolicy/busin ess.do; https://perma.cc/JQ4E-93ZS.

National Government of South Africa, *Department: Economic Development (EDD)*, available online at: https://nationalgovernment.co.za/units/view/13/Department-Economic-Development-EDD; https://perma.cc/F75D-VCHL.

National Index System, *Annual Public Official Status*, available online at: www. index. go.kr/potal/main/EachDtlPageDetail.do?idx_cd=1016; https://perma.cc/8M59-QYMP.

National Planning Commission, available online at: www.nationalplanningcommission. org.za/Pages/default.aspx; https://perma.cc/D2VQ-UZNE.

National Science and Technology Council, *The National Artificial Intelligence Research and Development Strategic Plan* (October 2016), available online at: www.nitrd.gov/ PUBS/national_ai_rd_strategic_plan.pdf; https://perma.cc/V49Y-94FW.

National Tax Service, *Capital Gains Tax* (in Korean), available online at: https://web.arch ive.org/web/20200422103312/www.nts.go.kr/support/support_11.asp?cinfo_key= MINF5720100720165645; https://perma.cc/Z2AA-C9FN.

Newsis, "Minister of Legislation (Announces) Exports of Advanced Korean Legal Systems" (in Korean), *Joongang Daily News* (April 16, 2013), available online at: http://article. joins.com/news/article/article.asp?total_id=11247168&ctg=1203; https://perma. cc/B464-5FXC.

Newton, Scott, "The Dialectics of Law and Development," *in* David M. Trubek and Alvaro Santos (eds.), *The New Law and Economic Development* (New York: Cambridge University Press, 2006).

North, Douglass C., *Structure and Change in Economic History* (New York: Norton, 1981).

North, Douglass C., *Institutions, Institutional Change and Economic Performance* (Cambridge: Cambridge University Press, 1990).

North, Douglass C., "Institutions" (1991) 5(1) *Journal of Economic Perspectives* 97–112.

North, Douglass C., "Big-Bang Transformations of Economic Systems: An Introductory Note" (2000) 156(1) *Journal of Institutional and Theoretical Economics* 3–8.

North, Douglass C. and Robert Paul Thomas, *The Rise of the Western World: A New Economic History* (New York: Cambridge University Press, 1973).

Nwapi, C., "Defining the 'Local' in Local Content Requirements in the Oil and Gas and Mining Sectors in Developing Countries" (2015) 8(1) *Law and Development Review* 187–216.

Nyaw, Mee-Kau and Chan-leong Chan, "Structure and Development Strategies of the Manufacturing Industries in Singapore and Hong Kong: A Comparative Study" (1982) 22(5) *Asian Survey* 449–469.

Nyombi, Chrispas, and Tom Mortimer, *Rebalancing International Investment Agreements in Favour of Host States* (London: Wildy, Simmons, and Hill Publishing, 2018).

Ohnesorge, John, "Developing Development Theory: Law and Development Orthodoxies and the Northeast Asian Experience" (2006) 28(2) *University of Pennsylvania Journal of International Economic Law* 219–307.

Oman, Charles P., "Corporate Governance and National Development," *OECD Development Centre Working Paper*, no. 180 (October 2001).

Oniemola, Peter and Oyinkan Tasie, "Engendering Constitutional Realization of Sustainable Development in Nigeria" (2020) 13(1) *Law and Development Review* 159–191.

Onishi, Norimitsu, "Jacob Zuma Resigns as South Africa's President," *The New York Times*, February 14, 2018, available online at: www.nytimes.com/2018/02/14/world/africa/jacob-zuma-resigns-south-africa.html; https://perma.cc/Y8SV-BER7.

Organisation for Economic Co-operation and Development, "'Indirect Expropriation' and the 'Right to Regulate' in International Investment Law," *OECD Working Papers on International Investment* 2004/04 (2004), available online at: www.oecd.org/daf/inv/investment-policy/WP-2004_4.pdf; https://perma.cc/9QGY-LUZ9.

Organisation for Economic Co-operation and Development, *Tax Incentives for Investment-A Global Perspective: Experiences in MENA and non-MENA Countries* (2007), available online at: www.oecd.org/mena/investment/38758855.pdf; https://perma.cc/ZKT3-XVV8.

Organisation for Economic Co-operation and Development, *Introductory Handbook for Undertaking Regulatory Impact Analysis (RIA)*, Version 1.0, October 2008, available online at: www.oecd.org/gov/regulatory-policy/44789472.pdf; https://perma.cc/8JN7-NNSW.

Organisation for Economic Co-operation and Development, *Divided We Stand: Why Inequality Keeps Rising* (Paris: OECD Publishing, 2011).

Organisation for Economic Co-operation and Development, "Contract Enforcement and Dispute Resolution," *Policy Framework for Investment*, available online at: www.oecd.org/investment/toolkit/policyareas/investmentpolicy/contractenforcementanddisputeresolution.htm; https://perma.cc/L2NX-EA7M.

Organisation for Economic Co-operation and Development, *Gross Domestic Product (GDP)*, available online at: http://stats.oecd.org/glossary/detail.asp?ID=1163; https://perma.cc/SE6A-2B8Q.

Organisation for Economic Co-operation and Development, *Hours Worked*, OECD Data, available online at: https://data.oecd.org/emp/hours-worked.htm; https://perma.cc/4JRJ-4HJS.

Organisation for Economic Co-operation and Development, *Regional Trade Agreements*, available online at: www.oecd.org/tad/benefitlib/regionaltradeagreements.htm.

Organization of American States, *Secured Transactions Reform in the Americas* (August 2013), available online at: www.oas.org/en/sla/dil/docs/secured_transactions_newsletter_aug_2013.pdf; https://perma.cc/V6UH-6TFT.

Othman, Aida, "Islamic Finance: Facing the Pandemic, Shaping the Future," *in* Salim Farrar and Paul Subramaniam (eds.), *Law and Justice in Malaysia 2020 and Beyond* (Thomson Reuters, 2021), at 203–212.

Packenham, Robert A. and William Ratliff, "What Pinochet Did for Chile," *Hoover Digest* (January 30, 2007), available online at: www.hoover.org/research/what-pinochet-did-chile; https://perma.cc/CJ6K-LXVC.

Pahuja, Sundhya, *Decolonising International Law: Development, Economic Growth and the Politics of Universality* (Cambridge: Cambridge University Press, 2011).

Pande, R., "Understanding Political Corruption in Low Income Countries," *in* T. Paul Schultz and John Strauss (eds.), *Handbook of Development Economics*, vol. 4 (New York: North-Holland, 2008).

Pangestu, Mari, "Industrial Policy and Developing Countries," *in* Bernard Hoekman, Aaditya Mattoo, and Philip English (eds.), *Development, Trade, and the WTO: A Handbook* (Washington, D.C.: World Bank Publications, 2002).

Park, Daekeun and Changyong Rhee, "A Study on the Savings Rates in Korea: Synthetic Cohort Analysis," *Korea Institute of Public Finance Research Report* (May 1997).

Park, Daekeun and Changyong Rhee, "Saving, Growth, and Demographic Change in Korea" (2005) 19(3) *Journal of the Japanese International Economies* 394–413.

Park, Soo Jin and Shin Ji Min, "One Year After the Implementation of Improper Solicitation and Graft Act," *The Hankyoreh*, September 25, 2017 (in Korean), available online at: www.hani.co.kr/arti/society/society_general/812409.html; https://perma.cc/2RC3-VQ45.

Pearl, Judea, *Causality: Models, Reasoning, and Inference* (New York: Cambridge University Press, 2000).

Perreau-Saussine, Amanda and James B. Murphy, *The Nature of Customary Law: Legal, Historical and Philosophical Perspectives* (New York: Cambridge University Press, 2009).

Perry, Amanda, "The Relationship between Legal Systems and Economic Development: Integrating Economic and Social Approaches" (2002) 29(2) *Journal of Law and Society* 282–307.

Peters, Pauline E., "Inequality and Social Conflict over Land in Africa" (2004) 4 *Journal of Agrarian Change* 269–314.

Peukert, Detlev J. K., *The Weimar Republic: The Crisis of Classical Modernity* (New York: Hill and Wang, 1993).

Pew Research Center, *Trends in Income and Wealth Inequality* (January 9, 2020), available online at: www.pewsocialtrends.org/2020/01/09/trends-in-income-and-wealth-inequality/#fnref-27657-5; https://perma.cc/SLX7-V49M.

Pflanze, Otto, *Bismarck and the Development of Germany, Volume II: The Period of Consolidation, 1871–1880* (Princeton: Princeton University Press, 1990).

Picker, Colin B., "International Trade and Development Law: A Legal Cultural Critique" (2011) 4(2) *Law and Development Review* 43–71.

Pinckney, Thomas C. and Peter K. Kimuyu, "Land Tenure Reform in East Africa: Good, Bad, or Unimportant" (1994) 3 *Journal of African Economics* 1–28.

Pipes, Richard, *Property and Freedom* (London: The Harvill Press, 1999).

Pisei, Hin, "Government Pushes for Land Registration by 2021," *The Phnom Penh Post*, March 14, 2019, available online at: www.phnompenhpost.com/post-property/government-pushes-land-registration-2021; https://perma.cc/8LJ5-KMTC.

Pistor, Katharina, "The Standardization of Law and Its Effect on Developing Economies" (2002) 50(1) *American Journal of Comparative Law* 97–134.

Pistor, Katharina and Chenggang Xu, "Governing Stock Markets in Transition Economies: Lessons from China" (2005) 7(1) *American Law and Economics Review* 184–210.

Pistor, Katharina and Philip A. Wellons, *The Role of Law and Legal Institutions in Asian Economic Development, 1960–1995* (New York: Oxford University Press, 1999).

Place, Frank, "Land Tenure and Agricultural Productivity in Africa: A Comparative Analysis of the Economics Literature and Recent Policy Strategies and Reforms" (2009) 37 *World Development* 1326–1336.

Place, Frank and Peter Hazell, "Productivity Effects of Indigenous Land Tenure Systems in Sub-Saharan Africa" (1993) 75 *American Journal of Agricultural Economics* 10–19.

Platteau, Jean-Philippe, *Institutions, Social Norms, and Economic Development* (Amsterdam: Harwood Academic Publishers, 2000).

Polishchuk, Leonid and Alexei Savvateev, "Spontaneous (Non)Emergence of Property Rights" (2004) 12(1) *Economics of Transition* 103–127.

"Political Will," *Oxford Living Dictionaries*, available online at: https://en.oxforddicti onaries.com/definition/political_will; https://perma.cc/FJZ2-GLN4.

Pooe, T. K., "Developmental State No Birth Right: South Africa's Post-1994 Economic Development Story" (2017) 10(2) *Law and Development Review* 361–387.

Pooe, T. K., "Law and Economic Development in South Africa: An Assessment through the General Theory of Law and Development" (2019) 12(2) *Law and Development Review* 377–401.

Porter, Andrew (ed.), *The Oxford History of the British Empire*, vol. III (Oxford: Oxford University Press, 2001).

Posner, Richard A., "Creating a Legal Framework for Economic Development" (1998) 13(1) *World Bank Observer* 1–11.

Posner, Richard A., *Economic Analysis of Law* (7th ed., New York: Aspen Publishers, 2007).

Post, Lori Ann, Amber N. W. Raile, and Eric D. Raile, "Defining Political Will" (2010) 38(4) *Politics and Policy* 653–676.

Prado, Mariana, "Institutional Bypass: An Alternative for Development Reform" (April 19, 2011), text available online on SSRN at: http://papers.ssrn.com/sol3/papers. cfm?abstract_id=1815442; https://perma.cc/ANR4-K8BS.

Priest, Brady P., "Steel Tariffs: A Shining Example of the Tension between Politics and Economics in the United States" (2002) 28(3) *Brooklyn Journal of International Law* 1025–1057.

Przeworski, Adam and Fernando Limongi, "Political Regimes and Economic Growth" (1993) 7(3) *Journal of Economic Perspectives* 51–69, cited *in* Michael J. Trebilcock and Mariana Monta Prado, *What Makes Poor Countries Poor? Institutional Determinants of Development* (Cheltenham: Edward Elgar, 2011).

Przeworski, Adam *et al.*, *Democracy and Development: Political Institutions and Well-Being in the World 1950–1990* (New York: Cambridge University Press, 2000).

Puig, Gonzalo Villalta and Omiunu Ohiocheoya, "Regional Trade Agreements and the Neo-Colonialism of the United States of America and the European Union: A Review of the Principle of Competitive Imperialism" (2011) 32(3) *The Liverpool Law Review* 225–235.

Pye, Lucian W., *Asian Power and Politics: The Cultural Dimensions of Authority* (Cambridge: The Belknap Press, 1985).

Qin, Liu, "China's Five-Year Plan to Radically Tighten Air Pollution Targets," *Climate Home News*, November 3, 2016, available online at: www.climatechangenews.com/ 2016/03/11/chinas-five-year-plan-to-radically-tighten-air-pollution-targets/; https://perma.cc/M3GF-L3AA.

Radaelli, Claudio M., "The Diffusion of Regulatory Impact Analysis: Best Practice or Lesson-Drawing?" (2004) 43(5) *European Journal of Political Research* 723–747.

Raheem, A. Abdul, *Islamic Banking: Principles, Practices and Performance* (New Delhi: New Century Publications, 2013).

Rajagopal, Balakrishnan, *International Law from Below: Development, Social Movements and Third World Resistance* (Cambridge: Cambridge University Press, 2003).

Republic of South Africa, *New Growth Path Framework* (November 23, 2010).

Republic of South Africa, *President Cyril Ramaphosa: South Africa's Economic Reconstruction and Recovery Plan* (October 15, 2020), available online at: www.gov.za/speeches/president-cyril-ramaphosa-south-africa%E2%80%99s-economic-reconstruction-and-recovery-plan-15-oct, accessed December 9, 2020.

Republic of South Africa (National Treasury), *Budget Review 2020*, available online at: www.treasury.gov.za/documents/national%20budget/2020/review/FullBR.pdf; https://perma.cc/CR2V-YV8E.

Reynolds, Susan, *Before Eminent Domain: Toward a History of Expropriation of Land for the Common Good* (The University of North Carolina Press, 2010).

Rice, Susan E. and Stewart Patrick, "Index of State Weakness in the Developing World," *Brookings Institution* (February 26, 2008), available online at: www.brookings.edu/wp-content/uploads/2016/06/02_weak_states_index.pdf; https://perma.cc/K2EV-AMXS.

Rittich, Kerry, "The Future of Law and Development: Second Generation Reforms and the Incorporation of the Social," *in* David M. Trubek and Alvaro Santos (eds.), *The New Law and Economic Development* (New York: Cambridge University Press, 2006).

Robinson, Joan, "Korean Miracle" (1965) 16(9) *Monthly Review* 541–549.

Rodrik, Dani, "Institutions for High-Quality Growth: What They Are and How to Acquire Them" (2000) 35(3) *Studies in Comparative International Development* 3–31.

Rodrik, Dani, *The Global Governance of Trade as If Development Really Mattered* (New York: UNDP, 2001).

Rodrik, Dani, "Industrial Policy for the Twenty-First Century," *John F. Kennedy School of Government, Harvard University Faculty Research Working Papers Series*, RWP04-047 (2004), available online at: https://drodrik.scholar.harvard.edu/files/dani-rodrik/files/industrial-policy-twenty-first-century.pdf; https://perma.cc/5ZUD-XBUC.

Rodrik, Dani, "Introduction: What Do We Learn from Country Narratives?" *in* Dani Rodrik (ed.), *In Search of Prosperity: Analytic Narratives on Economic Growth* (Princeton: Princeton University Press, 2005).

Rodrik, Dani, "Thinking about Governance," *in* World Bank, *Governance, Growth, and Development Decision-Making* (Washington, D.C., World Bank, 2008).

Rodrik, Dani, Arvind Subramanian, and Francesco Trebbi, "Institutions Rule: The Primacy of Institutions over Geography and Integration in Economic Development" (2004) 9(2) *Journal of Economic Growth* 131–165.

Rogerson, Christian, "Tracking Local Economic Development Policy and Practice in South Africa, 1994–2009" (2011) 22(2) *Urban Forum* 149–168.

Roh, Kihyun, "訴訟上における行政指導の権利救済の限界と克服方案―日本で の議論を中心に [Ways to Overcome the Limits on Judicial Remedy for Infringement of Rights by Administrative Guidance—Based on Discussions in Japan]" (2012) 15(2) *Inha Law Review* 85–116.

Rose-Ackerman, Susan, "Corruption and Development," paper prepared for the Annual Bank Conference on Development Economies, Washington, D.C. (1997).

Rose, Carol, "The 'New' Law and Development Movement in the Post-Cold War Era: A Vietnam Case Study" (1998) 32 *Law and Society Review* 93–140.

Rostow, W. W., *The Stages of Economic Growth* (Cambridge: Cambridge University Press, 1962).

Rotberg, Robert, "Failed States, Collapsed States, Weak States: Causes and Indicators," *in* Robert Rotberg (ed.), *State Failure and State Weakness in a Time of Terror* (Cambridge: World Peace Foundation, 2003).

Rouiller, Nicolas, *International Business Law: An Introduction to the Legal Instruments and to the Legal Environment of Business from an International Perspective* (Zürich: Schulthess, 2015).

Rowe, Peter G. (ed.), *A City and Its Stream: An Appraisal of Cheonggyecheon Restoration Project and Its Environs in Seoul, South Korea* (Cambridge: Harvard University Graduate School of Design, 2010).

Rutherford, Malcolm, "Institutional Economics: Then and Now" (2001) 15(3) *Journal of Economic Perspectives* 173–194.

Sachs, Jeffrey D. *et al.*, "Ending Africa's Poverty Trap," *Brookings Papers on Economic Activity*, 2004(1) (2004).

Salvatore, Dominick, *International Economics* (8th ed., Hoboken: John Wiley & Sons, 2003).

Salvatore, Dominick, *International Economics* (11th ed., Hoboken: John Wiley & Sons, 2013).

Santos, Alvaro, "The World Bank's Uses of the 'Rule of Law' Promise in Economic Development," *in* David M. Trubek and Alvaro Santos (eds.), *The New Law and Economic Development* (New York: Cambridge University Press, 2006).

Santos, Alvaro, "Labor Flexibility, Legal Reform and Economic Development" (2009) 50(1) *Virginia Journal of International Law* 43–106.

Schäfer, Hans-Bernd and Alexander Wulf, "Jurists, Clerics and Merchants: The Rise of Learned Law in Medieval Europe and Its Impact on Economic Growth" (2014) 11(2) *Journal of Empirical Legal Studies* 266–300.

Schäfer, Hans-Bernd and Ram Singh, "Takings of Land by Self-Interested Governments: Economic Analysis of Eminent Domain" (2018) 61(3) *Journal of Law and Economics* 427–459.

Schenk, Catherine, "Economic History of Hong Kong," *EH.Net Encyclopedia* (March 16, 2008), available online at: http://eh.net/encyclopedia/economic-history-of-hong-kong/; https://perma.cc/WV5J-6MJ4.

Schumpeter, Joseph A., *Capitalism, Socialism and Democracy* (London: Routledge, 1994).

Scribner, Marc, "The Limitations of Public-Private Partnerships: Recent Lessons from the Surface Transportation and Real Estate Sectors," *Issue Analysis* (Competitive Enterprise Institute) (January 2011).

Secured Transactions Law Reform Project, *Costa Rica*, available online at: https://securedtransactionslawreformproject.org/reform-in-other-jurisdictions/central-america/costa-rica/; https://perma.cc/YGP8-JY6X.

Secured Transactions Law Reform Project, *El Salvador*, available online at: https://securedtransactionslawreformproject.org/reform-in-other-jurisdictions/central-america/el-salvador/; https://perma.cc/XWL4-9TBH.

Sen, Amartya, *Development as Freedom* (New York: Oxford University Press, 1999).

Seth, Michael J., *A History of Korea: From Antiquity to the Present* (Lanham: Rowman & Littlefield Publishers, 2010).

Short, Jodi L., "The Politics of Regulatory Enforcement and Compliance: Theorizing and Operationalizing Political Influences," *Regulation and Governance* (December 12, 2019), available online at: https://onlinelibrary.wiley.com/doi/full/10.1111/rego.12291, accessed March 5, 2021.

Singapore Government Agency, *Economic Development Board Act*, available online at: https://sso.agc.gov.sg/Act/EDBA1961; https://perma.cc/MD7Q-YJEN.

Singer, Joseph William and Bethany R. Berger, *Property Law: Rules, Policies, and Practices* (New York: Aspen Publisher, 2017).

Singh, Aparna Shivpuri, "Banking and Financial System in GMS Countries, Its Relationship to Economic Development," *Policy Brief* (Hanoi Resource Center) (September 2007), available online at: http://cuts-international.org/HRC/pdf/; https://perma.cc/RS2G-9BFM.

Skidelsky, Robert, "The Wealth of (Some) Nations," *The Books, New York Times on the Web* (December 24, 2000), available online at: http://movies2.nytimes.com/books/00/12/24/reviews/001224.24skidelt.html; https://perma.cc/EWG8-CZR2.

Slides, John, "A Comprehensive Average of Election Forecasts Points to a Decisive Clinton Victory," *Washington Post*, November 8, 2016.

Smith, Adam, *An Inquiry into the Nature and Causes of the Wealth of Nations* (Chicago: University of Chicago Press, 1776).

Smith, Adam, *Lectures on Jurisprudence* (New York: Oxford University Press, 1978).

Sokol, Daniel, Thomas K. Cheng, and Ioannis Lianos (eds.), *Competition Law and Development* (Stanford: Stanford University Press, 2013).

Sonin, Konstantin, "Why the Rich May Favor Poor Protection of Property Rights" (2003) 31 *Journal of Comparative Economics* 715–731.

Soon, Teck-Wong and C. Suan Tan, *Singapore: Public Policy and Economic Development* (Washington, D.C.: World Bank, 1993).

South African History Online, *Apartheid Legislation 1850s-1970s*, available online at: www.sahistory.org.za/article/apartheid-legislation-1850s-1970s; https://perma.cc/VQ9M-VP47.

South African History Online, *South Africa's Key Economic Policies Changes (1994–2013)*, available online at: www.sahistory.org.za/article/south-africa%E2%80%99s-key-economic-policies-changes-1994-2013; https://perma.cc/MJU4-NP3N.

Sovann, Sar, "Land Reform in Cambodia," paper prepared for FIG Congress 2010 (2010), available online at: www.fig.net/resources/proceedings/fig_proceedings/fig2010/papers/ts07j/ts07j_sovann_4633.pdf; https://perma.cc/68Y8-5LHN.

Spence, David B., "The Political Economy of Local Vetoes" (2014) 93(2) *Texas Law Review* 351–413.

Srinivasan, T. N., "Trade, Development, and Growth," *Princeton Essays in International Economics*, no. 225 (December 2001).

Statistics South Africa, *Inequality Trends in South Africa: A Multidimensional Diagnostic of Inequality, 2017*, Report-03-10-19 (November 14, 2019), available online at: www.statssa.gov.za/publications/Report-03-10-19/Report-03-10-192017.pdf; https://perma.cc/U9J6-MLA6.

Statistics South Africa, *Quarterly Labor Force Survey* (Quarter 4: 2019), available online at: www.statssa.gov.za/publications/P0211/P02114thQuarter2019.pdf; https://perma.cc/6GB9-FKHD.

Stigler, George J. and Paul A. Samuelson, "A Dialogue on the Proper Role of the State," *University of Chicago Graduate School of Business Selected Papers*, no. 7 (1968).

Stiglitz, Joseph, "Globalization and the Economic Role of the State in the New Millennium" (2003) 12(1) *Industrial and Corporate Change* 3–26.

Strittmatter, Anthony and Uwe Sunde, "Health and Economic Development—Evidence from the Introduction of Public Health Care" (2013) 26(4) *Journal of Popular Economics* 1549–1584.

Suliman, Osman (ed.), *China's Transition to a Socialist Market Economy* (West Port: Praeger, 1998).

Tadelis, Steven and Oliver Williamson, "Transaction Cost Economics," *in* Robert Gibbons and Johnson Roberts (eds.), *The Handbook of Organizational Economics* (Princeton: Princeton University Press, 2013).

Tamanaha, Brian, "The Lessons of Law-and-Development Studies" (1995) 89(2) *American Journal of International Law* 470–486.

Tamanaha, Brian, *On the Rule of Law: History, Politics, Theory* (Cambridge: Cambridge University Press, 2004).

Tamanaha, Brian, "A Concise Guide to the Rule of Law," *Legal Studies Research Paper Series, St. John's University School of Law*, #07-0082 (September 2007), available online at: http://content.csbs.utah.edu/~dlevin/conlaw/tamanaha-rule-of-law.pdf; https://perma.cc/UZ2W-FLXU.

Tan, Augustine, "Official Efforts to Attract FDI: Case of Singapore's EDB," *in* 1999 EWC/KDI Conference on Industrial Globalization in the 21st Century: *Impact and Consequences for East Asia and Korea* (1999).

Tanzi, Vito, "Corruption around the World: Causes, Consequences, Scope and Cures" (1998) 45(4) *Staff Papers* (International Monetary Fund) 559–594.

Tanzi, Vito and Hamid Davoodi, "Corruption, Public Investment, and Growth," *in* Hirofumi Shibata and Toshihiro Ihori (eds.), *The Welfare State, Public Investment and Growth* (Springer, 1998).

"This Is Who Is Paying South Africa's Tax," *Business Tech*, October 26, 2017, available online at: https://businesstech.co.za/news/finance/207631/this-is-who-is-paying-south-africas-tax/; https://perma.cc/6TYK-RLBX.

Thompson, Mark R., *Authoritarian Modernism in East Asia* (New York: Palgrave Pivot, 2018).

Thornton, Songok Han and William H. Thornton, *Development Without Freedom: The Politics of Asian Globalization* (Abington: Routledge, 2008).

Thorson, Mitchell, Janie Haseman, and Carlie Procell, "Four Maps That Show How America Voted in the 2020 Election with Results by County, Number of Voters," *USA Today*, November 20, 2020, available at: www.usatoday.com/in-depth/graphics/2020/11/10/election-maps-2020-america-county-results-more-voters/6226197002/; https://perma.cc/93NV-M2XY.

Torriti, Jacopo and Ragnar E. Lofstedt, "The First Five Years of the EU Impact Assessment System: A Risk Economics Perspective on Gaps between Rationale and Practice" (2012) 15(2) *Journal of Risk Research* 169–186.

Traniello, Marisa, "Power-Sharing: Lessons from South Africa and Rwanda" (2007) 3(2) *International Public Policy Review* 28–43.

Transparency International, 1995 *TI Corruption Index*, available online at: www.transparency.org/files/content/tool/1995_CPI_EN.pdf; https://perma.cc/EG7D-WD8A.

Transparency International, *Corruption Perceptions Index 2019*, available online at: www.transparency.org/en/cpi/2019/results/table; https://perma.cc/M236-9W5J.

Trebilcock, Michael J., *The Limits of Freedom of Contract* (Cambridge: Harvard University Press, 1997).

Trebilcock, Michael J., "Between Theories of Trade and Development: The Future of the World Trading System" (2015) 16(1) *Journal of World Investment & Trade* 122–140.

Trebilcock, Michael J., "Between Universalism and Relativism: Reflections on the Evolution of Law and Development Studies" (2016) 66 *University of Toronto Law Journal* 351–352.

Trebilcock, Michael J. and Jing Leng, "The Role of Formal Contract Law and Enforcement in Economic Development" (2006) 92 *Virginia Law Review* 1517–1580.

Trebilcock, Michael J. and Mariana Monta Prado, *What Makes Poor Countries Poor? Institutional Determinants of Development* (Cheltenham: Edward Elgar, 2011).

Treuhaft, Sarah and David Madland, *Prosperity 2050: Is Equity the Superior Growth Model?* (Washington, D.C.: Center for American Progress, April 2011), available online at: https://cdn.americanprogress.org/wp-content/uploads/issues/2011/04/pdf/prosperity_2050.pdf; https://perma.cc/UZT4-W5YL.

Trubek, David M., "Toward a Social Theory of Law: An Essay on the Study of Law and Development" (1972) 82(1) *Yale Law Journal* 1–50.

Trubek, David M., "The 'Rule of Law' in Development Assistance: Past, Present, and Future," *in* David M. Trubek and Alvaro Santos (eds.), *The New Law and Economic Development* (New York: Cambridge University Press, 2006).

Trubek, David M., "Law and Development 50 Years On," *University of Wisconsin Legal Studies Research Paper*, no. 1212 (2012), available online at: http://ssrn.com/abstract=2161899, accessed January 7, 2021.

Trubek, David M. and Alvaro Santos, "Introduction: The Third Moment in Law and Development Theory and the Emergence of a New Critical Practice," *in* David M. Trubek and Alvaro Santos (eds.), *The New Law and Economic Development* (New York: Cambridge University Press, 2006).

Trubek, David M. and Marc Galanter, "Scholars in Self-Estrangement: Some Reflections on the Crisis in Law and Development Studies in the United States" (1974) *Wisconsin Law Review* 1062–1103.

Tsui-Auch, Lai Si, "Has the Hong Kong Model Worked? Industrial Policy in Retrospect and Prospect" (1998) 29 *Development and Change* 55–79.

Tu, Wei-Ming, *Confucian Traditions in East Asian Modernity* (Cambridge: Harvard University Press, 1996).

United Nations, *High-level Event of the General Assembly on the Contributions of Human Rights and the Rule of Law in the Post-2015 Development Agenda* (June 9–10, 2014), available online at: https://sustainabledevelopment.un.org/index.php?page=view&type=13&nr=719&menu=3; https://perma.cc/EBR4-XURM.

United Nations, *LDC Identification Criteria & Indicators*, available online at: www.un.org/development/desa/dpad/least-developed-country-category/ldc-criteria.html; https://perma.cc/8S66-MZDL.

United Nations, *Least Developed Countries (LDCs)*, available online at: www.un.org/development/desa/dpad/least-developed-country-category.html; https://perma.cc/6A6X-MK7S.

United Nations, "Low Growth with Limited Policy Options? Secular Stagnation—Causes, Consequences and Cures," *Development Issues*, no. 9 (March 1, 2017), available online at: www.un.org/development/desa/dpad/wpcontent/uploads/sites/45/publication/dsp_policy_0.pdf; https://perma.cc/U43H-5P83.

United Nations, *National Accounts Main Aggregates Database*, available online at: https://unstats.un.org/unsd/snaama/countryprofile; https://perma.cc/LF7T-GBPU.

United Nations, *Sustainable Development Goals*, available online at: www.un.org/sustainabledevelopment/sustainable-development-goals/; https://perma.cc/HQ6H-JJNQ.

United Nations, *The Millennium Development Goals Report 2015* (2015), available online at: www.un.org/millenniumgoals/2015_MDG_Report/pdf/MDG%202015%20rev%20(July%201).pdf; https://perma.cc/23WM-CXF5.

United Nations, *Treaty Collection*, available online at: https://treaties.un.org/pages/ViewDetails.aspx?src=TREATY&mtdsg_no=X-10&chapter=10&clang=_en; https://perma.cc/HW7M-WVZE.

United Nations Conference on Trade and Development, "Expropriation," *UNCTAD Series on Issues in International Investment Agreements II* (2012), available online at: https://unctad.org/system/files/official-document/unctaddiaeia2011d7_en.pdf; https://perma.cc/Q8PR-UGUP.

United Nations Conference on Trade and Development, *Achieving the Sustainable Development Goals in the Least Developed Countries* (2018), available online at: https://unctad.org/system/files/official-document/aldc2018d4_en.pdf; https://perma.cc/8S49-2864.

United Nations Development Programme, *What Is Human Development?*, available online at: http://hdr.undp.org/en/content/what-human-development; https://perma.cc/2PD3-8XZL.

United Nations Educational, Scientific, and Cultural Organization, *Abu Simbel: The Campaign that Revolutionized the International Approach to Safeguarding Heritage*, available online at: https://en.unesco.org/70years/abu_simbel_safeguarding_herit age; https://perma.cc/VJL9-LCY5.

United States Bureau of Labor Statistics, *Labor Force Data by County, 2019 Annual Averages,* available online at: www.bls.gov/lau/laucnty19.xlsx; https://perma.cc/QEU3-5AXN.

United States Bureau of Labor Statistics, *Labor Force Statistics from the Current Population Survey* (last modified December 4, 2020), available online at: www.bls.gov/web/empsit/cpseea10.htm; https://perma.cc/7DLW-PFLA.

United States Census Bureau, *2019 Poverty and Median Household Income Estimates,* available online at: www2.census.gov/programs-surveys/saipe/datasets/2019/2019-state-and-county/est19all; https://perma.cc/GC4D-BAT6.

United States Census Bureau, *Median Household Income of the Total Population by County: 2019,* available online at: www.census.gov/content/dam/Census/library/visualizations/2020/demo/p30-08/f1-mp-19.pdf; https://perma.cc/ZJ6K-YS5V.

United States Census Bureau, *Poverty Thresholds,* available online at: www.census.gov/data/tables/time-series/demo/income-poverty/historical-poverty-thresholds.html; https://perma.cc/7NCE-X972.

United States Census Bureau, *Small Area Income and Poverty Estimates,* available online at: www.census.gov/content/dam/Census/library/visualizations/2004/demo/2002-state-county-maps/med-hh-inc2002.pdf; https://perma.cc/S5BD-53XC.

United States Department of Agriculture Economic Research Service, *Geography of Poverty,* available online at: https://web.archive.org/web/20180109092507/www.ers.usda.gov/topics/rural-economy-population/rural-poverty-well-being/geography-of-poverty.aspx; https://perma.cc/N847-9UVR.

United States Department of State, *Hurricane Katrina: What Government Is Doing,* available online at: https://2009-2017.state.gov/documents/organization/150082.pdf; https://perma.cc/N7TX-DES7.

United States Department of Treasury, *The CARES Act Works for All Americans,* available online at: https://home.treasury.gov/policy-issues/cares; https://perma.cc/XEB4-87PC.

United States International Trade Commission, *U.S.-Korea Free Trade Agreement: Potential Economy-Wide and Selected Sectoral Effects* (2007), Investigation No. TA-2104-24, USITC Publication 3949, available online at: www.usitc.gov/publications/pub3949.pdf; https://perma.cc/H69M-PSMN.

United States Trade Representative, *Fact Sheet: Four Year Snapshot: The U.S.-Korea Free Trade Agreement* (March 2016), available online at: https://ustr.gov/about-us/pol icy-offices/press-office/fact-sheets/2016/March/Four-Year-Snapshot-KORUS; https://perma.cc/8RXL-8A7L.

United States Trade Representative, *2017 Trade Policy Agenda and 2016 Annual Report,* available online at: https://ustr.gov/sites/default/files/files/reports/2017/Annua lReport/Chapter%20III%20-%20Bilateral%20Trade%20Agreements.pdf; https://perma.cc/L9JU-GCVN.

Upham, Frank, "Mythmaking in the Rule of Law Orthodoxy," *Carnegie Papers, Rule of Law Series* (2005), available online at: http://carnegieendowment.org/files/wp30.pdf; https://perma.cc/AT6P-WUVW.

Upham, Frank, "The Paradoxical Roles of Property Rights in Growth and Development" (2015) 8(1) *Law and Development Review* 253–269.

Upham, Frank, *The Great Property Fallacy* (New York: Cambridge University Press, 2018).

US Real GDP Growth Rate by Year, available online at: www.multpl.com/us-real-gdp-growth-rate/table/by-year; https://perma.cc/5YCY-DYQH.

Van Den Meerssche, Dimitri, "The Evolving Mandate of the World Bank: How Constitutional Hermeneutics Shaped the Concept and Practice of Rule of Law Reform" (2017) 10(1) *Law and Development Review* 89–118.

Van Elkan, Rachel, "Singapore's Development Strategy," *in* K. Bercusson (eds.), *Singapore: A Case Study in Rapid Development* (Washington, D.C.: International Monetary Fund, 1995).

Veblen, Thorstein, *The Theory of the Leisure Class: An Economic Study of Institutions* (New York: Palgrave Macmillan, 1915).

Von Benda-Beckmann, Franz, "Legal Pluralism and Social Justice in Economic and Political Development" (2001) 32(1) *Institute of Development Studies Bulletin* 46–56.

Vreeland, James Raymond, *The IMF and Economic Development* (New York: Cambridge University Press, 2003).

Wachman, Alan M., *Taiwan: National Identity and Democratization* (Abington: Routledge, 2016).

Wade, Robert H., "The Economic Bureaucracy," *in* Robert Wade (ed.), *Governing the Market: Economic Theory and the Role of Government in East Asian Industrialization* (Princeton: Princeton University Press, 1990).

Wade, Robert H., "The Paradox of US Industrial Policy: The Developmental State in Disguise," *in* José Manuel Salazar-Xirinachs, Irmgard Nübler, and Richard Kozul-Wright (eds.), *Transforming Economies: Making Industrial Policy Work for Growth, Jobs and Development* (Geneva: ILO, 2014).

Waelde, Thomas W. and James L. Gunderson, "Legislative Reform in Transition Economies: Western Transplants: A Short-Cut to Social Market Economy Status?" (1994) 43(2) *The International Comparative Law Quarterly* 347–378.

Wagner, Wencelas J., "The Law of Contracts in Communist Countries (Russia, Bulgaria, Czechoslovakia and Hungary)" (1963) 7(4) *Saint Louis University Law Journal* 292–310.

Wang, Jiangyu, "The Evolution of China's International Trade Policy: Development through Protection and Liberalization," *in* Yong-Shik Lee (ed.), *Economic Development through World Trade: A Developing Country Perspective* (Alphen aan den Rijn: Kluwer Law International, 2008).

Watson, Alan, "Legal Change: Sources of Law and Legal Change" (1983) 131(5) *University of Pennsylvania Law Review* 1121–1157.

Weber, Max, *Law in Economy and Society* (translated by Max Rheinstein) (New York: Simon and Schuster, 1954).

Weber, Max, *The Protestant Ethic and the Spirit of Capitalism* (New York: Charles Scribner, 1958).

Wehner, Joachim, "Development Strategies in Post-Apartheid South Africa" (2000) 35(2) *Afrika Spectrum* 183–192.

Westphal, Larry E., "Industrial Policy in an Export Propelled Economy: Lessons from South Korea's Experience" (1990) 4(3) *Journal of Economic Perspectives* 41–59.

Wilber, Charles K. and Kenneth P. Jameson (eds.), *Socialist Models of Development* (Oxford: Pergamon, 1982).

Williamson, John, "What Washington Means by Policy Reform," *in* John Williamson (ed.), *Latin American Readjustment: How Much Has Happened* (Washington, D.C.: Peterson Institute for International Economics, 1990).

Wily, Liz Alden, "The Law and Land Grabbing: Friend or Foe?" (2014) 7(2) *Law and Development Review* 207–242.

Winck, Ben, *The $5 Trillion in Pandemic-era Stimulus Is More Than Triple Great Recession-era Aid—And Suggests a Permanent Shift in the Way Congress Spends,* Business Insider (May 10, 2021), available online at: www.businessinsider.com/stimulus-package-pandemic-surpass-great-recession-fiscal-plans-recovery-2021-3; https://perma.cc/PE2X-93SR.

Wolfensohn, James, D., *Comprehensive Development Framework* (February 9, 2000), available online at: http://documents1.worldbank.org/curated/en/20863158318 5352783/pdf/The-comprehensive-development-framework.pdf; https://perma.cc/D57N-6Y7X.

Wolfowitz, Paul, "Good Governance and Development—A Time for Action," remarks at Jakarta, Indonesia (April 2006), cited *in* Jean-Marie Baland, Karl Ove Moene, and James A. Robinson, "Governance and Development," *in* J. Baland, Dani Rodrik, and M. R. Rosenzweig (eds.), *Handbook of Development Economics,* vol. 5 (North Holland, 2009).

World Bank, *The East Asian Miracle* (New York: Oxford University Press, 1993).

World Bank, *The World Bank and Human Rights: The Role of the World Bank* (Washington, D.C.: World Bank, 1998).

World Bank, *Comprehensive Development Framework: Meeting the Promise?* (September 17, 2001), available online at: http://documents1.worldbank.org/curated/en/593 291468779076728/pdf/303650CDF0meeting0the0promise.pdf; https://perma. cc/L4HJ-CFW5.

World Bank, "Engendering Development—Through Gender Equality in Rights, Resources and Voice," *World Bank Policy Research Report* (2001), available online at: http://documents.worldbank.org/curated/en/512911468327401785/pdf/multi-page.pdf; https://perma.cc/TL3T-QHCX.

World Bank, *World Development Report 2005: A Better Investment Climate for Everyone* (2004), available online at: https://openknowledge.worldbank.org/handle/10986/5987; https://perma.cc/5TNP-DQJC.

World Bank, "Cambodia: Land Management and Administration Project," *Investigation Report,* no. 58016-KH (November 23, 2010).

World Bank, *Initiatives in Justice Reform 1992–2012* (2012), available online at: http://documents.worldbank.org/curated/en/575811468175154113/pdf/707290WP 0Full000Box370050B00PUBLIC0.pdf; https://perma.cc/CR77-N2WB.

World Bank, *Credit Reporting* (October 5, 2015), available online at: www.worldbank.org/en/topic/financialsector/brief/credit-reporting; https://perma.cc/AAX7-FZD3.

World Bank, *World Development Report 2017: Governance and the Law* (Washington, D.C.: World Bank, 2017).

World Bank, *Doing Business* (Washington, D.C.: World Bank, 2018).

World Bank, *World Governance Indicators* (dataset 2019), available online at: http://info.worldbank.org/governance/wgi/#reports; https://perma.cc/L682-PZK2.

World Bank, *Doing Business: Case Study of Peru* (March 2020), available online at: www.doingbusiness.org/content/dam/doingBusiness/media/Reforms/Case-Studies/2008/DB08-CS-Peru.pdf; https://perma.cc/933R-QFZN.

World Bank, "The Global Economic Outlook During the COVID-19 Pandemic: A Changed World," *Who We Are/News*, June 8, 2020, available online at: www.worldbank.org/en/news/feature/2020/06/08/the-global-economic-outlook-during-the-covid-19-pandemic-a-changed-world; https://perma.cc/6244-VECZ.

World Bank, *CPIA Property Rights and Rule-Based Governance Rating*, available online at: https://data.worldbank.org/indicator/IQ.CPA.PROP.XQ; https://perma.cc/3QLT-XW9Y.

World Bank, *Data: Country and Lending Groups*, available online at: http://data.worldbank.org/about/country-and-lending-groups; https://perma.cc/X9A6-FRYK.

World Bank, *Doing Business: Registering Property*, available online at: www.doingbusiness.org/en/data/exploretopics/registering-property; https://perma.cc/8KD4-YYWR.

World Bank, *Global Economic Prospects* (January 2018), available online at: https://openknowledge.worldbank.org/bitstream/handle/10986/28932/9781464811630.pdf?sequence=16&isAllowed=y; https://perma.cc/767X-Q6RJ.

World Bank, *GDP (Current US$)*, available online at: https://data.worldbank.org/indicator/NY.GDP.MKTP.CD; https://perma.cc/L3X3-WN3Y.

World Bank, *GDP Growth (Annual %)*, available online at: https://data.worldbank.org/indicator/NY.GDP.MKTP.KD.ZG; https://perma.cc/ZRJ4-VEV5.

World Bank, *GDP Growth (Annual %)—Cambodia*, available online at: https://data.worldbank.org/indicator/NY.GDP.MKTP.KD.ZG?locations=KH; https://perma.cc/63VX-9AJL.

World Bank, *GDP Growth (Annual %)—South Africa*, available online at: https://data.worldbank.org/indicator/NY.GDP.MKTP.KD.ZG?end=2019&locations=ZA&name_desc=false&start=1961; https://perma.cc/LMA4-EBHS.

World Bank, *GINI Index (World Bank Estimate)*, available online at: https://data.worldbank.org/indicator/SI.POV.GINI?locations=ZA-KR; https://perma.cc/XZF9-HSYR.

World Bank, *GNI per Capita, Atlas Method (Current US$)*, available online at: https://data.worldbank.org/indicator/NY.GNP.PCAP.CD; https://perma.cc/SKQ7-PXTK.

World Bank, *GNI per Capita Growth (Annual %)—United States, South Africa*, available online at: https://data.worldbank.org/indicator/NY.GNP.PCAP.KD.ZG?locations=US-ZA; https://perma.cc/6VKT-JXJX.

World Bank, *PovcalNet*, available online at: http://iresearch.worldbank.org/PovcalNet/povDuplicateWB.aspx; https://perma.cc/Q8GU-2PQF.

World Bank, *Rwanda Overview*, available online at: www.worldbank.org/en/country/rwanda/overview; https://perma.cc/9QXL-LJVQ.

World Bank, *Unemployment, Total (% of Total Labor Force) (National Estimate)*, available online at: https://data.worldbank.org/indicator/SL.UEM.TOTL.ZS; https://perma.cc/YY3N-GUN6.

Word Bank, *Worldwide Governance Indicators*, available online at: http://info.worldbank.org/governance/wgi/index.aspx#reports; https://perma.cc/48X8-KP2W.

World Justice Project, *Rule of Law Index* (2020), available online at: https://worldjusticeproject.org/sites/default/files/documents/WJP-ROLI-2020-Online_0.pdf; https://perma.cc/XU6Z-AE6S.

World Trade Organization, *Singapore Ministerial Declaration*, WT/MIN(96)/DEC (December 18, 1996).

World Trade Organization, *Preparations for the 1999 Ministerial Conference*, WT/GC/W/354 (October 11, 1999).

World Trade Organization, "Members Divided on Way Forward for Rules of Origin," *2013 News Items* (September 26, 2013), available online at: www.wto.org/english/news_e/news13_e/roi_26sep13_e.htm; https://perma.cc/3ZLX-9ZL8.

World Trade Organization, *Special and Differential Treatment Provisions in WTO Agreements and Decisions—Note by the Secretariat*, WT/COMTD/W/239 (October 12, 2018).

World Trade Organization, *Report (2020) of the Committee on Anti-Dumping Practices*, G/L/1366, G/ADP/27 (October 20, 2020).

World Trade Organization, *Aid for Trade*, available online at: www.wto.org/english/tratop_e/devel_e/a4t_e/aid4trade_e.htm; https://perma.cc/J4K8-KAFG.

World Trade Organization, *Anti-dumping Measures: Reporting Member vs Exporter 01/01/1995—30/06/2020*, available online at: www.wto.org/english/tratop_e/adp_e/AD_MeasuresRepMemVsExp.pdf; https://perma.cc/3UFS-H25C.

World Trade Organization, *Countervailing Measures: By Reporting Member 01/01/1995—30/06/2020*, available online at: www.wto.org/english/tratop_e/scm_e/CV_MeasuresByRepMem.pdf; https://perma.cc/S4KX-ZA3G.

World Trade Organization, *Disputes by Member*, available online at: www.wto.org/english/tratop_e/dispu_e/dispu_by_country_e.htm; https://perma.cc/J6H8-FFPJ.

World Trade Organization, *Dispute Settlement: The Disputes—Disputes by Agreement*, available online at: www.wto.org/english/tratop_e/dispu_e/dispu_agreements_index_e.htm; https://perma.cc/44R4-2M2P.

World Trade Organization, *Least-Developed Countries*, available online at: www.wto.org/english/thewto_e/whatis_e/tif_e/org7_e.htm; https://perma.cc/49RV-5EVS.

World Trade Organization, *Members and Observers*, available online at: www.wto.org/english/thewto_e/whatis_e/tif_e/org6_e.htm; https://perma.cc/QJR3-JMVN.

World Trade Organization, *Regional Trade Agreements*, available online at: www.wto.org/english/tratop_e/region_e/region_e.htm; https://perma.cc/4Q2K-5ZZG.

World Trade Organization, *Revised Agreement on Government Procurement*, available online at: www.wto.org/english/tratop_e/gproc_e/gp_revised_gpa_e.htm; https://perma.cc/GZF5-UAFN.

World Trade Organization, *The Doha Round*, available online at: www.wto.org/english/tratop_e/dda_e/dda_e.htm#development; https://perma.cc/MS28-LK2F.

World Trade Organization, *Trade Facilitation*, available online at: www.wto.org/english/tratop_e/tradfa_e/tradfa_e.htm; https://perma.cc/A9QK-FEL4.

Wu, Junjie and Munisamy Gopinath, "What Causes Spatial Variations in Economic Development in the United States?" (2008) 90(2) *American Journal of Agricultural Economics* 392–408.

Xu, Guangdong, "Property Rights, Law, and Economic Development" (2013) 6(1) *Law and Development Review* 117–142.

Yang, Lixia, Shaofeng Yuan, and Le Sun, "The Relationships between Economic Growth and Environmental Pollution Based on Time Series Data: An Empirical Study of Zhejiang Province" (2012) 7(1) *Journal of Cambridge Studies* 33–42.

Yasuda, Nobuyuki, "Law and Development in ASEAN Countries" (1993) 10(2) *ASEAN Economic Bulletin* 144–154.

YCHARTS, *US Real Nonresidential Fixed Investment QoQ*, available online at: https://ycharts.com/indicators/us_change_in_real_nonresidential_fixed_investment; https://perma.cc/B83K-PRPF.

Yonglai, Rachelle, Doug Palmer, and Teresa Carson, "Financial Crisis Caused by 'Greed and Stupidity': Geithneer," *Reuters* (April 25, 2012), available online at: www.reuters.com/article/us-usa-economy-geithner/financial-crises-caused-by-stupidity-and-greed-geithner-idUSBRE83P01P20120426, accessed October 12, 2020.

Yu, Guanghua, "Open Access Order and Interconnected Institutions in Brazil: A Challenge" (2018) 12(1) *Law and Development Review* 1–40.

Zwier, Paul, "Human Rights for Women in Liberia (and West Africa): Integrating Formal and Informal Rule of Law Reforms through the Carter Center's Community Justice Advisor Project" (2017) 10(2) *Law and Development Review* 187–235.

Cases

Government of the Republic of South Africa and Others v. Grootboom and Others (October 4, 2000), ZACC 19, 2001 (1) SA 46 (CC), 2000 (11) BCLR 1169 (CC) (South Africa).
Melms v. Pabst Brewing Co., 79 N.W. 738 (1899) (United States).
Obergefell v. Hodges, 135 S. Ct. 2584 (2015) (United States).
Pennsylvania Coal Co. v. Mahon, 260 U.S. 393 (1922) (United States).

Covenants and declarations

United Nations, *Universal Declaration of Human Rights*, G.A. Res. 217A (III), U.N. Doc. A/810 (December 10, 1948).
United Nations, *International Covenant on Civil and Political Rights*, G.A. Res. 2200A (XXI) 21, U.N. GAOR Supp. (No. 16) at 52, U.N. Doc. A/6316 (December 16, 1966a), 999 U.N.T.S. 171.
United Nations, *International Covenant on Economic, Social and Cultural Rights*, G.A. Res. 2200A (XXI) 21 U.N.GAOR Supp. (No. 16) at 49, U.N. Doc. A/6316 (December 16, 1966b), 993 U.N.T.S. 3.
United Nations, *Declaration on the Right to Development*, G.A. Res. 41/128, annex, 41 U.N. GAOR Supp. (No. 53) at 186, U.N. Doc. A/41/53 (December 4, 1986).

Decisions

General Agreement on Tariffs and Trade, Decision of 29 November 1957, B.I.S.D. 6S/18 (1958).
World Trade Organization, *Duty-Free and Quota-Free (DFQF) Market Access for Least-Developed Countries, Ministerial Decision of 7 December 2013*, WT/MIN(13)/44, WT/L/919 (December 11, 2013).
World Trade Organization, *Preferential Rules of Origin for Least-Developed Countries, Ministerial Decision of 7 December 2013*, WT/MIN(13)/42, WT/L/917 (December 11, 2013), available online at: www.wto.org/english/thewto_e/minist_e/mc9_e/desci42_e.htm; https://perma.cc/6YP4-VNLY.
World Trade Organization, *Preferential Rules of Origin for Least-Developed Countries, Ministerial Decision of 19 December 2015*, WT/MIN(15)/47, WT/L/917 (December 21, 2015), www.wto.org/english/thewto_e/minist_e/mc10_e/l917_e.htm; https://perma.cc/4Q85-S44D.

International treaties

Agreement on Implementation of Article VI of the General Agreement on Tariffs and Trade 1994, World Trade Organization Agreement, Annex 1A, 1868 U.N.T.S. 201 (April 15, 1994).
Agreement on Safeguards, World Trade Organization Agreement, Annex 1A, 1869 U.N.T.S. 154 (April 15, 1994).

Agreement on Subsidies and Countervailing Measures, World Trade Organization Agreement, Annex 1A, 1869 U.N.T.S. 14 (April 15, 1994).

Agreement on Trade-Related Intellectual Property Rights, World Trade Organization Agreement, Annex 1C, 1869 U.N.T.S. 299 (April 15, 1994).

Agreement on Trade-Related Investment Measures, World Trade Organization Agreement, Annex 1A, 1868 U.N.T.S. 168 (April 15, 1994).

Berne Convention for the Protection of Literary and Artistic Works, 28 U.S.T. 7645, 1161 U.N.T.S. 30 (September 9, 1886).

General Agreement on Tariffs and Trade, 1867 U.N.T.S. 194 (October 30, 1947).

Paris Convention for the Protection of Industrial Property, 21 U.S.T. 1583, 828 U.N.T.S. 11851 (March 20, 1883).

Understanding on Rules and Procedures Governing the Settlement of Disputes ("DSU"), World Trade Organization Agreement, Annex 2, 1869 U.N.T.S. 401, 33 I.L.M. 1226 (April 14, 1994), available online at: www.wto.org/english/docs_e/legal_e/legal_e.htm#dispute; https://perma.cc/G8RU-VEX8.

Proclamations

Proclamation 9704 of March 8, 2018, *Adjusting Imports of Aluminum into the United States*, Federal Register, vol. 83, no. 51 (March 15, 2018), doc. 2018-11619.

Proclamation 9705 of March 8, 2018, *Adjusting Imports of Steel into the United States*, Federal Register, vol. 83, no. 51 (March 15, 2018), doc. 2018-11625.

Statutes

섬유공업근대화촉진법 [Act on Promotion of Modernization of Textile Industries of 1979] (South Korea).

비철금속제련사업법 [Act on Refining Service of Non-Ferrous Metals of 1971] (South Korea).

섬유공업시설에 관한 임시조치법 [Act on Temporary Measures for Textile Industrial Facilities of 1967] (South Korea).

수출장려보조금교부에 관한 임시조치법 [Act on Temporary Measures for the Grant of Export Subsidies of 1961] (South Korea).

African Growth and Opportunity Act of 2000, Public Law 106-200, 114 Stat. 251, U.S.C. ch. 23 § 3701 *et seq.* (United States).

Agreement on Trade-Related Aspects of Intellectual Property Rights, April 15, 1994, *Marrakesh Agreement Establishing the World Trade Organization* (WTO Agreement), Annex 1C, 1869 U.N.T.S. 299, 33 I.L.M. 1197.

Appalachian Redevelopment Act of 1965, 40 U.S.C. § 14101 *et seq.* (United States).

Bayh-Dole Act of 1980, 35 U.S.C. §§ 200–212 (United States).

Broad-Based Black Empowerment Act of 2003 (South Africa).

Bürgerliches Gesetzbuch (BGB) (civil code of Germany).

공무원윤리강령 [Code of Ethics for Government Officials] (South Korea).

Civil Code of Korea § 534 (South Korea).

Civil Rights Act of 1964, 42 U.S.C. § 2000d *et seq.* (United States).

Constitution of the Republic of South Africa 1996 [assented to December 16, 1996].

Control of Manufacture Ordinance of 1959 (Singapore).

Economic Expansion Incentives Act, passed in 1967 (Singapore).

전자공업진흥법 [Electronic Industries Promotion Act of 1969] (South Korea).

수출진흥법 [Export Promotion Act of 1962] (South Korea).

Humphrey-Hawkins Full Employment Act of 1978, 15 U.S.C. §§ 3101–3152 (expired in 2000) (United States).

부정청탁 및 금품 등 수수의 금지에 관한 법률 [Improper Solicitation and Graft Act of 2016] (South Korea).

Industrial Expansion Ordinance of 1959 (Singapore).

정보공개법 [Information Disclosure Act of 1996] (South Korea).

Jobs and Growth Act of 2012, S.C. 2012, c. 31 (Canada).

Loi 2010-1192 du 11 octobre 2010 interdisant la dissimulation du visage dans l'espace public

[Law 2010-1192 of October 11, 2010, banning the covering of one's face in public] (France).

기계공업진흥법 [Mechanical Industries Promotion Act of 1967] (South Korea).

석유화학공업육성법 [Petrochemical Industries Facilitation Act of 1970] (South Korea).

Prevention and Combating of Corruption Act of 2004 (South Africa).

Pioneer Industries Ordinance of 1959 (Singapore).

Public Works and Economic Development Act of 1965 (PWEDA), as amended, 42 U.S.C. § 3121 *et seq.* (United States).

Regulation (EU) No 978/2012 of the European Parliament and of the Council of 25 October 2012 (applying a scheme of generalized tariff preferences and repealing Council Regulation (EC) No 732/2008), OJ L 303 (October 31, 2012).

조세감면규제법 [Regulation of Tax Reduction and Exemption Act of 1965] (South Korea).

Securities Act of 1934, 15 U.S.C. §§ 1–16 (United States).

조선공업진흥법 [Shipbuilding Industries Promotion Act of 1967] (South Korea).

Small Business Innovation Development Act of 1982, 15 U.S.C. § 638 (United States).

獎勵投資條例 [Statute for Encouragement of Investment] (Taiwan).

促進產業升級條例 [Statute for Upgrading Industries] (Taiwan).

철강공업육성법 [Steel Industries Facilitation Act of 1970] (South Korea).

Stevenson-Wydler Technology Innovation Act of 1980, 15 U.S.C. §§ 3710–3753 (United States).

Tariff Act of 1930 (Smoot-Hawley Tariff Act), 19 U.S.C. §§ 1201–1641 (United States).

Trade Act of 1974, 19 U.S.C. § 2271 *et seq.* (United States).

Trade Expansion Act of 1962 (amended in 1974), 19 U.S.C. §§ 1911–1920 and §§ 2341–2356 (United States).

무역거래법 [Trade Transactions Act of 1967] (South Korea).

Uniform Commercial Code (UCC) (United States).

Uniform Electronic Transactions Act of 1999 (United States).

Index